THE RECONSTRUCTION OF INTERNATIONAL MONETARY ARRANGEMENTS

Also by Robert Z. Aliber

THE FUTURE OF THE DOLLAR AS AN INTERNATIONAL CURRENCY

GUIDELINES, INFORMAL CONTROLS, AND THE MARKET PLACE (*co-editor*)

THE INTERNATIONAL MARKET FOR FOREIGN EXCHANGE (*editor*)

THE INTERNATIONAL MONEY GAME

WORLD INFLATION AND MONETARY REFORM

NATIONAL MONETARY POLICIES AND THE INTERNATIONAL FINANCIAL SYSTEM (*editor*)

EXCHANGE RISK AND CORPORATE INTERNATIONAL FINANCE

THE POLITICAL ECONOMY OF MONETARY REFORM (*editor*)

YOUR MONEY AND YOUR LIFE

MONEY BANKING AND THE ECONOMY (*co-author*)

MONETARY REFORM AND WORLD INFLATION

THE RECONSTRUCTION OF INTERNATIONAL MONETARY ARRANGEMENTS

Edited by
Robert Z. Aliber

St. Martin's Press   New York

© Graduate School of Business, University of Chicago, 1987

First published in the United States of America in 1987

Printed in Hong Kong

ISBN 0-312-66590-3

Library of Congress Cataloging-in-Publication Data
The Reconstruction of international monetary arrangements.
Bibliography: p.
1. International finance. 1. Aliber, Robert Z.
HG3881.R33 1987   332'.042   86-3758
ISBN 0-312-66590-3

Contents

Notes on the Contributors

Robert Z. Aliber is Professor of International Economics and Finance at the University of Chicago.

Jacques R. Artus is on the staff of the International Monetary Fund.

K. Alec Chrystal is Professor of Economics at the University of Sheffield.

Richard N. Cooper is Maurits Boas Professor of Economics at Harvard University.

Michael P. Dooley is on the staff of the International Monetary Fund.

Robert P. Flood is Professor of Economics at Northwestern University.

Peter M. Garber is Professor of Economics at Brown University.

Robert J. Gordon is Professor of Economics at Northwestern University.

Herbert G. Grubel is Professor of Economics at Simon Fraser University.

Hans Genberg is Professor of Economics at the Graduate Institute of International Affairs, Geneva.

David A. Hsieh is an Associate Professor of Economics at the University of Chicago.

John Huizinga is an Associate Professor of Economics at the University of Chicago.

Rachel McCullough is Professor of Economics at Northwestern University.

Peter M. Oppenheimer is Reader in Economics, Christ Church, Oxford.

Jeffrey R. Shafer is with the Division of Monetary and Fiscal Affairs, the Organization for Economic Cooperation and Development.

Alexander K. Swoboda is Professor of Economics at the Graduate Institute of International Affairs, Geneva.

Georges M. von Furstenberg is the Rudy Professor of Economics, Indiana University.

Introduction: The Reconstruction of International Monetary Arrangements

ROBERT Z. ALIBER

The agenda at conferences on policy issues in international finance tend to reflect the concern with the adequacy of existing monetary arrangements. In July 1972, at the conclusion of the first Wingspread Conference on International Monetary Problems, one participant noted that the Bretton Woods system of pegged exchange rates was breaking down and was beyond repair. Several other participants agreed; one suggested that the only alternative was a system of floating exchange rates. Although the Bretton Woods system of pegged exchange rates had been patched in the context of the Smithsonian Agreement at the end of 1971 and the US dollar had been devalued by more than 10 per cent relative to the currencies of the other major industrial countries, the US balance of payments deficit remained extremely large. The British authorities had ceased supporting the pound at its Smithsonian parity several weeks before the Conference.

By the time of the second Wingspread Conference in July 1974, the international economic environment had changed sharply. The currencies of the major industrial countries had been floating for more than a year, and the US dollar had depreciated sharply. The market price of gold was more than four times higher than two years before. The world price of oil had increased from $2.75 a barrel to $12.50 a barrel as a result of supply constraints adopted by Saudi Arabia and other members of the Organization of Petroleum Exporting Countries (OPEC) at the end of 1973. There was widespread concern whether many countries would be able to obtain the foreign exchange to finance their imports of oil. The

1

United States and other industrial economies were experiencing a more rapid rate of inflation than at any previous time in the post-war period; the term 'double-digit inflation' had become part of the vocabulary. The amplitude of the movement of exchange rates during the first year's experience with the new system was large. Nevertheless, most analysts accepted the view that the adjustments of most countries' payments positions to the sharp increase both in the price of oil and in the foreign exchange cost of oil imports would be easier with floating exchange rates than with parities.

After the move to floating rates, the United States eliminated many of the controls and restrictions on international payments that had been adopted in the 1960s to reduce the payments deficits associated with an increasingly overvalued dollar. Some analysts believed that the movements in exchange rates might be less abrupt as participants in the foreign exchange market gained more experience with the new system. A few skeptics, in contrast, believed that floating rates would be unlikely to work satisfactorily, and that large swings in exchange rates would lead to increased demands for protection in those countries whose currencies were becoming increasingly overvalued.

After nearly a decade, however, the sharpness and amplitude of the exchange rate movements has not led to the conclusion that the system of floating exchange rates has been operating effectively. In the late 1970s, the foreign exchange value of the US dollar was extremely low and the dollar was significantly undervalued. Foreign tourists trooped to the United States because of the substantial bargains. Some foreign central banks were reducing the proportion of dollar-denominated assets in their holdings of reserve assets and acquiring reserve assets denominated in some other currency. Considerable support was given to the proposal for a Reserve Substitution Account, which would be attached to the International Money Fund and acquire part or all of the excess dollar holdings from foreign central banks. By the early 1980s, however, the US dollar appeared strong and substantially overvalued. The price of the dollar in terms of the German mark and the Japanese yen had increased by nearly 50 per cent even though the price levels in both countries were rising less rapidly than the US price level. The international competitive position of US firms declined sharply; the US trade balance went from a surplus of $2 billion in 1975 to a deficit of $43 billion in 1982. As the dollar became increasingly overvalued, the demands for protection in the United States increased; monetary issues had important trade consequences.

The movements on the foreign exchange value of the US dollar were related to changes in the US monetary and fiscal policy and especially to changes in the perceptions about the strength of the US government's commitments to achieving a low inflation rate. In the late 1970s, the weakness of the dollar reflected investors' belief that the US government had a stronger interest in a high level of employment than in a low rate of inflation. The sharp appreciation in the foreign exchange value of the dollar was associated with the change in the operating procedures of the Federal Reserve System in October 1979. The shift towards monetarist policies led to an unexpected surge in the interest rates on dollar assets; the foreign demand for dollar assets increased sharply, and so did the foreign exchange value of the dollar. The monetary authorities in Western Europe and Japan then faced the choice between permitting their currencies to depreciate (and being subject to upward cost-push pressures on their domestic price levels from the higher price of imports) or permitting interest rates on assets denominated in their currencies to increase in response to the increase in interest rates on dollar assets.

The United States was exporting monetary contraction. One consequence of the worldwide decline in economic activity was that excess supply developed rapidly in the world petroleum market; the price of oil began to fall in the spot market and the current account surplus of the OPEC countries declined sharply. The payments positions of some of the oil-exporting countries like Mexico and Venezuela quickly worsened, and their ability to borrow in international markets declined as lenders revised downward their estimates of the oil price in the future. Moreover, the ability to borrow of oil-importing developing countries like Brazil and Chile also declined sharply in the face of the surge in interest rates and the decline in their export earnings. Because the developing countries could not borrow, their ability to make debt service payments on schedule declined sharply. The surge in interest rates on their external debt loans complicated their payments problems. The inability or reluctance of Mexico, Argentina, Brazil and Venezuela and other developing countries to make debt service payments on schedule raised questions about the value of these loans. Since the loans of the US money center banks to the developing countries exceeded the value of shareholders equity in these banks, the stability of these banks was questioned.

At a minimum, the developing countries were illiquid, for their holdings of international reserve assets were modest in relation to their external debt, and to their annual debt service payments. Their shortage of liquidity placed attention on the adequacy of member country quotas in the International Monetary Fund, and the adequacy of IMF holdings of usable national currencies to fund member country loans. Possibly some of these countries were insolvent or lacked the willingness to repay. The concern about solvency or willingness to repay of the developing countries led to renewed attention to the adequacy of lender-of-last resort arrangements in the international monetary system.

One of the paradoxes of the decade with floating exchange rates was that the supply of international reserve assets increased much more rapidly in the 1970s than in the 1950s and the 1960s when the currencies were pegged, even though one of the advantages attributed to the floating exchange rate system had been that the need for international reserves would decline. In part the expansion in the volume of international reserve assets reflected that the demand for reserves might increase in a period of rising price levels. The international reserve assets of some of the OPEC countries had increased as a result of the surge in their export revenues. And the international reserve assets of many industrial countries increased when they intervened in the foreign exchange market to limit the appreciation of their currencies. The counterpart to the rapid growth in international reserve assets was the rapid growth in the external debt of numerous developing countries; they financed their balance of payments deficits by liability management – by borrowing from the international banks.

The increase in the volume of international reserve assets in the most recent decade has been much larger than the increases in any previous period, especially if gold is valued at or near the market price. While few central banks have traded gold, many countries value gold in their official holdings at or near the market price. Nevertheless, the need to increase IMF quotas because of the extreme shortage of liquidity of the developing countries might lead to the conclusion – given the large increase in the volume of reserve assets – that reserve arrangements have been less than optimal.

As a consensus develops that the current monetary arrangements are less than optimal, attention is being given to the plausible modifications of current arrangements. The objective of this Conference was to assess the current arrangements and to consider some of the alternatives. One concern was the options to the system of floating exchange rates. A second concern was the adequacy of international reserves and of lender-of-last resort arrangements in the international system.

Part I
The Recent Past

1 The Evolving International Monetary System: Past Plans and Optimality

HERBERT G. GRUBEL

In the middle of 1960 the world of international finance was shaken by a momentous event which for most people today in retrospect is nothing but a minor incidence: wealthholders throughout the world were selling dollars and bought other currencies and assets. For the first time in nearly thirty years central banks had to purchase massive amounts of dollars. Almost simultaneously as these events were taking place in financial markets a book by Triffin (1960) appeared on the market in which he not only predicted this crisis but also diagnosed its causes and presented a remedy. In the following years many prominent economists and important policy-makers produced a plethora of reactions to the Triffin plan and alternative plans for reform of the international monetary system. In the first section below I present a brief anatomy of these plans, which were reprinted in my collection (Grubel, 1963), emphasizing that they were characterized by a remarkable absence of theoretical reasoning and of any kind of model of an efficient monetary system towards which reform plans could be directed. Similarly, the Bellagio Group (1964) publication and the studies of crawling pegs contained essentially pragmatic recommendations for changes to the existing system.

A detailed evaluation of actual reforms since 1971 in the light of the many divergent proposals would reveal a list of winners and losers, but would not be of lasting value or interest. For this reason I review only briefly the changes in the system most widely discussed before 1971, the increased flexibility of exchange rates, the problem of liquidity and the issue of confidence. However, in the second section I turn to the sketch of a model of an efficient international monetary system and its price-

7

theoretic foundations. In the concluding section I evaluate recent changes in the system in the light of this model and demonstrate that they have tended to raise efficiency.

ANATOMY OF PROBLEMS AND SOLUTIONS

With the help of perspectives gained in 20 years I would group the plans for reform of the international monetary system hatched during the 1950s and early 1960s under the following headings: (a) pragmatist perfection of existing gold exchange standard and (b) advocacy of traditional pure models of freely floating rates and the gold standard.

The 1950s was the period when intellectuals and economists in Western countries were in a euphoric state in which they believed that the science of economics would make it possible to engineer an economically perfect and equitable world. The creation of central banks in all Western countries was considered to have provided the essential tool for the maintenance of full employment and governments increasingly promoted equity through tax and expenditure policies. Triffin's idea for the creation of a world central bank, though he was reluctant to call it such,[1] captured public imagination precisely because such an international organization leading eventually to a world government represented the continuation, if not crowning achievement, of the era of economic engineering for full employment and an equitable income distribution. A re-reading of Triffin's proposal strikes one through its almost complete absence of concern over the issues which dominate today's era, when the euphoria over the possible gains from economic engineering has been replaced by deep pessimism and a return to faith in decentralized market solutions. What rules should guide the creation of reserves with respect to quantity and timing? What mechanism would assure the efficient adjustment of exchange rates? How much should they be allowed to fluctuate? The ability of well-meaning politicians and bureaucrats to find answers to these questions was assumed implicitly to be forthcoming once they had the appropriate institutions and tools provided by reform.[2]

The pragmatists of the era made proposals for the improvement of the system which had as the only, though powerful, theoretical rationale that evolution was better than revolution.[3] After all, the chaos of the 1930s had been changed into the order and prosperity of the post-war years by the pragmatic gradualism of engineering in small steps free from influence by ideology or idealism. If price theoretic norms or concerns with efficiency guided any of the pragmatist recommendations, they were well hidden.

Proponents for reform of the international monetary system towards the traditional models of the pure gold standard and freely floating exchange rates written during this period[4] were similarly devoid of modern price-theoretic reasoning. In a sense, of course, the standard case for freely floating rates rests on an understanding of the role of relative prices in the allocation of resources in a form as pure as it can be made. This characteristic provides it with its enormous appeal to those who understand fully the central role of prices in the Walrasian system. Yet the exposition of the case for freely floating rates at the time, like most of those presented even today, tend to leave readers with the impression that something is missing from the argument. In a very important sense that we now understand with the help of theories about the nature of contracts and uncertainty, there are essential differences between markets for potatoes on the one hand and for foreign exchange and labor on the other.

By analogy, the case for the pure gold standard rests on an implicit model of zero adjustment costs and of the absolute superiority of automatic over discretionary market processes. Its proponents were persuasive in their arguments for the need to curb the economic engineering instincts of politicians. But, as in the case of freely floating exchange rates, readers of these arguments were and are left with the feeling that something is missing from the analysis. Armed with today's theories concerning the nature of uncertainty, contracts and money we can readily see what the omitted variables are.

The cumulative disequilibria in the balance of payments of the United States, Germany and Japan during the 1960s provided continuous stimulus for rounds of conferences between academics and policymakers designed to shorten the lag between academic insights and their implementation in the real world. The so-called Bellagio Group[5] meetings performed a useful, educational role, passing on the conventional wisdom of the period and, as its central objective, attempted to dispel the notion that greater exchange rate flexibility would be disastrous for international trade and finance. However, a reading of the Group's manifesto shows that it is almost totally devoid of any theoretical model that could have provided answers for those who were convinced that greater flexibility of exchange rates was needed but who wanted to know how much more flexibility and what was wrong with the integration and stability provided by the fixed exchange rates under the gold standard? Or for those who accepted the validity of the argument that reserves should be created centrally and in an orderly fashion with an equitable distribution of seigniorage, who wanted to know how many reserves, at what price and seigniorage distributed by what criteria of equity?

After the growing size of the US deficits forced the demise of the dollar gold exchange standard in 1971,[6] pragmatists continued to dominate academic discussions of reform of the international monetary system. An unwarranted amount of resources was devoted to the formulation and analysis of automatic and binding rules for exchange rate adjustment.[7] In these discussions practically no effort was made to justify rules on price-theoretic grounds as leading to optimal exchange rate adjustment paths. In the place of such arguments were judgments about political matters and other non-quantifiable needs for constraints of national monetary authorities. In retrospect, it is no wonder that it was impossible to reach international agreement on the implementation of these rules as there was a plethora of judgments of political matters leading to a large number of feasible and defensible rules.

While academic discussions about international monetary reform took place during the 1960s and 1970s, there were parallel negotiations among governments and with the IMF. Solomon (1977) surveys such negotiations from the point of view of an insider and shows them to have had two outstanding features. First, they were concerned overwhelmingly with the solution of current crises. Second, discussions about longer-run reforms always were heavily influenced by current or immediately past problems, showed no reference to any consistent model of an ideal system, and were practically devoid of references to ideas and models worked out by academics. In the entire book I could find only one reference to Triffin's idealist solution. A few other prominent economists of the era were cited in a perfunctory manner.

Events and Reform Plans

In spite of the absence of any logically rigorous model of an efficient international monetary system by which to judge modifications and reforms of the system in recent decades, it is possible to find a broad consensus about the ailments of the Bretton Woods system in the majority of writings on international monetary problems in the post-war years. The Bellagio Group's taxonomy of the need for greater flexibility, liquidity and confidence neatly summarizes this consensus. It can be used to evaluate superficially the success of the reforms in recent years.

Flexibility of exchange rates was achieved at first without international agreement when major currencies were simply declared to be without parity pegs, and then officially after the 1976 Jamaica Accords[8], when free floats and all pegging arrangements were sanctioned as long as they did not harm the interests of the world community. By all criteria these developments were a great success since in most countries they removed exchange rate adjustments from the political arena, where in the past they had so often been delayed by non-economic criteria.

Liquidity was an area of concern in which consensus was minimal with respect to adequate quantities and appropriate sources, gold, SDRs and national currencies. Because of the absence of a consensus for needed reform it is impossible to say whether the rapid growth in reserves that took place during the 1970s was adequate or excessive and whether the components of the growth in the form of gold value increases, SDRs and national currencies was desirable. It is remarkable, however, that in 1980 the proportion of gold valued at market prices in total reserves, the ratio of total reserves to world trade and the US liquidity position (ratio of gold reserves to short-term obligations to foreign official holders) were roughly in the same relationship that they had been before the first crisis in 1960 and after a long period of often great deviations.[9] In my view, however, we have simply no relevant criteria by which to judge whether the market solution to the provision of liquidity is efficient, though I will return to this topic below.

The *confidence problem* of the 1960s was considered to be due solely to the convertibility of dollars into gold. The 1971 cessation of such convertibility by these criteria thus solved the problem of confidence. However, it was replaced by the much more pervasive and disruptive problem of the lack of confidence in individual currencies and the accompanying switching of assets and liabilities and exchange rate instabilities. Criteria of success are difficult to design and evaluate since the exchange rate instabilities in principle could be autonomous sources of difficulties for national economies or simply the manifestations of exogenously determined national instabilities which no international monetary institution can or should prevent.[10]

To the preceding list of needed reforms inspired by the Bellagio Group manifesto, I would like to add the need to reform the IMF, which was so central to Triffin's proposals. During the last two decades the IMF has grown in size,[11] prestige and operating experience. It has become a superb forum for international consultation and the production of economic statistics and intelligence. It has improved the quality of SDRs, but it has failed miserably as a source of liquidity for the world.

SDRs have never exceeded 5 per cent of the world total of owned official reserve assets and were only 2 per cent in 1980. Most disturbing to me have been politically powerful attempts to turn the IMF from a supplier of liquidity and an arbiter of adjustment policies into an instrument for economic justice as perceived by the political majority and poor of the world. Demands for the *link* between SDR creation and international assistance and the extension of medium-term credits for other than strictly balance of payments adjustment are the most visible of such attempts. Seen from the perspective of the modern theory of bureaucracy and interest group politics, they raise serious questions about the merit of relying on centralized, democratic solutions to the supply of liquidity, unless the power of the institution is limited strictly through constitutional provisions that protect the minority from the tyranny of the majority much like constitutionally determined constraints on monetary and fiscal policy sovereignty of democratic governments are expected to do.

In sum, it seems that actual developments in the international monetary system since 1971 cannot be evaluated unambiguously in the light of reform proposals of the post-war period, except for the abandonment of the parity exchange rate system which was considered desirable by almost all post-war critics. This ambiguity in the evaluation of reform proposals is due to the absence of a comprehensive, price-theoretic model of an ideal international monetary system, which in turn had made it possible for academics to propose reforms of a wide range and claims with relative impurity that a pursuit of their particular vision of the world would maximize welfare. These conditions lead me to suggest that academic economists take on as a priority research agenda the construction of models of an efficient international monetary system which could serve as both a guide for future reforms and as a standard by which the merit of past reforms can be evaluated.

I have in the past attempted the construction of such a model (1973; 1977a; 1977b). While the more popular version in the textbook must have been read by many people if sales are a guide to readership of books, the basic idea has had zero influence on the profession capable of evaluating and improving it and pushing it (or a substitute) in official use. In the remainder of this paper I will sketch the outline of an efficient international monetary system and the theoretical justification for its outstanding features which are drawn from modern theories concerning the role of prices, contracts and interest groups. This model is then used to provide some new perspectives on the reforms that have taken place in recent years.

A MODEL OF AN EFFICIENT INTERNATIONAL
MONETARY SYSTEM

An efficient international monetary system must take as given a world of nation states with independent central banks in which business cycles and random shocks affecting demand and supply of tradables and comparative advantage are a continuous phenomenon. In addition, national economic and social policies themselves must realistically be considered to be the source of frequent shocks to stability. The ideal international monetary system must allow the family of nations to minimize the cost of such business cycles and disturbances in terms of real income levels and stability.

I will now summarize briefly the characteristics of such an international monetary system and then sketch the theoretical justification of each key feature. Every country's exchange rate adjustments are chosen freely to accommodate their own peculiar needs and problems. However, most countries can be expected to *use reserves to stabilize exchange rates* through time and permit the formation of more or less formal currency areas. Major countries and currency areas use the strategy of *leaning against the wind* to reduce exchange rate instabilities without preventing basic adjustments necessitated by shifts in comparative advantage, long-term capital flows and terms of trade. *Liquidity* required for the policies of leaning against the wind is provided by SDRs, which the IMF supplies in quantities that grow at a steady annual rate and by national currencies used as reserves in response to excess demand.

In my view the central feature of the efficient system described is an exchange rate regime which has neither the permanently fixed rates of the gold standard nor rates that are freely floating. The theoretical justification for a regime of managed rates is found in the concepts of optimal currency areas due to Mundell (1961) and its logical extension to optimum exchange rate stability attempted in my publications noted above. Most analysts now agree that in an uncertain world with significant transaction and information costs, the enlargement of geographic areas within which one currency provides the services of money leads to benefits in the form of greater economic and price stability for all regions of the area and to costs through reduced ability to use exchange rate changes to accommodate changes in comparative advantage, tastes and other real disturbances of subregions necessitating changes in sticky factor incomes. For all possible combinations of regions in the world there exists a network of associations which represents optimum currency areas in the sense that any further recombinations would result in a loss of welfare due to an excess of marginal costs of adjustment over the marginal benefits in the form of levels and stability of income, all in a world of a given pattern of random disturbances.

The price theoretic core of the arguments for optimum currency areas is that the benefits and costs associated with changes in the geographic domain of currencies accrue in the form of externalities. The formation of nation states and in modern times of currency unions are seen from this point of view as the response of market participants to create new organizations and institutions that internalize the externalities in a manner that is perfectly consistent with the ideas of Coase (1966) about the way in which free markets deal with externalities. In a private conversation Milton Friedman answered my question about the effect of the optimum currency area argument upon his views of the optimality of freely floating rates: 'I never would have recommended that a small country like Panama should have its own currency and a freely floating rate'. By this answer even Friedman admitted indirectly, and by shifting the argument to the question of optimum domain of national currencies, that institutional arrangements can influence the optimality of signals and allocative effects provided by exchange rates.

I have elsewhere developed fully the nature of the costs and benefits associated with currency area formation to show that benefits occur in the form of greater price stability, which in turn increases the usefulness of money and raises the benefits from specialization and exchange in a money economy, paralleling the arguments of Klein (1977) made in another context. The costs take the form of slower adjustment and longer unemployment in response to real disturbances than would be required if exchange rate changes brought about the required adjustments in real incomes and relative prices of traded and non-traded goods.

I believe that the same price-theoretic arguments which imply that optimum efficiency requires the existence of a global network of optimum currency areas are also directly relevant for the concept of an optimum exchange rate stability through time. Private speculation may reasonably be assumed to result in the stabilization of exchange rates of optimum currency areas through time, as the speculative activity is pushed to the point where the marginal private productivity of resources in this activity are equal to marginal private costs. However, the remaining variance of exchange rates results in variance of domestic prices and externalities in the form of reduced usefulness of money. To eliminate these externalities, it is rational to form exchange stabilization funds which push the use of resources to the point where the marginal social benefits equal the marginal cost of doing so.[12]

It may be useful briefly to draw parallels between contract theory in labor markets and the theory of the optimality of exchange rate management. Today few economists believe that it would be optimal for every worker to renegotiate a pay contract in auction markets every minute, hour or even day. Allocative efficiency that takes proper account of uncertainty and transactions costs requires clearly that there is an optimal length of contract both privately and socially. In the same way, exchange rates determined continuously in auction are unlikely to be optimal in the sense noted above, and optimal stability through time exists much like there is an optimal stability of wage contracts.

One of the central arguments against official exchange rate management is that it requires the exchange stabilization authorities to know the equilibrium path of exchange rates. I am convinced of the evidence that the implicit forecasting record of authorities has indeed been poor. However, there exists a model of behavior for authorities which results in stabilization without requiring knowledge of equilibrium exchange rate paths. This behavioral model involves a policy of leaning against the wind. It can be shown by simulation that in a market where private market participants produce exchange rate fluctuations that follow a random walk, leaning against the wind results in the narrowing or the variance of exchange rates. Rules can be designed so that even if there are drifts in the random walk, the variance can be reduced consistently. In basic concept, the behavioral rules vary the magnitude of intervention according to the deviation of actual from a normal target level of reserves. When there is no drift or growth, the target level remains stationary. In a world of drift revealing itself in a persistent deviation from the target, the target itself can be changed. Under reasonable sets of assumptions, leaning against the wind must always reduce exchange rate variance, though the exact amount of reduction depends among other variables on the level and cost of reserves.[13] The intervention rule does not require authorities to know more about future equilibrium prices than private speculators.

My price-theoretic model of the efficient international monetary system is closed by the use of Friedman's (1969) optimum quantity of money argument which suggests in this context that the creation of reserves should be pushed until the marginal cost of producing and marginal benefits of using them are equal. Given the low marginal cost of producing SDRs, the optimum quantity of money argument implies that the real interest rate on reserves should be close to the marginal productivity of resources so that the opportunity cost of holding reserves is near zero and therefore equal to the cost of producing them. The setting of such interest rates and the mechanism for administering them is within the capability of the IMF and in recent years has in fact been accomplished. However, since it is not possible to determine simultaneously an equilibrium efficient quantity and cost of reserves, and because the creation of efficient quantities can be observed only indirectly, it appears desirable that SDRs should be created at rates of growth roughly equal to the real growth rate of international transactions, expressed as a moving average or set at a steady rate for a number of years.

Under such rules of reserve growth, global shortages would manifest themselves in two ways. First, national currencies would be used to supplement reserve holdings in the form of SDRs. Second, the incidence of restrictions of trade and capital flows and the frequency of exchange rate changes would increase. A monitoring of these reserve adequacy indicators could be used to determine SDR growth rates through time. While it seems unreasonable to link the creation of SDRs entirely to objective rules, recent experience with national monetary and fiscal policies of many countries suggests that deviations from certain norms should be permitted only through qualified majority voting.[14]

Elsewhere I have presented the preceding ideas in a somewhat more rigorous and integrated fashion and have considered such other key topics as the role of gold and of transition. Such efforts quickly become very long and tedious. It is quite possible that the problem is so complex that a model of an optimally efficient international monetary system can never be constructed with the rigor used in other macroeconomic models and within the normal constraints of length of articles the profession is prepared to read and study. However, I am obviously convinced that work on such a model is needed and that the theoretical concepts for its construction are available.

SUMMARY AND CONCLUSIONS

In this paper I have attempted to analyse the changes in the international monetary system that have taken place since 1971 in the light of the proposals for reform which were made in the post-war years. A review of the reform proposals has revealed that they are severely lacking in common assumptions about the nature of the problems to be solved by the system and in a common framework for analysis. As a result, the proposals contain a plethora of reform measures which their authors claim would improve the efficiency of the system but for which insufficient theoretical and empirical justifications are provided to permit them to be evaluated objectively. As a result, the greater flexibility of exchange rates since 1971 is considered a success by those who deplored the rigidity of the parity system, but falls short of the ideals of those who wanted freely floating rates and those who considered optimal a return to the gold standard. The endowment of the IMF with the capability to create SDRs and make them of stable value is consistent with proposals made by idealist planners but violates the objectives of those who recommend the market regimes of freely floating rates or the gold standard. The small share of SDRs in total world reserves, on the other hand, is inconsistent with those who proposed a replacement of national currencies by SDRs as a means for greater stability and a more equitable sharing of seigniorage. The list could be extended, but the above examples suffice to make the point that the present state of the art permits us only to prepare a taxonomy of reform proposals that were realized and that were rejected. Such a taxonomy of winners and losers may be fun but is hardly of lasting interest or value.

In this paper I have therefore suggested that there exists the need for the construction of models of an efficient international monetary system based on widely accepted price-theoretic assumptions and reasoning. Such a model is badly needed as a norm for the evaluation of past reforms and as a guide for future modifications. The sketch of such a model of an efficient international monetary system, together with an outline of the price-theoretic reasoning underlying its key features, represents a first attempt. Its usefulness and accuracy must await future events and scrutiny.

However, I believe that as it stands it permits me to make the judgment that three important developments in the system since 1971 represent a move towards greater efficiency: first, the almost universal adoption of the managed float; second, the formation of currency areas in the sense that countries have chosen more or less rigorous links of their exchange rates to national currencies, the SDR and regional norms of the type created for the European monetary system;[15] and third, the raising of the interest rates on SDRs to a weighted average of major national money market averages has achieved the dual objectives of assuring their real exchange value, since interest rates tend to reflect on real rate plus an expected inflation rate, and has made the opportunity cost of holding and using them equal to the efficient level suggested by the optimum quantity of money theory.

By the criteria of the proposed theoretical model, therefore, the reforms of the international monetary system since 1971 represent decisive moves toward the construction of an efficient system. The need for the future, by these criteria, lies in the area of making SDRs grow at steady and adequate rates and replacing national currencies as reserves in the portfolios of central banks.

NOTES

1. The Triffin XIMF, as one analyst called it, would have engaged in open market operations to distribute liquidity in the form of its own obligations. It thus would have performed the same function as central banks which acquire assets of a certain liquidity and provide liabilities with greater liquidity. However, Triffin liked to emphasize the elements distinguishing the XIMF from a central bank. Its liabilities did not circulate in the private sector and therefore did not compete directly with national currencies. In addition, the XIMF liabilities did not serve as a high-powered base for the expansion of national money supplies. In my view, however, there is little doubt that the ultimate objective of idealist reform planners was the creation of a genuine world central bank.

2. Triffin's concerns, which were borne out of his experiences during the period of nationalism of the 1930s, were with the creation of a spirit of co-operation, which would pave the way ultimately for greater economic integration and union.

3. References to pragmatist reform proposals are Bernstein, Harrod, Perjacobsson, Lutz, Machlup, Roosa, Wallich and Zolotas. The contributions by these authors are reprinted in Grubel (1963).

4. See contributions by Meade, Rueff, Heilperin, Yeager and Balogh reprinted in Grubel (1963).

5. See International Monetary Arrangements (1964), which reports on the deliberations of a study group of thirty-two economists who first met at the Rockefeller Foundation's center at Bellagio. The group was largely created by and functioned under the leadership of F. Machlup. It met at irregular intervals throughout the 1960s.

6. On 15 August 1971 the United States declared unilaterally the cessation of its traditional obligation to convert into gold US dollars held by foreign central banks at $35 an ounce. I believe that this date marks the end of the Bretton Woods system and the beginning of a new era. A chronology and major changes in the system after this date is found in Grubel (1981).

7. A summary of the doctrinal and official history of proposals for crawling pegs and similar innovations is found in Williamson (1981).

8. See Haberler (1977) for an analysis of the Jamaica Accord.

9. See Grubel (1982) for a study of the growth and composition of liquidity in the post-war years in the light of Triffin's reform proposals.

10. Willett (1968) has argued and attempted to show empirically that the exchange rate instabilities of the early 1970s simply accommodated the disturbances which were caused by exogenous supply shocks and national economic mismanagement. In an important sense, however, it could be argued that most of these disturbances were endogenous to the system in which international monetary discipline was absent and national monetary policies could be irresponsibly expansionary, causing even the supply shocks to have been endogenous to the global explosion of aggregate demand.

11. For a history of the IMF see Southard (1979).

12. I must admit to the failure of having considered the implication of rational expectations on the preceding ideas. However, unless all human events are pre-ordained, the formation of new institutions and their policies must have some effect on the economy.

13. P. Dee, a PhD student at Simon Fraser University, is analyzing the merit of leaning against the wind policies in her dissertation.

14. The entire role of centrally created reserves in an efficient international monetary system needs to be studied carefully. I am especially unhappy with the practice noted above that SDR interest rates are given exogenously by market developments while the IMF (in political consultations) determines the quantity of SDRs created. Perhaps the creation of SDRs through discounting would provide a more likely creation of equilibrium quantities. Or perhaps there are no valid efficiency arguments for any centrally created reserves and the world would be wise to stick to Hayek's principles concerning the efficiency of private money supplies.

15. See Heller (1979) for evidence that the arrangements chosen appear to be consistent with price-theoretic choice criteria.

REFERENCES

Bellagio Group (1964) see *International Monetary Arrangements*.

Coase, R. (1966) 'The Problem of Social Cost', *Journal of Law and Economics*, October.

Friedman, M. (1969) *The Optimal Quantity of Money and Other Essays* (Chicago: University of Chicago Press).

Grubel, H. (ed.) (1963) *World Monetary Reform: Plans and Issues* (Stanford: Stanford University Press).

Grubel, H. (1973) 'The Case for Optimum Exchange Rate Stability', *Weltwirtschaftliches Archiv*, 109 (3).

Grubel, H. (1977a) *The International Monetary System* (London: Penguin, third edn).

Grubel, H. (1977b) 'How Important is Control over International Reserves', in R. A. Mundell and J. J. Polak (eds) *The New International Monetary System* (New York: Columbia University Press).

Grubel, H. (1981) *International Economics* (Homewood, Ill.: Irwin, 2nd edn).

Grubel, H. (1982) 'Gold and the Dollar Crisis: Twenty Years Later', in R. N. Cooper, *et al.*, *The International Monetary System Under Flexible Exchange*

Rates, Essays in Honor of Robert Triffin (Cambridge, Mass.: Ballinger).

Haberler, G. (1977) 'The International Monetary System after Jamaica and Manila', in *Contemporary Economic Problems* (Washington: American Enterprise Institute).

Haberler, G. and Willett, T. (eds) (1968) *US Balance of Payments Policies and International Monetary Reform* (Washington: American Enterprise Institute).

Heller, H. R. (1979) 'Exchange Rate Flexibility and Currency Areas', *Zeitschrift für Wirtschafts und Sozialwissenschaften*, 1/2.

International Monetary Arrangements: The Problem of Choice (1964) Report on the Deliberations of an International Study Group of 32 Economists, (Princeton: Princeton University Press).

Klein, B. (1977) 'The Demand for Quality-adjusted Cash Balances: Price Uncertainty in the US Demand for Money Function', *J.P.E.*, 85(4), August, pp. 691–715.

Mundell, R. A. (1961) 'A Theory of Optimum Currency Areas', *American Economic Review*, September.

Solomon, R. (1977) *The International Monetary System 1945–76* (New York: Harper & Row).

Southard, F. A. (1979) *The Evolution of the International Monetary Fund*, Princeton Essays in International Finance, No. 135, December.

Triffin, R. (1960) *Gold and the Dollar Crisis* (New Haven, Conn.: Yale University Press).

Willett, T. (1968) see Haberler and Willett (1968).

Williamson, J. H. (1981) *Exchange Rate Rules: The Theory, Performance and Prospects of the Crawling Peg*.

2 Unexpected Real Consequences of Floating Exchange Rates[1]

RACHEL McCULLOCH

After a decade of floating exchange rates, international monetary reform is again in the air, and it is thus timely to ask how well (or badly) the current system is functioning. But compared to what? Because the current monetary arrangements came into effect following years of vigorous debate on the merits of exchange rate flexibility, some observers appear to forget that these arrangements were not in reality 'adopted', let alone 'designed.'[2] Rather, they were initiated by the collapse of the Bretton Woods regime and given markedly after-the-fact approval by an International Monetary Fund whose members were unable to agree upon an alternative, i.e. any system imposing even minimal restraints on the national policies of members. Since the present time seems no more propitious than the early 1970s for the willing sacrifice of national sovereignty by IMF members,[3] any argument for system reform must be solidly grounded in the accumulated experience of floating, not the dogmas of the Bretton Woods era.

This paper is an eclectic assessment of the floating-rate experience, with particular reference to the ways in which events have confounded both advocates and critics of floating. Although there is some discussion of the consequences of the floating-rate regime for macroeconomic performance worldwide, the main focus is on microeconomic issues – specifically, the role of floating rates in facilitating or retarding the growth of world trade and investment.

INTERNATIONAL MONEY AND THE GOALS OF BRETTON WOODS

National money, in its time-honored functions as medium of (indirect) exchange, unit of account, standard of deferred payment, and store of value, is supposed to facilitate the efficient allocation of resources in production and consumption. Although the precise nature and magnitude of such efficiency gains have never been spelled out fully in economic analyses, monetary history gives clear evidence of significant real resource costs (and unanticipated redistribution of wealth) entailed when money fails to perform the traditional microeconomic functions. At the same time, control of the nation's money supply also constitutes a potent tool of macroeconomic management and an alternative to taxation as a means of financing government expenditure. Thus there are conflicting objectives confronting those who exercise monetary policy, and both microeconomic and macroeconomic bases on which to judge their performance.

Analogously, a system of international money is supposed to facilitate the efficient allocation of resources worldwide, presumably through trade guided · by comparative advantage, but also has important consequences for global macroeconomic conditions. This twofold function was explicitly recognized in the Articles of Agreement of the International Monetary Fund approved at Bretton Woods in 1944, which listed among the purposes of the Fund:

> To facilitate the expansion and balanced growth of international trade, and to contribute *thereby* to the promotion and maintenance of high levels of employment and real income and to the development of the productive resources of all members as primary objectives of economic policy.[4]

As inadequacies in the Bretton Woods system became apparent during the 1960s, criticisms and proposals for reform of the system likewise fell into two distinct categories.

MACROECONOMIC PERFORMANCE

In the pre-1973 macroeconomic arguments for system reform and especially increased exchange-rate flexibility, the common theme was increased macroeconomic independence for IMF member nations.[5] The system was held to impart a deflationary bias to the world economy on account of the asymmetrical positions of creditor and debtor countries (at least in the rules if not the actual behavior of member nations). At a time when the prospects for 'fine tuning' of national macroeconomic performance seemed bright, obligations of member nations under the Bretton Woods rules appeared to limit the ability of elected governments to provide their constituents with the nationally mandated combination of inflation and unemployment.[6] Although control of two potent instruments – monetary policy and fiscal policy – in theory allowed enlightened policy-makers to achieve both 'internal balance' and 'external balance', thoughtful analysts soon recognized that still other objectives, notably adequate long-run growth, could be jeopardized by this textbook solution.[7]

Subsequent events suggest that advocates of increased flexibility failed to distinguish adequately between institutional and economic constraints on the actions of national policy-makers. The collapse of the Bretton Woods system clearly increased national sovereignty of IMF members with regard to macroeconomic policy but had a debatable effect on economic independence of member nations. Even so, the failure of the macroeconomic benefits of floating to materialize after 1973 had less to do with independence or the lack of it than with the now-evident flaws in 1960s-vintage macroeconomic paradigms of either the Keynesian or monetarist variety. That national economies failed to respond according to the predictions of ingenious 1960s models can be blamed on many aspects of human behavior that are usually assumed away for analytic convenience. Perhaps most important and surely most striking is the demonstrated capacity for profitable innovation – a description more optimistic than the pejorative 'structural instability' sometimes conjured up to explain the failure of econometric models to predict human behavior in times of rapid economic and social change.[8]

A related issue in the pre-1973 debate concerned the implications of the exchange rate regime for the propensity of national officials to engage in inflationary policies. According to one standard argument, 'the need to defend a fixed rate or a par value induces monetary and fiscal authorities to take greater care to prevent inflation; if floating rates were adopted, discipline would be weakened and countries would be more likely to pursue inflationary policies.'[9] Indeed, the case for flexibility as a means of increasing macroeconomic independence implies precisely that some nations will opt for higher inflation rates when freed of the 'external constraint' of a fixed parity. A similar but distinct argument is that a democratic government (or even one that is not so democratic) may find defense of a par value a politically acceptable reason to resist the competing claims of various domestic groups for increased shares of a relatively fixed national income.[10]

The standard arguments also sometimes noted the potential inflationary impact of exchange-rate changes themselves (for both fixed and flexible rates), but only after 1973 did attention shift to this line of causation from the 'nail-the-flag-to-the-masthead'[11] argument for fixed rates. Although the inflationary pressures attending any devaluation or depreciation had long been acknowledged by experts on less developed countries, analyses for the industrialized nations tended to ignore this, perhaps because of their Keynesian underpinnings.[12] But the post-1973 inflationary experience was too dramatic to be ignored. Much subsequent debate has centered on whether flexibility provides an independent source of inflationary pressure via a 'ratchet' mechanism that pushes domestic prices upward when a currency's value declines but fails to ensure a corresponding fall at times of currency appreciation. Empirical evidence on the ratchet issue appears to be inconclusive. However, one important competing explanation for the *ex ante* underestimates of the inflationary impact of devaluation or depreciation was the failure to assess correctly the true openness of industrial economies, or, more precisely, the strength of the linkage between international prices of traded goods and the domestic prices of nontraded goods.[13]

LIVING WITH EXCHANGE RISK

Pre-1973 microeconomic arguments for floating exchange rates stressed their role in encouraging 'unrestricted multilateral trade'.[14] While rigidly fixed exchange rates like those of the classical gold standard were conceded to provide transactors with many of the benefits of a single world money, the Bretton Woods system of adjustable pegs had major shortcomings. Balance-of-payments disequilibria were frequently met by direct controls on trade and capital flows rather than the domestic macroeconomic policy responses prescribed under the 'gold standard rules of the game'. Flexible-rate advocates argued that appropriate exchange rate movements would ensure prompt balance-of-payments adjustment, thus obviating the need for direct controls that distort global resource allocation.[15] Furthermore, the pegged rates could and did change. The appropriate comparison was therefore not between floating and fixed rates, but between rates changing by small amounts on a day-to-day basis and those changing at longer intervals by substantial percentages and usually only after macroeconomic policy debacles, welfare-reducing direct controls, and repeated foreign exchange market crises.[16]

But would the day-to-day movements in fact be small? Skeptics envisioned low price elasticities, long lags, exchange rate overshooting, destabilizing speculation, and resulting wide fluctuations in market-determined rates – a spector of the 1930s that (along with competitive devaluation) the IMF was specifically pledged to exorcise.[17] Large fluctuations in rates would increase the uncertainty facing international traders and investors. Although forward markets and a variety of other, more complicated mechanisms could provide transactors with insurance against rate changes, the additional cost would push world trade back towards barter.[18]

Post-1973 events have provided ample reason for extreme modesty on the part of prognosticators in either camp. Market-determined exchange rates have exhibited wild instability beyond the fondest nightmares of fixed-rate fanatics, yet trade and investment flows seem relatively unaffected by these changes.[19] The reconciliation of these apparently contradictory phenomena may be provided by the observation that the only alternatives to risky international transactions are risky domestic transactions. Of the many large risks of all types that any commercial endeavor now entails, exchange rate uncertainty may be relatively minor in relation to the benefits of foreign trade and investment, i.e. the risk appreciable but the profitability even more so. Foreign exchange risk is highly diversifiable, so that international operations provide an important means of diversifying risks associated with domestic transactions, rather than an independent addition to them.

The central message of the post-1973 experience is that the foreign exchange market is an asset market and that the economic laws governing exchange rates are fundamentally similar to those governing other asset prices, with stock and bond markets providing obvious domestic analogies.[20] In fact, while exchange rates have indeed been volatile, their volatility has been less than that of stock prices.[21] A related finding is that purchasing power parity, which perhaps ought not to have held in any case, has evidently 'collapsed'[22] in the 1970s, and that the celebrated 'law of one price' is not strictly enforced. As a consequence, the role of exchange rate movements in equilibrating international transactions must be re-evaluated.

A market-determined exchange rate necessarily equates day-to-day supply and demand for a nation's currency, whether or not supplemented by official reserve transactions. Thus the need for direct controls motivated by overall balance-of-payments considerations is indeed eliminated by floating rates. The result has been, as predicted, an important reduction in the use of capital controls for balance-of-payments purposes. But since asset preferences can and do produce significant prolonged divergences between the market price of a currency and its apparent 'real' worth as determined by purchasing power parity, there is no reason to expect a floating-rate system to eliminate incentives for direct controls motivated by current account considerations.[23] While current account balances have exhibited surprising (though lagged) responsiveness to rate movements, the reverse effect of current account imbalances on exchange rate movements is evidently much weaker. Indeed, the floating rate reacts only to the extent that current account imbalances constitute one type of 'news' affecting asset preferences.[24] Thus incentives for protection on macroeconomic grounds, i.e. as a means of increasing domestic aggregate demand, as well as for the more typical protection intended primarily to achieve sector-specific goals, are largely unaffected by floating rates.

The actual post-1973 experience has been characterized by a persistence and even extension of sectoral protection in the major industrialized countries, mainly for industries that are losing their competitiveness in relation to counterparts in Japan and especially the 'newly industrializing countries' (NICs). In contrast, there is no apparent trend toward the increased use of protection (or competitive devaluation) as a means of macroeconomic stimulus.[25] Further aspects of the relationship between protection and exchange rate movements are considered in subsequent sections.

FOREIGN DIRECT INVESTMENT

The 'overvalued' dollar of the 1960s was singled out as an (or perhaps even the) important reason for the large volume of US direct investment abroad, particularly in Europe. Through acquisitions of existing national enterprises and construction of new plant and equipment, US-based multinationals achieved a major presence in the protected markets of the newly created European Economic Community – investments all the more attractive at prevailing exchange rates. This role of disequilibrium exchange rates in foreign investment decisions was initially confirmed by events of the 1970s. As the dollar plummeted in relative value through two devaluations and post-1973 market depreciation, foreign direct investment in the United States grew with unprecedented rapidity – enough to make the United States the world's leading *host* country (in absolute but not relative terms) by the end of the decade. Yet strengthening of the dollar since 1978 has not stemmed the flow of new foreign direct investment, and volatility has had no noticeable impact on its volume.

Why have foreign investors been undeterred by exchange-rate turbulence since 1973? There are several plausible lines of explanation, not mutually exclusive. These considerations basically reflect the *relative* advantages of multinational firms over national enterprises. Thus the finding that foreign investment continued to increase after 1973 does not rule out large real costs resulting from increased exchange rate uncertainty.

As already noted, one anticipated benefit of floating that has materialized is a marked reduction in the use of direct capital controls. This trend facilitates new or expanded investments, while at the same time increasing their attractiveness by improving prospects for unimpeded repatriation of profits and royalties. Moreover, direct investment decisions are based on long-term planning, for periods during which even a pegged rate might well be expected to change. Over the life of an investment, the effects of volatility on profits largely cancel out; cumulative movements in exchange rates, whether pegged or floating, should mainly compensate for differential rates of domestic inflation or productivity growth across countries. A floating-rate system might ease such compensating exchange rate adjustments, reducing the likelihood of new direct controls on capital or trade flows during the investment period.

Foreign direct investment is also influenced by many considerations apart from exchange risk or the lack of it. If, as past studies suggest, protection is an important motive for direct investment, the recent protectionist swing in the United States – both actual and threatened new barriers to trade – may have elicited investments intended to protect large expenditures already incurred in development of the lucrative US market. Recent Japanese investments in the United States may fall into this category. Furthermore, the accumulation of wealth by OPEC surplus nations has given rise to increased demands for assets for all kinds.[26] However, available statistics are uninformative on this point, since many direct OPEC investments are presumably held through anonymous third country intermediaries.

Finally, as suggested above and exactly contrary to pre-1973 conventional wisdom, floating may provide an important independent source of gains from foreign direct investment. Input-price uncertainty is a recognized motive for vertical integration; a regime of floating rates accordingly provides incentives for vertical multinational integration. Together with centralized management, vertical integration allows substantial reduction in variability of profits due to exchange rate movements between input source countries and downstream users.[27] This explanation fits the Canadian floating-rate period, which was marked by continued expansion of US direct investments in Canadian extractive industries. Likewise, this may be a second motive (in addition to increased actual and threatened protection) for recent Japanese investments in US production facilities. Horizontal global expansion may similarly be favored by floating rates. For production operations in which minimum efficient scale is relatively low or scale economies unimportant, global diversification of production facilities allows firms some opportunity to optimize with respect to medium-term movements in real exchange rates as well as a means of smoothing profits associated with these operations.[28]

Both vertical and horizontal expansion motivated by exchange-rate variability also help to explain the rapid growth of intra-industry and intra-firm trade during the 1970s. They have opposite implications for the responsiveness of trade flows to movements in exchange rates, however. While vertical integration in effect allows a firm to ignore changes in the rate, horizontal integration offers opportunities to profit from them through rapid adjustments in trade flows.

EXCHANGE RATES, RELATIVE PRICES AND COMPETITIVENESS

A major surprise of the 1970s was the discovery that the United States is not a closed economy.[29] This erroneous characterization rested in part on a confusion of *traded* and *tradable* goods; for a large country like the United States, openness is consistent with low ratios of exports and imports to total domestic shipments. Closely linked was the failure to anticipate the importance of exchange rate changes for domestic prices. Early and crude estimates of the inflationary impact of dollar devaluation assumed that only the prices of imported goods would be affected.

Analysts had been misled in part by the traditional elasticities approach to exchange rate changes. The elasticities approach entailed a basically Keynesian view of price movements. Domestic currency prices (or supply curves) for exports and import substitutes were assumed to be independent of the exchange rate. A related, crucial but always implicit assumption was that domestic and foreign goods are not highly substitutable, so that domestic producers of tradables face appreciably downward-sloping demand curves for their outputs even in the longer run. Given these assumptions, the primary effect of a devaluation would be to alter the relative price of domestic goods and their foreign counterparts, shifting domestic and foreign demand towards domestic goods. A devaluing nation with some excess capacity could therefore expect a durable improvement in the international price competitiveness of its export- and import-competing industries and a resulting durable improvement in its trade balance. The same logic was carried over to open economy versions of Keynesian macroeconomic models, in which the exchange rate served as a policy instrument for switching aggregate expenditure between foreign and domestic markets.

The unexpectedly large impact of exchange rate changes on domestic prices in the United States, along with the observed failure in many cases of devaluation to produce a durable improvement in the trade balance, led analysts to discard the elasticities approach and its underlying assumptions. With considerable fanfare, the era of the monetary approach was ushered in. Central to the elasticities approach is the implicit assumption that the law of one price is not applicable; domestic currency prices of domestically produced tradables are able to move independently of the domestic currency prices of their foreign counterparts. Monetary approach analysts chose an opposite but equally extreme assumption, making the law of one price the centerpiece of their models. Domestically produced exports and import-competing goods were now taken to be perfect substitutes for their foreign counterparts; accordingly, their domestic currency prices were necessarily identical at all times. Under these circumstances, a devaluation must increase the price of domestically produced tradables to restore equality with the price of their foreign substitutes; for a small country, the domestic price of all tradables would rise by exactly the amount of the devaluation. An exchange rate change then affects primarily the relative price of tradables and non-tradables, rather than the relative price of domestic and foreign goods. While the higher relative price of tradables implies an increase in their domestic supply, domestic demand is shifted *away* from all tradables towards non-tradables, eventually raising the prices of the latter and restoring the initial allocation of resources in domestic production. A key implication of such models is that devaluation cannot improve the international price competitiveness of domestic suppliers.

But again events confounded theories, and again the problem centered on the law of one price – unduly disregarded in the elasticities approach but exalted beyond its empirical justification by monetary approach analysts. As producers of almost any tradable good will be happy to affirm, exchange rate movements *are* an important ingredient of the overall international competitiveness of domestic industries; for some non-negligible period, exchange rate movements can and do alter the relative prices of foreign and domestic goods.

While the law of one price (for any one 'good') assumes a high degree of substitutability in consumption or production between domestic tradables and their foreign counterparts as well as markets that are highly competitive, empirical investigation reveals that these conditions do not hold for most tradable goods, at least over the relatively short periods with which macroeconomic policy is concerned. Rather, for reasons including product differentiation, trade barriers, delivery lags, distribution and servicing, tradables are heterogeneous in their adherence to the law of one price, or, more precisely, in their adherence to its preconditions.[30] Recognizing that tradable goods are heterogeneous brings the analysis almost full circle to a framework in which elasticities again play a key role. An important implication is that the price effects of devaluation are not uniform across industries producing tradable goods.[31]

SECTORAL CONSEQUENCES OF CHANGES IN EXCHANGE RATES

Where substitutability and therefore cross-price elasticities are high and markets competitive, there will be strong forces equating the domestic currency price of foreign-produced goods with that of domestically produced versions. A devaluation will therefore cause domestic price to rise – by the full amount of a devaluation for a small country that has no appreciable effect on the international price. Domestic supply, employment and profits will rise; domestic consumption will fall.

For industries in which domestic and foreign versions are highly imperfect substitutes, devaluation has much weaker short-run consequences for the domestic price. The increased domestic currency price of the imperfect foreign substitute results in an outward shift in the domestic industry's downward-sloping demand curve.[32] The effects on equilibrium price thus depend crucially on conditions of domestic supply. Domestic output, employment and profits will rise; and domestic and foreign consumption of the industry's output will rise on account of the favourable movement in its relative price. Moreover, with goods or services that are highly differentiated, each *producer* faces a distinctly downward-sloping demand curve for the product, so that markets may be characterized by price discrimination. In such markets an exchange rate change may actually have a 'perverse' effect on output and price, although not profits.[33]

Exchange-rate changes also affect industry supply curves through their consequences for the domestic currency prices of tradable inputs. As noted above, the size of price changes depends critically upon the extent to which foreign and domestic versions are highly substitutable; the speed with which these price changes are reflected in higher production costs depends on the extent to which suppliers are bound by long-term commitments. One measure of the total impact of devaluation on a given industry through both output and input markets is the *net* effect on industry value-added.[34] Only for an industry in which domestic and foreign goods are highly substitutable both on the output and the input side *and* effects on world prices of the industry's output sales and input purchases negligible will a devaluation raise domestic currency value-added by exactly the amount of the devaluation. Otherwise, either a smaller or larger increment is possible.

A last dimension of the sectoral consequences of devaluation concerns the division of increased industry value-added between industry-specific and mobile factors. If the supply of mobile factors ('labor') is available at a fixed nominal reward (as in the case of a binding minimum wage), industry profits would increase by the full increment in value-added. But because devaluation raises the cost of living and also tends to increase the demand for variable factors of production, there may be some upward adjustment in wages, whether determined by a competitive market, union contract negotiation, or legislation of a real minimum wage. On the other hand, devaluation (as opposed to depreciation of a floating rate) is often accompanied by an 'income policy' intended to hold down wage adjustments, thus reducing the real wage and raising the proportion of increased industry value-added accruing as profits.[35]

ADJUSTMENTS TO REAL SHOCKS

Although real shocks were hardly new in the 1970s, their interaction with a floating-rate system provided beleaguered policy analysts with considerable food for thought. As predicted, floating rates prevented the recurring exchange market crises that no doubt would have otherwise accompanied the OPEC price shocks and ill-advised policy responses to them.[36] Indeed, even those basically opposed to floating rates readily acknowledge that no alternative system is likely to have remained intact during the stormy 1970s. On the other hand, the actual adjustment process was quite different than that anticipated by most analysts, principally because of the unexpected ways in which OPEC surplus nations spent their vastly increased earnings.

But according to the standard pre-1973 debate, flexible rates were supposed to have the merit of insulating a country from external shocks, while fixed rates would allow the burden of internal shocks to be shared with trading partners.[37] As already noted, the increased macroeconomic independence offered by flexible rates proved to be largely illusory. Moreover, the standard fixed-versus-flexible arguments, based on conclusions from one-sector macroeconomic models, necessarily ignored the sector-specific impact of many shocks and thus obscured the sector-specific aspects of the resulting adjustment process. In response to this latter discovery, enterprising theorists have recently come forward with models of such hitherto uncelebrated maladies such as 'Dutch disease'.[38]

As in the analysis of exchange-rate changes, the crucial missing insight was that 'the' tradables sector is in fact a set of heterogeneous industries. In particular, each has at any point in time a collection of industry-specific factors that can be shifted elsewhere only at considerable cost. In a floating-rate system, the good fortune of one tradable goods industry, whether technological progress, mineral discoveries or favorable price movements in the world market, can become bad news for other tradable goods industries through two mechanisms: exchange rate appreciation and bidding up of rewards to factors mobile between sectors. The result is 'Dutch disease' or 'de-industrialization' or 'lagging sectors', i.e. ones in which output falls and the rewards to industry-specific factors decline. Moreover, 'the decline in the relative size of non-booming sectors is a necessary component of the economy's adjustment toward a higher level of income'.[39] Thus a conflict arises between efficient resource allocation and certain other national objectives, such as developing and maintaining an industrial sector of a certain size or maintaining incomes of sector-specific factors.

All this assumes, of course, that the exchange rate moves in the direction suggested by the effect on the current account balance, a mechanism that in practice may be weak. Furthermore, a national government wishing to avoid the consequences of appreciation can intervene in the foreign exchange market, directly or indirectly, thus protecting other tradables sectors from injury.[40] In this case, or with a pegged rate that is not revised upward, the good news would mean reserve accumulation and attendant inflationary pressure, rather than appreciation. Thus the problem of adjustment can at least be postponed, for better or worse. If the good news were temporary or reversible, a stable rate could eliminate the unpleasant and perhaps undesirable squeeze on other tradables, although probably at the cost of some inflation.

While a sensible comparison of effects under the two regimes requires some specification of private and official expectations formation, it is possible that the outcomes may be quite similar. The reason is that a macroeconomic policy cannot eradicate the 'super-competitiveness' of one tradable goods sector over the rest. Through internal general equilibrium mechanisms such as competition for inputs, the less competitive sectors will still be squeezed. For example, it is noteworthy that the balance (in current dollars) of US trade in 'high-technology' industries has grown almost exponentially since 1960, while the trade balance of all other manufacturing industries is roughly its mirror image.[41] There is no apparent discontinuity in this pattern between the 1960s and 1970s, except for a higher variability that probably reflects underlying macroeconomic fluctuations and large jumps in real exchange rates over that period. But for a government determined to slow the movement of resources out of uncompetitive tradables industries, there is still an obvious solution in the form of sectoral intervention or 'industrial policy'.[42]

CAUSES AND CONSEQUENCES OF PROTECTION

Freer trade was one widely anticipated advantage of flexible exchange rates[43] that failed to materialize. While the conventional wisdom predicted that exchange rate flexibility would facilitate trade liberalization, the post-1973 period has in fact been marked by proliferation of new and subtle trade-distorting measures. Furthermore, there is some evidence that exchange-rate volatility has actually exacerbated the ever-present clamor for more and better protection from foreign competition.[44]

According to the usual pre-1973 argument, exchange-rate flexibility should eliminate the perceived need for protection and in any case neutralize its benefits. This argument rested on errors concerning both the motives for protection and its consequences in a flexible-rate system. A floating rate obviates the perceived need for direct controls on foreign transactions only to the extent that they are motivated by overall balance-of-payments considerations; possible incentives for protection as a tool of macroeconomic stabilization or to achieve sector-specific goals remain. The assumption that balance-of-payments considerations dominated trade policy choices before 1973 may have stemmed from a confusion of the underlying motives for protection with the public rhetoric used to justify it.[45] Since overall balance-of-payments considerations were in most instances merely a secondary motive for protection, the elimination of this motive has had only minor consequences for its use.

Gains achieved by protected domestic industries would be completely offset by resulting exchange rate movements[46] only under highly implausible circumstances. The notion that it is irrational for industries to seek protection which will be offset by currency revaluation is another example of the misleading conclusions to be drawn from macroeconomic models with insufficient 'structure'. Both in industrialized and developing countries, real-world protection is a microeconomic, industry-specific phenomenon. Although broad national coalitions may form to support or oppose major changes in national trade legislation, the level and form of actual protection is almost always determined on an industry-by-industry basis. Even the 'across-the-board' tariff cuts achieved in the Kennedy Round of multilateral trade negotiations in fact singled out numerous specific industries for exemption from these cuts. Recent macroeconomic analyses of protection are based on models in which only one good is produced domestically.[47] These models provide useful insights concerning asset-market channels through which protection can have unanticipated and complex general equilibrium consequences. But because they necessarily omit the important sector-specific effects that are at the very heart of trade policy, they can provide only partial, and sometimes misleading, information concerning the real-world policies that presumably motivate their construction.[48]

As soon as its industry-specific nature is recognized, the analysis of protection becomes identical to that of the industry-specific shocks discussed in the previous section. Protection of some tradables is likely to worsen the economic prospects of other, less-favored tradables. As before, whether the protection of some industries transforms others into lagging sectors depends in part on whether the exchange rate actually appreciates; in the case of protection, the outcome has an additional element of ambiguity, since some protective devices such as 'voluntary' export restraints can cause a deterioration rather than an improvement in the trade balance and hence (to the extent that the trade balance does influence the exchange rate) a depreciation rather than an appreciation.[48] Adequate analysis of these effects requires a model with at least two sectors producing tradable outputs.

Identification of sectoral consequences also helps to clarify the underlying rational motives for apparently irrational policies. One particularly interesting example is the prevalence of overvalued exchange rates among developing countries, along with extensive trade and credit controls. Taken together as a coherent policy package, this adds up to a hefty subsidy to a preferred sector, typically import-competing industrial production. While trade barriers protect domestic markets, an overvalued exchange rate allows required capital equipment and intermediate inputs to be purchased at bargain prices, and capital-export prohibitions facilitate access to low-cost credit. The resulting disadvantage to producers of other tradables is one important reason for the much-remarked failure of Third World agriculture to achieve the production levels suggested by its obvious comparative advantage.[50]

VOLATILITY AND PROTECTIONISM

The volatility of the dollar since 1973 has resulted in prolonged departures from purchasing power parity and large exogenous swings in the international competitiveness of US producers of tradable goods. Taken together with the unexpected increase in protectionism over the same period, this raises the question of whether the current system has actually been an important *cause* of increased protectionism.

A recent suggestion is that there is a 'ratchet' effect of exchange rate fluctuations on the average level of protection.[51] While prolonged overvaluation of the dollar gives rise, as in 1981 and 1982, to new arguments for all manner of sectoral protection, any new protection enacted is likely to persist long after the overvaluation has disappeared. Moreover, even undervaluation might add to protectionist pressures by attracting resources into industries with secularly declining international competitiveness, or at least slowing their exit. When the inappropriately low currency value finally moves upward again, protection will be demanded.

While this hypothesis is intuitively appealing and seems consistent with the recent protectionist fever in the US Congress, there is again a problem of distinguishing appropriately between the underlying motives for protection and its public justification. The quest for favorable government intervention (in all forms, including but certainly not limited to trade policies) is a fact of economic life. As long as governments are responsive to demands for sectoral intervention, efforts to obtain, retain and increase such benefits represent a capital investment comparable to R & D, advertising and other intangibles that have a favorable impact on profits.[52] However, since managers, union officials and the public all tend to view asymmetrically profits versus losses and overtime versus lay-offs, both the industry 'demand' for government intervention and its politically determined 'supply' may be expected to increase when national unemployment is high, as in 1981–2. Furthermore, while protection is only one possible type of favorable legislative or administrative action among many,[53] the political cost of intervention in the particular form of protection is probably less when the exchange rate is widely acknowledged to be overvalued, as in 1981–2.

For these political economic reasons, it is plausible to expect industry-specific intervention to increase when national unemployment is high and to take the specific form of new trade barriers when the dollar is overvalued. But the actual cases cited to support this link between protection and overvaluation (e.g. textiles, steel, sugar, shoes) are ones with chronic competitiveness problems, not fundamentally healthy industries put temporarily into the red by an overvalued dollar. For some, protection from imports is a national vice extending back into the 1950s. This suggests that exchange rate overvaluation can provide the politically expedient occasion for new protection of declining industries, interacting with other determinants of increased protectionism. However, the empirical evidence for the persistence of sectoral intervention seems to be weak. Because of strong domestic lobbies against, as well as in favor of, protection, for many industries import relief provides only a brief respite from the consequences of shifting comparative advantage.[54]

CONCLUDING REMARKS

Much of the pre-1973 debate on international monetary reform proved to be irrelevant for two reasons. First, international political realities precluded the 'choice' or 'design' of a new system. Perhaps Bretton Woods was a unique phenomenon, at least for modern times. But, more important, the post-1973 system of flexible exchange rates has functioned in ways that are markedly different from the predictions of most analysts on either side of the debate.

In many regards, the academic arguments in favor of increased flexibility never improved on Friedman's (1953) pioneering case. Yet Friedman as well as most others erred in their most fundamental prediction, that flexible rates would be stable if national monetary policies were stable. We live in times of too much daily economic 'news' from other sources to avoid large fluctuations in market-determined exchange rates.[55] Moreover,while these fluctuations do probably imply significant real costs to those engaged in international commerce, their effects on trade and investment flows are very different than anticipated. In particular, day-to-day movements in currency values offer an independent motive for international transactions as a means of diversifying exchange risk, as well as for several other reasons discussed above.

If there is a single salient lesson to be learned by scrutinizing academic research on exchange rates in the light of post-1973 events in the international monetary system, it is the great potential mischief arising from insufficient attention to economic structure in macroeconomic analysis. While theorists necessarily strip reality down to a bare minimum of basic relationships, the same basics are not appropriate for all questions. In particular, for the large number of policy issues concerning the interactions of individual industries within a single economy, macroeconomic models with only one aggregate tradable can provide at best a partial understanding and sometimes a seriously flawed account.

NOTES

1. This paper was prepared for the Wingspread Conference on the Evolving Multiple Reserve Asset System, July 28–30, 1982. I am grateful to J. David Richardson for extensive and stimulating discussions of the subject. I am indebted also to Robert E. Baldwin, Peter B. Kenen, Charles P. Kindleberger, Michael Rothschild, Andre Sapir, Janet Yellen, and conference participants at Wingspread and the 1982 National Bureau of Economic Research Summer Institute for helpful suggestions, and to the University of Wisconsin Graduate School for financial support.
2. For example, Bergsten and Williamson (1982, p. 11). As late as 1972, the Executive Directors of the IMF apparently rejected floating even as a viable option (IMF, 1972). An official 1970 document devotes one of 78 pages to floating rates (IMF, 1970).

3. This central problem was identified by Cooper (1968) in his remarkably prescient discussion of interdependence. On the implications of the same issue for trade, see Blackhurst (1981).
4. Articles of Agreement, Article I(ii) (emphasis added).
5. Cooper (1968, p. 263) suggested that wider exchange rate margins would be one means of reducing interdependence. Interestingly, he noted as a disadvantage of this approach 'from the viewpoint of fostering international cooperation . . . of *not* affording an occasion for close international consultation'.
6. On the trade-off argument for flexibility, see the incisive account by Artus and Young (1979, pp. 656–9).
7. See Haberler's (1969, p. 357) comments on the need for increased exchange rate flexibility, for example.
8. Meese and Rogoff (1982) found that a random walk performed as well out-of-sample as any estimated structural model of exchange rate determination. In an earlier version of the same paper (Meese and Rogoff, 1981), the authors attributed the poor out-of-sample performance to 'structural instability'. But, as the authors noted in the revised version, it is more accurate to describe the problem as one of omitted variables or other misspecification of the underlying structural relationships. In other words, simple models cannot predict complex responses. On some of the private-sector financial innovations contributing to this complexity, see Hester (1981).
9. Solomon (1977, p. 287). Curiously, although this is widely acknowledged to be a traditional argument, I have been unable to find a single clear example of its use by an advocate of fixed rates.
10. Caves and Jones (1973, p. 444). As the authors note, however, a government might just as well point to 'disgraceful' depreciation of a flexible rate. In the post-1973 period some have done exactly that.
11. Caves and Jones (1973).
12. For example, the 'absorption' literature stressed the importance of aggregate excess capacity in determining the degree to which the effects of a devaluation would be quickly offset by induced inflation. See Alexander's (1952) classic article.
13. Chipman (1981) provides a useful framework for analyzing this issue, as well as an illuminating historical account of its treatment. Also see McKinnon (1981).
14. Friedman (1953, p. 137).
15. Although proponents of flexible rates were virtually unanimous on this point, some critics foresaw incentives for protectionism. For instance, see Wallich's comments in Haberler *et al.* (1969, p. 362).
16. Mundell's observation (1969, p. 324) that 'an international crisis is one means by which a government can dramatize the need for an alteration in its policies and shift much of the blame for unpopular features of the new policy from the national government to the international community' applies equally to the more recent period. Compare, for example, official European pronouncements on the dollar and American monetary policy in 1978 and in 1982.
17. Articles of Agreement, Article I(iii).

18. Kindleberger (1970, p. 224).
19. Blackhurst and Tumlir (1980, pp. 13–16) have noted that world trade volume continued to grow more rapidly than production throughout the 1970s, consistent with their hypothesis that the major determinant of changes in the level of trade is underlying GNP growth. Examining the effects of exchange rate uncertainty on multilateral and bilateral trade flows of the United States, Germany, and several other industrial countries for the period 1965–1975, Hooper and Kohlhagen (1978, p. 505) 'found absolutely no significant effect on the volume of trade (at the 0.95 level) despite considerable effort and experimentation'. The authors did find a significant impact on prices, suggesting that the absence of a significant impact on volume might reflect relatively inelastic short-run supply of exports or, alternatively, substantial hedging by importers and exporters.
20. The pre-1973 concern about volatility in exchange markets was often linked to predicted speculative capital flows. The post-1973 experience suggests that exchange rate movements may in part substitute for actual flows of capital in maintaining covered interest parity. This form of arbitrage was far less important in the earlier period, when spot and often forward rates were highly constrained.
21. Frenkel and Mussa (1980). Some recent literature has attemped to judge whether volatility of observed asset prices is 'excessive', i.e. unjustified by movements in their fundamental determinants. Shiller (1981) found evidence that the volatility of stock prices is excessive in relation to underlying uncertainty about future dividends, at least if risk neutrality is assumed. Although Shiller's statistical methodology has been questioned by subsequent researchers, a similar test in the case of exchange rate movements rests on still shakier ground. As Meese and Singleton (1982) have pointed out, any test of whether exchange-rate volatility is excessive must be predicated on the validity of a particular structural model (of several active contenders). Furthermore, as Frenkel and Mussa note, even a finding of excessive volatility has no obvious policy implications.
22. Frenkel (1981). Although there is a rich literature spanning at least four decades on the reasons why purchasing power parity need not hold over short or even long time periods, the notion persists that its absence somehow violates fundamental precepts of rational economic behavior. A recent paper by Jones and Purvis (1981) shows that in a model with internationally traded 'middle products', the law of one price can obtain at all times and yet purchasing power parity does not hold.
23. Bergsten and Williamson (1982).
24. Dornbusch (1980).
25. However, an assumed net gain in aggregate employment is customarily used to bolster the case for proposed sectoral interventions, especially when large industries such as apparel and automobiles are involved. In England, the Cambridge Economic Policy Group has promulgated a macroeconomic case for across-the-board protection of British industry, but with no noticeable effect thus far on the policies of the Thatcher government. Japan is sometimes accused of engaging in policies to prevent appreciation of the yen, especially through restrictions on inward foreign investment. But the main evidence presented in support of this hypothesis is unbalanced

bilateral trade with the United States, a condition that also accompanied the allegedly overvalued yen in previous years.

26. Moreover, the post-1973 'internationalization' of the supply of saving suggested by Branson (1981) probably favors US assets because of the relative size and stability of the American economy.

27. Centralized management also facilitates optimization of foreign exchange exposure, reducing the need for forward-market cover. Aliber (1982) has suggested that the lower cost of internal cover provides an advantage of multinational firms over domestic ones. Burtle and Mooney (1978, p. 158) cite evidence from a survey conducted by Michael Jilling and William R. Folks, Jr. that multinational firms have moved towards greater management centralization since 1973.

28. Despite all the good reasons adduced by economic theorists to show that rational managers should be indifferent to variability of accounting profits, managers persist in their concern about period-to-period fluctuations in reported earnings. FASB Statement Number 8, the Financial Accounting Standards Board's first attempt to develop standardized accounting principles for a world of day-to-day movements in exchange rates, resulted in large and probably meaningless fluctuations in reported earnings (Hekman, 1981). The resulting storm of protests produced FASB Statement Number 52, which broadens the definition of exposure and calls for an adjustment to net worth rather than earnings.

29. See, for example, comments by Wallich in Haberler *et al.* (1969, pp. 360–1). Openness also increased in the 1970s, as implied by Branson's (1981) analysis of the effects of OPEC surpluses. Interestingly enough, authors of textbooks on macroeconomics continue to relegate any consideration of openness to the final chapters.

30. According to Isard, 'substantial changes in exchange rates typically have substantial and persistent effects on the relative common currency prices of closely matched manufactures produced in different countries' (1977, p. 948).

31. Although industry-specific consequences within the aggregate of 'tradables' have attracted little attention from theorists accustomed to highly aggregated models, econometric modelers have attempted to build into their estimations some of the effects discussed in this section. See Hooper and Lowrey (1979) and Deardorff and Stern (1982 and many similar papers).

32. Because different countries produce different products and different variants within a product category, a uniform exchange rate change may have non-uniform consequences for import demand across suppliers.

33. See Panagariya and Owen (1982).

34. As in the analysis of the 'effective protection' afforded to a given industry by a nation's tariff schedule, i.e. the percentage by which industry value-added per unit can exceed its free trade level, a calculation can in principle be made of the *net* effect of 'exchange rate protection' on an industry's value-added.

35. On the crucial role of 'structural' considerations such as supply elasticities and wage rigidities or indexation in open economy macroeconomic analysis see Branson (1982) and references cited there.

36. Although floating rates themselves did little to assist the adjustment problem of less-developed oil importers (most of which still peg their rates in

any case), a largely private recycling process solved the immediate problem of inadequate balance-of-payments financing. See Cohen (1982) and Branson (1981).

37. For example, see Kenen's comments in Haberler *et al.* (1969, pp. 362–3) and Caves and Jones (1973, pp. 442–3).

38. Including Corden (1981), Corden and Neary (1982), Neary (1982), and many others. Also see Branson (1982).

39. Neary (1982, p. 20).

40. Corden (1981) has suggested that this is a primary motive for 'exchange rate protection'.

41. General equilibrium consequences of expanded research and development and their implications for the overall competitiveness of US manufactured goods are considered in McCulloch (1978, pp. 24–6).

42. Blackhurst (1981) notes the blurring in recent years of the distinction between trade policies and domestic policies, at least on the basis of outcomes as opposed to instruments.

43. Among many others, see Baldwin (1970, pp. 20–1) and Bergsten (1972, pp. 8–9), two writers whose views reflected considerable experience in US agencies shaping the nation's trade policy decisions.

44. Bergsten (1982), Bergsten and Williamson (1982), Aho and Bayard (1982).

45. Two indirect pieces of evidence are levels of protection that vary markedly across industries and the use of quantitative restrictions with ambiguous balance-of-payments consequences. However, any positive balance-of-payments consequences can be viewed as reducing the political cost of providing protection to favored sectors. See Brock and Magee (1980) on the political determination of equilibrium protection levels.

46. See, for example, Friedman (1981).

47. For example, Eichengreen (1981), Krugman (1982), and Richardson (1982). Boyer (1977) assumes one aggregate tradable.

48. Also see my comments (McCulloch, 1982) on Krugman (1982).

49. This possible ambiguity, which was noted in Meade's classic analysis (1951, Chapter XXI), is central to Richardson's (1982a) treatment of 'modern' commercial policy.

50. Like all generalizations regarding developing countries, this one obviously disregards many important national differences. However, the pattern seems to fit a large number of countries. On its applicability to Sub-Saharan Africa, see World Bank (1981).

51. Bergsten and Williamson (1982). The paper calls for policies to ensure that the value of the dollar does not stray too far from its 'fundamental equilibrium rate', defined by analogy to the Bretton Woods criterion of fundamental disequilibrium for a parity change and distinguished from day-to-day market equilibrium. But while uncontroversial arguments in favor of greater stability constitute much of the paper, there is no indication of how the authors' proposed solution (which amounts to a wide-bands peg and would thus appear to share many of the flaws that led to the end of the Bretton Woods system) could be successfully implemented.

52. One important difference is that the investment in obtaining favorable government intervention is usually undertaken by an industry trade association or a labor union, rather than by a single firm. This poses a 'free

rider' problem that does not occur for advertising or R&D.
53. 'Domestic' policies with similarly favorable consequences for those with the political clout to obtain them include government procurement, regulatory or tax relief, technical assistance, and subsidized credit.
54. The AFL–CIO (1982, p. 21) cites color television, specialty steel and fasteners as examples of US industries that have recently lost temporary relief from import competition.
55. As Mussa (1979a, p. 9) puts it, 'the smoothly adjusting exchange rate is, like the unicorn, a mythical beast'.

REFERENCES

Aho, C. Michael and Tom Bayard (1982) 'The 1980s: Twilight of the Open Trading System', Office of Foreign Economic Research, US Department of Labor, May.
Alexander, Sidney S. (1952) 'Effects of a Devaluation on a Trade Balance', *IMF Staff Papers*, 2, April, pp. 263–78.
Aliber, Robert Z. (1982) 'Money, Multinationals, and Sovereigns', paper prepared for the Middlebury Conference on the Multinational Corporation in the 1980s, Middlebury, Vermont, April 15–17.
American Federation of Labor and Congress of Industrial Organizations (1982) *The National Economy 1981* (Washington, DC: AFL–CIO).
Artus, Jacques and John H. Young (1979) 'Fixed and Flexible Exchange Rates: A Renewal of the Debate', *IMF Staff Papers*, 26, December, pp. 654–98.
Baldwin, Robert (1970) *Non-Tariff Distortions of International Trade* (Washington, DC: Brookings).
Bergsten, C. Fred and John Williamson (1982) 'Exchange Rates and Trade Policy', paper prepared for the Institute for International Economics Conference on Trade Policy in the eighties, Washington, DC, June 23–25.
Bergsten, C. Fred (1972) *The Cost of Import Restrictions to American Consumers* (New York: American Importers Association).
Bergsten, C. Fred (1982) 'The Villain is an Overvalued Dollar', *Challenge*, March/April, pp. 25–49.
Blackhurst, Richard (1981) 'The Twilight of Domestic Economic Policies', *The World Economy*, 4, December, pp. 357–73.
Blackhurst, Richard and Jan Tumlir (1980) *Trade Relations Under Flexible Exchange Rates* (Geneva: General Agreement on Tariffs and Trade).
Boyer, R. S. (1977) 'Commercial Policy Under Alternative Exchange Rate Regimes', *Canadian Journal of Economics*, 10, May, pp. 218–32.
Branson, William H. (1981) 'OPEC Lending, LDC Growth, and US Trade', NBER Working Paper No. 791, November.
Branson, William H. (1982) 'Economic Structure and Policy for External Balance', paper prepared for the NBER/IMF Conference on Policy Interdependence, August 31.
Brock, William A. and Stephen P. Magee (1980) 'Tariff Formation in a Democracy', in J. Black and B. Hindley (eds) *Current Issues in Commercial Policy and Diplomacy* (London: Trade Policy Research Centre).

Burtle, James and Sean Mooney (1978) 'International Trade and Investment Under Floating Rates: The Reaction of Business to the Floating Rate System', in Jacob S. Dreyer, Gottfried Haberler and Thomas D. Willet (eds), *Exchange Rate Flexibility* (Washington DC: American Enterprise Institute), pp. 151–8.

Caves, Richard E. and Ronald W. Jones (1973) *World Trade and Payments* (Boston: Little, Brown and Company).

Chipman, John (1981) 'Internal-External Price Relationships in the West German Economy, 1958–79', *Zeitschrift für die gesamte Staatswissenschaft*, 137, September, pp. 612–37.

Cohen, Benjamin J. (1982) 'Balance-of-Payments Financing: Evolution of a Regime', *International Organization*, 36, Spring, pp. 457–78.

Cooper, Richard N. (1968) *The Economics of Interdependence* (New York: McGraw-Hill for the Council on Foreign Relations).

Corden, W. M. (1981) 'Exchange Rate Protection', in R. N. Cooper *et al.* (eds) *The International Monetary System Under Flexible Exchange Rates: Global, Regional, and National* (Cambridge, Ma: Ballinger).

Corden, W. M. and J. P. Neary (1982) 'Booming Sector and De-Industrialization in a Small Open Economy', Seminar Paper No. 195, Institute for International Economic Studies, Stockholm, February.

Deardorff, Alan V. and Robert M. Stern (1982) 'Tariff and Exchange-Rate Protection under Fixed and Flexible Exchange Rates in the Major Industrialized Countries', in J. Bhandari and B. Putnam (eds) *Economic Interdependence and Flexible Exchange Rates* (Cambridge, Ma: MIT Press).

Dornbusch, Rudiger (1980) 'Exchange Rate Economics: Where Do We Stand?', *Brookings Papers on Economic Activity*, 1, pp. 143–85.

Eichengreen, Barry (1981) 'A Dynamic Model of Tariffs, Output and Employment Under Flexible Exchange Rates', *Journal of International Economics*, 11, August, pp. 341–59.

Frenkel, Jacob A. (1981) 'The Collapse of Purchasing Power Parities During the 1970s', *European Economic Review*, 16, May, pp. 145–65.

Frenkel, Jacob A. and Michael L. Mussa (1980) 'The Efficiency of Foreign Exchange Markets and Measures of Turbulence', *American Economic Review*, 70, May, pp. 374–81.

Friedman, Milton (1953) 'The Case for Flexible Exchange Rates', in *Essays in Positive Economics* (Chicago: University of Chicago Press).

Friedman, Milton (1981) 'Do Imports Cost Jobs?', *Newsweek*, 9 February, p. 77

Haberler, Gottfried, Henry C. Wallich, Peter B. Kenen and Fritz Machlup (1969) 'Round Table on Exchange Rate Policy', *American Economic Review*, 59, May, pp. 357–69.

Hekman, Christine R. (1981) 'Foreign Exchange Risk: Relevance and Management', *Managerial and Decision Economics*, 2, pp. 256–62.

Hester, Donald D. (1981) 'Innovations and Monetary Control', *Brookings Papers on Economic Activity*, 1, pp. 141–83.

Hooper, Peter and Steven W. Kohlhagen (1978) 'The Effect of Exchange Rate Uncertainty on the Prices and Volume of International Trade', *Journal of International Economics*, 8, November, pp. 483–51.

Hooper, Peter and Barbara Lowrey (1979) 'Impact of the Dollar Depreciation on the US Price Level: An Analytical Survey of Empirical Estimates',

International Finance Discussion Paper Number 128, Board of Governors of the Federal Reserve System, January.

International Monetary Fund (1970) *The Role of Exchange Rates in the Adjustment of International Payments* (Washington, DC: International Monetary Fund).

International Monetary Fund (1972) *Reform of the International Monetary System* (Washington, DC: International Monetary Fund).

Isard, Peter (1977) 'How Far Can We Push the "Law of One Price"?', *American Economic Review*, 67, December, pp. 942–8.

Johnson, Harry G. (1970) 'The Case for Flexible Exchange Rates, 1969', in C. Fred Bergsten *et al.*, *Approaches to Greater Flexibility of Exchange Rates: The Bürgenstock Papers* (Protection: Princeton University Press), pp. 91–111, reprinted in Robert E. Baldwin and J. David Richardson (eds) *International Trade and Finance: Readings* (Boston: Little, Brown and Company, 1974).

Jones, Ronald W. and Douglas D. Purvis (1981) 'International Differences in Response to Common External Shocks: The Role of Purchasing Power Parity', paper prepared for the Vth International Conference of the University of Paris-Dauphine on Money and International Monetary Problems, June 15–17.

Kindleberger, Charles P. (1970) 'The Case for Fixed Exchange Rates, 1969', in *The International Monetary Mechanism* (Boston: Federal Reserve Bank of Boston, March), pp. 93–108, reprinted in Charles P. Kindleberger, *International Money* (London: Allen & Unwin, 1981).

Kindleberger, Charles P. (1970) *Power and Money* (New York: Basic Books).

Krugman, Paul (1982) 'The Macroeconomics of Protection with a Floating Exchange Rate', *Carnegie-Rochester Conference Series on Public Policy*, 16, Spring, pp. 141–81.

Magee, Stephen P. and Ramesh K. S. Rao (1980) 'Vehicle and Nonvehicle Currencies in International Trade', *American Economic Review*, 70, May, pp. 368–73.

McCulloch, Rachel (1978) *Research and Development as a Determinant of US International Competitiveness* (Washington, DC: National Planning Association).

McCulloch, Rachel (1982) 'The Macroeconomics of Protection with a Floating Exchange Rate', *Carnegie-Rochester Conference Series on Public Policy*, 16, Spring, pp. 183–5.

McKinnon, Ronald I. (1981) 'The Exchange Rate and Macroeconomic Policy: Changing Postwar Perceptions', *Journal of Economic Literature*, 19, June, pp. 531–57.

Meade, James E. (1951) *The Balance of Payments* (London: Oxford University Press).

Meese, Richard and Kenneth Rogoff (1981) 'Empirical Exchange Rate Models of the Seventies: Are Any Fit to Survive?', International Finance Discussion Paper Number 184, Board of Governors of the Federal Reserve System, June.

Meese, Richard A. and Kenneth Rogoff (1982) 'Empirical Exchange Rate Models of the Seventies: Do They Fit Out of Sample?', April 1982, forthcoming in *Journal of International Economics*.

Meese, Richard A. and Kenneth J. Singleton (1982) 'Rational Expectations and the Volatility of Floating Exchange Rates', unpublished paper.

Mundell, Robert A. (1969) 'Real Gold, Dollars and Paper Gold', *American Economic Review*, 59, May, pp. 324–43.

Mussa, Michael (1979a) 'Empirical Regularities in the Behavior of Exchange Rates and Theories of the Foreign Exchange Market', *Carnegie-Rochester Conference Series on Public Policy*, 11, pp. 9–55.

Mussa, Michael (1979b) 'Macroeconomic Interdependence and the Exchange Rate Regime', in Rudiger Dornbusch and Jacob A. Frenkel (eds) *International Economic Policy: Theory and Evidence* (Baltimore: Johns Hopkins), pp. 160–204.

Neary, J. Peter (1982) 'Real and Monetary Aspects of the "Dutch Disease"', paper prepared for the International Economic Association Conference on Structural Adjustment in Trade-Dependent Advanced Economies, Yxtaholm, Sweden, 2–6 August.

Panagariya, Arvind and Robert F. Owen (1982) 'Monopoly and Devaluation: A General Equilibrium Analysis', Social Systems Research Institute Discussion Paper 8211, University of Wisconsin, April.

Richardson, J. David (1982a) 'Four Observations on Modern International Commercial Policy Under Floating Exchange Rates', *Carnegie-Rochester Conference Series on Public Policy*, 16, Spring, pp. 187–220.

Richardson, J. David (1982b) 'The New Nexus Among Trade, Industrial and Exchange-Rate Policies', paper prepared for a conference on the Future of the International Monetary System, New York University, October.

Salop, J. and E. Spitaeller (1980) 'Why Does the Current Account Matter?', *IMF Staff Papers*, 28, March.

Shiller, Robert J. (1981) 'Do Stock Prices Move Too Much to be Justified by Subsequent Changes in Dividends?', *American Economic Review*, 71, June, pp. 421–36.

Solomon, Robert (1977) *The International Monetary System, 1945–1976* (New York: Harper & Row).

World Bank (1981) *Accelerated Development in Sub-Saharan Africa: An Agenda for Action* (Washington, DC: The World Bank).

3 Toward a More Orderly Exchange Rate System[1]

JACQUES R. ARTUS

INTRODUCTION

There is at present a widespread feeling of dissatisfaction with the exchange rate system born out of the 1971–3 crisis, in particular because of the instability that has so far characterized floating exchange rates. This feeling is not new, but it has grown considerably over the past four years with the extreme weakness, then extreme strength, of the US dollar. Partly in reaction against the instability of floating exchange rates, several European countries have created the European Monetary System, and the seven major industrial countries have recently started a joint study of the role of official intervention in foreign exchange markets. In my view, the risk of a shift back towards exchange rate rigidity with all its distorting effects is small, but it is there, and to argue that swings in exchange rates of 30 per cent or more are the healthy manifestation of an efficient market does not help to reduce it. Rather the time has come to assess the causes and effects of floating exchange rates, and to consider possible remedies that would not take us from Charybdis to Scylla.

The focus of this paper is on how to strengthen the present system. The second section below considers the causes and effects of exchange rate instability, without making any attempt to compare floating rates with fixed rates. The third section considers possible remedies for the instability of floating rates. Most of the discussion in that section focuses on the need for stable, credible and balanced domestic policies, and on the role of official intervention. The section concludes with a brief discussion of the risks inherent in a multicurrency reserve system. Because all the issues discussed here have been debated so many times before, I will stress points which I believe are often misunderstood, without making any attempt at comprehensiveness.

THE INSTABILITY PROBLEM

Floating exchange rates are more and more often described as unstable, volatile or erratic. No matter which adjective is used, the idea is the same: floating exchange rates move too much. In part, the concern arises from short-run movements that often exceed 1 per cent from day to day and 10 per cent from quarter to quarter. But the concern arises even more from longer-run movements that often exceed 30 per cent over a period of two to three years. It is these longer-run movements on which I intend to focus.

Nature and Causes of Instability

There is by now an overflow of evidence that floating exchange rates are unstable in the sense that their variability is much greater than the variability of the relative national price levels of the corresponding countries (Figure 3.1). Several explanations of this instability suggest that we should not be worrying about it. However, none is convincing. For example, we know that deviations of exchange rate movements from movements in relative national price levels – that is changes in real exchange rates – are justified whenever international comparative advantages or the underlying determinants of domestic saving and investment change, but it is difficult to accept the view that these factors have changed so much, so fast, so frequently. Even the major changes in comparative advantages related to the differential impact of the two waves of oil price increases and the emergence of North Sea oil only required relatively moderate changes in the real exchange rates of the major industrial countries, except possibly for the United Kingdom (see McGuirk, 1982).

We also know that exchange rates have the property of any asset prices of reflecting anticipated future developments, but this would explain why movements in exchange rates take place before movements in relative prices or other changes in underlying economic conditions, rather than why exchange rates are more variable. No doubt, exchange rates could be more variable than relative prices simply because prices are sticky – that is, they adjust slowly to unanticipated disturbances. Going to extremes, exchange rates would be viewed as indicating the long-run equilibrium values of relative prices. But this explanation fails to recognize that exchange rates are much more variable than relative money stocks (Figure 3.1), which can also be viewed as indicators of the long-run equilibrium values of relative prices[2] and which are not sticky.

Convincing reasons for the longer-run instability of exchange rates are to be found elsewhere, and in a direction that is more worrisome. The first reason is that an unanticipated disturbance affecting the supply or the demand for money tends to have an initial effect on the exchange rate that is much larger than the one that will ultimately be necessary to offset the effect of the disturbance on relative national price levels. The exchange rate 'overshoots', then gradually moves back towards its long-run equilibrium value. The mechanism behind this overshooting is simple. An unanticipated reduction in money growth, for example, is followed by an initial period during which prices keep rising as fast as before because of built-in rigidities in the goods and labor markets. The ratio of available money to nominal income declines and the real interest rate rises. The exchange rate then has to appreciate to a level which exceeds the one expected to prevail in the future by an amount that offsets the favorable international differential in real interest rates. The size of the initial appreciation is directly related to the size of the initial increase in the real interest rate and to the expected persistence of the period of the high real interest rate.

When the overshooting related to the interest rate effect was first emphasized by Dornbusch (1976), it was viewed as accounting for changes in the exchange rate of a few percentage points lasting for a few months because monetary shocks were supposed to have only a small and brief effect on real interest rates. To illustrate, say a major monetary contraction causes an immediate 2 per cent increase in the short-term real interest rate and this effect is expected to last for six months. The corresponding initial exchange rate overshooting will be 1 per cent. By now, we know better. The data on short-term real interest rates shown in Figure 3.2 suggest that a fairer estimate is that a major monetary contraction may cause the short-term real interest rate to rise by as much as five percentage points and that the effect may last for several years.[3] Therefore, we should not be surprised to observe a large and persistent overshooting of the exchange rate as a result of a monetary shock. Again for illustration purposes, a five-percentage-point increase in the short-term real interest rate expected to last for three years will cause an initial exchange rate overshooting of 15 per cent.

49

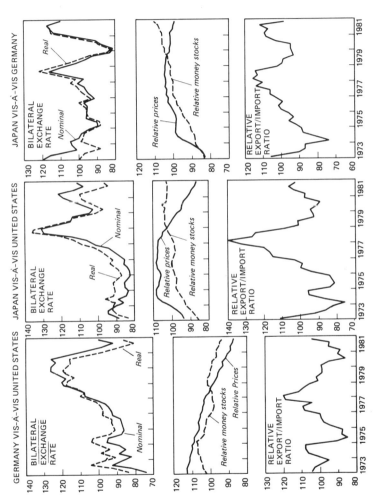

FIGURE 3.1

50

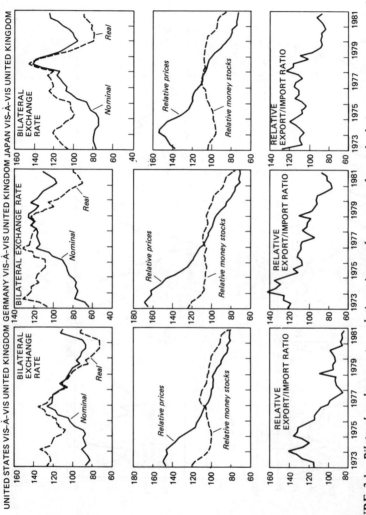

FIGURE 3.1 *Bilateral exchange rates, relative prices and money stocks, and relative current account positions*[1]

1. The bilateral real exchange rate is calculated as the bilateral nominal exchange rate (period average) adjusted for changes in GNP deflators expressed in local currencies. The data on relative prices also refer to the GNP deflators. The data on money stocks refer to M2 (average of end-of-month series). The relative export/import ratios refer to goods and services. All data except for bilateral exchange rates are seasonally adjusted.

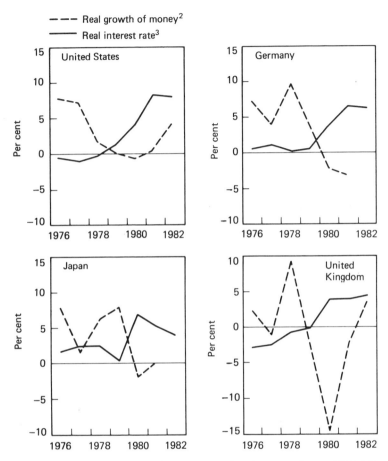

FIGURE 3.2   *Real growth of money and real interest Rates, 1976–82*[1]

1. Data for 1982 are the average of the observations for the first half of the year.
2. The real growth of money is calculated by subtracting the growth in GNP deflators from the growth in M1 (M2 in the case of the United States).
3. The real interest rate is calculated by deflating the monthly averages of daily rates on money market instruments of about 90 days' maturity by an estimate of inflation. This measure is proxied by a weighted average of the rate of inflation in the current quarter and the next two quarters, with the deflator of private final domestic demand being used as the price variable. Staff projections of this deflator are used for the end-of-period observations.

The second reason is that an unanticipated disturbance that affects the current account balance tends also to have an initial effect on the exchange rate that exceeds the change that will ultimately be necessary. (See Dooley and Isard, 1979, for a recent analysis of this issue.) For example, an adverse change in the terms of trade will lead to a worsening of the current account and a period of adjustment during which private wealth is shifted from domestic residents to non-residents, who have a weak preference for the form that this wealth takes. This weak preference is due to the exchange risk that arises from the denomination of most of residents' wealth in their own currency. In addition, there is the political risk that is associated with the possibility that the government will penalize foreign holdings of claims on domestic residents. Therefore, immediately after the disturbance, private market participants will bid down the exchange rate to a level which falls short of the one expected to prevail in the future by an amount that is sufficient to provide an adequate risk premium for what is expected to be the needed transfer of wealth. Then, gradually, the exchange rate will move back to its long-run equilibrium value at the same time as the current balance strengthens, private wealth flows back, and the need for a risk premium disappears.

It is difficult to assess the size of the overshooting arising from a current account imbalance. There is a propensity among many economists to believe that it is small because even a sizeable imbalance looks small by comparison with the stock of assets of a major industrial country. However, comparing a flow to a stock is misleading. What is relevant is the expected value of the stock of assets that will have to be used to finance the imbalance over its duration. Because the effects of relative price changes on trade flows tend to be slow, a given disturbance may lead to a large cumulative current account imbalance. Furthermore, private market participants normally shy away from assuming exchange or political risk and have a strong preference for domestic assets (see McKinnon, 1976). Thus even a small international transfer of private wealth may imply that the share of assets denominated in a country's currency in the portfolios of non-residents may have to go from 1 per cent to 2 per cent. This may not be easy to achieve unless the currency of this country depreciates significantly. I believe that over the past ten years there were at least three cases, namely the surges in the deutsch mark and the yen in 1977–8, and in the pound sterling in 1978–80, where the current account imbalance was a factor contributing to overshooting (Figure 3.1).

The third reason for the longer-run instability is that the future is highly uncertain. The size of the overshooting of the exchange rate due to the effect of unanticipated disturbances on the real interest rate, or on the current account, has just been described as related to the expected duration of this effect. In practice, it is extremely difficult to forecast how fast the real interest rate, or the current account, will move back to its long-run equilibrium level. Therefore, private market participants will often have to revise their forecasts on the basis of current developments. In turn, these revisions will lead to exchange rate movements. For example, it is clear that in 1979, when the US monetary authorities shifted to a policy of reduction in money growth, private market participants did not expect that US short-term interest rates would still be around 8 per cent in real terms by mid-1982. Thus the overshooting of the US dollar related to the interest rate effect did not develop fully in 1979; it developed gradually during 1980 and 1981 when private market participants came to realize how persistently high US interest rates were to be.

The uncertainty concerning the future also leads to the indeterminacy of the expected long-run equilibrium exchange rate. Private market participants have fairly limited information on what underlying economic conditions are going to be a few years ahead. This is particularly true at present, as it has been during most of the 1970s, because practically all industrial countries are engaged in a difficult fight against stagflation, with the outcome of the fight remaining highly uncertain. Private market participants still have to form a view as to the evolution of underlying economic conditions over the next few years, but, given the circumstances, it should not come as a surprise that they change their view frequently on the basis of whatever new information comes along, even if it is tenuous. In addition, national authorities are at times directly responsible for exchange rate swings because they let the economic conditions and expectations deteriorate gradually to a point where the exchange rate has been pushed so far that they feel obliged suddenly to shift to a policy of strict monetary restraint. (On this last point, see Mussa, 1981.)

Nevertheless, the difficulty of predicting underlying economic conditions should not be exaggerated, at least as far as crucial variables such as prices and money stocks are concerned. As noted above, what is striking when we consider the evolution of relative GNP deflators or relative money stocks among major industrial countries over the past ten years is that they have often followed relatively regular trends with fluctuations of limited amplitude.[4] If private market participants do not systematically exaggerate the risk of sudden divergences, it is difficult to see why such trends would lead to wild gyrations in expectations. This leads me to believe that political factors were as important as economic factors in affecting exchange rate expectations, in part because they affected the perceived riskiness of the physical assets located in, or the financial assets issued by, the various countries. Such political factors tend to evolve in an unpredictable way from year to year, and the implications for the long-run equilibrium values of exchange rates are difficult to gauge. Thus here again there is ample room for frequent changes of views based on tenuous information.

The factors of long-run instability discussed so far have nothing to do with market inefficiencies. Indeed, the view is that it is because exchange rates reflect all available information that they often tend to overshoot and to vary considerably from year to year. Whether we should also recognize that, at times, private market participants are victim of speculative crazes or other 'bandwagon' forms of behavior is more controversial. My view is that there is no scientific way to prove or to disprove the existence of such forms of behavior. For example, one may find it difficult to believe that the change in the outlook for underlying economic and political conditions in the United States and Germany, from January 1980 to August 1981, was so large that it justified a 54 per cent appreciation of the US dollar vis-à-vis the Deutsch mark in real terms. But that is a matter of judgment. Possibly the information available in January 1980 suggested that the United States was on the verge of runaway inflation. Possibly the information available in August 1981 suggested that the US inflation problem had been solved, while the situation in Eastern Europe was on the verge of dealing a deadly blow to the German financial system. I do not believe either one, but I cannot prove that such judgments were inconsistent with the information available at the time.

The Costs of Instability

The costs of exchange rate instability take many forms. The static welfare loss derived from production and consumption decisions based on exchange rates that are out of line with long-run needs is probably small. Even if the amount of economic resources being moved in and out of various sectors is large, only trade flows that are marginal in terms of their contribution to welfare are likely to be affected. From a welfare standpoint, what is far more important are the actual costs of moving resources. Given existing rigidities in goods and labor markets, such moves will lead to transitional unemployment of both labor and capital, and perhaps also a permanent loss of resources when some workers are forced to go into early retirement and some capital equipment is scrapped. There may also be inflation when the industries that start to expand bid for the necessary resources.

These sectoral shifts, with accompanying loss of resources, can be on a fairly large scale. Looking again at Figure 3.1, what is striking is that fluctuations in nominal exchange rates are accompanied by fluctuations in exchange rates of similar amplitude. If there were ever any doubt that nominal exchange rate changes could affect real exchange rates, by now there is no more doubt. There is also no more doubt that changes in exchange rates of 30 per cent or more in two or three years have major effects on the structure of production. For illustration purposes, Table 3.1 presents some estimates derived from the Fund Multilateral Exchange Rate Model (see Artus and McGuirk, 1981). In the five major industrial countries, an appreciation in the effective exchange rate of 30 per cent leads to a decline in the production of finished manufactures of 6 to 10 per cent. There is also a large decline in the production of semi-

TABLE 3.1 *Effects of a 30 per cent appreciation of the effective exchange rate*[1] *(in per cent)*

	France	*Germany*	*United Kingdom*	*Japan*	*United States*
Export volume					
Semi-finished manufactures	− 16.5	− 13.7	− 7.2	− 23.0	− 26.4
Finished manufactures	− 22.4	− 17.8	− 12.5	− 31.1	− 31.5
Other goods	− 14.1	− 9.1	− 5.0	− 23.5	− 18.2
Import volume					
Semi-finished manufactures	15.6	15.4	8.0	20.1	27.2
Finished manufactures	24.3	24.7	17.9	33.3	30.4
Other goods	4.0	4.9	4.2	3.3	6.3
Terms of trade	11.3	10.4	8.0	15.0	14.2
Volume of production					
Semi-finished manufactures	− 10.3	− 9.6	− 10.1	− 6.8	− 1.8
Finished manufactures	− 7.2	− 9.5	− 7.6	− 7.7	− 6.3
Other tradable goods	− 3.2	− 2.1	− 1.1	− 6.4	− 4.3
Non-tradable goods	3.2	5.8	3.3	3.5	1.5
Prices					
Consumption deflator	− 16.2	− 15.2	− 18.8	− 9.6	− 10.1
GNP deflator	− 6.8	− 6.5	− 8.0	− 4.1	− 4.6

1. The estimates presented here are derived from the IMF's Multilateral Exchange Rate Model (see Artus and McGuirk, 1981). They refer to medium-term effects (three to four years) of an appreciation of the exchange rate over and above the exchange rate change corresponding to the differential in underlying rates of inflation. In the simulations used to derive these estimates, the level of real GNP is constrained to remain unchanged in order to focus attention on the effects of the appreciation on the structure of the economy.

finished manufactures, except in the United States. By contrast, the production of non-tradable goods rises significantly. These estimates are subject to a significant margin of error, but they give a fair indication of the order of magnitude of these effects. In addition, they help to explain why, in certain cases, national authorities of countries experiencing a large exchange rate appreciation find it difficult to resist the call for protectionist measures.

Another source of concern is that the uncertainty concerning longer-run changes in real exchange rates that is generated by the type of instability considered here may lead to a shift of resources away from the more exposed traded-goods sectors. The consequences may be slower growth of foreign trade, a weaker competitive climate, and decreased incentives for growth and productivity, but such consequences are quite complex and difficult to measure.

The main problem is that the uncertainty concerning longer-run changes in real exchange rates cannot be easily hedged in the forward markets. Other forms of hedging have to be used, and some of them may be quite costly in terms of resource allocation. Firms may, for example, set up separate production units in each of their major national markets so as to minimize the risk of sudden movements in the ratio between costs and product prices. They may also try to decrease their net risk position by importing more from countries to which they are exporting, or by exporting more to the countries from which they are importing. In all these cases it is clear that the decrease in the volume of international trade could be small, but that the move away from a full exploitation of the comparative advantages of the various countries could be quite significant.

Similarly, the fact that the level of foreign direct investment is not decreased does not indicate that resource allocation is not impaired. The diversification of production units among countries could lead to an increase in the global amount of foreign direct investment that in fact would be undesirable. What is more relevant in the present context is the amount of savings transferred among countries. If investors are risk-averse, an increase in exchange rate uncertainty should, in itself, generate a decrease in the amount of savings transferred among countries (as economic agents refrain from accumulating financial assets denominated in foreign currencies in their portfolio). Apart from the question of transfers of savings, there could also be a fragmentation of the international capital markets so that the comparative advantages of each market over different types of transactions and maturities could not be fully exploited.

The econometric evidence available thus far casts little, if any, light on the issues concerning the effects of exchange rate uncertainty. Certainly, the tests indicate that exchange rate instability of the kind experienced so far does not lead to a major decline in foreign trade. But the tests are not powerful enough to judge whether exchange rate instability leads, or does not lead, to a decline in foreign trade of a magnitude that is significant from an economic standpoint. More importantly, the tests give no information on the issue of resource misallocation since, as noted above, the volume of foreign trade is not a good indicator of the degree of optimality of resource allocation.

It is even more difficult to assess the effects of real exchange rate instability on long-term international capital flows through econometric techniques. So far there is little evidence that enterprises have significantly curtailed international capital movements in response to exchange rate fluctuations. One can only say that the magnitude of long-term international investment flows continued to grow rapidly during the 1970s.

Available studies of how businesses view exchange rate developments are also inconclusive on these points. The surveys published in Germany and the United Kingdom were fairly broad in scope, seeking answers to such questions as: (a) Do you prefer flexible or fixed exchange rates? (b) Are you concerned by the instability of exchange rates? Not surprisingly, the answers contained little useful information. A survey undertaken by the Group of Thirty (1980) is more useful because it is based on more detailed and more carefully selected questions, but, even in this case, the findings are rather unclear. The respondents stated that floating rates had added a 'new dimension' of risk (or uncertainty) of both trade and investment, but few of them deemed the added risk to be material. They viewed volatility as a damaging element, but not floating rates *per se* (sic).

A further cost of exchange rate instability is that, at times, it makes it more difficult for the authorities to achieve stable domestic economic conditions. One reason is that, as discussed above, a disturbance in a major country may push its exchange rate to overshoot because of its effects on real interest rates and the current balance. In turn, the overshooting will present authorities in trading-partner countries with a dilemma, namely, to accept the changes in their exchange rates, with their accompanying effects on domestic costs and prices, or to change their monetary policies. Both alternatives may be extremely costly. For example, a simulation reported in Artus (1982), which is based on a schematic description of the effects of the 1979 shift to monetary restraint in the United States, indicates the following effects on the German economy.

If the German monetary authorities do not change their rate of money growth, prices increase substantially in Germany; after three years, the GDP deflator is nearly 4 per cent higher than in the control solution corresponding to no shift to monetary restraint in the United States, and the domestic demand deflator is nearly 10 per cent higher. Furthermore, output decreases substantially in Germany by comparison with the control solution. The cumulated lost output amounts to 2.2 per cent of a year's GDP after three years and 5.4 per cent after five years. It is true that all these effects unwind in the long run, but the long run seems so far away in this case as to be irrelevant.

If the German monetary authorities respond to the changes in US policy by adopting an equivalent policy of monetary restraint and if other industrial countries follow suit, Germany benefits from a marked decline in its inflation rate, but the cost in terms of lost output is extremely large. After a year, the rate of inflation, in terms of the GDP deflator or domestic demand deflator, has declined by about one percentage point (at a quarterly rate), and the lower level persists in subsequent years. The output gap increases gradually to reach about eight percentage points after two years, before declining slowly. By the end of the fifth year, the cumulated lost output amounts to 21.5 per cent of a year's GDP.

To be fair, I have to recognize that, in an inflationary world, exchange rate instability has certain advantages. In particular, it favors authorities that are inclined to follow a policy of monetary restraint because the appreciation of their exchange rates will help the domestic fight against inflation. Similarly, it penalizes authorities that are inclined to follow loose monetary policies because the depreciation of their exchange rates will contribute to inflation and send a clear signal to the electorate that their governments are following unwise policies. The problem is that there are countries such as Japan, and to a lesser extent Germany, that have already largely reduced their domestic inflation, in part thanks to relatively well-functioning labor markets. These countries no longer have a pressing need for an externally imposed discipline and, therefore, do not appreciate the choice given to them between exchange rate depreciation and abnormally high real interest rates.

POSSIBLE REMEDIES

Given the costs associated with instability in real exchange rates, major changes in real rates that are not truly needed from the standpoint of adjustment in the goods markets should be viewed with concern. An exchange rate change that reflects a case of overshooting is not truly needed because it is transitory. An exchange rate change that reflects a change in expectations based on tenuous information is not truly needed either because the probability of its need is too small to warrant incurring the costs associated with the exchange rate change. The issue is how we can reduce the occurrence of such unnecessary exchange rate changes without introducing other problems involving equal or even greater costs.

The Need for Stable, Credible and Balanced Domestic Policies

It is a truism, but a truism that cannot be repeated too often, that the important prerequisite for more exchange rate stability is to have national authorities follow more stable, credible and balanced domestic policies to deal with their inflation problems. The policies need to be more stable and credible for at least two reasons. First, stable exchange rate expectations are necessary to the proper functioning of the floating exchange rate system, or for that matter to the proper functioning of any system. However, stable expectations simply cannot exist unless market participants have some reliable information that allows them to form a view as to where exchange rates are likely to be a few years in the future. If market participants do not have a clue as to what the domestic policies will be a few years in the future, exchange rate movements are bound to be unstable since they will be dominated by very short-term factors, rumors and other tenuous information. Second, only stable and credible domestic policies can gradually lead to the winding down of inflationary expectations that must take place if inflation is to be reduced. As long as no progress is made on the inflationary front, the domestic situation is bound to remain unstable.

It is also necessary for domestic policies to be more balanced. In part this means that a restrictive monetary policy should be accompanied by a restrictive fiscal policy, but this is not the only or even the main element. As already discussed in the last section, a program of monetary restraint has a tendency to cause exchange rate overshooting. The overshooting results from the rise in real short-term interest rates, the decline in economic activity, and the strengthening of the current account caused by monetary restraint. This rise can, under certain circumstances, be amplified by an excessive fiscal deficit, but in the main it reflects the failure of prices and nominal factor incomes to respond quickly to monetary restraint. This failure is often the result of the rigidities that limit the rapidity with which prices and wages adjust to changes in inflationary expectations, as well as to changes in supply and demand. It is also often the result of a lack of credibility – the authorities have so often failed to carry through their program of monetary restraint in the past because of the costs involved that nobody seriously believes that this time they are going to do it. If the degree of overshooting is to be reduced, monetary restraint must be accompanied by other policy measures that facilitate the adjustment of prices and wages. There are only two ways to facilitate this adjustment: (a) to rely on market forces, which assumes that most of the rigidities that limit the role of these forces are eliminated; or (b) to rely on incomes policy, which assumes that a suitable social and political framework is established.

National authorities should also keep an eye on the exchange rate in conducting their monetary policy. Technological and regulatory developments in financial markets are currently affecting the meaning of the various monetary aggregates in a number of countries. In addition, in countries such as the United Kingdom, where residents are free to substitute assets denominated in foreign currencies for domestic money holdings, shifts in expectations about exchange rates or relative interest rates can affect the normal relationship between the monetary aggregates and domestic nominal demand. Even in other countries, this normal relationship can be affected by changes in foreign demand for the local currency. For all these reasons, seeking a constant rate of growth of certain monetary aggregates may, at times, destabilize the real economy and the exchange rate. On such occasions, movements in the exchange rate can be viewed as a useful indicator of shifts in money demand that should be offset by shifts in domestic money supply.[5]

However, the use of the exchange rate as an additional indicator of monetary policy requires careful judgment. Exchange rate movements that are needed to offset inflation rate differentials or other changes in underlying economic conditions do not call for changes in domestic money supply. Similarly, as discussed above, the authorities may rightly hesitate to change domestic money supply when the instability of the exchange rate reflects the instability of monetary policies abroad. Finally, even if a convincing case can be made that an exchange rate appreciation reflects an increase in money demand, the authorities must assess whether allowing a sustained expansion in domestic money supply will not be misinterpreted by private market participants as an indication that the monetary authorities are giving up the fight against inflation.

So far, I have considered only policy measures that would be beneficial to the countries taking them as well as to their trading partners. By definition, such measures do not involve the need for international policy co-ordination in any true sense of the term, even though pressures from abroad can sometimes be useful to push a country to adopt measures for their own good. However, there are cases where exchange rate instability results from a difference of interests between countries. For example, in my view there is a difference of interests, at least in the short run, between countries where deeply embedded wage rigidities make it necessary to maintain high real interest rates for a sustained period in order to reduce inflation, and countries where a greater flexibility of nominal wages allows a reduction of inflation without having much recourse to high real interest rates. Some reconciling of the different interests must take place, and, in this process, one may have to accept some exchange rate instability in the short run for the sake of achieving a reduction of inflation in countries with inflexible nominal wages. But, in the longer run, there is no doubt that the domestic and international interests would best be reconciled by a gradual elimination of the wage rigidities.

It is because of this close interdependence between domestic policies and exchange rates that the IMF responsibility under the Articles of Agreement includes exercising surveillance over domestic policies that affect exchange rates. In fact, for the major industrial countries, this is certainly the most important aspect of surveillance. (On this point, see Artus and Crockett, 1978.) For obvious reasons this is also an aspect of surveillance where the role of the IMF is limited by the sensitivity of national authorities to criticism of their domestic policies and by the understanding of the political and social constraints that they face. Nevertheless, this is a domain where the role of the IMF should be increased.

Intervention and the Formation of Currency Blocs

Although more stability could be introduced into the system through more efficient domestic policies and more effective IMF surveillance over domestic policies, it would be unrealistic to expect that such changes would completely solve the problem of exchange rate instability. In any case, progress on these two fronts will be difficult and slow. Thus, it is easy to understand that many countries are looking for means to control their exchange rates through various forms of intervention in foreign markets,[6] and through the formation of currency blocs. In my view, both approaches are potentially useful, but only under certain conditions that are not easy to satisfy in practice.

Concerning intervention, it must be recognized that countries differ substantially as to how much the authorities can rely on this policy instrument to control their exchange rate. There is a whole spectrum ranging from countries that have primitive domestic trade and financial markets completely isolated from world markets by direct controls to a country such as the United States that has large and highly developed domestic markets fully integrated with world markets. At one end of the spectrum, intervention can keep the exchange rate fixed for many years almost no matter what (although a black market may develop), while, at the other end, intervention is unlikely to have a sustained effect.

The experience of recent years also suggests that the effectiveness of intervention depends on whether the authorities intervene to defend some specific objectives (either a specific rate or a lower or upper bound) to which they have in some way committed themselves over the short run, or only try to influence the evolution of rates that are basically floating. In the first case, members of the EMS have demonstrated that countries can maintain exchange rates among themselves within narrow bands for substantial periods of time, even though they have widely different domestic policies and inflation rates. In the second case, the experiences of countries such as Germany (with respect to the DM/$ rate), Japan and the United Kingdom suggest that intervention as part of a managed float tends to have a limited effect.[7] There are two main reasons for this difference in effectiveness. First, here as in the case of the current balance effect, a major factor influencing the exchange rate is the expectation that there will have to be a significant and persistent change in the shares of domestic and foreign securities in private portfolios at home and abroad. If there is no clear intervention policy, intervention on any given day is unlikely to give rise to such an expectation. Second, if the commitment of the authorities is credible because it is realistic, private speculators will greatly enhance the effectiveness of intervention by moving funds in the same direction.

The preceding remarks would suggest that, whenever feasible, an effective way to avoid the instability of a floating rate system is to use some form of pegging, with the peg crawling or revised at discrete intervals. This is what practically all developing countries, as well as the countries that participate in the exchange rate arrangements of the EMS, have done. But the major risk is that a system that aims at avoiding undue exchange rate movements is often soon transformed into a system that aims at postponing needed exchange rate changes. This general discussion being left aside, I would like to turn my attention to the specific case of the EMS, because of its importance for the whole international monetary system.

Apart from important political aspects, the EMS can in many ways be viewed as an attempt to solve the problems described in this paper on a regional basis. It purports to do it through the development of the ECU – in certain respects a substitute for the SDR – and through a system of exchange rate arrangements. So far, the EMS has been relatively successful in stabilizing nominal exchange rates among the countries that participate in its exchange rate arrangements, but not real rates (Figure 3.3). In addition, developments have made it obvious that the costs involved in such an approach are extremely high when inflation-prone countries are not able rapidly to adjust their rates of growth of labor costs to whatever levels are consistent with the rate in the least inflation-prone country (that is, Germany), allowance being made for relative changes in productivity and international comparative advantage.

There are basically three types of costs. First, there is the case of relatively small countries, such as Belgium, which had enough control on their labor costs through the 1970s to avoid having to devalue *vis-à-vis* Germany, but not enough to avoid a profit squeeze in the open sector that gradually led to a shrinkage of that sector and a worsening of the balance of payments problem. Second, there is the dynamic instability of interest rates implied by fixed, but adjustable, exchange rates between countries with widely different inflation rates. In schematic form, after an initial fixing of reasonable parities, market participants expect these parities to persist for at least a few months and purchase assets denominated in the currencies of countries with high inflation rates and high nominal interest rates. Thus countries with high inflation rates are pushed to have relatively expansionary monetary policies, while countries with low inflation rates are pushed to have relatively deflationary monetary policies. Then, a few months later, market participants begin to anticipate a new realignment and the relative policy stances of the two groups of countries have to be reversed gradually. The case of France and Germany over the past two years provides an illustration of the mechanism involved. Third, there is the inherent instability of a system where significant changes in parities are frequent. Market participants soon start anticipating these realignments and the ability of the authorities to control their exchange rates through intervention declines rapidly.

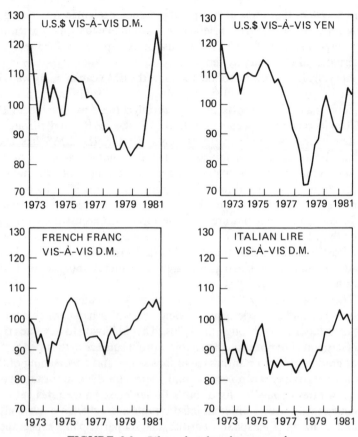

FIGURE 3.3   *Bilateral real exchange rates*[1]

1. The bilateral real exchange rate is calculated as the bilateral nominal exchange rate adjusted for changes in GNP deflators expressed in local currencies.

The point to emphasize is that for such blocs to be useful rather than harmful, the basic rule of the game must be clearly understood. The rule is not that you must have co-ordination of policies, since there is no reason why the least inflation-prone country should move in the direction of other countries. It is not even sufficient to have countries with high inflation rates move to the inflation rate of the least inflation-prone country, as the case of Belgium demonstrates. The rule of the game is that countries must be able to adjust their rates of growth of labor costs to levels that are consistent with the rate in the least inflation-prone country. This requires that countries be willing to adopt financial policies that foster the achievement of this target within a few years. This also requires a certain flexibility of nominal wage rates if restrictive financial policies are not to lead to a vicious circle of profit squeeze, low investment and declines in productivity calling for reductions in real wage rates.

Issues Raised by a Multicurrency Reserve System

In my view, the exchange rate instability caused by changes in the composition of official portfolios has been small, if not negligible, so far, but the potential for instability has increased in recent years, as many central banks began diversifying the composition of their foreign exchange reserves (see Table 3.2).[8] This diversification has given rise to two interrelated problems. First, sudden changes in the composition of official portfolios could destabilize exchange rates. Second, the longer-run investment strategies of central banks could place sustained upward or downward pressures on the exchange rates of major currencies.

The first problem should not be exaggerated. There is no evidence that central banks tend to make large and sudden changes in the composition of their portfolios. Furthermore, even if they did, such changes could often be offset either by stabilizing private capital flows or by the use of swap arrangements between affected central banks. Nevertheless, there is a risk that under certain circumstances a number of central banks could join private market participants in forming a 'bandwagon'.

The second problem is already with us to some extent. As central banks increase their reserves of Deutsch marks, yen, Swiss francs and a few other currencies, they place some upward pressures on the values of these currencies. This effect may be welcomed by the countries whose currencies are being purchased when their currencies are weak, but it is usually less welcome when the currencies are already strong. A further source of concern is that longer-run investment strategies can change. For example, the pound sterling which was in strong demand by official as well as private agents as a 'petro-currency' in 1979–80, was much less in demand in 1981 when a glut of oil developed.

There are two possible approaches to these problems: to regulate the composition of currency reserves or to make the SDR the primary reserve asset of the system. Both approaches are reviewed very briefly here.

The regulation approach does not appear promising. To be meaning-

TABLE 3.2 *Share of national currencies in SDR value of total identified official holdings, end of selected quarters, 1973–80[1] (in per cent)*

	1973(I)	1977(IV)	1978(IV)	1979(IV)	1980(IV)	1981(IV)
	All IMF members					
US dollar	78.4	79.4	76.9	73.8	68.3	70.6
Pound sterling	6.5	1.6	1.5	1.9	2.9	2.3
Deutsch mark	5.5	8.3	9.9	11.5	13.9	12.5
French franc	0.9	1.0	0.9	1.0	1.3	1.1
Swiss franc	1.1	2.0	1.4	2.3	3.1	2.8
Netherlands guilder	–	0.4	0.5	0.7	0.9	1.0
Japanese yen	–	1.2	2.5	2.9	3.8	4.1
Unspecified	7.3	6.2	6.3	5.9	5.8	5.6
Total	100.0	100.0	100.0	100.0	100.0	100.0
	All non-industrial IMF members					
US dollar	55.2	68.6	62.6	62.6	58.1	61.7
Pound sterling	13.4	2.8	3.0	3.4	5.3	4.1
Deutsch mark	13.2	12.9	15.0	16.1	15.4	13.8
French franc	3.1	2.0	2.2	2.0	2.6	2.3
Swiss franc	2.0	3.4	2.9	3.3	4.8	4.3
Netherlands guilder	0.6	0.7	0.9	1.0	1.3	1.3
Japanese yen	0.2	2.2	4.0	4.0	4.9	5.2
Unspecified	12.3	7.4	9.3	7.5	7.6	7.3
Total	100.0	100.0	100.0	100.0	100.0	100.0

1. The detail in each of the columns may not add to 100 because of rounding. The SDR value of ECUs issued against US dollars has been added to the SDR value of US dollars, and the SDR value of ECUs issued against gold has been excluded from the total distributed here.

SOURCES Various Fund publications and Fund staff estimates.

ful, countries would have to accept the principle that they cannot accumulate currencies of other countries in their reserves without some agreement with the countries whose currencies are being used and with the IMF. There is no sign that countries are willing to accept such a constraint, which would go further than the existing rule under IMF surveillance of exchange rate policies that members should take into account in their intervention policies the interest of other members. A partial solution would be for non-dollar reserve centers to become more willing to authorize other central banks to have access to their domestic financial markets, rather than oblige them to hold Eurocurrencies, in return for some agreements on their longer-run investment policies. But I am afraid that many central banks would choose to keep the freedom that they have in Eurocurrency markets.

The SDR approach should in principle be easier to implement, since countries have already agreed to Article XXII of the amended Articles of Agreement of the IMF, which stipulates that each participant to the SDR arrangements undertakes to collaborate with the IMF and with other participants with the objective of making the SDR the principal reserve asset in the international monetary system. However, by end-1980, holdings of SDRs accounted for only 5.2 per cent of holdings of total reserves minus gold of all IMF members, about three percentage points less than at end-1975. If there is no new allocation of SDRs in 1982, the importance of the SDR is likely to decline even further in the period immediately ahead. In brief, we are far from having the SDR as the principal reserve asset, and we are not moving in that direction.

Even if the SDR were to become the primary reserve asset of the system, the problems arising from a multicurrency reserve system would only be mitigated. As long as various national currencies are also used as reserves, the potential for exchange rate movements caused by changes in the composition of official portfolios would remain. Ultimately, informal co-ordination of reserve policies among important central banks will have to continue to play an important role.

CONCLUSION

An underlying theme of this paper is that an international monetary system must largely take the world as it is, rather than try to mold it. The present system of floating exchange rates among the major currencies meets this requirement. A centralized and regulated system that would aim at re-establishing more rigid exchange rates on a global level would not meet this requirement. Rather than constraining national authorities to follow wise domestic policies, it would simply lead them to use direct controls on international trade and financial transactions. But the present widespread feeling of dissatisfaction with the instability of floating exchange rates cannot and should not be ignored.

There is a number of approaches that can be used to reduce exchange rate instability. By far the most promising one is to move towards more stable, credible and balanced domestic policies. Given the present inflationary conditions, of particular importance would be policy measures that would reduce rigidities in labor markets in order to enhance the effect of monetary restraint on the growth of nominal wages. This would shorten the period of high real interest rates and reduce the overshooting of the real exchange rate. However, progress in this direction is likely to be slow. Another approach is to rely more heavily on official intervention. No doubt there are clear limits to the effectiveness of intervention, as well as clear dangers, but I believe that we should keep an open mind on the usefulness of intervention under certain circumstances. In this context, regional monetary blocs could contribute to a more orderly global system, but only if member countries are able to adjust their rates of growth of labor costs to the rate in the least inflation-prone country. Finally, co-ordination of reserve policies among important central banks will have to continue in order to prevent potentially destabilizing changes in the composition of their portfolios of foreign currencies.

NOTES

1. The views expressed in this paper represent the opinions of the author and should not be interpreted as official Fund views.
2. The expression long-run equilibrium value, whether related to prices or the exchange rate, is used to indicate the value which would clear markets in the long run assuming no further disturbances.
3. Chart 2 has only an illustrative value. Monetary policy is obviously only one of the factors influencing real interest rates. Furthermore, it is difficult to measure real interest rates because of the lack of reliable data on inflationary expectations, although this source of errors is limited when the period concerned covers only the next few months.
4. The evolution of relative money stocks has probably been even more regular than suggested by Figure 3.1 because some of the variations in the statistical series may be attributed to changes in the definition of the variables and other statistical problems.
5. The interest rate can also be used as an indicator to detect shifts in money demand, but, as is well known, there is a risk that a change in the nominal interest rate may reflect a change in inflationary expectations rather than a shift in money demand. This can lead to costly policy mistakes; in particular, an expansion of domestic money supply may feed the rise in inflationary expectations at a time when they should be subdued by a contraction.
6. Intervention can be financed from owned reserves, use of swap facilities, or borrowing from private international markets. Directives or incentives given to state agencies or private banks to lend or borrow abroad are also forms of intervention. It is assumed here that effects of intervention on high-powered money are being offset. If not, we are speaking of a change in monetary policy, albeit a possibly marginal one if the intervention is not large and sustained.
7. This judgment must be qualified by noting that since 1973, and contrarily to what many people think, the major industrial countries have not had an active policy of sterilized intervention. (This point is carefully documented in Dooley (1982).)

8. Gentlemen's agreements among central banks of industrial countries tend to restrict the use of non-dollar national currencies in their reserves. However, other central banks can use the Eurocurrency markets as means of diversifying into the currencies of those countries that do not wish to encourage the reserve-currency role of their national currencies.

REFERENCES

Artus, Jacques R. (1982) 'Effects of US Monetary Restraint on the DM-$ Exchange Rate and the German Economy', Working Paper No. 926, National Bureau of Economic Research Inc., July.
Artus, Jacques R. and Anne K. McGuirk (1981) 'A Revised Version of the Multilateral Exchange Rate Model', IMF *Staff Papers*, Vol. 28, June, pp. 275–309.
Artus, Jacques R. and Andrew D. Crockett (1978) *Floating Exchange Rates and the Need for Surveillance*, Essays in International Finance, No. 127, International Finance Section, Princeton University, May.
Dooley, Michael P., 'An Analysis of Exchange Market Intervention of Industrial and Developing Countries,' forthcoming in IMF *Staff Papers*.
Dooley, Michael P. and Peter Isard (1979) 'The Portfolio-Balance Model of Exchange Rates', Federal Reserve Board, *International Finance Discussion Paper No. 141*, May.
Dornbusch, Rudiger (1976) 'Expectations and Exchange Rate Dynamics', *Journal of Political Economy*, Vol. 84, December, pp. 1161–76.
Group of Thirty (1980) *Foreign Exchange Markets Under Floating Rates* (Group of Thirty, New York).
McGuirk, Anne K. (1982) 'The Oil Price Increase and Real Exchange Rate Changes Among Industrial Countries', unpublished, International Monetary Fund, July.
McKinnon, Ronald I. (1976) 'Floating Foreign Exchange Rates 1973–74: The Emperor's New Clothes', *Institutional Arrangements and the Inflation Problem*, ed. by Karl Brunner and Allan H. Meltzer, Carnegie-Rochester Conference on Public Policy, Vol. 3, Amsterdam, pp. 79–114.
Mussa, Michael (1981) *The Role of Official Intervention*, Occasional Papers No. 6, Group of Thirty, New York.

4 The Wage and Price Adjustment Process in Six Large OECD Countries[1]

ROBERT J. GORDON

INTRODUCTION

The American literature on the dynamics of aggregate supply behavior is dominated by the issue of nominal wage stickiness. The less responsive the nominal wage rate is to changes in the growth rate of nominal GNP, the greater is the output cost of a disinflationary monetary policy and, because of these costs, the less likely it is that such a policy will be adopted.[2]

Within the context of recent developments in international monetary economics and comparative macroeconomics, the American obsession with nominal wage rigidity appears narrow and incomplete in its isolated one-country orientation. International monetary economists have called attention to 'the collapse of Purchasing Power Parity' (PPP) and its implications for key issues (see especially Frenkel, 1981). The domestic price adjustment literature translates the phrase 'collapse of PPP' into an equivalent proposition, the 'incomplete adjustment of domestic price deflators to changes in exchange rates'. PPP would be maintained in the standard case of an inflation-prone Latin American country that experiences an annual inflation rate 100 per cent faster than that of the US, together with a simultaneous and continuous depreciation against the dollar of 100 per cent per year. Yet PPP is not maintained, and nominal exchange rate changes are translated into changes in real exchange rates, when the domestic price level responds less than one-for-one to changes in the nominal effective exchange rate. As one extreme case, the typical US domestic Phillips curve equation allows for no response at all to exchange rate changes. Nevertheless, the domestic wage stickiness literature helps us to understand why PPP might 'collapse', since the causal factors explaining nominal wage rigidity, including multi-year wage-contracting institutions, also help to explain the incomplete response of domestic prices to exchange rate movements. The distinction between traded and non-traded goods contributes an extra factor of delay in the transmission of exchange rate changes into wages in the domestic non-traded goods sector.

A second issue, as common in European discussions as it is absent in US macroeconomic debates, concerns the alleged rigidity or non-responsiveness of real wages to supply shocks. As popularized by Branson and Rotemberg (1980) and Sachs (1979), the rigid real-wage hypothesis interprets the multifold increases in European unemployment in the late 1970s relative to the 1960s as due to excessive real wages. In the simple Branson–Rotemberg story, real wages fail to respond to economic slack. In the more sophisticated Sachs account, real wages may be quite variable and exhibit a considerable growth-rate slowdown after 1973, but this slowdown may nevertheless be insufficient to offset the slowdown in productivity growth and to avert an increase in the share of employee compensation in national income. When profits are squeezed by an increase in the growth rate of real wages relative to productivity, firms may be induced to create otherwise unnecessary unemployment, as well as to cut back on investment and hence on the long-run growth of output (Malinvaud, 1982).

Further, if nominal wage rates are relatively sticky in the US and real wage rates relatively sticky in Europe, domestic demand expansion will have uneven spillover effects in the two regions. A US monetary expansion that raises the growth rate of nominal GNP will boost US output more than US prices, whereas the spillover of the US expansion to Europe will raise prices there more than output. A European monetary expansion will not raise output, due to inflexible real wage rates, and instead all of the output benefit will accrue to the United States. As worked out in a detailed theoretical exercise by Branson and Rotemberg (1980), these asymmetries appear capable of explaining why the US was more eager than the Europeans to promote worldwide demand expansion during the Carter years, particularly 1976–8.

This paper provides a new characterization of differences among six major industrialized nations (France, West Germany, Japan, Italy, the UK, the US) in the domestic wage and price adjustment process. The discussion of nominal wage rigidity takes as its point of departure my recent claim (Gordon, 1982a) that nominal wage rates are much less responsive to changes in nominal GNP in the US than in the UK and Japan. Do response patterns in the three additional countries, France, West Germany and Italy, resemble more closely those in the US or the UK and Japan? A limitation of the earlier paper was its concentration on wage rates to the exclusion of price deflators; an incomplete responsiveness of wage rates to changes in nominal GNP implies fluctuations in output only if price movements mimic wage movements. If price changes were to absorb nominal GNP changes entirely, real output growth might remain stable even if nominal wages were rigid. Thus, for all six countries, results on nominal wage responsiveness are supplemented by parallel equations that measure the responsiveness of price deflators.

This paper also goes beyond the traditional US concern with nominal price and wage responses to domestic demand variables by quantifying the extent of domestic price adjustment to nominal exchange rate movements (thus contributing to the understanding of PPP and its collapse), and the extent, if any, of short-run real wage rigidity. After preliminary sections that report summary statistics on the behavior of nominal wages and prices and of the real wage, the main empirical results consist of econometric wage and price equations estimated on quarterly data for the six countries covering a uniform sample period extending from 1961 to 1981. Responses are exhibited and compared for the reaction of domestic wage and price measures to changes in lagged wages, prices, exchange rates, and proxies for domestic demand and supply shocks.

In addition to the usual problems that afflict comparative macroeconometric studies, this paper suffers from two separate limitations on the cross-country comparability of data sources. First, the nominal wage data for the US consist of an index that corrects average hourly earnings in the non-farm private economy for cyclical shifts in overtime pay and the mix of employment, whereas wage data for most other countries are unadjusted indexes of earnings or compensation in manufacturing (not the whole economy). Either the lack of cyclical adjustment or the narrower manufacturing source could reduce the cross-country comparability of estimated coefficients. Second, the exchange rate data are based on the IMF multilateral exchange rate model and cover only the period 1973–81. Changes in bilateral exchange rates prior to 1973 are not taken into account (e.g. the pound–dollar devaluation in 1967); to be accorded parallel treatment, they would require the development of appropriate trade weights.

BASIC CHARACTERISTICS OF THE DATA

Means and Standard Deviations

This section presents statistics on means, standard deviations and simple correlation coefficients for quarterly changes in nominal GNP, the wage rate, the GNP deflator, and the real product wage. Table 4.1 displays means and standard deviations for two portions of the 1960–81 sample period, divided at the end of 1972. West Germany and Japan stand out as having achieved a slower growth rate of nominal GNP in the second period than in the first, thus helping to explain why these two nations also achieved the lowest rates of inflation in the second period. France, Italy and the UK all experienced sharp jumps in nominal GNP growth and even greater accelerations in the inflation rate, since in all countries real GNP grew more slowly in the second period. The overall similarity in the experience of Italy and the UK may justify the verdict that the Italians have caught the 'English disease'. Despite a doubling of inflation, France stands out in the second period as having managed to escape with the smallest slowdown in real GNP growth among the six nations. On most of the comparisons across the two periods the US lies in the middle, with a modest acceleration of nominal GNP growth and of inflation, and with the third smallest slowdown in the growth rate of real GNP.

The countries are grouped differently in the behavior of the mean growth rates of the real wage. Here Italy stands out, with an acceleration in real wage growth between the two periods combined with a marked slowdown in output growth. In France, Germany, the UK and the US, the slowdown in the growth rate of the real wage is roughly parallel to the slowdown in real output growth. In Japan real wage growth fell much less than output growth, raising a question (to be investigated below) as to how the Japanese have avoided a substantial increase in unemployment of the 'classical' type.

The bottom half of Table 4.1 exhibits standard deviations of the same variables for the same sub-periods, based on four-quarter overlapping rates of change to eliminate seasonal variation (the data are a mixture of seasonally adjusted and unadjusted data). The US experienced the least variability in its nominal and real wage, and Germany in the second sub-period experienced the second lowest degree of variability. The US price deflator was not unusually stable, however, with a standard deviation similar to that in France and Germany in both sub-periods and to Japan in the first sub-period. At the other extreme, nominal wages, real wages and the price deflator were much more volatile in Italy, Japan and the

TABLE 4.1   *Means and standard deviations of changes in wage rates and GNP deflator, quarterly data expressed at annual rates, 1960(3)–1981(4)*

	France	Germany	Italy	Japan[1]	UK[2]	US
A. Means						
1. 1960(3)–1972(4)						
(a) Nominal GNP	9.9	8.5	10.0	15.2	7.3	7.1
(b) Wage	8.5	8.4	9.1	11.3	7.5	4.7
(c) Price	4.7	4.0	4.9	5.0	4.9	3.1
(d) Real GNP	5.2	4.5	5.1	10.2	2.4	4.0
(e) Real wage	3.8	4.4	4.2	6.4	2.6	1.6
2. 1973:1–1981:4						
(a) Nominal GNP	14.5	6.9	18.3	10.7	15.3	9.9
(b) Wage	13.9	6.9	20.6	10.8	15.2	7.7
(c) Price	10.1	4.8	15.8	6.8	13.9	7.5
(d) Real GNP	4.4	2.1	2.5	3.9	1.4	2.4
(e) Real wage	3.7	2.2	4.7	4.0	1.2	0.2
B. Standard deviations[3]						
1. 1960(3)–1972(4)						
(a) Nominal GNP	1.9	3.2	2.2	3.9	2.3	2.2
(b) Wage	2.8	3.0	4.8	2.8	3.1	1.5
(c) Price	1.3	1.9	2.2	1.4	2.2	1.5
(d) Output	1.1	2.7	2.4	3.2	1.5	2.1
(e) Real wage	2.1	2.1	3.4	2.9	2.2	0.5
2. 1973:1–1981:4						
(a) Nominal GNP	1.6	2.1	4.3	4.7	5.0	1.9
(b) Wage	2.0	1.9	4.2	6.1	4.6	1.1
(c) Price	1.8	1.5	3.3	5.2	5.7	1.6
(d) Output	1.3	2.7	4.1	3.5	3.2	3.0
(e) Real wage	1.7	1.2	3.6	3.0	3.3	0.8

Notes
1. Data end in 1981(3).
2. Data end in 1981(1).
3. To avoid seasonality effects, standard deviations are reported for four-quarter overlapping changes in quarterly data.

UK in the second sub-period than in France, Germany and the US.

Another interesting contrast is evident in the ratios of the standard deviation of the price deflator to that of real GNP. In both sub-periods real GNP was more volatile than the price deflator in the US, as well as in Germany and Italy. This was also true of Japan in the first sub-period. Prices were more volatile than real GNP in France and the UK in both periods, and Japan in the second sub-period.

Overall, the results provide an interesting perspective on my recent contrast (Gordon, 1982a) of inertia-bound US wage behavior with highly variable wage changes in the UK and Japan. It appears that (a) the contrast for Japan is mainly attributable to the second sub-period, and particularly to the behavior of wages and prices at the time of the first oil shock; (b) the price deflator in Japan was not more volatile than the US in the first sub-period; and (c) France, Germany and Italy exhibit wage and price behavior intermediate in character between the extremes represented by the US and the UK.

Simple Correlations

Table 4.2 presents simple correlations that might be expected to reveal stark differences among countries in the extent of nominal and real wage rigidity, and of wage, price and output responsiveness to changes in nominal GNP. Correlations are presented for the same sub-periods as in Table 4.1. To control for the fact that some of the raw data are seasonally unadjusted, the rates of change in Table 4.2 are calculated on a four-quarter overlapping basis. This tends to exaggerate positive correlations and to highlight unusually low correlations.

In Section A the US and Japan appear to share the highest degree of positive serial correlation of the wage change series. While the high US correlation between the current and lagged nominal wage rate is

TABLE 4.2 *Simple correlations among changes in current and lagged wage rates, GNP deflator, and nominal GNP, four-quarter overlapping changes, 1960(3)–1981(4)*

	France	Germany	Italy	Japan[1]	UK[2]	US
A. Wage, lagged wage						
1. 1960(3)–1972(4)	0.80	0.87	0.89	0.93	0.81	0.99
2. 1973(1)–1981(4)	0.89	0.76	0.70	0.94	0.83	0.92
B. Wage, lagged price						
1. 1960(3)–1982(4)	0.65	0.59	0.71	0.15	0.64	0.95
2. 1973(1)–1981(4)	0.62	0.61	0.61	0.86	0.68	0.91
C. Wage, nominal GNP						
1. 1960(3)–1972(4)	0.75	0.69	0.32	0.08	0.72	0.38
2. 1973(1)–1981(4)	0.25	0.26	0.10	0.84	0.74	−0.34
D. Price, nominal GNP						
1. 1960(3)–1972(4)	0.84	0.57	0.40	0.65	0.77	0.42
2. 1973(1)–1981(4)	0.70	−0.05	0.43	0.76	0.77	−0.37
E. Real GNP, nominal GNP						
1. 1960(3)–1972(4)	0.79	0.80	0.54	0.94	0.41	0.75
2. 1973(1)–1981(4)	0.26	0.83	0.71	0.23	0.06	0.85

Notes
1. Data end in 1981(3).
2. Data end in 1981(1).

consistent with the Branson–Rotemberg–Sachs description of the US as having sticky nominal wage rates, their description of sticky real wage rates outside the US appears more problematical. In both sample periods the US has the highest correlation between current wage change and lagged price change, with Japan a close runner-up in the second sub-period. Interestingly, the correlation for Italy is relatively low, despite the existence of widespread indexation after 1974 (the *scala mobile*).

The next two sections of Table 4.2 present simple contemporaneous correlations between four-quarter changes in wage rates and nominal GNP (Section C) and the GNP deflator and nominal GNP (Section D). Here the US is joined by Germany and Italy as having relatively low correlations between wages and prices on the one hand, and nominal GNP on the other hand. In the second sub-period both correlations for the US are negative, which would be consistent with a 'non-accommodating' monetary policy in response to supply shocks. Similarly, Germany has a small negative correlation for prices in the second sub-period. At the other extreme, the UK has consistently high correlations in both Sections C and D in both sub-periods, and is joined by France and Japan for the price-to-nominal-GNP correlations. We see again, as in Table 4.1, that the character of Japanese wage behavior changed in the second sub-period, with much greater variability and a much higher correlation with nominal GNP changes. France appears to have changed in the opposite direction. These apparent shifts in structure can be explained by two special events, the 1968 wage explosion in France after the Grenelle Accord, and the upward surge of wage and nominal GNP growth in Japan in 1974–5 after the first oil shock.

The last section of Table 4.2 displays correlations between real and nominal GNP. Here again the US and UK represent the extremes, with nominal GNP changes being mainly reflected in output changes in the US and in price changes in the UK. Japan and France both shift between the two sub-periods, becoming more like the UK and less like the US. In both periods, Germany is the country displaying patterns for prices and output that are the most similar to those in the US.

Overall, no evidence in Table 4.2 warrants special treatment for the US as having unusually sticky nominal wage rates or unusually flexible real wage rates. If anything, the response of wage rates to lagged price changes, an indication of real wage stickiness, is higher in the US than elsewhere. Nominal GNP changes are accompanied mainly by output rather than price changes in the US, a sign of sluggish nominal price adjustment, but there is no apparent difference in behavior between the US and Germany in this regard.

Real Wages and Productivity in Manufacturing

A more direct test of the rigid real wage hypothesis emerges from a comparison of the growth rates of real wages and productivity in manufacturing. The basic idea, emphasized by Sachs (1979), is that an increase in the income share of employee compensation implies a squeeze on profits and investment together with the emergence of 'classical' unemployment. The income share of labor can be written as (WN/PQ), where W is the nominal wage rate, N is labor input, P is the value-added deflator, and Q is real value-added. Using lower-case letters to designate proportional rates of change, the growth rate of the labor's share is:

$$w - p - (q - n)$$

that is, the growth rate of the real wage minus the growth rate of labor productivity.

Table 4.3 exhibits data for the six countries on the annual average growth rates for 1960–73 and 1973–81 of the real wage and labor productivity in manufacturing. The productivity data are compiled on a comparable basis by the US Bureau of Labor Statistics from national sources, as are the data on nominal hourly employee compensation in manufacturing. There is a problem, however, in locating an appropriate price deflator for manufacturing value-added. The real wage data in Section A of Table 4.3 are based on the GNP deflator. Section C exhibits the difference between the growth rates of the real wage and productivity in the two periods, and line C3 computes the change between the two periods in this difference. A negative number supports the Sachs hypothesis by indicating that real wages grew faster relative to productivity in the second sub-period, and a positive number indicates the reverse. The hypothesis is supported for France, Germany, the UK and the US. The inclusion of the US on this list is surprising, since both Branson–Rotemberg and Sachs have contrasted the excessive growth of real wages in Europe with the supposedly more moderate behavior of real wages in the US.

An alternative measure of the difference is provided in Section D of Table 4.3, based on an alternative real wage measure calculated with the Wholesale Price Index rather than the GNP deflator. For Germany, the UK and the US, the WPI excludes crude materials, and thus covers mainly the manufacturing sector. By this measure only two nations, France and the UK, support the Sachs hypothesis, and four nations including the US exhibit greater decelerations in real wage growth than

TABLE 4.3   *Mean annual rates of change of real product wage and output per hour in manufacturing, 1960–73 and 1973–81*

	France	Germany	Italy	Japan	UK	US
A. Real wage						
1. 1960–73	4.3	5.2	6.9	9.1	3.5	1.6
2. 1973–81	4.3	4.7	2.1	3.0	3.2	1.6
3. 1 minus 2	0.0	0.5	4.8	6.1	0.3	0.0
B. Output per hour						
1. 1960–73	6.0	5.5	6.9	10.7	4.3	3.0
2. 1973–81	4.6	4.5	3.6	6.8	2.1	1.7
3. 1 minus 2	1.4	1.0	3.3	3.9	2.2	1.3
C. A minus B						
1. 1960–73	−1.7	−0.3	0.0	−1.6	−0.8	−1.4
2. 1933–81	−0.3	0.2	−1.5	−3.8	1.1	−0.1
3. 1 minus 2	−1.4	−0.5	1.5	2.2	−1.9	−1.3
D. Line C recalculated with WPI						
1. 1960–73	−0.6	1.9	1.6	−1.6	−0.8	−0.4
2. 1973–81	1.6	−0.8	−2.4	−4.1	1.1	−2.0
3. 1 minus 2	−2.2	2.7	3.6	2.5	−1.9	1.6
E. Ranks						
1. Line C3	5	3	2	1	6	4
2. Line D3	6	2	1	3	5	4

SOURCES by line:

A. Employee compensation from US Bureau of Labor Statistics (1982), GNP deflator from Federal Reserve Bank of St. Louis (1980, 1982).
B. From US Bureau of Labor Statistics (1982).
C. WPI from Federal Reserve Bank of St. Louis (1980, 1982), described as follows:
   France, Italy and Japan: 'Wholesale Prices'
   Germany: 'Wholesale Prices, Industrial Products'
   UK: 'Wholesale Prices, Industrial Output'
   US: 'Producers' Price Index, Finished Goods'

in productivity growth in the second sub-period. As shown by the ranks in Section E of the table, by both measures, Japan, Germany and Italy exhibit more 'reasonable' real wage behavior than the US, with France and the UK sharing last place.

Lines C1, C2, D1 and D2 of the table, which show differences between the growth rates of the real wage and productivity, should exhibit predominantly positive values if the share of employee compensation has increased. But there are seventeen negative values among the twenty-four numbers displayed on these four lines. Overall, the real wage appears to have grown more slowly than labor productivity; the differences averaged over the six countries are as follows:

	From Section C	From Section D
1960–73	− 1.0	0.2
1973–81	− 0.8	− 1.1

It is possible that improved data might reverse these conclusions. To do so, the alternative data would have to indicate some combination of (a) a greater acceleration of nominal compensation after 1973, (b) a lesser acceleration of inflation, and (c) a greater deceleration of productivity growth. It is suggestive of possible data problems that there are two important conflicts between Tables 4.1 and 4.3. Table 4.1 indicates no slowdown between the first and second sub-periods in the growth rate of the real wage for Italy, whereas Table 4.3 suggests that the growth rate declined by more than half, using either measure of prices. For Japan there is also an apparent discrepancy, since Table 4.1 reports that real wage growth slowed down less than real GNP, whereas Table 4.3 suggests that real wage growth decelerated more than manufacturing productivity. For Italy, the main source of the discrepancy is in the growth of nominal wage rates; the US BLS data for 1960–73 used in Table 4.3 exhibit much faster growth than the compensation data obtained directly from Italian sources in Table 4.1. For Japan, there is a similar excess of compensation growth in Table 4.3 for the first sub-period; in addition productivity growth in manufacturing (Table 4.3, Section B) decelerates much less than real GNP (Table 4.1, line 4).

Overall, the data sources used in Table 4.3 would appear to be more reliable, and therefore we find no obvious reason to doubt the results displayed there. Until alternative data sources can be located, we conclude by rejecting the Branson–Rotemberg and Sachs real-wage hypothesis. Not only is there no evidence of excessive real wage growth after 1973 for the average of the six countries, but, contrary to their hypothesis, the US does *not* appear to be distinguished by unique real wage behavior.

REPRESENTATIONS OF WAGE AND PRICE ADJUSTMENT

Reduced-form Equations

To this point our examination of the data has been limited to basic statistics, – means, standard deviations and simple correlations. Next, we develop specifications for multiple regressions explaining wage and price changes. The hypothesis that the growth rate of nominal wages adjusts slowly to economic forces can be translated into a partial adjustment equation:

$$w_t = \lambda w_t^* + (1 - \lambda)w_{t-1}, \quad 0 \leqslant \lambda \leqslant 1, \tag{4.1}$$

where lower-case variables again represent rates of change and w_t^* is the 'equilibrium' growth rate of the nominal wage. A value of zero for λ would indicate a totally rigid nominal wage, with no response to the economic variables determining w_t^*, whereas a value of unity for λ would indicate no inertia at all. A particularly simple representation of w_t^* can be written:

$$w_t^* = \alpha_0 + \alpha_1 p_{t-1} + \alpha_2 d_t + \alpha_3 z_t + \varepsilon_t. \tag{4.2}$$

The four right-hand variables are, respectively, the lagged change in prices (p_{t-1}), a vector representing the effect of demand pressure or slack (d_t), a vector of supply shocks and exchange-rate movements (z_t), and an error term (ε_t). If the d_t and z_t variables are defined so that zero values represent neutral demand pressure and the absence of supply shocks, then the constant term α_0 measures the equilibrium growth rate in the real wage.

Taken literally, the hypothesis of real wage rigidity would imply that the growth rate of the real wage does not respond at all to the effect of demand pressure or to supply shocks:

$$w_t = \alpha_0 + p_{t-1} \tag{4.3}$$

One way of testing for rigidity in the growth of real wages is to contrast (4.3) to the result when (4.2) is substituted into (4.1):

$$w_t = \lambda\alpha_0 + \lambda\alpha_1 p_{t-1} + \lambda\alpha_2 d_t + \lambda\alpha_3 z_t + (1 - \lambda)w_{t-1} + \lambda\varepsilon_t \tag{4.4}$$

In the context of (4.4), rigid real wage growth would require that $\lambda = \alpha_1 = 1$ and that $\alpha_2 = \alpha_3 = 0$. Rigid nominal wage growth would imply that $\lambda = 0$.

It would be undesirable, however, to identify the parameters directly from (4.4), because the specification of equilibrium real wage growth (4.2) imposes over-tight restrictions on the lag structure. If contract expiration dates are staggered over a year or more, then the observed wage change would be correlated with a moving average of past wage changes in the case of nominal wage rigidity, and a moving average of past price changes in the case of real wage rigidity. Also, in the specification (4.2) for the change in the equilibrium wage, p_{t-1} is sometimes replaced, as in Branson–Rotemberg, by the expectation of price change at time t, say Ep_t. If expectations are formed adaptively on a moving average of recent changes in prices and in demand and supply variables, then there is an additional reason to expect lagged values of all variables to enter in (4.4). Allowing each coefficient except the constant term in (4.4) to be replaced by a polynominal in the lag operator, we have:

$$w_t = \beta_0 + \beta_1(L)p_{t-1} + \beta_2(L)d_t + \beta_3(L)z_t + \beta_4(L)w_{t-1} + \eta_t \qquad (4.5)$$

where η_t is a new error term.

Now rigid real wage growth would require that the sum of the coefficients on lagged price change ($\Sigma\beta_{1i}$) be equal to unity, and that the coefficients on the other variables be equal to zero. The introduction of the lagged values thus clouds the concept of real wage rigidity, since if the β_1 lag distribution were stretched out over a substantial period of time, say two years, there would be considerable flexibility in the actual observed change in the real wage ($w_t - p_t$). In (4.5) nominal wage rigidity would require that the sum of the coefficients on lagged wage change ($\Sigma\beta_{4i}$) be equal to unity, and that the coefficients on the other variables be equal to zero.

As observed above, nominal wage rigidity does not give rise to output fluctuations if prices are sufficiently flexible. To supplement estimates of (4.5), we also provide estimates of a reduced-form price equation in which the lagged wage terms are recursively solved out of (4.5), and the resulting expression for wage change is substituted into a 'mark-up' equation which expresses price change as depending on w_t, as well on as current and lagged values of d_t and z_t:

$$P_t = \gamma_1(L)p_{t-1} + \gamma_2(L)d_t + \gamma_3(L)z_t + v_t \qquad (4.6)$$

In the process of substituting the wage equation into the price equation, the constant term cancels out on the condition that the equilibrium real wage growth term (α_0) equals the productivity term in the price mark-up equation.[3]

The reduced-form price-change equation (4.6) has clear implications for output fluctuations when the demand variable (d_t) is represented by the excess of nominal GNP growth (y_t) over 'natural' real GNP growth (q_t^*), or $\hat{y}_t = y_t - q_t^*$, and by the lagged log ratio of actual to natural real GNP ($\hat{Q}_{t-1} = Q_{t-1} - Q_{t-1}^*$):

$$P_t = \gamma_1(L)P_{t-1} + c_1\hat{y}_t + \gamma_2(L)\hat{y}_{t-1} + c_2\hat{Q}_{t-1} + \gamma_3(L)z_t + v_t \qquad (4.7)$$

To derive the output corresponding equation, we first write the log level of actual real GNP as equal by definition to its lagged value plus 'adjusted' nominal GNP growth ($\hat{y}$) minus price change:

$$\hat{Q}_t \equiv \hat{Q}_{t-1} + \hat{y}_t - p_t \qquad (4.8)$$

When (4.7) is substituted into (4.8), we obtain:

$$\hat{Q}_t = -\gamma_1(L)p_{t-1} - (1 - c_1)\hat{y}_t - \gamma_2(L)\hat{y}_{t-1} + (1 - c_2)\hat{Q}_{t-1}$$
$$- \gamma_3(L)z_t - v_t \qquad (4.9)$$

The sets of coefficients obtained from estimating (4.7) and (4.9) should be identical and should indicate how changes in nominal GNP are divided over time between price and output changes.[4]

Supply Shocks and Exchange Rate Movements

In previous research on historical US data I have identified changes in the relative price of food and energy, and the impact of programs of government intervention and the wage- and price-setting process, as the major types of supply shocks, represented above by the z_t vector. More recently, Gordon and King (1982) expanded the list to include changes in the relative price of imports and in the effective exchange rate of the dollar. In this paper the variables included in the z_t vector include changes in the relative price of imports and in the effective exchange rate, dummy variables for known periods of government intervention in the US and UK, and additional dummy variables for the episodes of autonomous wage push previously identified by Perry (1975) and myself (Gordon, 1977) for France in 1968, Germany in 1969–70, Italy in 1969–70, and the UK in 1970. The definitions of the dummy variables and their coefficients are listed in *Appendix A*.

There is a problem in defining the exchange rate variable in the estimation of the basic price adjustment equation (4.7). Imagine an artificial situation with zero inflation in the rest of the world, and full equilibrium in the subject country with $p_t = p_{t-1} = \hat{y}_t$, and with output at its natural level ($\hat{Q}_{t-1} = 0$). Assume also that all supply shocks are absent and that the exchange rate is depreciating at a rate equal to p_t. Then for the 'accelerationist' or 'natural rate' hypothesis to be valid, steady inflation in (4.7) would require that the coefficients on lagged inflation plus those on current and lagged nominal GNP change ($\hat{y}$) sum to unity. To achieve a zero value for every component of the z_t vector, the exchange rate change would have to be defined in real terms, i.e. as the nominal exchange rate depreciation (measured with a positive sign) minus the domestic rate of inflation.

Now imagine that there is a positive price change in the rest of the world. If that rest-of-world inflation is equal to the steady-state inflation in the subject country in the above example, then the nominal exchange rate change will be zero under purchasing-power-parity, and the above conditions on the sum of the p and $\hat{y}$ coefficients will be valid if the nominal rather than the real exchange rate change is included in the equation. If the rest-of-world inflation were slower than that in the subject country, then under PPP the nominal exchange rate would depreciate (its change would be positive). If short-run changes in the exchange rate help to explain price changes, then there would be a positive sign on the exchange rate variable, and a sum of coefficients on the p and $\hat{y}$ variables of less than unity. In the reverse situation, with rest-of-world inflation faster than in the subject country, the exchange-rate change would be negative, and this, multiplied by a positive coefficient, would require a sum of coefficients on the p and $\hat{y}$ variables of more than unity in a steady-state inflation.

None of this would be a problem if there were a readily available measure of 'rest-of-world inflation' for each subject country, using appropriate trade weights. Lacking such a measure, it appears more appropriate to use a nominal measure of exchange rate change, and to expect that in nations with inflation rates diverging substantially from that in the rest of the world, the sum of coefficients in (4.7) on the p and $\hat{y}$ variables may diverge from unity even if the accelerationist hypothesis is correct.

EMPIRICAL RESULTS

Responsiveness of Wages and Prices to Lagged Nominal GNP Changes

Before proceeding to the estimates of the wage equation (4.5), and price equation (4.7), we report a preliminary set of summary measures of wage and price responsiveness designed to parallel my earlier study of wages in the US, UK and Japan (1982a). There I reported sums of coefficients for regressions specified in the format of a Granger causality test, with wage changes regressed on lagged changes in wages and on lagged changes in nominal GNP, and a separate set of results with nominal GNP changes regressed on the same variables. With eight values of all lagged variables included in the equations, the results indicated much higher sums of coefficients on nominal GNP changes in the wage equation for the UK and Japan than for the US. This was interpreted as evidence of nominal wage flexibility in those two countries, and nominal wage stickiness in the US.

Table 4.4 exhibits coefficients from similar wage equations for all six countries. All equations include, in addition to the eight lagged changes in wage rates and nominal GNP, a constant term, seasonal dummy variables, and the full set of supply shock variables described above, including the change in the nominal effective exchange rate. Once again, as in the earlier paper, there is a sharp contrast between Japan and the UK, with sums of coefficients on nominal GNP near unity in line A1(b), and the US, with a sum of coefficients near zero. France shares with the US a sum of coefficients insignificantly different from zero, whereas Germany and Italy fall between the extremes, with sums of coefficients near 0.5. The sums of coefficients on lagged wages, as would be expected, have roughly the reverse ranking, with the highest sum in the US and the lowest (significantly negative) in the UK. The other countries exhibit sums of coefficients on lagged wages in an intermediate range between 0.36 and 0.58.

Not only does US wage behavior seem to be unique in the pattern of coefficients in Table 4.4, but also in the relatively low standard error in

TABLE 4.4   *Equations in which quarterly changes in wage rates and the GNP deflator are regressed on lagged values of the dependent variable and of changes in nominal GNP,[1] sample period 1961(1)–1981(4)[2]*

	France	Germany	Italy	Japan	UK	US
A. Wage change equation						
1. Sums of coefficients on:						
(a) Lagged wage changes	0.58***	0.36*	0.37**	0.49***	−0.86*	0.81***
(b) Lagged nominal GNP changes	0.25	0.46*	0.48**	0.87***	1.05*	0.08
2. Standard error of estimate	2.09	3.60	5.58	4.53	4.81	0.89
B. Price change equation						
1. Sums of coefficients on:						
(a) Lagged price changes	0.87*	0.29*	0.72**	0.52**	0.10	0.78***
(b) Lagged nominal GNP changes	0.14	0.47**	0.20	0.17	0.07	0.23**
2. Standard error of estimate	1.87	2.36	4.10	3.80	3.52	1.40

Notes
1. Asterisks designate significance levels of 10(*), 5(**), and 1(***) per cent.
2. Sample period extends to 1981(3) in Japan and 1981(1) in the UK.

the wage equation. As was suggested by the standard deviations in Table 4.1, wage changes in most other countries are much more variable than in the US. There is a possibility, however, that some of the extreme character of US wage behavior may be due to non-comparability of data. The US wage index covers average hourly earnings in the entire non-agricultural private sector, not just manufacturing as in the other countries, and is adjusted to eliminate the cyclical effects of changing overtime pay and the interindustry mix of employment. If the US wage equation in Table 4.4 had been based instead on the unadjusted data for average hourly earnings in manufacturing, as reported in the IMF International Financial Statistics, an entirely different picture would have emerged:

	US Results in Table 4.4	*Replicated with IMF wage data*
Sums of coefficients on:		
Lagged wage changes	0.81***	0.52**
Lagged nominal GNP changes	0.08	0.40**
Standard error	0.89	1.93

With IMF wage data, behavior in the US now falls into the intermediate category with that in Germany and Italy, and the standard error of the equation is almost as high as in France.

Not only do the manufacturing earnings data indicate less difference between the US and other nations, but so do the equations for changes in the GNP deflator, as reported in Section B of Table 4.4. Sharp differences among the countries disappear, and the sums of coefficients on lagged nominal GNP range only from 0.14 for France to 0.47 for Germany. The UK still has a relatively high coefficient, but insignificantly so, and Japan exhibits no evidence of a rapid price response to nominal GNP changes. France and Italy exhibit as much or more inertia and nominal price sluggishness than the US. The standard error in the US equation is still the lowest of the six countries, but is fairly close to that in France.

Estimates of Full Reduced-Form Equations for Wage and Price Changes

The next stage in the investigation is the estimation of regression equations corresponding to specification (4.5) above for wage changes and (4.7) for price changes. As in the previous results reported in Table 4.4, all equations include changes in the relative price of imports and in the nominal effective exchange rate, as well as dummy variables (defined in the *Appendix*) for episodes of government intervention and autonomous wage push. The wage equations all contain a single constant term, while the price equations exclude the constant.

The top half of Table 4.5 reports sums of coefficients for the quarterly wage change equations. In scanning these sums, we interpret relatively

TABLE 4.5   *Sums of coefficients on variables in basic wage and price change equations;*[1] *sample period 1961(4)–1981(4)*[2]

	France	Germany	Italy	Japan	UK	US
A. Wage equation[3]						
1. Sums of coefficients on:						
(a) Lagged wage change	0.34*	0.10	0.03	0.22	−2.35***	1.02***
(b) Lagged price change	−0.05	0.01	1.34**	0.32	2.45***	0.00
(c) Nominal GNP change	0.25	0.48**	−0.05	0.71***	0.51**	−0.04
(d) Lagged output ratio	−1.10***	0.60**	0.86*	0.12	1.05	0.21***
(e) Relative import price change	0.12**	0.06	−0.08	0.08	0.32***	0.06**
(f) Exchange rate change	0.10**	0.15*	0.26*	0.14	−0.11	0.00
2. Standard error of estimate	1.89	3.56	5.45	4.17	4.35	0.84
B. Price equation[4]						
1. Sums of coefficients on:						
(a) Lagged price change	0.50***	0.39***	0.41**	0.70***	0.25	0.83***
(b) Nominal GNP change	0.48***	0.40***	0.56***	0.21*	0.38	0.20***
(c) Lagged output ratio	0.20**	0.24**	0.20	0.31**	0.98**	0.27***
(d) Relative import price change	0.08***	0.17***	0.06	0.13***	0.14**	0.09***
(e) Exchange rate change	0.10***	−0.06	0.05	−0.07	0.33**	0.05
2. Standard error of estimate	1.43	2.30	3.27	3.07	3.10	1.21

Notes
1. Same as Table 4.4.
2. Same as Table 4.4.
3. The equation also includes a constant and the following number of lags: wage, 1–8; price, 1–8; nominal GNP, 0–4; output ratio, 1; relative import price, 0–4; exchange rate, 0–4.
4. Same as 3, except that the constant term and lagged wage changes are excluded.

large sums on lagged wage changes as evidence of nominal wage inertia, large sums on lagged price changes as evidence of real wage inertia, and large sums on nominal GNP change as evidence of a high degree of responsiveness to expansions in nominal demand generated at home or abroad. The coefficient on the lagged output ratio, representing the effect of the *level* of economic slack, should be positive to accord with the traditional slope of the Phillips curve. The sums of coefficients on changes in the relative price of imports and in the nominal effective exchange rate should both be positive.

The wage equation for the US again identifies the unique role of inertia in the wage change process, reflecting the role of three-year staggered and overlapping wage contracts. The output ratio coefficient is significant and has the expected sign. There is no evidence of feedback from prices or nominal GNP to wages. There is a small import price effect, but no impact of exchange rate changes. Once again the UK is at the other extreme. The sum of coefficients on lagged wages is negative, reflecting an odd pattern of negative serial correlation in the data that is not eliminated by seasonal dummy variables. There is strong positive feedback from price changes to wage changes, but strong feedback from nominal GNP as well, so that real wage changes are not rigid but rather are responsive to nominal demand. The output ratio coefficient is large but insignificant, while the import price coefficient is relatively large and significant.

The other countries can be described as falling between the extremes represented by the UK and the US. Italy exhibits coefficients that are consistent with relatively rigid real wages, although there is a large positive coefficient on the output ratio variable. Japan and Germany display similar patterns, with little evidence of nominal or real wage rigidity, together with relatively large and significant responses to nominal GNP changes. French behavior does not fall into any neat category, displaying modest wage inertia, no feedback from prices or nominal GNP, and a large and incorrect sign on the output ratio.

As in Table 4.4, the behavior of US price changes is much less different than wage changes. In fact, the coefficients for the US are remarkably similar to those in Japan. France, Germany and Italy display similar patterns of coefficients, while again the UK falls into an extreme category in its small and insignificant price inertia coefficient and its very large and significant response to the output ratio. Effects of the relative price of imports are mostly significant and fall into a narrow range, whereas exchange rate effects mainly lack statistical significance, except in France and the UK.

Differences across nations in the coefficients on the relative price of imports can provide additional evidence on the issue of real wage rigidity. The Branson–Rotemberg–Sachs hypothesis implies that in the US, because of sticky nominal wage rates, a supply shock reduces the real wage, in contrast to other countries in which real wages grow at a fixed rate and in which a supply shock requires some other type of adjustment, i.e. a profit squeeze and higher unemployment. The import price coefficients for the price equations in Table 4.5 can be subtracted from those in the wage equations, to indicate the implied response of the real wage to changes in the relative price of imports:

France	0.04	Japan	−0.05
Germany	−0.11	UK	0.18
Italy	−0.14	US	−0.03

By this measure, four of the six countries exhibit a decline in the real wage in response to an increase in the relative price of imports, but this negative effect in the US is weaker than in Japan, Germany and Italy.

SUMMARY AND CONCLUSIONS

Previous papers by Branson–Rotemberg and Sachs have popularized the characterization of the United States as having uniquely sluggish nominal wage adjustment, with changes in nominal demand mainly altering real output rather than prices in the short run, in contrast to other industrialized nations in which nominal wages are more flexible and changes in nominal demand alter real output to a lesser extent and prices to a greater extent. A second part of the Branson–Rotemberg–Sachs (B–R–S) analysis stresses the role of real wage inertia in explaining the unprecedented increase in unemployment in the 1970s in other industrialized countries, in contrast to the US in which nominal wage stickiness, together with a moderate degree of price flexibility, makes real wages responsive and flexible. This paper provides new evidence based on simple correlations and on quarterly time series regressions that bear on both parts of the B–R–S analysis. In addition, the paper examines the responsiveness of domestic wages and prices to changes in exchange rates, in order to provide an interpretation of the phenomenon identified by Jacob Frenkel as the 'collapse of purchasing-power-parity'. The major conclusions can be summarized as in Table 4.6.

1. Almost all of the evidence provided here supports the B–R–S

TABLE 4.6 *Summary of results in Table 4.5*

	France	Germany	Italy	Japan	UK	US
1. Extent of nominal wage inertia	Low	None	None	None	Negative	High
2. Extent of nominal price inertia	Medium	Medium	Medium	High	None	High
3. Overall responsiveness to demand expansion						
(a) Wages	None	High	Medium	High	High	Low
(b) Prices	Medium	Medium	Medium	Low	High	Low
(c) Real wages	Negative	Positive	Mixed	Positive	None	Negative
4. Extent of real wage inertia	None	None	High	None	High	None

identification of nominal wage changes in the US as being uniquely dominated by inertia. This evidence is also consistent with my recent contrast of US wage behavior with that in Britain and Japan. The only qualification to this point is the possible role of differences in the construction and scope of data; a crude index of average hourly earnings for US manufacturing displays less inertia than the adjusted index for the non-agricultural sector used here and in much previous research.

2. Changes in the US GNP deflator are not nearly as inertia-prone as changes in US wage rates. As shown in lines 2 and 3(b) of Table 4.6, the extent of price inertia and responsiveness to demand changes is almost identical in Japan and the US. There is less inertia, and more demand responsiveness, in France, Germany and Italy, with no inertia and very prompt demand responses in the UK. Thus it is true that a domestic demand expansion will raise output relatively more in the US, and the spillover from that expansion will raise prices relatively more elsewhere (as in the B–R–S hypothesis), although the differences in price adjustment behavior are not nearly as sharp as for wages.

3. There is no consistent set of responses of the real wage to changes in demand. In France as well as in the US, prices are more responsive than wages, and so the real wage tends to fall (or rise less than usual) during an expansion. In Germany and Japan the opposite is true, and the real wage tends to rise. In Italy and the UK there is no systematic response of the real wage to a demand expansion. This difference in real wage responses is a challenge to theorists of price adjustment. I would conjecture that the US pattern can be explained by short price contracts in contrast to three-

year wage contracts. Perhaps in Germany and Japan there are sufficient forward commitments in product markets, particularly in international trade, to make the effective contract length for prices longer than that for wages.

4. Changes in the relative price of imports make a modest contribution to explaining both wage and price changes in the 1961–81 period, with the predominant pattern for the real wage to be depressed by an increase in the relative price of imports. This evidence, and the pattern of feedback from prices to wages summarized on line 4 of Table 4.6, suggests that there is no evidence to confirm the second part of the B–R–S hypothesis that stresses real wage flexibility in the US and rigidity elsewhere. There is some evidence of sticky real wages in Italy and Britain, due to contractual indexation in the former and *de facto* indexation in the latter, but not elsewhere. By no measure is the real wage more rigid in France, Germany and Japan than in the US.

5. Data collected for the manufacturing sector also tend to reject the B–R–S hypothesis that real wage stickiness has been responsible for higher unemployment in countries outside the US in the 1970s. As shown in Table 4.3, Germany, Italy and Japan all showed a greater deceleration in real wage growth relative to productivity growth than did the US in the 1973–81 period. Only France and Britain exhibit the patterns necessary to lend support to the B–R–S hypothesis. But, again, real wage behavior in the US is not in a special category.

6. In all estimated equations (with the exception of the UK) domestic prices tend to exhibit small responses to exchange rate changes during the 1973–81 period. Thus a change in US monetary policy that causes a major dollar depreciation as in 1977–9, or an appreciation as in 1980–2, will have little short-run impact on domestic inflation differentials and will show up mainly as a change in real exchange rates.

7. Overall, we conclude that the US and UK represent extremes of behavior, with nominal wage stickiness in the US contrasting with rapid responses of both wages and prices in the UK. But there is little evidence that the other four non-US nations can be neatly defined by a simple characterization like the B–R–S hypothesis. US price behavior is very similar to that of Japan, and the US real wage exhibits responses to both demand and supply shocks that duplicate the responses in one or more of the other countries.

NOTES

1. This research is supported by the National Science Foundation. I am grateful to Stephen R. King for his careful work in developing the data file, and to Joan Robinson for her rapid and accurate production of the paper under last-minute deadline pressure.
2. Gordon and King (1982) present a comparison of alternative estimates of the output cost of disinflationary monetary policy in the US, using both traditional and vector-autoregressive econometric models.
3. In addition, the sum of coefficients on prices in the wage equation, and the current wage in the price equation, must be unity. In the simplest example:

   (a) $w_t = a_0 + p_{t-1} + a_2 d_t$;
   (b) $p_t = (w_t - c_0) + b_2 d_t$;

   and, substituting (a) into (b), if $a_0 = c_0$, we obtain:

   (c) $p_t = p_{t-1} + (a_2 + b_2) d_t$

4. Equations identical to (4.7) and (4.9), lacking only the lagged nominal GNP terms, have been used in Gordon (1982b) to evaluate the 'policy ineffectiveness proposition' on US quarterly data extending from 1890 to 1980.

REFERENCES

Branson, William H. and Rotemberg, Julio J. (1980) 'International Adjustment with Wage Rigidity', *European Economic Review*, Vol. 13, May, pp. 309–32.

Federal Reserve Bank of St. Louis (1980, 1982) *International Economic Conditions, Annual Data*, July 1980 and June 1982.

Frenkel, Jacob A. (1981) 'The Collapse of Purchasing Power Parities during the 1970s', *European Economic Review*, Vol. 16, May, pp. 145–65.

Gordon, Robert J. (1977) 'World Inflation and the Sources of Monetary Accommodation: A Study of Eight Countries', *Brookings Papers on Economic Activity*, Vol. 8, No. 2, pp. 409–68.

Gordon, Robert J. (1982a) 'Why US Wage and Employment Behavior Differs from that in the UK and Japan', *Economic Journal*, Vol. 92, March, pp. 13–44.

Gordon, Robert J. (1982b) 'Price Inertia and Policy Ineffectiveness in the United States, 1890–1980', *Journal of Political Economy*, December, forthcoming.

Gordon, Robert J. and King, Stephen R. (1982) 'The Output Cost of Disinflation in Traditional and Vector Autoregressive Models', *rookings Papers on Economic Activity*, Vol. 13, No. 1, forthcoming.

Perry, George L. (1975) 'Determinants of Wage Inflation Around the World', *Brookings Papers on Economic Activity*, Vol. 6, No. 2, pp. 403–35.

US Bureau of Labor Statistics (1982) 'International Comparisons of Manufacturing Productivity and Labor Cost Trends, Preliminary Measures for 1981', Release, 2 June.

Sachs, Jeffrey (1979) 'Wages, Profits and Macroeconomic Adjustment: A Comparative Study', *Brookings Papers on Economic Activity*, Vol. 10, No. 2, pp. 269–319.

5 Fixed Exchange Rates, Flexible Exchange Rates, or the Middle of the Road: a Re-Examination of the Arguments in View of Recent Experience[1]

HANS GENBERG and
ALEXANDER K. SWOBODA

INTRODUCTION

Dissatisfaction with the workings of flexible exchange rates has recently become rather widespread, in Europe at least. Concern with exchange rate movements is no longer confined to the business world and to economic journalists but is also increasingly expressed by academic economists. Two features of the post-Bretton Woods era have, in particular, been the source of much disenchantment with flexible exchange rates: wide ('excessive'?) movements and high short-run variability in both nominal and real exchange rates, and apparently strong transmission of economic disturbances across countries, especially from the United States to the rest of the world.

This paper discusses briefly the reasons for this disenchantment and compares them with those that led to dissatisfaction with the Bretton Woods system (the first two sections below). In one sense, there is a surprising similarity between complaints heard then and now, both in terms of inadequate adjustment of real exchange rates (though for different reasons) and in terms of lack of independence for national macroeconomic policy. We will argue that an important common reason for the shortcomings in the performance of both systems is failure to agree on, or to adopt, clear rules for the conduct of monetary policy. The appropriate focus of these rules depends of course on the exchange rate regime, but, contrary to popular belief, a system of flexible exchange rates does not remove the need for rules if that system is to function properly.

This last hypothesis is developed in the third section below, which argues that the need for policy responses which have the property of being medium- to long-term commitments does not change fundamentally with a change in the exchange rate regime, although the form of the commitment does change. To develop this conjecture, we draw on recent work on rules versus discretion and on the inconsistency of optimal plans, notably by Kydland and Prescott (1977), and by Barro (1982b). The final section briefly discusses the contribution of intermediate exchange rate arrangements (of the crawling peg, heavily managed, or regional EMS variety) to solving current policy problems; we argue that none of them are likely to remove the need for more predictable policy responses to be workable. More generally, we conclude that in the absence of such predictability one can expect strained monetary relations and increasingly frequent attempts to interfere with international trade in goods and assets justified by references to unsatisfactory exchange rate behavior.

THE CURRENT SYSTEM: TOO MUCH EXCHANGE RATE FLEXIBILITY?

Disappointment with the workings of flexible exchange rates since 1973 can perhaps best be understood in the light of the expected benefits from the changeover from the Bretton Woods system. A major contribution of the adoption of more flexible rates among major industrial countries, it was hoped, would be a smoother payments adjustment process. Nominal exchange rate changes would compensate for diverging national inflation rates, allowing for the maintenance of equilibrium real exchange rates and the avoidance of current account imbalances associated with the gradual build-up of under- or overvaluation of currencies in real terms. Should real exchange rate changes be required to adjust to changes in preferences, endowments and technology, nominal exchange rates would again provide the means in the face of inherently rigid domestic price structures. Flexible exchange rates would thus allow for international adjustment in the face of the desire for greater national monetary autonomy. In fact, they would allow for a high actual degree of monetary autonomy, an end of the transmission of inflation from country to country (imported inflation), and for a lessening of the transmission of real economic disturbances through the current account. Additional benefits could (or would) be the renunciation of the use of controls to shore up inappropriate nominal parities, the removal of the exchange rate from politics, a decreased need for international liquidity, and greater symmetry in the adjustment process.

Among these, two benefits seemed particularly important from a national policy point of view: smoothly adjusting exchange rates and insulation from foreign disturbances (with an associated increased national policy autonomy). These are also the two areas where there has been most disenchantment. The high actual degree of exchange rate variability stands in apparent contradiction to the ideal of smoothly adjusting rates, and disturbances appear to have been transmitted as strongly, if not more strongly, after 1973 as before, casting doubt on the insulating properties of floating exchange rates.

The high recent degree of exchange rate variability has been widely documented.[2] To take but one example, the standard deviation of changes in the DM–dollar rate (calculated from monthly observations on three-month changes) quintuples from the 1960–71 to the 1973–82 period.[3]

With relatively little increase in the variance of national inflation rates, this translates into a roughly equivalent increase in the standard deviation of the real exchange rate. In the words of Frenkel (1981), purchasing power parity has collapsed in the 1970s. The stylized facts about exchange rate variability are: (a) a strong increase in variability in nominal rates as between the pre-1971 and post-1973 periods, the increase tending to be larger in terms of bilateral than multilateral (effective) rates; (b) an equal increase in the variability of real exchange rates, movements in the latter being dominated by nominal exchange rate variations in the short run; (c) innovations in exchange rates seem to follow first- (or second-) order auto-regressive processes with a first-order coefficient close to one; (d) over longer time horizons there appears a tendency for purchasing power parity to hold, at least when appropriate corrections for time-trend are made; the evidence from single-country time series is tenuous, but that from cross-sections across countries is quite strong on that point.[4]

The important question, of course, is whether and in what sense current exchange rate variability is excessive. In a superficial sense, it is excessive simply because it is large by historical standards. It is also high when set against expectations held in the late 1960s, when small but persistent differences in yearly national inflation rates combined with fixed nominal exchange rates were deemed to result in cumulative disequilibria in real exchange rates and, hence, chronic payments imbalances. The fact that real exchange rates have been even more variable since 1973 was thus somewhat unexpected and disturbing. The fact that real exchange rates of several major currencies have undergone medium-term cycles (of, say, two to three years' duration) of significant amplitude leads to the suspicion, *ex post*, that these variations were not necessary. The question, of course, is whether the variations were excessive *ex ante* and whether they have had untoward economic consequences.

This last question is an empirical one but there is no simple way of assessing recent experience or, more generally, to measure the costs of variability in relative prices. There is a presumption, however, that unexpected real exchange rate and terms of trade changes do have an impact on real output (and its composition) as *a priori* reasoning predicts.[5] Moreover, high variability in prices by reducing the information content in price changes is likely to have efficiency costs and may well lead to reduced investment by raising risk premia. It may also inhibit effective current account adjustment. Be that as it may, whether exchange rate movements are excessive cannot be judged independently of the variability of other economic variables, in particular policy variables. In this respect, increased variability is not confined to exchange rates; it extends notably to monetary variables and to interest rates.[6] In other words, one wants to know *why* exchange rates, both real and nominal, have been as variable as they have been.

As is by now well known, there is no good, generally accepted, precise answer to this question. Simple empirical exchange rate models have not performed very well; their predictive ability has been quite poor.[7] One usual explanation is that exchange rates, being one element determining the expected yield of assets denominated in different currencies, behave like asset prices. This in turn means that expectations of the future course of exchange rates play a crucial role in determining current spot rates. To the extent that the variables (and economic relationships) on which expectations are based are subject to large unexpected variations – to the extent that there is 'news' – spot (and forward) exchange rates will undergo wide fluctuations. Since one important element entering expectations of future exchange rates is forecasts of the future course of macroeconomic and, in particular, monetary policy, increasing the predictability of future monetary policy becomes a prerequisite if exchange rate variability is to be reduced. The section below on 'rules, discretion and the exchange rate regime' argues that this may well require the adoption of rules rather than discretion in policy formation, since discretion tends to lead to an increase in predicted future variability of the determinants of exchange rates.

One main argument for reducing nominal (and, as a consequence, real) exchange rate variability is that short-run exchange rate variations act as a channel of transmission of disturbances across countries. The usual argument relies on differences in speeds of adjustment as between rapidly adjusting asset markets and slowly adjusting goods markets. With slowly adjusting goods prices, unexpected money supply disturbances result in short-run real exchange rate changes and in 'overshooting' of nominal exchange rates. Given speeds of adjustment and unexpected shocks, this is not necessarily a bad thing; the short-run overshooting of prices fulfills a useful function in that it gives correct information as to the direction in which adjustment should take place. Nevertheless, the flexible exchange rate system is robbed of its insulating characteristics.

Evidence on the extent of transmission of economic disturbances under flexible as opposed to fixed exchange rates is again not easy to assess. Simple correlations of GNP changes for major industrial countries for the pre- and post-1973 periods tend to show more rather than less correlation for the latter as compared with the earlier period. However, it is not clear whether this is evidence of transmission or of stronger common worldwide disturbances (oil-price shocks and the like). Similarly, there does not appear to be a reduction in the interdependence of interest rate movements with the move to floating rates – if anything, the contrary. Here again, existing correlations have to be interpreted carefully; they appear to reflect common movements in underlying variables as much if not more than direct transmission from the United States to Europe.[8] There is, of course, one instance of decreased transmission since 1973, namely that of inflation. The variance in OECD countries' inflation around the mean has increased very substantially since 1973 (as, unfortunately, has the mean).

The performance of flexible exchange rates thus appears to be poor both in terms of insulation and in terms of 'reasonable' stability in nominal and real exchange rates. It does remain possible that recent medium-term cycles in real exchange rates have played a useful role in the adjustment of current account balances to a variety of shocks.

To gain some empirical feeling for the adequacy of the adjustment process under the fixed and flexible exchange rate regime, one can investigate the time-series properties of the current or trade account of a country. Determining the time pattern of response of the trade balance to a once-and-for-all shock allows an answer to the question: 'taking account of all endogenous responses, how does a shock to the trade balance in period t influence the trade balance in subsequent periods $(t + i)$?' This rough and preliminary exercise was carried out for each of ten industrialized countries and indicates some interesting differences for the period 1962–71 as compared with the period 1976–82. Responses tend to be slightly more damped and less cyclical in the 'fixed' rate 1960s than in the 1970s, which include more explosive cases.[9] Again, the usual disclaimer applies here also: these findings may not have anything to do with the exchange rate regime *per se* but may, instead, reflect differences in the nature of the exogenous shocks observed in the two periods.

The shocks to which the world economy was subjected in the 1970s may well account for its relatively poor performance over the period, and much of the disenchantment with floating exchange rates may be misplaced. Still, we suspect that one reason for this relatively unsatisfactory performance has been the attempt to run a system of floating exchange rates without paying heed to the need for policy rules, whatever the exchange rate regime. Floating rates may remove nominal variables from being the subject of policy conflict, but not real variables. This has at least two implications: (a) that policy-makers should *not* attempt to influence real exchange rates (since one of the benefits of floating rates is purportedly to allow for market adjustment of relative prices); and (b) that monetary policy should be predictable enough not to lead to high variability of real exchange rates and, hence, to transmission of disturbances.

BRETTON WOODS: TOO LITTLE EXCHANGE RATE FLEXIBILITY?

If current international monetary arrangements are seen to produce excessive exchange rate variability, the Bretton Woods system was deemed to provide for too little exchange rate flexibility. It was, like the current system, blamed for excessive transmission of disturbances. The concern then, however, focused mainly on the transmission of inflation, from the United States to a number of purportedly inflation-averse countries such as West Germany or Switzerland.

The argument that the Bretton Woods System provided an inadequate degree of exchange rate flexibility was made forcefully in the early 1950s by Friedman (1953) and Meade (1955). Their case for flexible or variable exchange rates was essentially a case against fixed rates, and their reasoning was basically accepted and reiterated by most critics of Bretton Woods. The reasoning combined an analytical notion with an empirical (or normative) observation. The analytical notion was the Tinbergen–Meade principle on the required equality between the number of instruments and targets of policy. The observation concerned the downward rigidity of domestic prices (or of the price level), a rigidity that was either a matter of fact or the result of policies designed to avoid real deflation in a world of sticky nominal wages. A payments deficit, for instance, could be either financed by a sterilized decumulation of international reserves, or suppressed by resort to controls on trade in goods and assets, or eliminated through a fall in output, employment and imports. The first of these (financing) was thought of only as a short-run expedient, the second (controls) as inefficient and violating international agreements, and the third (deflation) as unacceptable politically and needlessly costly if an additional instrument of policy could be made available to cure external disequilibrium while maintaining internal balance through aggregate demand management. The additional instrument is, of course, the nominal exchange rate, variations in which result in variations in the real exchange rate and of the terms of trade provided prices expressed in domestic currency are sticky.[10] In Johnson's (1961) terminology these variations act as an expenditure-switching policy that can be combined with expenditure-changing financial policies to deal simultaneously with internal and external balance. Whatever the precise analytical framework, the key point from our point of view is that nominal exchange rate flexibility is deemed necessary to bring adjustment in the *relative* (or 'real') price of 'domestic' and 'foreign' goods.

With fixed nominal exchange rates and countries unwilling to sacrifice internal objectives to the requirements of external balance, a gradual build-up of external imbalances and inappropriate real exchange rates would take place. Although this is a bit of a caricature, the typical view of many economists in the 1960s went somewhat as follows. Some countries (e.g. the UK) have a tendency towards higher inflation than others (e.g. West Germany). As a result, with fixed nominal rates, the currency of low-inflation countries tends to become undervalued, that of high-inflation countries overvalued in real terms. At the same time, the former countries experience 'chronic' payments surpluses, the latter 'chronic' deficits. Inappropriate parities are defended by controls on trade in goods and assets, and occasionally by stop-go policies. At some stage, however, speculation sets in and abrupt changes in parities have to occur. Insufficient flexibility in nominal exchange rates in the short run thus leads to excessively abrupt changes (instability) in the long run.

The argument that nominal exchange rates under Bretton Woods were 'too fixed' or not flexible enough needs to be analyzed with some care. In particular, one needs to ask 'too fixed in terms of what criterion?' This also raises the question of whether there is an optimal degree of exchange rate flexibility. The Friedman–Meade argument referred to above argues for the degree of exchange rate flexibility needed to maintain equilibrium relative prices internationally in the presence of domestic price level rigidity – while maintaining full employment output at home. As Mundell's optimum currency area analysis points out (see Mundell, 1968), the argument assumes the existence of money illusion in that it implies that, in a country that experiences unemployment and a deficit, workers will accept a fall in real wages brought about by a rise in the price of imports but not by a fall in nominal wages. As a matter of fact, the degree of exchange rate flexibility becomes a matter of indifference from the point of view of the conflict between (real) internal and external balance in a world of full information and perfect wage-price flexibility. However, the degree of exchange rate flexibility is not a matter of indifference in a world where countries have diverging inflation targets. The focus shifts from insuring internal and external balance simultaneously to providing autonomy for national monetary policy, although, of course, the two issues are intimately connected. In this second view, the optimal degree of exchange rate flexibility is that which is needed to accommodate differences in national inflation rates (beyond the differences that would arise from the maintenance of changing equilibrium real exchange rates at constant nominal rates of exchange). Here the trouble with fixed exchange rates is that there is too much transmission of disturbances, particularly of price-level disturbances.

Looking back at experience in the 1960s, we would suspect that this second consideration was in fact probably more important than the first, even if more attention was paid to the first in the literature of the time. There are two ways in which one can view existing inter-country differences in inflation rates during the fixed-rate period. The first, mentioned above, is to view them as reflecting differences in *ex ante* national inflation rates (which thus have a certain amount of autonomy) and resulting in disequilibrium deviations from purchasing power parity. That is, they result in changes in real exchange rates when the latter's equilibrium value did not in fact change, or change as much. The second view is that these inflation differences reflect changes in equilibrium real exchange rates (or errors of measurement for that matter) and that the *ex ante* inflation rates might have been either larger or smaller had the nominal rate of exchange not been fixed. Without wishing to apportion exactly that part of the experience of the 1960s that reflects one or the other view, we should note that experience is not incompatible, *a priori*, with the second. In an inflationary world which is otherwise stable, small differences in national inflation rates should suffice to accommodate medium-term trend changes in real exchange rates. Moreover, existing studies document the very limited scope for policy autonomy with respect to inflation under fixed rates[11] and thus throw doubt on the extent to which disequilibrium in the real exchange rate can cumulate under fixed nominal exchange rates. Finally, that view is not incompatible with persistent payments disequilibria, the origin of which has to be sought, however, in inappropriate national monetary policies rather than, or together with, distortions in relative prices. In other words, the problem attempts at achieving autonomy of national monetary policy in an exchange rate system the logic of which denies the possibility of such autonomy.

These considerations may help explain why the Bretton Woods system began to break down in the late 1960s after having functioned quite satisfactorily earlier on (at least with the benefit of nostalgic hindsight). Much of the breakdown can be interpreted as the result of dissatisfaction with, and disagreement on, the rules implicit in, and needed to govern smoothly, a system of fixed exchange rates based on a reserve currency. In such a system, different rules apply to the center and other countries. The logic of a system of fixed exchange rates requires, by and large, that individual countries do not seek monetary autonomy but let their monetary policy be governed by the requirements of external balance. That is, the monetary mechanism of adjustment under fixed exchange rates must be allowed to work. In one sense, all that is required is that monetary authorities do whatever is needed to maintain the exchange rate fixed and that they make their commitment believable. This requires, in turn, a number of 'negative' rules to be observed. A first rule is that rigid targets for money growth should *not* be adopted; a second is that full sterilization should *not* take place.[12] This does not mean that some sterilization of reserve flows should not take place over, say, the business cycle, but that monetary autonomy should be confined to smoothing out temporary or cyclical disturbances. In the medium to longer run, fixed exchange rates do imply that the evolution of inflation and the business cycle might be dictated by the course of these variables in the rest of the world.

What that course will be depends very much on the system, or rules, governing the supply of international reserves and, in a reserve-currency system, on the behavior of the issuer of that currency. In principle, there are few policy constraints on the issuer of a reserve currency required by the maintenance of fixed exchange rates between that and other currencies – at least as long as other countries agree to follow whatever rules are necessary to keep their and the reserve currency convertible at a fixed rate. There are, however, at least two constraints on the center country if the system is to be viable in the long run. First, if convertibility between the reserve currency and some outside asset such as gold is to be maintained, proper rules for the sharing of responsibility for the maintenance of the gold–dollar ratio between center and other countries must be followed, as Mundell (1968) has pointed out in his analysis of the 'crisis problem'. Second, the center country must follow a macroeconomic policy that is broadly acceptable to other countries lest the latter find it advantageous to opt for autonomy of their monetary policy by opting out of the fixed exchange rate system. The next section argues that this may require the adoption of rules rather than discretion by the center country.

Much of the breakdown of the Bretton Woods system can be interpreted as a failure to agree on a proper framework for governing the supply and composition of international reserves, and of the 'world' money stock. As a result the course of macroeconomic policy, and of inflation in particular, implied by the policies pursued by the United States became unacceptable for a number of countries. They sought a higher (or smoother) degree of exchange rate flexibility in order to regain the autonomy denied them by the existing system. This was true not only of European countries but also of the United States, which apparently found adoption of the policy rules (and commitments) necessary for acceptance of fixed rates by the rest of the world too onerous.

It is ironic, though perhaps not surprising, that dissatisfaction with both Bretton Woods and with recent experience arises from 'inadequate' exchange rate behavior on the one hand, and excessive transmission of disturbances on the other. Unwillingness to submit to rules limiting national monetary autonomy seems to be at the root of the unsatisfactory performance of both systems. Yet, as we will argue in the next section, neither system is likely to function satisfactorily without some commitment to appropriate rules, even if their form should differ under different exchange rate systems.

RULES, DISCRETION AND THE EXCHANGE RATE REGIME

It is commonly held that a system of flexible exchange rates allows more discretion for national monetary policy than a system of fixed exchange rates. While this is certainly the case in the sense that a flexible exchange rate is *viable* without any explicit constraint on the conduct of monetary policy, it is also true that (a) it is only after the advent of floating rates in 1973 that a number of countries have experimented with growth rate rules for money supplies, and (b) many economists would argue that for a system of flexible exchange rates to work satisfactorily a great deal of stability and predictability of monetary policy is required. This suggests that rules for policy may be as necessary under flexible rates as they are under fixed rates. In this section we investigate this issue by discussing the room for discretionary monetary policy under fixed and flexible exchange rates and by comparing the nature of the necessary commitment concerning monetary policy under the two regimes. We also take up some possible consequences of failing to adhere to the commitment.

Fixed Exchange Rates

The adoption of a fixed exchange rate is a commitment by the central bank or exchange rate stabilization authority to buy or sell domestic money against foreign money at a fixed price. Many economists would also argue that such a system must imply a commitment to a particular type of monetary policy for the fixed exchange rate to be credible. The nature of the required monetary policy is well-known from writings in the tradition of the monetary approach to balance of payments theory and policy[13] and can be summarized briefly as follows.

For a country which is not a reserve currency country and which is 'small' in internationally integrated goods and asset markets, the quantity of money in circulation is in the longer run demand-determined. The demand for money is furthermore exogenously (relative to domestic monetary policy) determined, so that domestic open market operations will 'only' succeed in influencing the composition of the backing of the money supply between domestic and foreign assets. In the short run the scope for deviations from the passive role of monetary policy is larger and depends to an important extent on the degree of international capital mobility and substitutability between assets denominated in different currencies. As noted above, the empirical evidence on the last question tends to indicate rather strong, but not absolute, constraints on the amount of autonomy exercised by most European countries during the Bretton Woods years.

Considerations similar to those just mentioned led McKinnon at the previous Wingspread conference to propose a set of rules for the conduct of monetary policy which would be consistent with a fixed exchange rate system.[14] These rules included a fixed growth rate for the domestic asset component of the domestic money supply and a rule prohibiting complete sterilization of the effects of balance of payments flows on the money supply. A rigid rule for the growth of domestic assets is likely to be inappropriate (unless information is perfect and the rule can be made contingent on changes in the demand for money function). It is true that the rule has to be stated in terms of the domestic component of the money supply, but it should be made contingent on the level or growth of the country's international reserves, i.e. it should be designed to allow the monetary mechanism of payments adjustment to work. It is here that the prohibition on complete sterilization is essential.

For the reserve currency country the problem is different and, as far as the technical feasibility of fixed exchange rates is concerned, less constraining. Since the center country does not face the problem of running out of reserves, it can in principle choose to follow a discretionary monetary policy. But as the policy adopted will have to be accepted by the other countries, some form of constraint may be needed in order for the system to be politically feasible. It will in fact be argued shortly that purely discretionary policy on the part of the center country may lead to an inflation rate which is too high from a welfare point of view not only for the rest of the world but also for the center country itself.

The consequences of departing from the monetary policy dictated by the requirement of a fixed exchange rate are well known in the case of the non-reserve currency countries. Erring systematically either on the side of too rapid or too slow a rate of domestic credit creation is going to lead to 'chronic' (fundamental?) balance of payments problems which may be interpreted by the private sector as a weakening commitment to the fixed exchange rate. This in turn is likely to lead to currency crisis of the kind we saw towards the end of the 1960s.

The reserve currency country does not, as already noted, have to pre-commit its monetary policy in order for fixed exchange rates to be feasible. The arguments concerning the appropriateness of rules versus discretion in this case must be based on other considerations. Kydland

and Prescott (1977) have recently provided an interesting analysis which suggests that in a world where economic agents form expectations rationally,[15] discretionary policy by the government may lead either to time-inconsistent policies or to non-optimal outcomes compared to a policy *rule*. Discretionary policies are defined as those policies which do not effectively commit the government to follow a particular policy in the future. Instead the government is assumed to be setting current policy with the intent to maximize a social welfare function subject to the current state and structure of the economy and the current state of private sector expectations. The private sector is assumed to be aware of the authorities' objectives and to form expectations accordingly. Within this framework Kydland and Prescott demonstrate that an optimal policy strategy may be time-inconsistent in the sense that the future path of a policy variable chosen in period t will not be followed starting in period $t+1$ because it will then seem more advantageous to follow a different strategy. But if such a mid-course change in the path of the government policy instrument is undertaken, private agents will soon catch on to the fact that the original intentions of the government are not being followed, and they will modify their behavior accordingly. This will result in 'a breakdown in [the] ability either to predict the behavior of [agents] or to make an analytic statement about optimal government policy' (Lucas and Sargent, 1981, p. xxxvi).

Furthermore, in those situations where a time-consistent discretionary policy exists, Kydland and Prescott show that this policy can be dominated in a welfare sense by a rule commiting the policy-makers to future actions. The reason is that a discretionary policy does not take into account the effects of expected future policy decisions on current behavior.

Recently, Barro and Gordon (1981) and Barro (1982a, 1982b) have illustrated the results obtained by Kydland and Prescott in a context of inflation and unemployment determination. One conclusion of their analysis is that discretionary policy will lead to an excessive rate of inflation even in a model where there is no exploitable trade-off between inflation and unemployment. In the case of a reserve-currency country under fixed exchange rates, a possible implication of these findings is that even if this country adopts a cosmopolitan view and tries to pursue a discretionary policy aimed at maximizing a world welfare function, the resulting policy might be one in which the world rate of inflation is excessive. It is tempting to speculate about whether considerations of this type have anything to do with the fate of the Bretton Woods system. Be that as it may, they do indicate that some form of constraint of the monetary policies of the reserve currency country may be necessary under fixed exchange rates. This constraint may take the form of a rule[16] for the growth rate of some domestic monetary aggregate or be related to a convertibility requirement on the external liabilities of the reserve currency country. The essential requirement is that the rule should prevent the monetary authorities from seeking to reach short-term stabilization goals by generating unexpected movement in the money supply.

Flexible Exchange Rates

We have already noted that flexible exchange rates have not succeeded in insulating national economies from external shocks. Policy actions in one country will hence continue to affect economic conditions in others. Rules or guidelines may therefore be necessary in order to prevent inconsistencies between the intentions of individual governments. For example, domestic policies in each of two countries may be aimed at depreciating the home currency. Since this is obviously not possible for both countries simultaneously, it may be desirable to conclude agreements on what constitutes permissible monetary and financial policies from an international perspective. While such agreements are a form of commitment concerning future policies, they constitute an agreement about what policies will *not* be followed, rather than a statement about which policies *will* be followed. As this paper focuses on the latter type of commitment, we will not discuss further the former type, even though that too is an important ingredient in designing policy.

Two considerations suggest that constraint on the future path of monetary (and fiscal) policy may be as important under flexible rates as under fixed rates. The first is an implication of the so-called asset market view of exchange rate determination. According to this view, floating exchange rates are likely to be determined in a manner similar to prices of other durable assets in that they will depend on expectations of future events which determine the demands and supplies of the moneys involved. As noted above, if views about future events change frequently and abruptly, one would expect exchange rates to be quite volatile. In particular, it may be argued that monetary policy may contribute to this volatility unless it is conducted according to a generally known and enforced rule. The benefit of a rule, which to re-emphasize would not have to take the form of a *fixed* growth rate of some monetary aggregate but could involve feedback relationships to output, inflation or the exchange rate itself, would be that the forecasting problem of each economic agent would be simplified, since the path of monetary policy would be subject to less arbitrary variation. Changes in the expectations of future policy would be less frequent and the exchange rate would be less volatile.[17]

The second consideration pointing towards the potential usefulness of rules in the flexible exchange rate context relies on the Kydland and Prescott analysis reviewed above. Although formal modelling will be required in order to extract the implications of their framework for optimal policy in an open economy setting, we venture three hypotheses as to the outcome of such modelling. First, to the extent that the long-run effects of monetary policy in a country are bottled up by the purchasing power parity relationship, it is likely that the results of Barro and Gordon will be preserved; namely, that a time-consistent discretionary policy will lead to excessive inflation. This would hold independently for each country following such a policy. Second, if the optimal policy turns out to be time-inconsistent, the volatility of exchange rates may be increased as a result of the increased unpredictability of future policy. Since the optimal discretionary policy depends on the reaction of the private sector to a given policy, uncertainty about how agents modify their behavior in the light of the realization that monetary policy is subject to the time-inconsistency problem will lead to more uncertainty about future monetary policy. Third, since a flexible exchange rate does not seem to provide complete insulation from external shocks, it seems likely that even if the domestic policy-makers commit themselves effectively to a future policy, 'misbehavior' on the part of other countries is likely to have undesirable consequences for the domestic economy. Misbehavior in this context may involve the pursuit of the optimal discretionary policy analyzed by Kydland and Prescott, but it may also involve the optimal exploitation of the knowledge that the domestic country is following a rule for its policy. In this case the complexity of the modelling task is increased significantly, since it will be necessary to formalize the nature of the game not only between the dominant domestic policy-maker *vis-à-vis* the private sector but also between the two policy-makers.

The previous discussion has implicitly treated monetary policy and exchange rate policy as one and the same. Many economists would object to that and argue that under flexible exchange rates monetary policy-makers have two instruments available, monetary base control and interventions in the foreign exchange market. If this were the case then the latter instrument could be used, for instance, to smooth excessive fluctuations in the exchange rate, while the former could be used to influence aggregate demand. Consequently, some of the arguments in favor of rules based on their salutary effects on volatility would be weakened. It is thus necessary to comment at least briefly on the effectiveness and use of intervention policy under flexible rates.

The question of the effectiveness of sterilized intervention in the foreign exchange market is essentially the same as the question of the degree of monetary autonomy allowed by a fixed exchange rate. In both cases the answer depends on the degree of substitutability between domestic and foreign assets and the degree of capital mobility. Available evidence[18] suggests that both mobility and substitutability are sufficiently high in the medium term to ensure that sterilized intervention in and of itself will have quite small, if any, effects. Hence it appears that the treatment of monetary and exchange rate policy as two sides of the same coin is justified. This does not necessarily mean that countries should refrain from intervening in the market. For as Mussa (1980) and others have emphasized, it might be that intervening when the government is committed to a particular exchange rate level will be advantageous because it provides a signal to the market that the government intends to follow the monetary and fiscal policies necessary for the exchange rate target to be reached. Intervention then may become a potentially useful complement to pre-commitments in other policy matters. But in order to serve this purpose it is important that intervention policy should not be expected to accomplish too much. For instance, it might be tempting to announce and follow a growth rate rule for the money supply defined over a period of a year, say, and attempt to use intervention policy within the year to smooth exchange rate movements. Using arguments similar to those by Poole (1976) it can be shown[19] that such a strategy might lead to more rather than less exchange rate volatility.

In closing this section it may be useful to restate our contention that some form of effective pre-commitment of economic policy may be as necessary under flexible rates as under fixed rates. This leaves open questions concerning, on the one hand, the likelihood that policy rules will in fact be adopted, and on the other how monetary institutions could be designed in order to provide greater incentives to move in this direction. We do not take up these important issues here. Nor do we enter into a discussion of the determinants of trust in and credibility of government announcements stating their intention to let rules guide their future economic policies.[20] Our aim is the more modest one of pointing out that in the debate about optimal exchange rate regimes, the often repeated (but therefore not necessarily correct) argument that commitments to rules for policy are not politically feasible do not constitute a case for an international monetary system based on flexible rather than fixed exchange rates.

INTERMEDIATE EXCHANGE RATE REGIMES

As a result of views that a fixed rate system embodies excessively rigid rates and that a freely floating rate system leads to excessive volatility, a number of proposals for intermediate solutions have been made. One such solution involves some variant of a crawling peg, whereas another envisages more active and co-ordinated management of exchange rates without actually announcing parities. We shall comment on these proposals with particular reference to their implications for the issue of rules versus discretion.

Exchange rate adjustments can be achieved either by discretionary policy or on the basis of predetermined criteria both under a crawling peg and a managed floating-rate system. Nevertheless, differences exist between the formula variants of the two systems; these differences become blurred in the decision (discretion) variants. Under a decision variant of the crawling peg, the market would know exactly the rate at which the currency is being pegged *at each point in time*, whereas this would not be the case under managed floating. In this sense the crawling peg might contribute to reducing the uncertainty concerning official intentions. But since the peg can be changed at the discretion of the relevant policy-maker without reference to any rule governing such a change, the decision variant of a crawling peg is little different from a heavily managed float as regards *future* movements in the exchange rate.

To the extent that the Kydland and Prescott argument in favor of rules for policy instruments is valid in the variable exchange rate context, it is evident that it would apply to both the crawling peg and managed floating systems. In addition, the 'traditional' arguments focusing on international co-operation and co-ordination would still be relevant in order to avoid conflicting goals in the policies of individual countries. Such co-operation could be most easily conceived within the framework of a set of rules of acceptable conduct.

If one accepts the proposition that exchange rate and monetary policy should be conducted according to commitments constraining future actions, what are the advantages and disadvantages of the intermediate exchange rate regimes considered here compared to the polar cases of fixed or freely floating rates?

A case in favor of a crawling peg as opposed to a fixed exchange rate might be built on the proposition that contingent rules are likely to be superior to fixed rules for policy variables.[21] Contingent rules in this context would specify that the exchange rate peg would be altered in response to well-defined events in the future such as changes in income, the price level, the balance of trade, the stock of reserves, etc. A fixed rule, on the other hand, would specify a *predetermined* value of the peg or a *predetermined* rate of crawl. The superiority of contingent rules can be explained, with one exception noted below, by the fact that a fixed rule is simply a restricted sub-class of contingent rules and as such can at best be as good as the latter. In general, it is unlikely that it will be optimal not to allow the policy variable to respond to changes in future economic conditions.[22] An exception to this proposition may result if the simplicity and transparency of a rule is important for its effects on the economy. If the private sector can more easily understand and adapt its behavior to a fixed rule, it is possible that the outcome will be superior under such a regime. In addition, to the extent that the ability to monitor the policy-makers' adherence to the rule is important, the fixed rule may again be superior.

As in the case of fixed exchange rates, a crawling-peg arrangement imposes strict constraints on the monetary policies followed by the countries concerned. In particular, the non-sterilization rule is still crucial. Some commitment of the center country is also necessary for the same reasons as before. In addition, it is essential that the rules for the rate of crawl should be consistent across countries as well as consistent with market-determined equilibria. The latter requirement can be illustrated by analysing the frequently proposed purchasing power parity rule for the crawling peg.[23] According to such a rule, the exchange rate between two countries would always be adjusted so as to offset changes in the relative price levels. This effectively means that the real exchange rate, defined as the ratio of the price levels multiplied by the nominal exchange rate, would be fixed: this would preclude adjustments to real disturbances which require changes in relative prices. It is also likely that under this rule the domestic price level would become more variable, because any shock to it would be validated by a corresponding change in the exchange rate. The required monetary accomodation would be forthcoming through the balance of payments adjustment mechanism. For these reasons a purchasing power parity rule for a crawling peg would not be desirable. Other criteria determining the rate of crawl may, however, be found which have more attractive characteristics and which might, subject to the proviso concerning understand-ability noted above, be superior to a fixed rule.[24]

Turning to the management of floating exchange rates and its advantages over a freely floating rate, an argument can be made that is analogous to that in favor of contingent over fixed rules for a crawling peg. In this context it is important to remember that management of exchange rates does not have to take the form only of interventions in the foreign exchange market, but that it can be carried out by traditional forms of monetary policy. Hence, exchange rate management implies using movements in the exchange rate as one criterion in setting monetary policy. From this point of view it seems that making use of the information contained in exchange rate movements is likely to be superior to ignoring that information when the rules for policy are designed.[25] As in the crawling peg example, however, the presumed advantage of contingent rules must be set against the greater simplicity and enforceability of fixed rules for policy.[26]

NOTES

1. Research support from the Fonds National Suisse de la Recherche Scientifique under Grant No. 4.361-0.19.09 is gratefully acknowledged.
2. See Saidi and Swoboda (1981b) for a recent discussion and a number of references.
3. These figures are from Genberg, Saidi and Swoboda (1982).
4. See Saidi and Swoboda (1981a).
5. See Huber and Saidi (1982) for some evidence.
6. For some evidence on interest rate variability, see Genberg, Saidi, and Swoboda (1982).
7. See, for instance, Meese and Rogoff (1981).
8. See Genberg, Saidi, and Swoboda (1982) for evidence on the interdependence of interest rates.
9. The ten countries are Austria, Canada, France, West Germany, Italy, Japan, the Netherlands, Switzerland, the UK, and the USA. More detailed results are available on request.
10. The real exchange rate is defined as the ratio of a foreign to a domestic price level index multiplied by the nominal exchange rate.
11. See, for instance, Genberg (1977).
12. A further implication is that domestic credit rather than the monetary base, the money supply, or interest rates is the main instrument of monetary policy.
13. See Swoboda (1973) for an example.
14. See McKinnon (1977) and also Parkin (1977).
15. It is not necessary for the expectations to be fully rational in the sense of Muth for the basic conclusions of Kydland and Prescott's analysis to be valid. It suffices that 'agents have *some* knowledge of how policymakers' decisions will change as a result of changing economic conditions', and that they take this knowledge into account in forming their current decisions.

16. The rule need not to be of the fixed growth rate type but may be of the contingent variety.
17. This does not mean that flexible exchange rates would change very little through time. They might still be highly volatile due to other disturbances influencing the foreign exchange market. The claim is that the current level of volatility would be reduced.
18. See Genberg (1981a) for a survey and Obstfeld (1982) for a recent contribution to this evidence.
19. See Genberg and Roth (1979).
20. Aliber (1977) contains such a discussion in a context similar to ours.
21. See Barro (1982a), Buiter (1980) and Lucas and Sargent (1981).
22. This should not be interpreted to mean that *any* contingent rule is preferable to a fixed rule. An example of a contingent rule for a crawling peg which is distinctly worse than a fixed rule will be given below.
23. Only the bare bones of such an analysis is given here. See Genberg (1981b) for a more detailed treatment. Dornbusch (1982) contains a formal model yielding similar conclusions.
24. See the contributions in Williamson (1981) and the references therein for a further discussion.
25. See Boyer (1978) for an example where the information embodied in the exchange rate is used to design optimal monetary policy.
26. Adoption of a fixed rule (or a simple contingent one) may thus be more believable than adoption of a complicated contingent rule.

REFERENCES

Aliber, Robert Z. (1977) 'Monetary Rules and Monetary Reform', in *The Political Economy of Monetary Reform*, ed. by Robert Z. Aliber (London: Macmillan), pp. 3–12.

Barro, Robert J., and Donald G. Gordon (1981) 'A Positive Theory of Monetary Policy in a Natural-Rate Model', National Bureau of Economic Research, Working Paper No. 807, November, forthcoming in *Journal of Political Economy*.

Barro, Robert J. (1982a) 'Inflationary Finance under Discretion and Rules', National Bureau of Economic Research, Working Paper No.   , May 1982, forthcoming in *Canadian Journal of Economics*.

Barro, Robert J. (1982b) 'High and Volatile Inflation – the Role of Discretionary Monetary Policy', paper written for the *Conference on Monetary Policy, Financial Markets, and the Real Economy* (Geneva: International Center for Monetary and Banking Studies), June 1982.

Boyer, Russel S. (1978) 'Optimal Foreign Exchange Market Intervention', *Journal of Political Economy*, Vol. 86, December, pp. 1045–56.

Buiter, Willem H. (1980) 'The Superiority of Contingent Rules over Fixed Rules in Models with Rational Expectations', Discussion Paper 80/80, University of Bristol, May.

Dornbusch, Rudiger (1982a) 'PPP Exchange Rate Rules and Macroeconomic Stability', *Journal of Political Economy*, Vol. 90, February, pp. 158–65.

Dornbusch, Rudiger (1982b) 'Equilibrium and Disequilibrium Exchange Rates', paper prepared for the Conference on Monetary Policy, Financial Markets, and the Real Economy (Geneva: International Center for Monetary and Banking Studies), June.

Frenkel, Jacob (1981) 'The Collapse of Purchasing Power Parities during the 1970s', *European Economic Review*, Vol. 16, February, pp. 145–65.

Friedman, Milton (1953) 'The Case for Flexible Exchange Rates', in Milton Friedman, *Essays in Positive Economics* (Chicago: University of Chicago Press), pp. 157–203.

Genberg, Hans, 'Policy Autonomy of Small Countries', in *Inflation Theory and Anti-Inflation Policy*, proceedings of a conference held by the International Economic Association at Saltsjöbaden, Sweden, ed. by Erik Lundberg (London: Macmillan), pp. 183–208.

Genberg, Hans (1981a) 'Effects of Central Bank Intervention in the Foreign Exchange Market', International Monetary Fund, *Staff Papers*, Vol. 28, September, pp. 451–75.

Genberg, Hans (1981b) 'Purchasing Power Parity as a Rule for a Crawling Peg', in *Exchange Rate Rules*, ed. by John Williamson (London: Macmillan), pp. 88–106.

Genberg, Hans and Jean-Pierre Roth (1979) 'Exchange-Rate Stabilization Policy and Monetary Target with Endogenous Expectations', *Schweizerische Zeitschrift für Volkswirtschaft und Statistik*, Vol. 115, September, pp. 527–45.

Genberg, Hans, Nasser Saïdi and Alexander K. Swoboda (1982) 'American and European Interest Rates and Exchange Rates: US Hegemony or Interdependence?', paper prepared for the Conference on Monetary Policy, Financial Markets, and the Real Economy (Geneva: International Center for Monetary and Banking Studies), June.

Huber, Gérard and Nasser Saïdi (1982) 'Macroeconomic Fluctuations in Switzerland, 1960–1981' manuscript, Geneva, April 1982.

Johnson, Harry G. (1961) 'Towards a General Theory of the Balance of Payments', in Harry G. Johnson, *International Trade and Economic Growth: Studies in Pure Theory* (Harvard University Press), pp. 153–68.

Kareken, John and Neil Wallace (1979) 'International Monetary Reform: The Feasible Alternatives', *Quarterly Review*, Federal Reserve Bank of Minneapolis, Summer 1978, pp. 2–7.

Kydland, Finn E. and Edward C. Prescott (1977) 'Rules Rather than Discretion: the Inconsistency of Optimal Plans', *Journal of Political Economy*, Vol. 85, June, pp. 473–91.

Lucas, Robert E. Jr. and Thomas J. Sargent (1981) 'Introduction', in *Rational Expectations and Econometric Practice*, ed. by Robert E. Lucas Jr. and Thomas J. Sargent (London: Allen & Unwin), pp. xi–xl.

McKinnon, Ronald I. (1977) 'Beyond Fixed Parities: The Analytics of International Monetary Agreements', in *The Political Economy of Monetary Reform*, ed., by Robert Z. Aliber (London: Macmillan), pp. 42–56.

Meade, James E. (1955) 'The Case for Variable Exchange Rates', *Three Banks Review*, September, pp. 3–27.

Meese, Richard and Kenneth Rogoff (1981) 'Empirical Exchange Rate Models of the Seventies: Are Any Fit to Survive?', *International Finance Discussion*

Papers, No. 184 (Washington: Board of Governors of the Federal Reserve System).

Mundell, Robert A. (1968) *International Economics* (London: Macmillan).

Mussa, Michael (1980) 'The Role of Official Intervention', manuscript, February.

Obstfeld, Maurice (1982) 'Exchange Rates, Inflation, and the Sterilization Problem: Germany, 1975–1981', paper prepared for the International Seminar on Macroeconomics, Mannheim, West Germany, May.

Parkin, Michael (1977) 'World Inflation, International Relative Prices and Monetary Equilibrium under Fixed Exchange Rates', in *The Political Economy of Monetary Reform*, ed. by Robert Z. Aliber, (London: Macmillan), pp. 220–42.

Poole, William (1976) 'Benefits and Costs of Stable Monetary Growth', in *Institutional Arrangements and the Inflation Problem*, Carnegie-Rochester Conference Series on Public Policy, Vol. 3, ed. by Karl Brunner and Allan H. Meltzer (North-Holland Publishing Co.), pp. 15–50.

Saidi, Nasser and Alexander K. Swoboda (1981a) 'Exchange Rates, Prices and Money: Evidence from the 1920s and the 1970s', manuscript, Geneva, April 1981.

Saidi, Nasser and Alexander K. Swoboda (1981b) 'Real and Nominal Exchange Rates: Issues and Some Evidence', manuscript, Geneva, June 1981, forthcoming in *Unemployment and Inflation under Flexible Rates*, ed. by Emil Claasen and Pascal Salin (North-Holland).

Swoboda, Alexander (1973) 'Monetary Policy under Fixed Exchange Rates: Effectiveness, the Speed of Adjustment and Proper Use', *Economica* Vol. 40, May, pp. 136–54.

Tobin, James (1978) 'A Proposal for International Monetary Reform', Cowle Foundation Discussion Paper 506, Yale University.

Williamson, John (ed.) (198?) *Exchange Rate Rules, The Theory, Performance and Prospects of the Crawling Peg* (London: Macmillan).

Part II
International Reserves and International Money

Part II

6 Internationally Managed Money Supply[1]

GEORGE M. VON FURSTENBERG

Since the title of this paper is not self-explanatory, we start with a taxonomic section before discussing three possible forms of international management of national money supplies. Elements of such management can be achieved either by committee or by rules or by inventing a stateless money which has a chance of becoming dominant over national moneys in international use. History and prospects of attempts to bring greater international influence to bear on national money supply processes are appraised in the concluding section.

INTRODUCTION

At the present time there are no fully fledged internationally managed moneys, unless the SDR and the ECU, which are created by international agreements on allocations or swaps, are viewed as such moneys in spite of their restricted use in official transactions, their scant leverage over national policies, and their limited substitutability for foreign exchange.[2] In fact, internationally managed moneys may never have existed in the full sense in which this term has been understood.[3] For instance, for a long time, gold was a supranational money, but its supply and the resulting supply of central bank money were never managed internationally (Keynes discussed methods that could be used to achieve supranational management in this regard). Currencies freely convertible into gold at a fixed official price continued to be managed nationally, even though other countries had a means for bringing pressure to bear on the monetary policy of any country offering conversion. The multiple-currency system of floating among the major currencies that succeeded the gold exchange standard in the early 1970s provided for even less international influence over money supply growth in the United States and in other countries. In all these instances, either the 'moneyness' of internationally managed assets or the collectivity of their management have been insufficient to declare them internationally managed moneys.

Having winnowed the concept, what are the elements that remain? In theory, money could be managed by an international committee. If this is to be done in much the same way in which the US money supply is managed by the collective of governors of the different Federal Reserve districts, a monetary union would first have to be established for that purpose. If it is done by negotiating money growth among governments represented in an international institution, the authority and decision rules of that institution would determine whether national money supply growth is managed internationally in substance.

The money supply decisions of one country will tend to influence those of other countries under almost any system that may be applied in the modern world. If the ways in which these repercussions feed forward through the reaction functions of other countries are not subject to national control and discretionary modification, for instance, because of binding and 'unalterable' commitments to fixed exchange rates, and there are no significant feedbacks that could create mutual dependency, the result is hegemonial money. Under such a system the growth of 'world' money supply is decisively influenced by a nation such as the United States, regardless of whether that nation factors international ramifications into the design of its actions. However, if the feed-in mechanisms through which other countries translate US policy impulses are elective and subject to discretionary modification by those countries, there is no predictable global imprint and no semblance of money that is managed either by an international collective or for that collective by its dominant member. Even under those conditions it would remain sensible, of course, to speak of the international money supply and credit conditions which result from the interplay of national monetary policy systems and to analyze characteristic features of that interplay from an international perspective (see, for instance, McKinnon, 1982).

International money management could be conducted by rules rather than by discretion. If these rules are to govern national money supply growth, they must be tied to criteria of economic performance. A system of fixed exchange rates does not, by itself, afford such a link because it does not make the management of national moneys predictable under international rules. It would not, of itself, prevent countries from pursuing various inflationary policies jointly, even if they cannot choose to do so on their own without jeopardizing exchange rate fixity. If countries agreed to commit themselves to monetary policies compatible with stability of their domestic price levels (or with some other fixed target rate of inflation judged to be desirable in both principle and practice), internationally managed moneys could result. If the common rule could not be abrogated easily by any country and if the monetary antidotes to any price level movements that may occur were agreed to in advance and implemented predictably, then national discretion would be limited after the adoption of a suitable international convention. International management would then consist of the administration of that convention.

Finally, internationally managed moneys could conceivably arise not from discretionary agreements or firm conventions negotiated among governments, but by sponsorship of a stateless money, such as a currency-option money, by an international institution. (Another theoretical possibility, international sponsorship of a commodity money, is not considered in this paper.) If such a money should be able to compete successfully with national moneys in private use, it might help establish international monetary order by disciplining the growth rate of national moneys.

DISCRETIONARY MANAGEMENT

Major countries are aware of the costs of pursuing policies whose implications for inflation differ sharply from the inflation rates expected in other major countries. These costs include increased volatility of the terms of trade and increased risks of political and macroeconomic instability, government interference, and distortions. Whether or not countries feel bound to defend their exchange rate within narrow margins, they recognize the benefits of striving for international compatibility of policies. They thus seek to influence the policies of other countries as these countries attempt to influence theirs.

The resulting pressures tend to be conveyed with the help of positive images, such as the locomotive or convoy theories of the 1970s, or by appealing to international comity to reduce negative externalities arising from the domestic policies of particular countries for others. Appeals are based on notional deviations from economic principles and objectives to which most major countries appear to have subscribed in a general way, rather than on violations of codified rules. The exercise of surveillance by international organizations over major aspects of national policy, and advisory opinions issued about the appropriateness of such policies, help to crystallize and apply whatever standards appear to be acceptable to a qualified majority of countries as a basis for collective appraisal. Whether that appraisal is powerful in causing national policies to be modified depends in part on the degree to which costs of ignoring international advice can be brought home to the country concerned and on the strength and cohesion of the underlying coalition on which this advice rests.

APPLICATION OF RULES

Countries may be willing to agree to narrow the range of policy choices available to them if the freedom of action in other countries is likewise curtailed. Adopting a convention of common rules could generate greater predictability of future policies and of policy responses to unfolding events, thereby reducing the potential dispersion of standards and policies between countries.

In the trade area, an example of such an approach is GATT. The efficacy of that agreement is protected by countries being allowed to retaliate unilaterally against violators and to deny most-favored-nation treatment to countries which do not subcribe to the rules of GATT. It is much more difficult to devise rules in the monetary area that can be protected by credible threats of retaliation and discrimination against violators. Since there may be no effective way for countries to pressure others engaged in excessive money creation – although exchange markets may react by depreciating the currency involved by much more than in proportion to its extra rate of supply money growth, thereby inaugurating a vicious cycle – international rules may not be enforceable. In that case, any shared commitment to adhere to money supply growth compatible with domestic price stability or similar objective would be predicated on unanimity, i.e. voluntary compliance. There could be international prestige and economic benefit to belonging to a core group of countries seeking to achieve domestic price stability, but the costs of exit might not appear to be high from the point of view of an individual country contemplating such a move for domestic reasons.

To increase international leverage, a system of mutual dependency can conceivably be constructed from the top by specific undertakings of a single country. Thus the United States could pledge itself to rules which allow other countries to bring pressure on the United States to adjust its policies, thereby allowing the rules adopted by that country to be complemented by those of others. The end result could be an internationally managed system. For instance, when the United States stood ready to exchange dollars for a fixed quantity of gold and other countries endeavored to maintain fixed exchange rates with the dollar, they could, up to a point, attempt to discourage inflationary policies by the United States by threatening to convert dollars into gold (for details on how this threat has been appraised in past literature, see Cumby, 1982). If the United States had placed great store on maintaining the convertibility of dollars into gold at a fixed official price and other countries had valued fixed exchange rates with the dollar, a non-inflationary international monetary order might have resulted from the linking of rules.

AN ALTERNATIVE TO NATIONAL MONEYS

In theoretical discussions, money has commonly been described as a commodity or an asset with a comparative advantage in absorbing and disseminating information concerning transactions (see, for instance, Brunner and Meltzer, 1971). The degree of predictability of the exchange rate for commodities determines this comparative advantage. Moneys possessing lower cost of information on account of shorter transaction chains and a smaller variance of price quotations replace moneys with higher costs of information. Hence stability, predictability and uniformity of purchasing power in the international market would be among the prerequisites for a money to emerge dominant. A dominant money, in turn, exerts pressure on other countries to compete, for instance, by pegging the exchange value of their currency to the dominant money or by trying to achieve even lower rates of domestic inflation than the country that issues it.

To stimulate such competition, international sponsorship of a currency-option money could be contemplated by which such a unit could be enabled to become a legally accepted denominator for a wide variety of private claims. Such a money would retain its purchasing power to a greater degree than all or most national moneys on account of the option feature described below.[4]

A unit of currency-option money is here defined as being worth no less than $\bar{x}_i$ in any of i currencies, where the value of the fixed amounts $\bar{x}_i$, converted to any common currency, may be equal at the point of introduction. Subsequently, however, when exchange rates have changed, the market value of the option money in all currencies other than the one (or more than one, in a joint float) that has appreciated most will be higher. In other words, the option money will then (normally) be worth $x_i = \bar{x}_i$ (plus option premium) in only one of the i currencies, and $x_j > \bar{x}_j$ in all others ($j \neq i$), where x_j is derived from $\bar{x}_i$ by use of the current spot exchange rate, e_{ji}. Once x_j has moved far above the contractual minimum $\bar{x}_j$, a minimum of this type could be raised at periodic intervals. This could be done without loss of continuity in redemption value to restore the insurance value of the currency option which was lost when the market value of the currency-option money fell towards its exercise value.

To illustrate, if the value of the SDR in each of the five major currencies (US dollar, Deutsch mark, yen, pound sterling, and French franc) that prevailed at the end of June 1974 had been used to determine $\bar{x}_i$ and none of these minima had subsequently been changed through administrative action, the dollar redemption value of the option money, which would have been \$1.20635 in mid-1974, would have been \$1.34929 (x_j) eight years later, while the yen redemption value (342.72 yen) would have been the same in mid-1982 as at the beginning of the instrument ($\bar{x}_j$). For comparison, at the end of June 1982 the official SDR was worth 19 per cent less than a unit of the option money described here. The fact that the performance of such a currency-option money could be influenced greatly by the choice of the base period used to fix the $\bar{x}_i$ could be mitigated by building in some slack even at the time of origination ($x_j = e_{ji}\bar{x}_i > \bar{x}_j$) for those currencies believed to be undervalued. Even then, however, currency-option money could be used to hedge commitments in any one of i currencies or currency combinations up to the specified minima $\bar{x}_i$, $\bar{x}_j$. In many situations the same instrument would provide versatile cover regardless of changes in the currency composition of exposure.[5] Speculative investors would normally be willing to accept a lower interest rate on claims denominated in the option money than on claims denominated in the currently hardest currency contained in it, provided the option feature remains of value.[6] That feature promises compensation if the currency that is expected to appreciate, or to remain appreciated, the most from initial positions does not actually do so.

Because of its versatility and unexcelled maintenance of purchasing power, currency-option money could become an attractive denomination in international applications. If national authorities were to allow its use to spread, they might be induced to compete for the status of their money contributing the $\bar{x}_i$ in which the redemption value of the currency-option money is fixed. Such competition could reduce inflationary biases in the policies of major countries.

Under a par-value system such as the European Monetary System (EMS), institution of an 'asymmetrical basket' technique of valuation (for a description see IMF, 1974, p. 44) for the ECU could replicate many of the characteristics of currency-option money just described. The currency basket currently used to value the ECU (or the SDR) involves fixed amounts of national currencies whose share in the value of the currency basket varies directly with the ECU (SDR) value of each currency. Changes in that value, weighted by the corresponding national currency amounts, must always net to zero by the manner in which a unit of basket currency is defined under the standard technique. If an asymmetrical basket technique were applied instead, changes in central rates could always be expressed as devaluations of a particular currency against the basket currency unit, with a decline of the share of its value in the unit compensated by raising the amount of that national currency contained in it. Under such a valuation adjustment rule, the basket currency would retain its value as well as the hardest currency, or succession of hardest currencies, within it. However, once such successions occurred, all of the national currency amounts in the basket, and not just all but one of them, would be higher than at the institution of the basket, something that could not happen under the currency-option money previously described. Although no such succession (to the Deutsch mark) has as yet occurred among the EMS currencies that participate in its exchange rate and intervention mechanisms, currency-option money would be anchored rather more predictably than a currency basket with potentially leapfrogging elements of the kind just described.

HISTORY AND PROSPECTS

At various points in the preceding discussion it was suggested that elements of international management of national money supplies could be strengthened if means were found to make excessively inflationary policies and the resulting depreciations or devaluations more costly for major countries. Attempts to do so through discretionary management have sometimes led to conditions being attached to devaluations of major currencies in the Bretton Woods system or, more recently, in the EMS. These conditions could be imposed not because countries could have been denied the right to devalue under appropriate circumstances, but because the availability of international credits and the restoration of confidence could sometimes be predicated on countries agreeing to make their domestic policies more compatible with future maintenance of fixed exchange rates. However, if a compelling majority of major countries cannot be found which desire to emulate the price performance of the least-inflating country among them, the degree of international influence that can be exerted over any of the other countries is likely to be small.

Attempts have also been made to bring international influence to bear on a single country by adopting a set of rules. Such an opportunity could have arisen in connection with the substitution of SDR claims for foreign official holdings of US dollars that was proposed in 1979–80. One of the arrangements considered was for the substitution account, which could be established by the IMF, to cover the exchange risk arising between the interest-bearing dollar assets to be acquired and the SDR-denominated liabilities to be issued by making the United States government financially responsible for part of any deficit that might arise in the account from unanticipated depreciation of the dollar against other currencies contained in the SDR. Had such an arrangement been concluded, it could have put pressure on the United States to avoid policies that could lead to such a depreciation and budget exposure. If other countries had agreed to share the burden of the exchange risk to the account with the United States, they too would have had a financial stake in the strength of the dollar. It is doubtful, however, that a country will accept rules or international arrangements raising the penalties for poor performance unless it is convinced that there is an adequate *quid quo pro* other than putting it on its good behavior.

The last comment also applies to the willingness of countries to tolerate a parallel money in their jurisdiction that could offer corrective, but frequently undesired, competition to their national money. Although open capital markets already provide considerable freedom of denomination for domestic residents, national authorities may be disinclined to help increase the substitutability of instruments denominated in a foreign or stateless money for their own money. Denominating in currency-option money is discouraged by many national accounting, fiduciary and regulatory conventions because it does not allow the nominal future value of assets and obligations to be predetermined. Thus large strides can probably not be made under current circumstances in any of the directions that could lead to greater international control of money for the group of countries whose currencies figure prominently in international finance.

Nevertheless, possible structural reinforcements for such a development can be identified. For instance, discretionary management could be strengthened if those few countries who pay more than lip service to the goal of first attaining and then maintaining approximate stability of their domestic price level would bring their combined weight to bear on advancing that cause regardless of any regional groupings to which they may belong. Within regional groupings such as the EMS, which includes the countries with the highest rate of inflation among those whose currency is used extensively in international finance, changes in rules may also have some effect. For instance, the onus of inflationary policies leading to devaluations, expressed as increases in the central rate in domestic currency, could perhaps be aggravated by refusing to lower any other central rate, thereby strengthening resistance to inflationary policies and hardening the exchange value of the basket currency if the asymmetrical basket technique is judged workable. Internationalism would be preserved in this and other hypothetical schemes by allowing any of the participating national currencies to assume a leading role in international valuation of stateless money, either alone or in tie with a few other currencies, solely on the basis of exchange performance.

NOTES

1. The author is indebted to Robert E. Cumby for helpful suggestions and comments. The usual disclaimer of institutional responsibility applies.
2. Acceptance limits and other regulations limit the transfer of SDRs and ECUs among official holders. Limited substitutability in the private market is evidenced by the bid-asked spread on SDR-denominated deposits in Eurocurrency markets normally being twice as large as on Eurodollar deposits with the same term to maturity.
3. Robert Triffin (1961, pp. 146–7) has described the surrender of national sovereignty that would be implied by moving towards an internationally managed system as involving a trade of national policy instruments against international or supranational policy instruments adequate to serve the broad objectives of economic policy in the modern world.
4. The option feature serves to protect purchasing power even if the currency that appreciates the most over some period of time does not belong to the country with the lowest rate of inflation. In fact, currency-option money would then retain its purchasing power to a greater extent than if PPP held.
5. Conversely, covering the exposure that issuing liabilities in that unit may imply would involve no more than covering in that one of the *i* currencies, provided it is foreign to the borrower, which has appreciated the most since introduction of the instrument. Since that currency may be overtaken by another as time progresses, cover would have to be adjusted when such an event appears imminent.

6. Details would depend on whether a claim is payable in the currency-option money unit of denomination itself or redeemable at maturity in the governing $\bar{x}_i$ or its equivalent in other currencies. In the latter case, the loss of the option premium over the term of the contract would have to be weighed against the chance that the exercise price would have risen in the currently hardest currency by the maturity date.

REFERENCES

Brunner, K. and A. H. Meltzer (1971) 'The Uses of Money: Money in the Theory of an Exchange Economy', *American Economic Review*, December, 61, pp. 784–805.

Cumby, R. E. (1982) 'Special Drawing Rights and Plans for Reform of the International Monetary System: A Survey', unpublished paper prepared at the IMF, April 14.

IMF (1974) *International Monetary Reform*, documents of the Committee of Twenty, Washington DC.

Keynes, J. M. (19) 'Problems of Supernational Management', *A Treatise on Money*, Chapter 38, reprinted in *The Collected Writings of John Maynard Keynes*, Volume VI (London: Macmillan).

McKinnon, R. I. (1982) 'Currency Substitution and Instability in the World Dollar Market', *American Economic Review*, June, 72, pp. 320–33.

Triffin, R. (1961) *Gold and the Dollar Crisis* (New Haven: Yale University Press).

7 Changing Perceptions of International Money and International Reserves in the World Economy[1]

K. ALEC CHRYSTAL

The international monetary environment of the early 1980s is very different from that of the early 1960s or indeed the early 1970s. Despite the intentions of central bankers and finance ministers, in those distant days of the 1967 Rio de Janeiro meetings, to plan for the rational evolution of an official sector-dominated system, expediency appears to have dictated a seemingly haphazard development. Despite the occurrence of a period of severe economic difficulties in many countries – the UK is a good but extreme example where there has been little or no growth in a decade, inflation remains in or close to double figures and unemployment is at a forty-year high – there is no consensus on the proper shape of an international monetary system that would support a return to more prosperous times. Will any system do?

It is clear from recent high level meetings such as the June 1982 Versailles summit that there is no prospect of a major international initiative, nor is there even a serious concern to look for solutions in these directions. Accordingly, while membership of the club of international monetary economists used to be granted on the basis of expertise in the production of ingenious reform proposals, such exercises seem pointless in the current intellectual climate. Rather, the present paper will offer an analysis of two important aspects of change in the extant international monetary system. The first concerns both perceptions and reality of the role of pure international money. The second concerns the evolution of the position of international reserves and, by implication, of agencies such as the IMF.

INTERNATIONAL MONEY[2]

The question that this section addresses is the extent to which traditional monetary analysis can be applied to the international system. Is there any useful sense in which we can think of there being a 'transactions demand' for money at the international level? Do currencies fulfill a genuine 'money' role in the international economy? If so, how is that role likely to develop?

The first formal attempt of which I am aware to analyze international money from this point of view was by Swoboda (1968, p. 39), who made a direct application of the Baumol–Tobin transactions demand inventory model. If an importer must meet a stream of foreign currency payments M evenly over a period, and he withdraws cash in discrete lumps from domestic bonds, then his optimum average foreign cash balance will be

$$F = \sqrt{\frac{aM}{2r}}. \tag{7.1}$$

where a is the brokerage cost of moving from bonds to foreign cash (per transaction), and r is the interest rate on domestic bonds.

Now consider the problem of trading with n different currency areas. There will be n different expenditure streams, $M_1, M_2, \ldots, M_n$. So the importer will have to hold balances of n different currencies, $F_1, F_2, \ldots, F_n$. His total foreign currency balance will be

$$\sum_{i=1}^{n} F_i = \sum_{i=1}^{n} \sqrt{\frac{aM_i}{2r}} \quad i = 1, \ldots, n \tag{7.2}$$

However, if payments could be arranged so that all were made in a single currency, there would be a considerable saving of foreign cash balance. This would mean that more resources could be held in interest-bearing bonds. Assuming for simplicity that $M_1 = M_2 = \ldots M_n$, then the saving in cash balances would be

$$(n - \sqrt{n}) \sqrt{\frac{aM_i}{2r}} \tag{7.3}$$

This expression is definitely positive so long as $n > 1$ and $a, M_1, r > 0$. Swoboda concludes that 'This establishes the proposition that there are economic advantages to be derived from the use of vehicle currencies' (p. 41).

This is an important result because it breaks the common presumption that actors will only wish to hold working balances of either the money of the currency area in which they live or the money of an area with which they are actively trading. It would be quite rational to organize trade such that the settlement medium used over large areas of international trade was not the domestic money of either party to the trade. Helpful as it is, however, to establish this simple point, the above analysis is now recognized to be deficient for a number of reasons. These deficiencies have emerged both from empirical studies of the method of finance in foreign trade and from an increased understanding of the structure of foreign exchange markets.

The most important single piece of information arises from studies of the currency of invoice of foreign trade (Grassman, 1973, 1976; Page, 1977; Carse, Williamson and Wood, 1980; Magee and Rao, 1980). The greater part of trade in manufactured goods between developed nations is invoiced in the currency of the exporter. Of the remainder, the bulk is invoiced in the currency of the importer. Only a small proportion (probably less than 5 per cent) is invoiced in third party currencies. Grassman regarded this evidence as a death blow to the vehicle currency hypothesis and argued that the international monetary system was, after all, symmetrical in the sense that no single currency fulfilled the role of international medium of exchange. The remainder of this section is devoted to demonstrating that, while Swoboda's analytical framework is certainly inadequate in the light of the evidence, there is an important role for 'international money', irrespective of the evidence on invoicing patterns.

Even the invoicing evidence suggests some role for international moneys. In particular, it is clear that much of the external trade of Third World countries, especially trade in homogeneous primary commodities, is invoiced in third party currencies, notably the dollar. However, the most important datum that has to be incorporated into any relevant analysis of international moneys is the fact that foreign exchange markets are almost entirely intermediated. Goods traders do not buy or sell currencies directly in foreign exchange markets; rather this is done by the specialist foreign exchange divisions of commercial banks. The existence of universal intermediation presents prima facie evidence of significant non-convexities in transactions technology which would obviously be related to the economies of scale evident in Swoboda's model. However, the very existence of intermediation means that the foreign exchange market can be analyzed at two distinct levels – the levels of the goods trader and the level of the foreign exchange dealer. The present paper concentrates on the more important of these, namely the behaviour of those actively engaged in the foreign exchange markets.

There are in reality three major areas worthy of enquiry, though only one will be developed below.

1. First, there is the important question of the choice of currency in terms of which firms set their prices. McKinnon (1979) suggests it is rational for differentiated manufactures to be priced in local currency while homogeneous commodities are priced in terms of an international money. There must, however, be a margin of choice at which economic analysis becomes appropriate, though this issue will not be pursued here. Further discussion is also available in Magee and Rao.

2. For any given pricing and payments pattern traders still have to decide the size and composition of their money balances. All traders will presumably hold working balances of the local currency. The issue is the extent to which they will wish to hold balances of international money. There are two aspects to this – transactions demand and speculative demand. With regard to transactions demand, McKinnon argues that traders will in general have a 'preferred monetary habitat' in the local currency. Traders would only buy foreign exchange immediately prior to making payments and sell it immediately after receipt. This will only be true, of course, where there are no cost advantages to operating in foreign currency, such as lower brokerage fees.

There has recently been a growing literature pointing to the speculative demand for foreign exchange (Calvo and Rodriguez, 1977). This arises because citizens of high inflation countries will substitute into holdings of foreign currency at the margin. While it has been demonstrated that there is significant substitution between international moneys (Chrystal, 1977; Chrystal, Wilson and Quinn, 1979), it is not clear that high-inflation countries are substantial holders of foreign exchange (Chrystal, 1979). The reason for this is that high-inflation countries, for this very reason, impose severe foreign exchange controls.

A more fundamental problem with the currency substitution literature, however, is that the analysis should apply *mutatis mutandis* to all foreign currency denominated assets and not just to 'money.' The peculiarities of that literature arise from the fact that choice is restricted to two non-interest-bearing moneys. If the menu of assets available were broader, a domestic resident would *never* choose foreign money for speculative purposes if there was an interest-bearing asset of the same denomination to choose from. In other words, speculative arguments *per se* are not a sufficient explanation for holdings of foreign *money*. Some additional story is required about transactions costs or liquidity services, etc. On the other hand, once interest-bearing assets are entertained, the novel properties of currency substitution models disappear or at least merge into the more familiar capital flows literature. Accordingly, the speculative approach to international holdings will not be pursued here, although its potential importance should not entirely be ignored.

3. The final important area relates to the organization of the foreign exchange markets themselves. McKinnon argues that even if international moneys, such as the dollar, are not the settlement media in manufactured goods trade (apart from where the US is a party to the trade), they (especially the dollar) are used as media of exchange in the foreign exchange markets. Forward markets, in particular, are universally structured with the dollar as settlement medium. The vast bulk of trade of spot markets is also done through the dollar, although here a number of cross-markets do exist between major currencies, notably within Europe (including Japan).

Accordingly, the topic that will now be investigated further is the use and evolution of media of exchange within the market made up by foreign exchange dealers alone. The analysis now to be developed makes liberal use of the analysis applied by Jones (1976) to the emergence of a medium of exchange in goods markets. However, some aspects of this analysis seem even more appropriate when transformed to foreign exchange markets. What follows differs from the approach of Krugman (1980), who discusses the use of vehicle currencies in financing trade imbalances. Here trade is presumed to be in basic balance.

The foreign exchange market is presumed to be made up of a large number of individual foreign exchange dealers sitting by telephones but otherwise isolated. Each trader has a given order for various quantities of different currencies to be purchased within a given period. This demand is a derived demand, coming from the needs of goods traders. However, the dealer does not merely transfer each order directly into the market. Rather, he will go to the market with lumps of orders. The reason for this is that, although market clearing prices are presumed to be known, there still exists a significant set-up cost for each exchange. The intuition of this is that even though exchange rates are known to a close approximation, a dealer wishing to sell currency A for currency B has to telephone other dealers using expensive lines until he finds another dealer wishing to make the opposite exchange. It is cheaper to do this for a small number of large deals than for a large number of small deals. For the problem to be non-trivial, it is necessary to assume that dealers do not have complete prior information about other dealers' demands and supplies. However, they do have some subjective notion, based upon experience, of the relative scale on which various currencies are traded. For example, they know that the number of dealers selling dollars for sterling on a particular day is likely to be much greater than the number selling drachmas for cruzeiros.

What makes the problem interesting is that dealers who can be presumed to conduct their affairs so as to minimize expected costs of any ultimate exchange, may choose to structure their transactions via an intermediate currency (drachmas for dollars, dollars for cruzeiros, rather than drachmas for cruzeiros). It is the potential use of this intermediate currency that is of particular interest.

The trading space is presumed to contain n currencies and a large number of individual dealers. Currency units are defined so that all exchange rates are unity, and quantities exchanged in each trade are presumed to be all of equivalent value (e.g. 1 million dollars' worth per transaction). To accomplish any given exchange, say of currency i for currency j, a dealer searches randomly for another dealer who wishes to exchange currency j for currency i. The transactions cost to the individual dealer is assumed to be proportional to the time spent searching for a complementary trade. The dealer will seek to structure his trades so as to minimize this cost. His trading strategy will be chosen prior to entering the market (i.e. before picking up the phone) on the basis of his beliefs about the probabilities of finding takers for various deals. These beliefs are derived from his previous experience in the market, whereas the true probabilities are the fractions of traders offering to buy or sell each currency.

It is assumed that the subjective probability, P_i, that any randomly encountered dealer will want to buy currency i, is equal to the probability that any randomly encountered dealer will want to sell currency i. In other words, each dealer believes that currency markets will clear at the known prices on each and every day. Each dealer also assumes that the currency supplied by each other dealer is independent of the currency demanded. For example, sellers of dollars are not more likely to demand sterling than sellers of Deutsch marks. This allows us to state the subjective probability of another dealer wishing to trade currency i for currency j as $P_i P_j$. The objective of each dealer is to achieve a given ultimate exchange in the minimum time, i.e. with a minimum number of phone calls. If he does this by direct exchange, the expected number of phone calls is

$$\frac{1}{P_i P_j} \tag{7.4}$$

If he does this by indirect exchange, whereby i is traded for k and k for j, the expected number of phone calls is

$$\frac{1}{P_i P_k} + \frac{1}{P_k P_j} \tag{7.5}$$

The optimizing dealer will obviously choose the currency with the highest expected probability of being bought and sold as his intermediary currency. Define P_n as Max (P_k), then indirect exchange will be used as long as:

$$\frac{1}{P_i P_n} + \frac{1}{P_n P_j} > \frac{1}{P_i P_j} \tag{7.6}$$

Two other propositions immediately follow. First, the choice of currency n is independent of i and j. This follows from the assumed independence of currencies demanded and supplied, so P_n is invariant to the ultimate deal desired. Secondly, there is no longer transactions chain preferable to (7.5). This is because

$$\operatorname*{Min}_{k,\,1} \left(\frac{1}{P_i P_k} + \frac{1}{P_k P_1} + \frac{1}{P_1 P_j} \right) = \frac{1}{P_i P_n} + \frac{1}{P_n P_n} + \frac{1}{P_n P_j} \tag{7.7}$$

This involves a trade of currency n for itself, which is redundant.

To summarize so far, the use of a medium of exchange in currency markets is not hard to envisage. It could arise in the above model whenever $P_n > P_i + P_j$. In the real world it means that, since the market for dollars is clearly substantially larger than that of other currencies, the dollar could reasonably be a candidate for medium of exchange in currency markets irrespective of the evidence on invoicing patterns.

What, then, will the equilibrium trading structure look like if we allow the system to evolve from an initial position of total direct trade (barter)? Intuitively, the evolution is quite simple. If $P_n > P_i + P_j$ for any pair (i, j), indirect trade using currency n will be adopted. This will raise P_n and lower all other P_i $(i \neq n)$. This will increase the number of deals for which $P_n > P_i + P_j$, and the process will continue. Where will it stop? Some more analytical apparatus is required to answer this question.

Definitions

$P = (P_1, \ldots, P_n)$ is the vector of subjective probabilities of a randomly chosen dealer wishing to sell each currency $i = 1, \ldots n$.

$q = (q_1, \ldots, q_n)$ is the actual proportion of dealers selling currencies $i = 1, \ldots n$.

s is the fraction of ultimate exchanges executed indirectly using currency n as the medium of exchange.

m is the constant number of individuals entering the market each 'day' to initiate a given ultimate exchange. Those using indirect exchange complete the second deal the next day.

$U = (u_{ij})$ is the matrix of the fraction of dealers entering who wish *ultimately* to exchange currency i for currency j. U is constant and symmetric.

$u_i = \sum_{j=1}^{n} u_{ij} = u_{ji}$ is the fraction of new entrants ultimately demanding and supplying the ith currency.

$u = (u_i, \ldots u_n)$

It follows from the definitions of s and u from the previous argument that $0 \leqslant s \leqslant 1 - u_n$. This is because an ultimate demand for currency n will be achieved directly.

The total number of dealers in the market on a particular day is $m + ms$ (new entrants + those completing indirect exchange from previous day). The number of dealers demanding the nth currency is $mu_n = ms$. So

$$q_n \approx \frac{mu_n + ms}{m + ms} \approx \frac{u_n + s}{1 + s} \tag{7.8}$$

where $\approx$ arises from the fact that s today is only approximately equal to s yesterday. It is assumed that (7.8) holds with equality.

The number of dealers demanding currencies $i = 1, \ldots, n - 1$ is mu_i. So

$$q_i = \frac{mu_i}{m + ms} = \frac{u_i}{1 + s} \quad i = 1, \ldots, n - 1 \tag{7.9}$$

(7.8) and (7.9) may be rewritten as

$$q = u + \left(\frac{s}{1 + s}\right)(e_n - u) \tag{7.10}$$

where $e_n = (0, 0, 0, \ldots, 0, 1)$.

The dynamic adjustment of the system is determined by the assumption that P is revised each day in proportion to its distance from q.

$$\Delta P_t = \gamma(q_t - P_t) \qquad 0 < \gamma < 1 \tag{7.11}$$

The complete system is now described by equations (7.10) and (7.11) with the addition of the definition of s, which is:

$$s = \sum_x u_{ij} \qquad (x = i, j, \cdot \ni \cdot P_n > P_i + P_j) \qquad (7.12)$$

The existence of a solution to this system is easy to establish. The u_{ij} are parametric. In equilibrium $P_i = q_i$ for all i. Any q is associated with some value of s. The domain of q (and P) is a compact convex set with lower and upper bounds of u and $u + (e_n - u)$ $(1 - u_n)/(2 - u_n)$. From any initial value P always approaches q. So an equilibrium will always exist even if only at the boundary. However, an analytical solution for s cannot be obtained owing to the discontinuity of (7.12). This discontinuity arises from the fact that the addition of another currency whose trade is intermediated involves a discrete jump. So even though P is continuous, s will not be. The possibility of multiple locally stable equilibria may, however, be illustrated by defining an arbitrary variable s^e. This is the value of s that is consistent with any given value of the P vector and is defined by:

$$P = u + \left(\frac{s^e}{1 + s^e} \right)(e_n - u) \qquad (7.13)$$

Analytically, the role of s^e is as of the expected value of s, though no such direct expectations are held by the actors. The value of this, however, is that the system can now be reduced to a relationship between s and s^e (Jones, 1976, p. 770). As s^e rises, s moves up in steps. This corresponds to discrete increases in the number of currencies for which $P_n > P_i + P_j$. For given initial conditions s^e always adjusts towards s. Both s and s^e are bounded below by 0 and above by $1 - u_n$ and in equilibrium $s = s^e$. $s = 1 - u_n$ whenever $s^e > u_i + u_j - u_n$ for all $i \neq n$, $j \neq n$. These conditions determine only that a locally stable equilibrium will exist whenever $s = s^e$. Possible solutions are illustrated in Figure 7.1.

Starting at an initial point such as X, with $s^e = 0$, the function $s = (u, s^e)$ moves upward in steps until it reaches point B. At B all dealing is through an intermediary currency. However, *whenever* the function crosses the diagonal, there is a locally stable equilibrium such as at A. In principle, there may be a multiplicity of points such as A or there may be none at all. For domestic goods trade there can be a strong presumption that monetary exchange becomes almost universal, and once it is so, it is seldom reversed. In foreign currency dealing there can be no such presumption. The possibility of the system being in a point such as A and *occasionally moving* would seem quite strong. Let us return to the realities

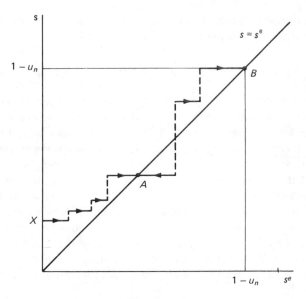

FIGURE 7.1

of the environment within which foreign exchange dealers exist.

Consider the world economy as it existed in the 1950s. The role of the dollar under the Marshall Plan for the reconstruction of Europe has been outlined by McKinnon (1979, Chapter 11). It is clear that during that period, not only was the US by far the largest economy in world trade but also other central banks were committed to using dollars to peg exchange rates. At this time the above analysis would suggest that the dollar would become the intermediary currency *par excellence*. The only obvious exception to this was the use of sterling among sterling area countries, although it is not clear to what extent sterling was used as an intermediary as opposed to a reserve asset. If it were used in the former capacity, it could only have been because of a violation of the assumption that the currency ultimately demanded is independent of the currency initially supplied.

However, over the past two decades important changes have taken place. Two have been gradual, one relatively sudden. First, the structure of world trade has changed. Clearly the share of the US in world trade has declined. It is less clear that dollar-denominated trade has reduced in share, particularly if capital markets are included. Nonetheless, it is probably true that currencies like the Deutsch mark and yen are closer substitutes for the dollar (in some sense) now than they were twenty-five years ago. In effect, there are now deep and active markets in many currencies other than the dollar. Some evidence on the declining relative use of the dollar is given by Magee and Rao (1980). Secondly, the information systems available to foreign exchange dealers have changed considerably, especially in the last decade. The Visual Display Units (VDUs) with which every dealer is now equipped, permit him or her to get prices currently quoted for the major currencies from any other major bank in the world. At present banks are not committed to deal at these prices, but it is understood that in the near future they will come to represent a binding commitment. In other words, the price at which a deal is actually made can still only be established by a telephone call, and presumably where bargaining is involved this will continue to be true. However, it does mean that, within the group of major currencies, the role of an intermediary currency is largely redundant. A dealer wishing to trade, say, sterling for Deutsch marks may do so directly in a well-developed market. The virtual certainty of finding a taker quickly at no great discount makes the use of an intermediary step through the dollar unnecessary. However, outside the major currencies (say, of the Group of Ten), it is still quite likely that the role of the dollar as intermediary is extremely important. This is reinforced by the fact that many currencies are still pegged to the dollar. However, it is not difficult to imagine rivals to the dollar being established. The Deutsch mark within the European countries is an obvious candidate for the role of intermediary currency.

The third important change has been the switch to floating exchange rates among the major currencies. If this had been associated with a major decline in the use of the dollar as an intervention currency, this could have reduced the use of the dollar as an intermediary currency, by changing the U matrix in the above analysis. It is not clear to what extent such a decline in dollar intervention actually took place, though presumably the *probabilities* of such intervention have changed.

In summary, there is a good case for thinking of the dollar as an intermediary currency in world exchange markets, although the changes of the last two decades should have reduced the *relative* importance of that role rather than enhanced it. This decline may, of course, be related to the apparent decline of the dollar as an invoicing currency, but clearly the relationship is quite loose. How the role of the dollar will develop in the future depends upon the balance of two competing forces. The first is gains from economies associated with the use of a unique monetary instrument and standard. This will tend to increase the role of the dollar as the only clear candidate for 'world money'. There are, however,

contrary pressures due to a combination of factors – changing information technology, changing intervention patterns, changing regional
groupings, changing trade patterns – which seem likely to work in the
opposite direction.

INTERNATIONAL RESERVES[3]

Traditionally the dominant focus of attention among international
monetary analysts has been official sector reserves. During the 1960s in
particular, the major topic of discussion in international fora was the
question of international liquidity. It was widely feared that if adequate
and rational provision was not made for growth of liquidity there would
be serious repercussions for world trade. Competitive devaluations and
restrictionism in general would be the order of the day, leading to an
inevitable slowdown of real growth. It is from the discussions of these
issues that the SDR emerged as the agreed 'solution' to the liquidity
problem. The prime movers in these discussions were the industrial
countries, and there can be little serious doubt that it was their own
position that was uppermost in their minds. However, in the last decade
the position of the industrial countries has changed considerably, both
with regard to liquidity and as a result of the move to floating exchange
rates. Consequently, international liquidity has become a much less
urgent issue, if indeed it is seen as an issue at all.

The purpose of the present section is to argue that, for a substantial
number of developing countries, international liquidity continues to be a
problem. This will not be argued on the basis of their projected deficits as
a group (though this makes individual country problems much worse)
but rather because of the necessity of exchange rate pegging in those
countries. The international liquidity problem has not gone away but has
merely shifted its locus from the developed to the developing world. In
what follows the first sub-section will provide a brief summary of the
background. The second sub-section will discuss the position of developing countries *vis-à-vis* the foreign exchange markets and the liquidity
position of developing countries, and the third sub-section will suggest
that the analysis indicates a strong case for a bias towards developing
countries in future SDR issues. This case, it should be emphasised, is
entirely separate from the notion of the 'Aid Link'.

International Liquidity: A History

In the nineteenth century and before, international debts were settled either by shipments of bullion or by the use of the major 'colonial' currencies. There was, however, no general concern about the stock of international liquidity *per se*. Such debates as there were typically considered the reverse, i.e. given the extant bullion stock, what was the correct level for the domestic note issue? Concern for international liquidity is largely a twentieth-century phenomenon which arose out of analysis of the experience of the inter-war period. First there were the episodes of hyperinflation in Central Europe, and secondly there was the Great Depression of 1929–33. In the 1930s in particular, many countries pursued policies that involved substantial trade restrictions, and there were several examples of competitive devaluations.

It was widely hoped that the post-Second World War period would turn out differently. There was a general belief that international co-operation could produce a more stable environment than trade warfare. It is well known that a key role in designing a new international monetary system fell to Keynes of the UK and White of the USA. International liquidity now came to the centre of the stage.

> Keynes was very strongly convinced that before the war the world was suffering from a shortage of international liquidity also. At the time of the World Economic Conference in London (1933), which was convened to deal with the great depression, he put forward a scheme for the issue of international 'gold notes'. Later his primary purpose in devising a plan for a 'clearing union' was to secure such increase of liquidity after the war as would facilitate a return to more liberal multilateral commercial policies. (Harrod, 1963, p. 296).

Keynes saw clearly what was necessary to build a rational system:

> We need an instrument of international currency having general applicability between nations, so that blocked balances and bilateral clearings are unnecessary . . . We need an orderly and agreed method of determining the relative exchange values of national currency units, so that unilateral action and competitive exchange depreciation are prevented.
>
> We need a *quantum* of international currency, which is neither determined in an unpredictable and irrelevant manner . . . nor subject to large variations . . . but is governed by the actual current require-

ments of world commerce, and is also capable of deliberate expansion and contraction to offset deflationary and inflationary tendencies in effective world demand . . .

We need a system possessed of an internal stabilizing mechanism, by which pressure is exercised on any country whose balance of payments with the rest of the world is departing from equilibrium *in either direction*, so as to prevent movements which must create for its neighbours an equal but opposite balance . . .

More generally, we need a means of reassurance to a troubled world, by which any country whose own affairs are conducted with due prudence is relieved of anxiety for causes which are not of its own making, concerning its ability to meet its international liabilities, and which will therefore make unnecessary those methods of restriction and discrimination which countries have adopted hitherto, not on their merits but as measures of self-protection from disruptive outside forces.

The White plan for a United Nations Stabilization Fund had similar aims. These were:

1. To stabilize the foreign exchange rates of the United Nations.
2. To encourage the flow of productive capital among the United Nations.
3. To liberate blocked balances.
4. To help correct the maldistribution of gold among the United Nations.
5. To facilitate the settlement and servicing of international debts – both public and private.
6. To shorten the periods of disturbing disequilibrium in the international accounts of member countries and help stabilize price levels.
7. To reduce the necessity and use of foreign exchange controls.
8. To eliminate multiple currency practices and bilateral clearing arrangements.
9. To promote sound note issuing and credit policies and practices among the United Nations.
10. To reduce barriers to foreign trade.
11. To promote more efficient and less expensive clearings of international exchange transactions. (IMF, 1969, p. 41)

It should be clear that the Keynes and White plans had similar aims although they were different in substance. However, it is now a matter of history that a conference was held on 1–22 July at the Mount Washington Hotel, Bretton Woods, New Hampshire. Here proposals were drawn up which led to the establishment of the International Monetary Fund and what came to be known as the Bretton Woods system. The provision of this system that is of central importance for present purposes is the commitment by all member countries to peg the exchange rates of their various currencies. This commitment could only be met given the availability of adequate liquidity, as Keynes had foreseen.

The reason that liquidity was important was that the mechanism of pegging exchange rates required central banks to hold reserves of key currencies (notably dollars) for the purpose of intervening in their own foreign exchange markets as and when their exchange rates deviated from their announced 'par values'. Reserves would, in effect, be a buffer stock which would enable stable exchange rates to be maintained across a trade cycle. The typical pattern might be as in Figure 7.2. During an initial period of surplus the central bank buys dollars to stop the domestic exchange rate from rising. This is followed by a period of deficit during which reserves are run down.

The liquidity problem may be defined as that of ensuring that central banks as a whole have sufficient reserves at each point in time so that

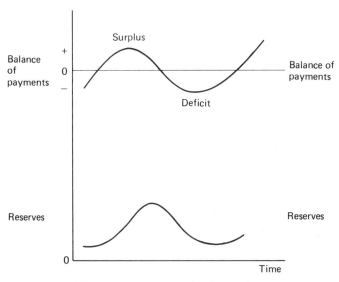

FIGURE 7.2 *Reserves and balance of payments*

they might reasonably expect to survive without restrictions or devaluations. It was widely anticipated that growing world trade would require growing balances of reserves to maintain any given level of security against running out of reserves. This is because the variance of the balance of payments will increase with the level of payments. Whether this relationship between world trade and reserves should be linear or not has been a matter of some dispute, but need not detain us.

Growth in reserves in the post-war period was provided almost entirely by growing dollar balances. The dangers of this were pointed out in 1961 by Triffin in his book *Gold and the Dollar Crisis*:

> The gold exchange standard *may*, but *does* not *necessarily*, help in relieving a shortage of world monetary reserves. It does so only to the extent that the key currency countries are willing to let their net reserve position decine through increases in their short-term monetary liabilities unmatched by corresponding increases in their own gross reserves. If they allow this to happen, however, and to continue indefinitely they tend to bring about a collapse of the system itself through the gradual weakening of foreigners' confidence in the key currencies.

The key problem was that as dollar liabilities rose relative to US gold reserves, belief in the convertibility of dollars into gold would become increasingly tenuous. This prognosis gained an important following and it was eventually agreed to introduce a new reserve asset, the SDR. This was intended to become the principal reserve asset of the international monetary system. The initial allocation of SDR 9 billion took place in the three years 1970–2, and a further allocation of SDR 12 billion has taken place in the period 1979–81. SDRs were allocated to IMF members in relation to quotas.

The events of 1970–3, however, completely changed the world monetary environment. First there was a substantial increase in the stock of dollars held by central banks, and second there was a switch to floating exchange rates by the major industrial countries. These changes posed serious questions about the relevance of previous concepts of international liquidity. In particular, it was felt – at least initially – that there was an excess of liquidity rather than a shortage. However, matters became more confused as a result of the oil price rise of 1973, which made the distribution of liquidity an issue in addition to the level of world reserves. As a result, the dominant topic of discussion in the mid-1970s was the 'recycling' of OPEC surpluses. In the event the bulk of such 'recycling' was achieved through the money markets with small supplementary assistance from IMF facilities.

By 1978 the OPEC surplus had all but disappeared, and a general increase in IMF quotas plus a new allocation of SDRs was deemed appropriate to catch up with the inflation of the previous decade. The period 1979–80 also saw another major rise in the price of oil which appears to be causing particular adjustment problems for the developing world. However, this specific problem is not of central concern here. Rather, the concern is with the 'normal' position of developing countries and in particular with the choices they face for managing their foreign exchange markets.

Foreign Exchange Markets in Developing Countries

The period since 1973 has been heralded as a period of floating exchange rates. However, as Table 7.1 indicates, this statement requires considerable modification. At the latest count there were 93 countries pegging their currencies to either identifiable currencies or currency baskets. Even of those not so classified the majority have exchange rates which are pegged on some basis, i.e. to an unknown basket or to a 'crawling' peg. Only the exchange rates of the currencies of the major

TABLE 7.1   *Exchange rate arrangements of IMF countries*

	Numbers of countries	
	30 June 1975	30 September 1980
Exchange rate pegged to:		
US dollar	54	40
French franc	13	13
Pound sterling	10	1
Spanish peseta	1	1
S. African rand	3	2
SDR	5	15
Other basket	14	21
Jointly floating (snake/EMS)	7	8
Floating or other intervention formula	18	38
	125	139

SOURCES   1975 IMF *Annual Report*; *IMF Survey*, 10 November 1980.

industrial countries are determined dominantly by or in the money markets. Even here major currencies are linked together through the EMS and all other floats are at best dirty. Nevertheless, there is a clear difference between the exchange markets of the industrial countries and those of the developing countries. This difference does not arise because of a conscious choice by developing nations to spurn the floating option. Rather it arises from structural considerations which make floating, in effect, a non-option.

The currencies of most developing countries are not fully convertible. One reason for this suggested by McKinnon (1979, p. 41) is that:

> Governments in less developed countries often lack the internal political power, and the accompanying fiscal and administrative capability, to allocate domestic resources directly by centralized fiat in the manner of the communist centrally planned economies. Nevertheless, these same governments are usually not enamoured with the idea of a decentralizing economic decision making through the unrestricted use of equilibrium prices and free markets. Rather, the government has a domestic plan and perhaps planning agency; its political office is seen as a mandate to control or influence as much economic activity as possible. However, the strongest instrument for internal control that can be freely manipulated by LDC governments is often the market for foreign exchange – where the clearing of international payments can be fairly easily brought under a single authority. Since imports and exports usually pass through centralized ports and border-crossing stations, they are more easily monitored and taxed by a weak governmental authority than is commerce in the domestic hinterland.

The corollary of this is that control over trade necessarily involves control over domestic access to foreign exchange.

> Clearly, if all domestic firms and individuals were free to spend the domestic currency for foreign goods – using commercial banks as unrestrained financial intermediaries – the government's control would be undermined. Therefore, the clearing of foreign payments usually devolves on the *central bank* in LDCs . . . Hence commercial banks are not free to create a unified market for foreign exchange, either spot or forward, as they might do with a floating convertible currency or one floating within given exchange margins.
>
> Willy-nilly the central bank is cast in the role of announcing

exchange rates for the various categories of transactions . . . and then providing the necessary foreign exchange to those traders satisfying the rules and regulations. (McKinnon, 1979, p. 41)

Thus in the cases that involve severe foreign exchange controls it should be clear that a fully operative foreign exchange market *cannot arise*. The problem, however, may be even more general than is suggested in the above quotations. It has been widely noticed that the exchange rates of the industrial countries have fluctuated considerably since the advent of floating, despite the fact that they have diversified trade composition and deep and sophisticated financial systems. In contrast the foreign exchange markets of developing countries would be extremely thin, and it is hard to believe that they could be anything but highly unstable if they attempted a free float. The experience of Israel would seem to confirm this. In this sense most developing countries may not be 'optimal currency areas'.

The importance of this argument should be clear. If the central banks of developing countries do not 'make' the foreign exchange market for their domestic currency, such a market as there would be could be highly inadequate. It would almost certainly exhibit a high degree of instability. In practice, therefore, central banks have little choice but to announce a price at which they will buy and sell foreign exchange to traders. This procedure is exactly what is understood by the term 'pegging' the exchange rate. Once pegging is a reality, of course, it becomes difficult to decide, *a priori*, whether the financial restrictions are to sustain trade controls or whether trade controls are necessary to maintain a particular exchange rate level or path. Certainly it would be reasonable to expect that, since central banks are obliged to peg exchanges rates, restrictions of foreign exchange holding, capital flows and trade would be necessary weapons for a government endowed with inadequate reserves.

It has often been argued that developing countries will need proportionately more reserves than developed countries. Triffin (1961), for example, argued that:

Reserves have to be higher in an unstable economic and political environment than in a world enjoying a greater degree of economic and political stability. Higher reserves are also needed by under-developed countries, with more volatile levels of export proceeds and capital imports, than by the richer and more diversified economies of the industrial countries. The burden of reserve accumulation, however, in relation to national wealth and savings on the one hand, and to competing needs for the financing of developmental imports on the other, will unfortunately be higher for the former countries than for the latter.

Triffin's argument is obviously quite plausible and was intended to apply in a situation where both developed and developing countries are pegging their exchange rates. However, in a situation, as at present, where developed countries are not pegging, there must be an overwhelming case for arguing that developing countries' reserve needs are proportionately greater. This theme will be expanded upon below.

It is worth considering what range of policies is open to central banks in the conduct of their foreign exchange operations. Three broad classes of operation can be identified: the sliding peg, the crawling peg and the stable peg. With a sliding peg the central bank announces the price at which it will buy and sell foreign exchange on a particular day, but this price is changed every few days or, at most, weeks. With the crawling peg exchange rate, adjustments are much less frequent, intervals being often pre-arranged and measured more in terms of months. Two broad scenarios for crawling may be identified. First, 'passive' crawling typically involves periodic devaluations to compensate for past domestic inflation. Second, 'active' crawling, which involves an announced *future* path or bounds for the crawl, may provide a feasible course in a transition to lower domestic inflation. The stable peg involves maintaining a particular exchange rate for a considerable length of time, usually measured in terms of years, with only occasional and infrequent changes.

There must be a strong presumption that, other things being equal, reserve needs would increase with the infrequency of exchange rate adjustments. However, this would not be a safe basis for making cross-country comparisons, since the exchange rate variations will themselves reflect balance of payments stability. In other words, two countries of comparable size may require very different reserve stocks to achieve the same degree of exchange rate stability. All central banks actively pegging need reserves, and greater reserves would enable any central bank to achieve greater stability or the same stability with less rationing.

There is no correct measure of reserve adequacy, and in reality each country should be looked at individually. However, there is a long history of reliance upon one particular measure and that is the ratio of reserves to annual imports. This is a very rough indicator, but strong trends in this ratio have been the main basis upon which judgments about the adequacy of liquidity have been made in the past. Table 7.2

TABLE 7.2 *Ratio of world reserves to world imports*

1928	0.42
1937	1.01
1938	1.17
1948	0.77
1957	0.49

SOURCE 'International Reserves and Liquidity', IMF, 1958.

contains the evidence of the obvious decline which led Triffin to his influential conclusions. Indeed, Triffin went so far as to suggest that countries with reserve–import ratios below 0.2 had found themselves in desperate positions, while those with ratios between 0.2 and 0.3 had been under severe pressure. These numbers may be used as benchmarks for looking at the current position, even though there may be a case for arguing that things are much more difficult in the current unstable environment. The reality of the situation is that large numbers of developing countries find themselves in a position of 'severe pressure' or worse. Chrystal (1981) reports that at the end of 1979, sixty-seven countries had reserve–import ratios of 0.3 or less. Thirty-seven of these had a ratio of 0.2 or less, and ten had ratios of 0.1 or less. These figures exclude gold holdings but these make little or no difference. If anything the position has deteriorated since 1979 due to the impact of oil price rises and high interest rates.[4]

The conclusion of this argument should be clear. There remains a severe international liquidity shortage for a substantial group of developing countries. These countries have been unable to benefit from any of the developments of the 1970s. They held little gold, they were allocated minimal quantities of SDRs, they are unable to permit a free float of their currencies, and yet they have been adversely affected both by the instability of commodity prices and the instability of the major exchange rates.

Implications

The founding fathers of the IMF had it in mind to establish an institution that would assist central banks to stabilize their exchange rates without excessive recourse to trade controls, restrictions on capital flows and exchange controls. Only the central banks of developing countries really find themselves in a position similar to that feared by Keynes and White nearly forty years ago. It is thus they for whom the IMF is really important, and it is no coincidence that only developing countries have borrowed from the Fund recently. Without a substantial improvement in their international liquidity position it is hard to imagine that many countries will be able to survive without periodic draconian economic policies or worse.

It is hard to see that any co-operative action by the developing countries as a group could alleviate their situation. It may be true that reserve pooling within the European Monetary System (EMS) has assisted the stabilization of exchange rates within Europe. However, the position of the EMS provides a good example of why the developing countries could not easily form a similar system. One obvious, but probably lesser, problem is that reserve pooling requires the presence of excess reserves on the part of some members at all times. In this sense the 'poorest' nations could not go it alone. The real problem, however, is that for a system like the EMS to work, central banks have to be prepared to transact in each other's currencies. This does not require any net additions of *external* reserves. However, developing countries would find such a system difficult, if not impossible, to operate owing to the inconvertibility of the constituent currencies.

If the liquidity shortages of developing countries are to be relieved in any way at anything short of drastic costs in human terms, there is only one solution that suggests itself. This is a substantial allocation of SDRs in favor of the developing countries. In the past, SDRs have been allocated only in proportion to IMF quotas. This is now inequitable for two reasons. First, the rich countries have benefitted most from gold revaluation. Second, and perhaps more importantly, the reserve needs of developing countries are far greater (proportionately) owing to the necessity of foreign exchange market interventions, as discussed above. Intervention activity for most industrial countries is voluntary. For developing countries it is compulsory.

One objection that will be raised is that such an SDR allocation amounts to a proposal for an 'Aid Link'. This is not true. If the SDR, as proposed, bears a market interest rate, there is no direct resource transfer involved in new allocations. The benefit to the developing countries is that it gives them automatic unconditional credit at market interest rates, whereas the poorest nations may only be able to borrow commercially at above-market rates. The net gain comes from international risk pooling. The benefits to the industrial countries could be considerable, particularly if the allocation were accompanied by mutual trade liberalization. The simplest form of such an allocation would be a lump sum to all countries or to all countries with pegged exchange rates or to all non-oil developing countries. The goodwill resulting from such an allocation could be enormous, and it would serve the agreed goal of promoting the SDR as the centrepiece of the international monetary system.

NOTES

1. I am grateful to the discussants, Helmut Mayer and Charles Lipson, for their thoughtful comments.
2. This section draws heavily on my paper 'On the Theory of International Money' presented to the Annual Conference of the International Economics Study Group, September 1982, and forthcoming in the proceedings (ed. G. Dorrance, Macmillan).
3. The argument in this section is a summary of that set out in my paper 'International Liquidity and the Position of Developing Countries in the 1980s', Unctad INT/75/015. Opinions expressed are solely the responsibility of the author.
4. A full analysis would, of course, require a consideration of the external debt as well as just the level of owned reserves. This is unlikely to improve the picture for most countries.

REFERENCES

Calvo, G. A. and C. A. Rodriguez (1977) 'A Model of Exchange Rate Determination Under Currency Substitution and Rational Expectations', *Journal of Political Economy*, 85, June, pp. 617–25.

Carse, S., J. Williamson and G. Wood (1980) *The Financing Procedures of British Foreign Trade* (Cambridge: Cambridge University Press).

Chrystal, K. A. (1977) 'Demand for International Media of Exchange', *American Economic Review*, 67, December, pp. 840–50.

Chrystal, K. A. (1978) 'International Money and the Future of the SDR', *Princeton Essays in International Finance*, No. 128, June.

Chrystal, K. A. (1979) 'Some Evidence in Defense of the Vehicle Currency Hypothesis', *Economic Letters*, Vol. 3, No. 3, pp. 267–70.

Chrystal, K. A., N. D. Wilson and P. Quinn (1979) 'Demand for International Money, 1962–77', UC-Davis Working Paper No. 140, November.

Chrystal, K. A. (1981) 'International Liquidity and the Position of Developing Countries in the 1980s', UNCTAD, Project INT/75/015, January.

Grassman, S. (1973) *Exchange Reserves and the Financial Structure of Foreign Trade*, (London: Saxon House).

Grassman, S. (1976) 'Currency Distribution and Forward Cover in Foreign Trade', *Journal of International Economics*, 6, May, pp. 215–21.

Harrod, R. (1963) 'Liquidity', reprinted in H. G. Grubel (ed.) *World Monetary Reform* (Stanford University Press).

IMF (1969) Keynes and White Plans in *The International Monetary Fund 1945– 1965*, Vol. III, IMF.

Jones, R. A. (1976) 'The Origin and Development of Media of Exchange', *Journal of Political Economy*, Vol. 84, No. 4, pp. 757–75.

Krugman, P. (1980) 'Vehicle Currencies and the Structure of International Exchange', *Journal of Money Credit and Banking*, 1980.

Magee, S. P. and R. K. S. Rao (1980) 'Vehicle and Nonvehicle Currencies in International Trade', *American Economic Review*, 70, No. 2, May, pp. 368– 73.

McKinnon, R. I. (1977) 'The Eurocurrency Market', *Princeton Essays in International Finance*, No. 125, December.

McKinnon, R. I. (1979) *Money in International Exchange* (Oxford: Oxford University Press).

Page, S. A. B. (1977) 'Currency of Invoicing of Merchandise Trade', *National Institute Economic Review*, August, pp. 77–80.

Swoboda, A. K. (1969) 'The Euro-Dollar Market: An Interpretation', *Princeton Essays in International Finance*, No. 64, 1968, in R. Z. Aliber (ed.) *The International Market for Foreign Exchange* (New York: Praeger).

Triffin, R. (1961) *Gold and the Dollar Crisis* (New Haven: Yale University Press).

8 Gold: Does it Provide a Viable Basis for the Monetary System?[1]

RICHARD N. COOPER

Prompted by the acceleration of inflation, the decline in real rates of economic growth, and the general rise in economic uncertainty that occurred during the decade of the 1970s, many people have begun to consider whether a revival of a monetary role for gold would offer a way out of our travail. Professor Robert Mundell of Columbia University has called for a return to gold convertibility (*Wall Street Journal*, 30 September, 1981), several bills have been submitted to Congress calling for a return to one variant or another of the gold standard by the United States, President Reagan has allegedly expressed a positive view on the issue, and a Gold Commission was established to examine the question.

This widespread interest would have been difficult to imagine twenty, ten or five years ago. Is it just misplaced nostalgia for a non-existent golden past, or is there a basis in gold for a less uncertain, less troublesome monetary system? This paper tries to examine the possibilities for using gold as a basis for the monetary system in the future. It finds that there are probably insuperable difficulties in doing so. Before we turn to the various possible roles for gold and the difficulties inherent in all of them, however, it will be useful first to make some distinctions concerning what we mean by the monetary system, and then to take a brief excursion into the characteristics and performance of the historical gold standard.

GOLD AND THE MONETARY SYSTEM

Gold can play and has played a role in *domestic* monetary arrangements and in *international* monetary arrangements. We look to domestic monetary arrangements to provide for smooth, steady, non-inflationary growth in economic activity, providing the right combination of monetary discipline to prevent inflation, monetary stimulus to encourage economic growth, and monetary flexibility to accomodate shifts in the demand for money so as to insulate real economic activity from them. We look to international monetary arrangements to provide the international counterpart of domestic monetary systems, accomodating them, reconciling them, and providing some discipline to prevent them from straying too far from the optimal combination of attributes. In addition, we have looked to gold-based international monetary arrangements to provide for fixed exchange rates among currencies, on the usually implicit assumptions that fixed exchange rates not only fostered international transactions, but also reduced uncertainty and provided the appropriate degree of international discipline on national monetary systems. In an extreme case, of course, national monetary systems cease to have an independent existence, being merely geographic components of an international system in which gold is universal money, both national and international, and it is not supplemented by any form of national money. But that is an unreal idealization which has not existed at any time since the formation of identifiable nation states.

Return to a system of fixed exchange rates is an important and extensive topic by itself. Since the use of gold in monetary systems is not a necessary nor even an important facilitative condition for a return to fixed exchange rates, this paper will not deal with that question, but rather will focus on the role of gold as a source of monetary discipline, both nationally and internationally. We can have fixed exchange rates without gold if we are willing to devote monetary policy to that end, as is also necessary under a gold standard; and from a mechanical point of view the system of fixed exchange rates can even be currency-neutral (that is, not focused around a single intervention currency such as the US dollar) by using the SDR or the ECU, first as a unit of account (with intervention in the relevant combination of currencies), and ultimately, with the development of markets in SDR- or ECU-denominated assets, directly in those assets. So the question of fixed exchange rates is analytically separable from the issue of the use of gold in the monetary system.

THE HISTORICAL GOLD STANDARD

The international gold standard, meaning a system in which the major countries defined their currencies in terms of a given quantity of gold and stood ready to buy or sell gold against their currencies with respect to domestics and foreigners alike at (approximately) the definitional rate of exchange, and in which gold could be freely exported and imported, existed only from the 1870s to 1914, with a brief revival for a few years in the late 1920s. This system implied severe limitation of movement in exchange rates among currencies, because gold arbitrage – or the mere possibility of it – kept exchange rates within the gold points. Britain was on a *de facto* gold standard after 1717, when Sir Isaac Newton (then Master of the Mint) mistakenly undervalued silver relative to gold, which led to the export of Britain's full-bodied silver coins. But most countries used both gold and silver. The United States went on a *de facto* gold standard in 1879 (*de jure* in 1900) with the resumption of gold convertibility against US currency after a seventeen-year period of inconvertibility, and with the dropping of the standard silver dollar. All European countries suspended their convertibility during the First World War, resuming briefly after 1925. Gold coins were also called in from circulation. Britain suspended again in 1931. The United States suspended in 1933, and it too called in the gold coins in circulation. Gold convertibility of the US dollar resumed (at a price of $35 an ounce, up from $20.67) in 1934 and continued until 1971, but only for foreign official holders of dollars. US residents were not permitted to hold gold for monetary purposes after 1933. Such gold convertibility as remained in Europe ceased during the Second World War (1954 for Switzerland) and has never resumed. The Bretton Woods system, embodied in the Articles of Agreement of 1946, accorded gold a central role in the system, but only in the background, an ultimate reserve asset and (in the form of the 'Gold Dollar of 1944') unit of account, but playing only a negligible role in operational terms. Its ultimate role was formally abandoned with the amendments of the Articles of Agreement in 1978.

In the United States gold continued until 1968 to provide legal backing for Federal Reserve liabilities, declining in two steps (1945 and 1965) from the levels set in 1934 before they were eliminated.

The historical gold standard is sometimes looked back on as a period of economic progress and stability. It is difficult to evaluate the period as a whole in any simple way, but the data in Table 8.1 cast some doubt on this proposition for the leading country of the period, Britain, and the lead emerging country, the United States, even during the so-called heyday of the gold standard – that is, leaving aside the fact that the First World War and the Great Depression of the 1930s both occurred when gold reigned supreme in the monetary arena.

Table 8.1 shows that the average rate of inflation over the entire pre-

TABLE 8.1 *Economic variables under the gold standard and since the Second World War*

| | The gold standard | | Post-Second World War | |
	UK 1870–1913	US 1879–1913	UK 1946–79	US 1946–79
Average annual percentage change in wholesale prices	−0.7	0.1	5.6	2.8
Standard deviation of price change (per cent)	4.6	5.4	6.2[3]	4.8[3]
Annual growth in real per capita income	1.4	1.9	2.4	2.1
Coefficient of variation of annual percentage changes in real per capita income	2.5	3.5	1.4	1.6
Average unemployment rate	4.3[1]	6.8[2]	2.5	5.0
Average annual percentage growth in money supply	1.5	6.1	5.9	5.7
Coefficient of variation of growth in money supply	1.6	0.8	1.0	0.5

Notes
1. 1888–1913
2. 1890–1914
3. 1929–1979

SOURCE Cooper, 'The Gold Standard: Historical Facts and Future Prospects', *Brookings Papers on Economic Activity,* 1982, No. 1.

First World War period was considerably lower, both in the United States and especially in Britain, than in the thirty-year period following the Second World War. But growth in per capita income was also lower during the earlier period, and average unemployment rates were higher. Moreover, the variation in the rate of inflation was higher in the earlier period for the United States (though not for Britain), the variability of real growth was higher, and the variability in the growth of the money supply was higher. To the extent that variability is a source of uncertainty, the earlier period did not provide greater certainty than the latter one; on the contrary.[2]

It is sometimes claimed that the gold standard provided a secure basis for long-term lending. It is true that bonds floated in the United States around the turn of the century occasionally carried 100-year maturities, and of course Britain issued its famous consols, with no maturity. But it was not the case that a gold standard secured certainty in real interest rates over all planning horizons (or holding periods). On the contrary, while price stability obtained over certain periods of time, *ex post*, cumulative price movements were often substantial, with the general price level in most major countries moving up (and down, which marks the major difference from recent experience) by as much as 50 per cent twice during the century 1816–1914. The financial market did not adequately adjust to these great swings in prices (which were the original observations for the Kondriateff cycles). Interest rates adjusted only sluggishly, and with a long lag, to changes in the price level, with the result that over the medium run there were large movements in real interest rates. For example, for a twenty-year holding period (many bonds carried an original maturity of twenty years) real interest rates in the United States varied from 10.5 per cent in 1872 (a price peak) to 1 per cent in 1896 (a price trough).

The vigorous debate over the 'nature of the standard' in late nineteenth-century United States indicated that contemporaries were well aware of the implied redistribution from debtors to creditors brought about by the steady decline in prices. This period saw the emergence of populism as a political movement and the strong pressure for monetary expansion through free coinage of silver. Hardly a year went by without vigorous debate on monetary questions in Congress, and the Presidential election of 1896 was the only one fought principally over the question of the monetary standard. So while the gold standard emerged (for a time) victorious, this was not a period of serene stability, either economic or political, in the monetary arena.

A FUTURE GOLD STANDARD?

Notwithstanding the not-very-encouraging history of the gold standard, and the fact that with today's expectations regarding economic performance the historical gold standard would not have survived politically, a number of serious proposals for re-instituting a monetary role for gold have been made. I will consider the viability of these proposals, which fall under two broad headings, and assess whether they could perform the desired function of exerting sufficient monetary discipline to avoid inflation. The first class of proposals involves some form of convertibility of money into gold; the second involves legally required gold backing for the money supply or some portion of it, without convertibility. Finally, I will consider briefly the possible role of gold as a form of international reserves, for settlement of international obligations.

Gold Convertibility Proposals

Proposals involving convertibility vary, at one extreme calling in effect for full convertibility of all Federal Reserve notes and 100 per cent gold money thereafter. Banknotes could be issued by private banks, but they would in effect be depository receipts for gold. Others are more limited, for example calling for restoration of the pre-1971 gold convertibility for foreign monetary authorities. The focus of these proposals has been the United States, acting on its own, and they will be evaluated here first on those terms. We can then turn to the additional complications that would arise if several major countries moved to gold convertibility of their currencies.

While the *modus operandi* would vary substantially from one proposal to another, the underlying idea is the same: the possibility of conversion exerts discipline on the monetary authorities and limits the growth of the money supply. Whenever some substantial group of the relevant dollar holders becomes dissatisfied with monetary developments and unsure about the future value of the dollar, they can and presumably will convert their dollars to gold. These conversions in turn will require the Federal Reserve to defend its gold reserves by tightening credit conditions or otherwise persuading the relevant public that gold conversions are unwarranted. The system in principle would be symmetrical: as gold reserves increase, the money supply will increase. This feature has not been emphasized by most proponents of gold convertibility, but it would be crucial in its international versions. Historically, central banks have often offset, or 'sterilized', the expansionary effects of gold inflows, as the United States did during the late 1930s and again during the late 1940s. Sterilization, of course, would not be possible where gold (or gold certificates) was the sole form of money.

Since new gold production is small relative to outstanding gold stocks, the requirement for convertibility, it is argued, will automatically limit the rate of money creation, and hence inflation, since there seems to be a natural limit to how rapidly gold reserves can grow. Too rapid monetary growth would lead to conversion, which in turn (to preserve convertibility) would necessitate monetary retrenchment.

Note that most proposals for convertibility – those that fall short of

100 per cent gold money – provide for some elasticity to the supply of money, provided the relevant public is not of a disposition to convert dollars into gold. This feature could indeed conceivably be a source of instability, since in periods of high 'animal spirits' in the business and financial community Federal Reserve credit could rise substantially, only to be sharply reduced as the buoyant spirits give way to pessimism and a period of heavy conversion sets in, leading to a drop in Federal Reserve credit below its historical trend under the regime.

There are three fundamental difficulties with restoring gold convertibility at the present time. One has to do with prospective gold supply relative to secular demand. A second has to do with finding an appropriate initial price for gold in terms of currency, one that will simultaneously persuade a skeptical public that convertibility is here to stay, yet at the same time provide the desired discipline on monetary policy. The third concerns the need to persuade a skeptical (and learned) public that once a price has been chosen, it will endure. But before turning to each of these points, it will be useful to review the fundamental assumption underlying the proposition that a monetary standard based on gold convertibility will assure secular price stability.

The objective is stability in some general index of money prices, P. The instrument is to fix credibly the money price of gold, P_g. The instrument is related to the objective by the identity $P = P_g \times T$, where T is the terms of trade between gold and the general bundle of goods (and services) in the index P, or the gold price of goods. Fixing P_g will stabilize P over the long run only if T is stable over the long run. But there is no reason either in theory or in history to expect T to be stable over time. As a depletable resource, Ricardian theory would suggest a secular decline in T, as lower quality ores are needed to sustain gold production. One would need a strong hypothesis about induced discovery and induced technical change, such as to hold the real commodity value of gold (and other depletable resources?) constant over time, to support the proposition that fixing P_g will also fix P. And while it is true that emerging shortages of gold have sometimes been relieved by new discoveries or new (lower cost) techniques of extraction, these have by no means kept T constant over time. William Stanley Jevons and Alfred Marshall both remarked on the instability of prices during the gold standard era of the late nineteenth century, and Irving Fisher even went so far as to propose his 'tabular' standard, whereby P_g would be consciously varied to compensate for changes in T, so as to hold the general level of money prices constant in the face of variations in the real price of gold.[3]

So the assumption that gold convertibility at a fixed money price will stabilize the general level of prices is based on a fundamentally erroneous proposition. The difficulties are borne out by the current outlook for the supply of gold. World gold production (exclusive of the Soviet Union) currently runs around 30 million ounces a year, down over 25 per cent from the peak production in the mid-1960s, despite a trebling in the real price of gold between 1969 and 1975 and a further sharp rise since the mid-1970s. Soviet sales augment this flow by about 10 per cent on average. World monetary gold stocks total about 1,100 million ounces, with private holdings of gold being perhaps 50 per cent above that. Thus new gold supplies increase total gold stocks by about 1.2 per cent annually. New gold supplies amount to about 3 per cent of monetary gold stocks, but in recent years all new supplies have gone to private holders.

Thus if gold is to be the basis for the monetary system, it will not sustain steady growth in the world economy at its potential for growth of 3–4 per cent a year at a constant price level. The general price level would have to decline over time in the absence of some dramatic change with respect to the supply of gold. It is, of course, possible to imagine a world with a secularly declining price level – those concerned with achieving the optimum holdings of currency would even see some merit in it – but historical periods of declining prices have been noteworthy for their economic distress and political unrest; and in any case it would involve abandonment of the objective of price stability, which opens up possibilities in the other direction as well. In addition to being inadequate in the long run, gold supplies are likely to be variable and to experience long lags in response to changes in the real price of gold. These factors are not propitious for the re-establishment of gold convertibility.[4] That fact will itself raise doubts about the durability of any commitment to convertibility, and will provoke speculative runs on official gold holdings from time to time.

The second fundamental difficulty of returning to gold convertibility concerns the choice of a price (in dollars) at which the US authorities would commit themselves to buy and sell gold. For gold convertibility to be durably credible, the United States would have to hold ample gold stocks against potential claimants, and to be seen to be doing so. But the volume of outstanding dollar assets around the world has grown to huge proportions. Federal Reserve liabilities (including currency) at the end of 1980 were $158 billion, compared with $3.5 billion when the Federal Reserve began in 1914, and $9.5 billion at the time of the Banking Act of 1934. The US money supply was $416 billion ($M_1$) or $1,669 billion ($M_2$) in 1980; foreign monetary authorities held an estimated $250 billion in liquid dollar claims ($157 billion directly in the United States and the remainder in various 'Eurodollar' centers around the world), and other foreigners held an additional $700 billion, give or take several tens of billions, in dollar deposits (other than European inter-bank deposits) outside the United States. US gold reserves, by contrast, amounted to only $11.1 billion at the official price of $42.22 an ounce,[5] and $111 billion at $422 an ounce (which has no virtue beyond being ten times the US official price and roughly equal to the market price at the end of 1981; the market price fell substantially below that in early 1982).

Full convertibility would hardly be credible, given the relationship of assets to potential claims. Of course, not all outstanding liquid dollar claims would formally be convertible into gold; presumably the convertibility requirement would strictly apply only to Federal Reserve liabilities. But that provides no comfort, since the financial system functions on the supposition that all liquid dollar claims can on short notice be converted into claims on the Federal Reserve, either Federal funds or currency. To deny or repudiate this more general convertibility is tantamount to a breakdown in the financial system, domestic and international. Moreover, a major strength of the international financial system at present is that for large holders (that is, leaving aside banknotes) it is a *closed* system, so funds can be moved around in it but cannot be withdrawn from it (except by the Federal Reserve System). This feature served the international economy well in 'recycling' the large OPEC surpluses during the last decade. This feature would be altered by gold convertibility, which would provide a potential leakage to the system at the initiative of dollar holders, and thus could threaten the system as a whole.

With too little gold relative to the potential for conversion, a gold-convertibility system would be seen as a fair-weather system, expectations about future economic developments would not be changed radically, and the real costs of monetary adjustments would continue to be high, casting further doubt on the political sustainability of a gold-convertibility regime.

A straightforward way to deal with these problems is to set a price of gold sufficiently high that there cannot be any doubt about the ability of the United States to sustain even large-scale conversion, at least for some time. If $422 an ounce will not be persuasive, perhaps $844 an ounce would be, and $1266 an ounce certainly should be (the latter figure would result in a valuation of $333 billion on the existing US gold stock).

But with a much higher price, another, equally acute, problem arises:

not only will new gold production increase substantially, but sales from the large existing gold stocks and hoards would take place. The US authorities would find themselves flooded with gold. Consider the privately held stocks first. Much of the estimated 1,600 million ounces of privately held gold no doubt is held for traditional reasons, partly for ornament, partly as precautionary protection against untoward political or economic events. But much of it, especially during the 1970s, was also acquired as an investment. With a credibly high official price of gold, the prospect for further capital gains on these investments vanishes, and gold as an investment would lose its lustre, except to a small degree for portfolio diversification against remote contingencies. Thus there would be large-scale dishoarding.[6] Even some central banks might sell their gold under these circumstances, and for similar reasons: prospective earnings on alternative assets would be much higher.

With respect to new production, it is unclear what the supply schedule is, although it is presumably upward-sloping with respect to the price of gold in terms of other goods and services. In any case, production is not determined simply by marginal costs today, but rather is subject to oligopolistic manipulation by the two major suppliers, South Africa and the Soviet Union, which are large enough to face a downward-sloping demand schedule for gold. With a high and credible US official price of gold, in contrast, the demand schedule becomes perfectly elastic even for large producers, and there would then be no reason for them not to produce as much gold as it is economic to produce at that price.

Thus there would be a flood of gold into the United States, on a more modest scale if convertibility were limited to foreign monetary authorities, on a vast scale under full convertibility. What should the United States then do? To monetize the gold would be strongly expansionary.[7] This expansion would presumably endure until the price level had risen sufficiently to reduce new gold production to the point at which it just satisfies the growth in demand for gold. That prolonged adjustment hardly satisfies the expectation of price stability sought by advocates of gold convertibility. The monetary authorities could, of course, sterilize the monetary impact of the additional gold, as they did at various times past. But then we would be back to a world of discretionary monetary policy much as we had from 1934 to 1971, during which we rely on the monetary authorities, not gold convertibility, for monetary restraint.

With large holdings of (sterilized) gold in official hands, there would be ample room for monetary expansion without threatening convertibility, and when that room was exhausted many years later, the public would rightly wonder why suddenly this constraint of gold supply, which had not been operative for many years, should induce a rush to convert, provoking a restrictive monetary policy. Legislatures would simply remove the constraint.

Is there a price that just balances these conflicting considerations – too low a gold stock to make a continued convertibility credible, or such a high gold stock that it would exert no monetary discipline and we would *de facto* be in a regime of discretionary management? Conceivably there could be such a price, one that would persuade enough hoarders to disgorge enough gold such that a combination of the higher price and the enlarged quantity of monetary gold would make the system credible but not too undisciplined. My guess is that there is no such price. The relevant public would be skeptical about continued convertibility up to quite a high price, and only then would be won over; but the price that would be persuasive would be too high to provide the discipline.

Whether there is such a price or not is irrelevant, however, since we have no way of finding it. Any guess, however well informed or rationalized, would obviously be seen to be a conscious policy choice. And therein lies the third fundamental difficulty with a restored gold standard as a source of monetary discipline and automaticity: once the price is recognized as a discretionary variable, the discipline that a gold standard could conceivably exert would be lost. As we have seen, the choice of a price for gold plays a central role in the viability of any restoration of gold convertibility. Yet the choice of a price, while crucial, is unavoidably arbitrary and is known to be arbitrary. So long as this is so, a rule based on a supposedly fixed price of gold cannot be a credible rule. If gold were to become unduly constraining, its price could be changed, and that would be widely known – indeed, it is intrinsic to the process of setting a price in the first place. In this respect, the situation today is fundamentally different from the situation in the nineteenth and early twentieth centuries. Then the dollar price of gold was *historically given* and not open to question (except for minor adjustments on several occasions to preserve the relationship to silver). The price was not conceived as a policy variable. Now it is, indeed must be. Yet gold ceases to provide monetary discipline if its price can be varied. So long as the price of gold is a policy variable, a gold standard cannot be a credible disciplinarian. It provides no escape from the need for human management, however frail that may seem to be.

The discussion thus far has focused on re-establishing gold convertibility in a single country, the United States. Are the difficulties eased in any respect if several major countries were to restore convertibility in collaboration? On the contrary, the difficulties of convertibility by several major countries would if anything be even more acute. In addition to the problems mentioned above, gold convertibility (at a fixed price) by several countries would also establish virtually fixed exchange rates between their currencies, so the difficulties of maintaining fixed exchange rates would be added to those of gold convertibility as such. That the conditions to maintain gold convertibility do not automatically satisfy the conditions for fixed exchange rates is suggested by the possibility that a country's payments position may worsen for reasons that have nothing to do in the first instance with its monetary or macroeconomic policies. Yet under a regime of gold convertibility and fixed exchange rates the entire burden of payments adjustment would be thrown on monetary contraction – assuming the gold price were inviolable – no matter what the source of the imbalance. The problem would be compounded – as it is in any system of purportedly fixed exchange rates that are not entirely credible – by speculative conversion of the threatened country's currency into gold if its commitment to gold convertibility were in any respect in doubt. The resulting leakage of gold into private hands would put pressure on the entire gold-convertible monetary system, not just that of the country in deficit.

Furthermore, if as argued above there would be a likely secular shortage of gold in the absence of major increases in new production, the fact that the monetary systems of more than one country depended upon gold would lead to some competition for the limited gold supplies, possibly resulting in trade restrictions in order to avoid gold losses (or to augment gold increases) through the country's external accounts – a revival of mercantilism, in its classical meaning. But the more fundamental difficulties have already been mentioned, and they would remain.

Gold Reserve Requirements

Gold could be used to 'back' all or some portion of the central bank's liabilities even if they were not literally convertible into gold. The idea behind gold backing without convertibility is to limit the growth in the supply of money and presumably also to bolster psychological support for the currency by those who still attach monetary significance to gold and do not fully comprehend that money, whatever its form, is ultimately a social convention.

The most limited proposal for gold backing calls for stipulating that the currency circulation must be backed by the existing official gold stock of the United States at its current official price of $42.22 an ounce, and that the allowable growth in an outstanding currency should be limited to 3 per cent a year after a transition period, assured by revaluing the existing gold stock by 3 per cent a year.[8] For the indefinite future, this proposal amounts only to a monetary rule in (thin) disguise; gold plays no essential role. One might just as well back the currency with the Washington Monument or the Statue of Liberty, endowing each with an initial value and stipulating that that value should increase at the fixed rate of 3 per cent a year.

Gold backing for all or some portion of the money supply could also be required at a fixed price of gold, or at the market price of gold, which fluctuates substantially. If the gold backing requirement does not bind – that is, if the value of the monetary gold exceeds the requirement for gold reserves – then we are in the realm of discretionary monetary policy, as at present. When the reserve requirement does bind, the monetary authorities would have to buy gold in order to increase the money supply. Unlike under a regime of convertibility, the purchase would be at the discretion of the monetary authorities.

This kind of arrangement poses difficult but not insuperable technical problems over the valuation of monetary gold, since in general the market price must deviate from the official price if orderly monetary growth is to be maintained (otherwise the permissable monetary base would fluctuate – wildly, on recent experience – with the market price of gold). For example, the Treasury Department could buy gold necessary for increasing the money supply at market prices, and resell it to the Federal Reserve Banks at the fixed official price, absorbing the difference as an expenditure (or, if the official price were above the market price, as a receipt).

But the key point is that this would be a discretionary regime, not an automatic one, unless in addition a rule governing monetary growth were also imposed. It would involve extra discipline only insofar as OMB directors and their superiors balk at budgeting for gold when market prices are considerably higher than the official price, or Treasury secretaries balk at the balance-of-payments implications of gold purchases. An idea of the magnitudes involved are suggested by the fact that a 4 per cent growth in the official US gold stock – implying a 4 per cent growth in that component of the money supply covered by gold reserves, if the reserves are binding – would involve a gross expenditure of $4.2 billion if the market price were $400 an ounce, and a net expenditure on the budget of $3.75 billion if the gold were resold to the Federal Reserve at the present official price. If the official price were increased, say, to

$200 an ounce (with a corresponding increase in the required gold reserve, to keep it binding), the gross expenditure by the Treasury for 4 per cent growth would be the same, and the net expenditure would be reduced to $2.1 billion. Of course, official US purchases of the 10.6 million ounces a year required for 4 per cent annual growth, amounting to 35 per cent of current world gold production, would very likely drive up the market price of gold considerably.

In short, gold backing by itself does not provide monetary discipline. The United States had backing for many years, and during most of that period the gold reserve requirements were not binding. The gold reserves would have permitted much more rapid growth than took place. On the occasions when the reserve requirement became binding, it was lowered, and eventually removed. The national debt ceiling provides an analogous restraint on US government borrowing; it is there in principle, but in practice it is regularly overridden by other considerations, even by 'conservative' Congresses.

Switzerland is the only country that currently requires gold backing for its banknotes, in a ratio of 40 per cent. (Switzerland ceased to provide for convertibility of its banknotes into gold in 1954, the year the London gold market re-opened.) Swiss official gold holdings grew only 7 per cent during the inflationary decade of the 1970s, but the Swiss money supply grew by 75 per cent. How was this possible? Switzerland entered the period with ample gold holdings relative to the required backing, more than double the legal requirement in 1970. The ratio fell steadily through the decade to 53 per cent in 1981, still well above the required 40 per cent. The restraint in Swiss monetary expansion has been discretionary, not conditioned by a binding gold reserve requirement.

What will happen when the reserve requirement becomes binding? Switzerland would have two options, apart from relaxing the requirement itself. It could raise its official price of gold (which stands at 4,596 Swiss francs a kilogram, about $70 an ounce at current exchange rates), which is well below the market price, and which can be changed by simple government decree (after consultation with the Swiss National Bank). Or it could buy sufficient gold at market prices, something even Switzerland could probably not do without affecting the market price for gold. Either action would be discretionary in nature.

Gold as International Reserves

If gold cannot provide a viable basis for the monetary system, is there any role for officially-held gold? Or should it simply be disposed of as an infertile asset? Fellner concludes – illogically, following his trenchant analysis on why gold supplies are both too inadequate and too variable to support its re-establishment in a monetary role – that we should not sell official gold stocks on the grounds that the underlying situation might change.[9] No doubt there is a 'national security' rationale for retaining some official gold so long as it remains an asset that is internationally acceptable and can be readily sold in case of emergency. But that rationale could be satisfied with a far smaller gold stock than the United States holds at present, or indeed than many countries hold. This suggests that at least some substantial portion of the gold could be sold, with a view to reducing the borrowing requirements, and hence the future debt-servicing obligations, of the government. Because of the demonstrated thinness of the gold market – that is, its limited capacity for absorbing increased gold supplies without a sharp drop in price – a revenue-maximizing strategy would necessarily involve stretching the sales out over a prolonged period of time.[10] Of course, if an objective is to penalize the Soviet Union at a time when it must sell gold to acquire foreign exchange, the government might wish to sell more gold than would be indicated by a revenue-maximizing strategy.

Finally, gold can be used for international settlement in any international monetary regime that has not accepted freely floating exchange rates. Because of ambiguities surrounding the present appropriate and future price for official international transactions in gold, gold has become virtually immobilized as international reserves, even though it still accounts for an important part (at market prices, the bulk) of the external reserves of monetary authorities. Under the revised Articles of Agreement of the International Monetary Fund, gold lost the special legal status it once held in the international monetary system. By the same token there is now no legal obstacle to prevent governments or central banks from undertaking any transactions they wish to in gold. But the choice of an appropriate price is a snag. Contrary to the usual assumption, gold really is *not* a liquid asset – in the sense that it can be sold quickly and at a known price – when dealt with on the scale of major central banks. Governments have been reluctant to sell gold for a variety of no doubt deeply rooted psychological reasons, as well as because of its price-depressing effects; but governments have also been reluctant to buy gold, because they are unclear what they are buying, other than a speculative asset.

Gold as reserves are effectively mobilized within the European Monetary System by the European Monetary Co-operation Fund. The arrangements provide for 'deposits' by member countries in the EMCF of 20 per cent of their gold and dollar reserves, updated quarterly, against which the members are credited with an equivalent value of ECUs (European Currency Units, a composite of European currencies), where gold and dollars are valued at approximately their market rates. This process thus involves a considerable increase in the valuation of gold compared with the official price of thirty-five SDRs an ounce still used by many countries, including some members of the EMS. The scheme 'liquifies' gold reserves at market prices without putting pressure on the gold market. The mobilization is limited, however, since the ECUs can be used only for intra-European settlements. And the scheme is basically somewhat fraudulent, since the gold and dollars deposited in the EMCF remain under national ownership and the ECU transfers among member countries are subject to holding limits, so practically speaking the ECUs are lines of credit. The same effect could be achieved with an initial allocation of ECU credit lines to member countries, without any so-called deposit of gold and dollars. This alternative would have the additional advantage that the book value of the ECUs would not vary capriciously with the market price of gold, as it does under present arrangements. But such is the residual psychological hold of gold that, despite its disadvantages, its invocation can occasionally help launch a scheme that could not be negotiated without it.

NOTES

1. This paper draws heavily on my longer and more fully documented paper, 'The Gold Standard: Historical Facts and Future Prospects', *Brookings Papers on Economic Activity*, 1982, No. 11. References to most of the facts cited can be found in that paper.
2. This statement has to be qualified in one respect. The figures shown in Table 8.1 concern *annual* variability. If instead one takes five-year periods of observation, the variability of inflation rates was lower during the pre-1914 period. See Cooper, 'The Gold Standard: Historical Facts and Future Prospects', p. 7n.
3. See Jevons (1875) *Money and the Mechanism of Exchange* (London: Kegan Paul); and his essays of the 1860s, which inagurated the development of index numbers; Alfred Marshall (1926), testimony before the Royal Commission of the Depression in Trade and Industry, 1886, printed in *Official Papers by Alfred Marshall* (London: Macmillan), pp. 10–15; and Irving Fisher (1920) *Stabilizing the Dollar* (New York: Macmillan).
4. William Fellner has emphasized both variability and the long-run inadequacy of gold supplies as decisive disadvantages of an early return to gold convertibility, although he does not rule out some (unpredictable) improvement in this regard in the long run. See his 'Gold and the Uneasy Case for Responsibly Managed Fiat Money', in *Essays in Contemporary*

Economic Problems (Washington: American Enterprise Institute), 1981.

5. US official gold holdings were $1.5 billion in 1914 and $8.2 billion in 1934.

6. To the extent that private gold holdings are solely yield-oriented investments, private gold holdings are fundamentally unstable. Gold convertibility at a credible price would lead *all* private gold to be sold to the monetary authorities; if the price were considered not credible, there would be a run on official gold and all of it would pass into private hands. For an analysis of alternative government gold policies on the path of gold prices and on private behavior, see Stephen W. Salant and Dale W. Henderson (1978) 'Market Anticipations of Government Policies and the Price of Gold', *Journal of Political Economy*, 86, July, pp. 627–48.

7. It is for this reason that Sir Roy Harrod over the years favored an increase in the official price of gold. See, for example, his *Reforming the World's Money* (London: St. Martin's Press), 1965, Chapter 3.

8. Robert E. Weintraub, 'Restoring the Gold Certificate Reserve', Appendix to the 'The Gold Standard: Its History and Record Against Inflation', US Congress, Joint Economic Committee, September 1981.

9. 'Gold and the Uneasy Case for Responsibly Managed Fiat Money'.

10. Salant and Henderson ('Market Anticipations') show that the anticipation of sales by the government can have substantial impact on price, and in their model the present-value-maximizing strategy is to sell *at once* all the gold that the government plans to sell, because the price obtainable at future auctions rises at a rate lower than the (constant) interest rate. But their model assumes known yet-to-be-mined gold reserves, stationary demand, gold disappearance (literal consumption, like oil, not merely transformation), and a universally known 'choke price' at which demand for gold drops to zero (p. 14). Relaxation of these assumptions will weaken their strong conclusion. In particular, private uncertainty about yet-to-be mined reserves, about the motives for private holdings of gold, about future government sales, and about future interest rates, will impart a downward slope to the demand schedule for gold. If it is steep enough, it leads to the conclusion stated in the text.

9 Gold in the International Monetary System: A Catalog of the Options

ROBERT Z. ALIBER

For much of the last decade, one of the apparent paradoxes has been the contrast between the attitudes toward gold as an international reserve asset by officials in monetary institutions, especially in the Anglo-Saxon world, and the attitudes of investors and market participants. The monetary authorities in the United States and several other countries have sought to demonetize gold or to move gold from 'the center of the international monetary system'. If their views prevail, the likelihood that the real price of gold would rise significantly is low, primarily because central banks might sell gold from their holdings so that the market price of gold would be depressed. Yet in the last decade, investors and market participants have priced gold as if they expect its price to rise indefinitely, and by as much or more than the increase in the consumer price level. They view gold as an inflation hedge, even though there is modest evidence to suggest that gold should be a better inflation hedge than most other storable commodities. Apparently the investors and market participants do not believe that the monetary authorities will sell much of their gold, even though over the decade they sold about 5 per cent of their gold to private parties.

The reasons given for seeking to demonetize gold differ. Many authorities view the need to peg their currencies as a constraint or anchor on their policy choices. The proponents of SDR as the major reserve asset believe that including gold as a reserve asset would reduce the interest in producing more SDR. The monetarists are concerned that gold inflows and outflows would limit their ability to manage the predictable and constant growth in the monetary base or the monetary aggregates. Many view gold as a 'barbarous relic'. In contrast, the proponents of gold believe that a restoration of gold convertibility would prove a constraint on the rates of money supply growth, and, paradoxically, that the ability to convert moneys into gold would reduce the demand for gold.

These differences in views about the future role of gold were evident in the statements made to the US Gold Commission (Commission on the Role of Gold, 1982). One group wants to restore the gold standard because of 'the virtue of monetary discipline'; they are primarily concerned with the domestic impacts of setting a new parity for gold, any international impacts being secondary. A second group in contrast belittled the likelihood that a return to the gold standard would bring the well-advertised advantages of demonetarization of gold. The Commission's report focused almost exclusively on the domestic impacts of a new monetary role for gold; relatively little attention was given to the usefulness of gold as an international reserve asset, and the advantages for the United States of using gold as a reserve asset. (Indeed, the Commission put virtually all significant issues concerning gold on hold, as well as a number of non-significant ones).

One of the paradoxes of the 1960s was the view that gold should be phased out as an international reserve asset, at a time when gold was the single most important reserve asset and there was a shortage of international reserves. So SDR was produced as a fiat substitute for gold. The increase in the market price of gold in the 1970s led to an increase in the market value of monetary gold reserves that dwarfed the increase in SDR. Since US gold holdings are larger than those of any other country (indeed, as large as those of the next three largest holders combined), the United States has a significant vested interest in the role of gold as money. Thus if there are proposals to increase the supply of reserves, a key question is whether the United States would be as well off if measures were adopted that would achieve the same effective increase in reserves by enhancing the usefulness of gold as a reserve asset as by producing more SDR. A related question is whether efforts to reduce the international monetary role of gold should be continued, or whether gold should again be used as an international reserve asset.

In retrospect, then, the concern with the reserve shortage in the 1960s seems somewhat ironical. The increase in the value of international reserves that occurred as a result of market processes was very much larger than the increase that resulted from the planned processes associated with the increases both in SDR and in IMF quotas.

The paper deals with the national options toward gold as an international reserve asset, especially with the US national options. The

TABLE 9.1 Components of international reserves, 1965–1982 (millions of US dollars)

	1965	1970	1975	1980	1982 (April)
Foreign exchange	23,993	45,432	162,392	378,120	323,705
IMF reserve position	5,377	7,697	14,778	21,472	25,170
SDRs	–	3,724	10,260	15,061	14,153
Total reserves without gold	29,370	56,253	187,430	414,653	363,028
Gold @ $35/oz	41,528	36,989	35,690	33,348	33,352
Gold @ $100/oz	118,652	105,683	101,970	95,281	95,291
Gold @ $200/oz	237,304	211,366	203,940	190,562	190,582
Gold @ $300/oz	355,956	317,049	305,910	285,843	285,873
Total reserves, with					
Gold @ $35/oz	70,898	93,242	223,120	448,001	396,380
Gold @ $100/oz	148,022	161,936	289,400	509,934	458,319
Gold @ $200/oz	266,674	267,619	391,370	605,215	553,610
Gold @ $300/oz	385,326	373,302	493,340	700,496	648,901
Note: gold, million oz	1,186.521	1,056.831	1,019.701	952.81	952.91

SOURCE International Financial Statistics

future role of gold as an international reserve asset involves answers to three issues: the price of gold in transactions both between national monetary institutions and between national monetary institutions and international monetary institutions; the terms or conditions that might apply to transactions in gold between monetary institutions; and the impact of gold purchases and sales by monetary institutions in different countries on the monetary base. These issues or questions are central both to the analysis of the role of gold historically and to the current options toward gold as a monetary asset. This paper discusses the first two of these questions.

The first section of this paper presents some stylized facts on the development of gold as money. The second section reviews gold's role under the gold exchange standard. The third section discusses the US options toward gold.

THE DEVELOPMENT OF GOLD AS MONEY: STYLIZED FACTS

The development of gold as money predates written history and even the monetary institutions (Hicks, 1969). Initially gold was almost certainly one of several commodity moneys – commodities used as a means of payment, a unit of account, and a store of value were a money. Commodity moneys were in implicit competition with each other. The commodity money that had the most attractive set of attributes eventually dominated the competition. The price of other commodities that had also served as moneys declined in terms of gold as the monetary demand for these commodities fell; however, because of this decline, these moneys would continue to be used for specialized purposes. Gold could become a monopoly commodity money only as a result of a planning process which would effectively prohibit the low-price commodity competitors.

The monetary authorities preferred to avoid the uncertainty associated with changes in the price of gold in terms of other commodity moneys, so they attempted to stabilize the prices. The ability of the authorities to peg the price of gold in terms of other commodity moneys was challenged whenever any structural disturbances affected the supply–demand relationship in one commodity money relative to the other.

Many of the problems inherent in bimetallic systems reappeared in a mixed system of a commodity money and a fait money. Yet there were differences, for the authorities could manage the production of the fiat money and they could alter interest rates on fiat money assets. Fiat moneys developed as an alternative to gold in response to efforts to economize on the costs of transactions. The usual story involves transactions in warehouse receipts that represent title to the ownership of gold. These receipts were a money – they were stores of value, means of payment, and units of account. Even though owners of gold were charged storage costs by the warehouse, they realized other savings; transactions costs or payment costs were lower. Initially each warehouse receipt was fully backed by gold; the receipt represented title to a specified amount of gold. The monetary authority – the managers of the warehouse – had a passive role; they issued more receipts for gold if the public wished to store more gold, and they bought back these receipts if the public wanted more gold. (These transactions were a form of open market operations.) Owners of these receipts might trade them: there would be incentives for a market to develop in warehouse receipts.

Similarly, other commodity moneys might be warehoused, and trading might occur in these warehouse receipts. Silver warehouse receipts would be held by individuals and firms that found ownership of gold warehouse receipts too expensive. So the price of gold warehouse receipts would vary in terms of the price of silver warehouse receipts.

The owners of the warehouses received a payment for providing a storage service, much like banks now rent safe deposit boxes. The owners of the warehouses sought additional income by issuing identical receipts in exchange for assets other than gold as a way to increase their profits. So the managers of the warehouse might issue claims on themselves, convertible or payable in gold. These certificates were indistinguishable from the warehouse receipts offered in exchange for gold. Yet these certificates were indistinguishable from other certificates, for they were claims on the warehouse rather than claims to particular units of gold. The owners of the warehouse then had to decide how large a volume of these certificates to issue; they could no longer take a passive approach.

Competition among warehouses meant that they began to pay interest on the certificates, both those issued in exchange for gold and those issued in exchange for other assets. The interest payments compensated the owners of these certificates from the risk of a possible loss in purchasing power in terms of gold if these certificates could no longer be converted into gold on demand. Depending on their attitudes toward risk and their demands for returns, some investors preferred to hold these certificates while others preferred to hold gold. As the volume of outstanding certificates increased relative to the volume of gold in the warehouses, the issuers of these certificates might be required to pay higher interest rates on the certificates to attract holders. The limit to the volume of outstanding certificates is posed by the ultimate ability or capacity of borrowers to pay the interest rates charged by the issuers of these certificates.

An increase in the gold holdings of the warehouses, perhaps a result of new gold discoveries, reduced the risk attached to these certificates and permitted the producers to increase their purchases of other assets. As the volume of outstanding certificates increased relative to the volume of gold in the warehouse, the risk of a credit deflation or a credit collapse increased should a shock occur; and the owners of certificates rushed to convert them into gold. The 'house of cards' of the fractional credit system might tend to topple in response to a surge in the demand for gold. The issuers of certificates might raise the interest rates on the certificates; however, they could not afford to pay more in interest than they were receiving in interest, at least for an extended period. So mechanisms were established to produce a superior form of certificate.

The central bank – the certificate-issuing authority – could 'manage' the system by altering the interest rate payable on the certificates. Raising the interest rates on the certificates increased the demand as long as investors believed that the risk attached to the certificates was unchanged. If, however, investors believed the certificates were more risky, then higher interest rates might be associated with reduced demand for certificates; the authorities might have to raise interest rates further to 'protect' their gold holdings from the risk of a run.

The Bank of England managed the system while holding gold that was modest in amount relative to the forms of fiat money. Changes in interest rates necessary to protect its gold were also modest. The reason that such modest changes in interest rates were adequate is that the credibility of the gold parity was rarely, if ever, seriously doubted.

GOLD AND THE GOLD EXCHANGE STANDARD

At the beginning of the First World War, the authorities in most countries prohibited the export of gold, in part because of the submarine crises; gold convertibility was suspended. After suspension, the authorities were able to increase the supply of certificates outstanding relative to their gold holdings. So investors held more certificates than they would have preferred at the prevailing interest rates and the traditional or customary relationship between the price of gold in terms of the price of the certificates, but the conversion possibility was foreclosed. After the war, the problem of restoring gold convertibility was severe because of the surge in the non-gold component of the world moneys. The options open to the authorities included a reduction in the non-gold monetary liabilities and presumably a reduction in commodity price levels, an increase in monetary gold holdings effected either by an increase in the price of gold in terms of the certificates or from the chance of new gold discoveries, and an increased demand for certificates prompted by either higher interest rates or new reserve requirements or portfolio regulations. All three factors occurred; there was a decrease in the supply of certificates as a result of deflation, especially in 1920–1, and through the devaluations of numerous currencies in terms of gold. Several international meetings were designed to increase the demand for certificates relative to the demand for gold.

Whether there was in fact a gold shortage in the 1920s is conjectural. The argument that there was a gold shortage is based both on the much higher price levels after the First World War than before and the increase in the price of gold in the 1930s, which is viewed as a belated response to the earlier shortage. The argument that gold holdings were adequate in the 1920s is based on the data that suggest that central bank gold holdings were increasing – gold production was not much smaller than a decade before the war. While individual central banks were concerned about the inadequacy of their gold holdings, their currencies were overvalued relative to the US dollar.

Because of the sharp increase in the price of gold in the 1930s and the decline in the US (and world) price level, gold production was stimulated. Moreover the monetary value of existing gold holdings surged. There was an excess supply of gold, and a 'Golden Avalanche' resulted. For a while, at least, the US authorities lost control of the monetary base.

The monetary history of the 1960s echoes that of the 1920s. There was concern about a gold shortage because the non-gold component of international reserves had increased relative to the gold component; the world price level had risen during the Second World War and then again at the time of the Korean War. US gold holdings peaked in 1949 and then began to decline, for the United States 'managed' the world's buffer stock in gold – or the warehouse. The policy options in the 1960s were the same as in the 1920s – the demand for gold might decline if the supply of non-gold moneys (and the world price level) could be reduced, the supply of gold could be increased by raising the monetary price on a worldwide basis or by discovering more gold, and the demand for the non-gold component of reserves could be increased by raising interest rates and by promoting the sale of assets that are alternatives to gold (including new assets), perhaps through reserve requirements or portfolio measures.

The international monetary system broke down in the late 1960s when the private demand for gold surged in anticipation that convertibility might be suspended, and the price of gold might then increase. Once the market price of gold increased relative to the official price, following the move to the two-tier system, official institutions became reluctant to sell gold; gold was 'paralyzed' in reserve holdings.

The effect of the increase in the price of gold in the 1970s was to increase the ratio of gold to other assets in investor, and central bank, portfolios. The market price of gold at any moment reflects the implicit convenience yield or real return and an inflation premium. Investors acquired gold if they anticipated a higher return from these two factors relative to the returns on other assets. The convenience yield is not likely to change significantly when the inflation rate changes.

CHANGES IN GOLD POLICY: THE OPTIONS

Gold is now in monetary limbo. Gold is held as a reserve asset even though central bank transactions in gold have been modest. At recent market prices – indeed, at any market price above $350 an ounce – monetary gold holdings are the largest component of international reserves. Central bank intervention in exchange market has been extensive, indeed more extensive than under pegged exchanged rates. The rules or procedures for transactions in gold by monetary institutions are virtually non-existent, with the exception of those that operate through the European Monetary Arrangement. Nevertheless, central banks buy and sell gold in the commodity markets. Central banks differ in how they value gold when presenting data on their reserve assets; some value gold at its last parity, while others value gold at or near current or recent market prices. Yet few investors and market participants are unaware of the magnitude or market value of central bank gold holdings. When investors price the stock of gold, it is likely that they include official gold holdings in the stock. So the key questions involve the costs and benefits of altering the monetary role of gold.

The monetary role for gold might be altered by changing the price of gold in transactions between monetary authorities in different countries, or the terms on which these institutions might trade gold with each other. To assess the significance of these changes, these prices and terms should be compared with the prices and terms according to which monetary authorities might trade gold in the private market.

There are a number of rationales or motives for altering the monetary role of gold. One motive for changing gold market arrangements is to enhance exchange rate stability by increasing the value of international reserves; central banks will then be able to intervene more extensively in the foreign exchange market. Gold now can be used to obtain foreign exchange for exchange market intervention in several different ways (in the European Monetary Fund, by borrowing foreign exchange using gold as collateral, and by selling gold in the private market). Hence the key question involves the impact of changing the terms on which central banks might trade gold with other central banks on their willingness to intervene in the foreign exchange market. Since central banks can already deal in gold with the market, the significance of this argument depends on the price at which central banks might trade gold with each other relative to the market price if there is no change in gold market arrangements. The higher the price and the grater the assurance that they might trade at these prices, the more significant is this argument.

A second reason for altering the role of gold in the system is to meet the demand for international reserves. If there is a shortage of international reserves currently or if a shortage develops, then this demand might be satisfied by setting a parity for gold somewhat above the prevailing market price, or by increasing the confidence that monetary institutions can sell the gold with less uncertainty about its future value. While the surge in the level of reserves in the last decade might suggest that the likelihood of a shortage in the near future is modest, the system already may have adjusted to the level of reserves available. The alternatives to increasing reserves by altering the role of gold include increases in both IMF SDR and in reserves denominated in the dollar, the Deutsch mark, the Japanese yen, the Swiss franc and other currencies. Difficulties and concern about increasing these other types of reserves might lead to the conclusion that the monetary role of gold should be enhanced. One primary advantage of gold is that gold is already there; a second is that gold is a form of outside money, so that increases in monetary gold holdings are not associated with increase in some country's debt.

From the US point of view, developing a less uncertain role for gold in the system, even if only by valuing US gold holdings at or near the market price when presenting data on the US reserve position, would improve the US balance sheet in international reserve assets. Foreign holdings of liquid dollar assets exceed $250 billion (much of which involves holdings in dollar deposits in Euro-banks) while foreign claims on the United States total $150 billion. US gold holdings would be valued at $90 billion at a market price of $300 and at $120 billion at a market price of $400. This change would increase the confidence in the foreign exchange value of the dollar; foreign holders of dollar assets might come to the conclusion that the US authorities would be in a better position to support the foreign exchange value of the dollar. Hence their demand for dollar assets might be stronger.

Many holders of dollar assets must already recognize implicitly the market value of the US Treasury's gold holdings, even if the US Treasury does not explicitly value the US gold holdings on the basis of prevailing market prices. Nevertheless, a firmer statement that the US gold holdings would be valued on the basis of market price might carry the implication that US gold holdings would be used as part of an exchange market intervention policy. The US authorities would be in a position to sell gold for foreign currencies that they might wish to use in exchange market intervention, or to sell gold in exchange for the excess dollar holdings of foreign official institutions.

A third reason for enhancing the role of gold in the international monetary system is that the net worth of central banks that own gold would increase. Commercial banks in a number of countries have incurred large losses. While their central banks may wish to act as lenders-of-last-resort, these central banks may feel constrained in providing credit because their own liquidity position would be weakened. The willingness of central banks to act as lenders-of-last-resort would increase if gold could be traded at its market price. Thus the change in gold policy would have a wealth effect. Once again the issue of additionality arises, for some of these central banks already value gold at or near the prevailing market price. Strengthening the arrangements under which gold might be traded among central banks would enhance their willingness to extend credit.

A fourth reason for altering the terms on which central banks buy and sell gold involves the search for a mechanism to achieve domestic price level stability. Changes in central bank gold holdings would then provide the basis for changes in their monetary liabilities; the monetary rule would be based on gold. While this rationale, unlike the first several, primarily has a domestic orientation, there would be some international implications: other countries might peg their currencies to the dollar (or to gold) if the dollar is again pegged to gold. Hence there is an asymmetry: changes in the domestic monetary role of gold have significant implications for its international role, while changes in the international monetary role of gold have far less extensive implications for changes in the domestic role. The argument for a return to convertibility as a way to strengthen constraints on credit expansion is based on the association between long-run price level stability in the nineteenth century and rapid economic growth in a gold standard environment. The traditional inference is that the gold standard led to the price level stability. An alternative interpretation of this experience is that rapid growth, a result of abundant investment opportunities, may have led to price level stability. The evidence that the 'rules of the game' were followed in the nineteenth century has been questioned extensively. Changing US gold policy to achieve this objective would lead to very sharp changes in the operating procedures of the Federal Reserve – so sharp that the political feasibility of the change is doubtful.

One of the basic concerns with any proposals to rely more extensively on gold in international monetary arrangements involves the costs to the system. Many of these costs were identified in the 1960s, when Milton Gilbert, Roy Harrod and others recommended that the monetary price of gold should be increased. Because of a concern with these costs, increasing the monetary price of gold was deemed too expensive a policy change. One alleged cost involved the inflationary impacts of the increase in the monetary gold price. Now, however, the market price of gold has increased, so that most or all of any inflationary impact has already been felt, unless the price at which official institutions might deal in gold is set at a level substantially above the market price. Just as the advantages of altering the terms on which monetary institutions might deal in gold are limited because so many value gold at its market price, so the costs of changing the terms and price are limited because gold is already valued at market price. Another alleged cost involved the subsidy to the gold producers. Here, too, any additional subsidy would involve a comparison between the anticipated market price with and without a change in the monetary role of gold. In the 1960s political costs were attached to the process of changing the gold price; now that the gold price has been changed, this argument would appear to have much less force. The political costs of altering the terms on which central banks might trade gold appear to be significantly smaller than the costs of increasing the monetary gold price in the 1960s.

The monetary role of gold can be changed by altering the terms that apply to gold transactions between central banks, and the price at which they deal in gold with each other. The terms include whether the monetary authorities have a call (a right to buy at a stipulated price) and a put (a right to sell at a stipulated price) and whether there are limits to the call and the put, or whether the amounts which can be bought and sold are unlimited amounts at the prevailing price. Under the Bretton Woods system, foreign official institutions had an unlimited call at $35 plus a handling charge and an unlimited put at $35 minus a handling charge. Under the gold standard, each monetary authority offered both an unlimited call and an unlimited put. The range of possible prices include the market price or a price keyed to the market price or a parity. If there are limits to the volume of transactions, then the market price of gold might differ from the price of gold in transactions between official institutions.

One extreme is a return to an arrangement like that of Bretton Woods: the US authorities would set the price at which they are prepared to buy and sell gold in unlimited amounts, while monetary institutions abroad decide on the amounts of gold they wish to buy or sell at this price. Under this arrangement the foreign central banks would have an unlimited put at the US Treasury's gold buying price and an unlimited call at the US Treasury's gold selling price.

Table 9.2 shows possible combinations of the prices and of the terms on which gold might be traded. Four possible price arrangements are noted, and range from a parity to the market price. Three different sets of terms are noted. The least ambitious arrangement would involve changes in the terms on which central banks might deal in gold with each other at the market price; this arrangement is in the southeast cell. The Bretton Woods system is represented in the northwest cell.

TABLE 9.2 *Possible gold trading arrangements*
Price in central bank transaction

Terms/Amounts	Parity	Parity plus charges	Average market price	Actual market price
Unlimited				
Limited				
Conditional				

Movements toward the northwest cell increase the wealth of national monetary authorities, since they can have greater assurance about the price at which they can buy and sell the gold, and the amounts of gold which they might buy and sell at these prices.

The terms on which central banks deal in gold might be altered by facilitating off-market transactions at market prices or at market-referenced prices. The US Treasury might agree to lend dollars against gold. Or the US Treasury might agree to buy gold spot and to sell gold forward in transactions with foreign central banks. The US Treasury might arrange a series of gold standby arrangements with various other countries, along the lines of the reciprocal credit arrangements; each country might be able to obtain a specified amount of the currency of the other participant by a sale of gold at market or market-referenced price.

These various types of gold transactions might be arranged on a conditional basis, so that either country might refuse to participate in the arrangement; the arrangement would be pre-negotiated, but either party would have a veto over its implementation. Alternatively, these standbys might be arranged on an unconditional basis, so that either party could initiate the transaction without fear that the other party might veto the transaction. Or the arrangements might involve a combination of an unconditional and a conditional standby.

Inevitably, world gold policy will largely reflect US gold policy. If gold is to have a larger monetary role, the US authorities must decide the price at which they will buy and sell gold, and whether the price will be fixed as a parity or variable and related to the market price. There appear to be no good historic counterparts to this decision – frequently, for example, a new parity has been set on the basis of a parity established earlier, or on the basis of a previous parity adjusted for the change in international competitive position. In 1933–4, the US authorities sought to increase the dollar price of gold by 100 per cent to compensate for a decline in the US price level of 30 per cent. But there appears to be no good analogy to the current situation, because the discontinuity between the previous gold parity and current gold price is so large.

Setting a price at which the US authorities might buy and sell gold is central to the re-entry problem, because the market price for gold in most recent years has been so much higher than estimates of an equilibrium price based on increases in national price levels in the last decade. The price of gold, like many other real assets, began to incorporate an inflation premium. For example, if a PPP approach is taken to the market price of gold, the 'predicted' 1980 price might be about three times as high as the mid-1960s price. If the equilibrium mid-1960s price is $70 (or twice the then US parity), the appropriate price in the mid-1980s might be $200 an ounce. If the market price is used as the basis for setting a new parity at the time when the inflation premium remains high, the parity might be excessively high if the inflation rate were to drop substantially, with the consequence that there might be a new 'Golden Avalanche'. If the parity is set at a level that is below the market price, there is a risk of a 'run' on the US Treasury's gold holdings; investors would sell dollars and buy gold.

Or the US authorities might announce a target for the parity, perhaps together with the view that this parity would be effective at a particular date in the future. Even then, however, the authorities encounter the risk that they might subsequently be subject to very large gold inflows or outflows at that future date. The British learned in 1926 that setting a parity for sterling that might be effective some months into the future would not mean that this new parity would be appropriate after its adoption.

The US authorities might adopt a parity together with very wide support limits. If they adopt a parity of $350, they might adopt support limits of plus or minus $50, or $75, or $100. Support limits might be progressively narrowed.

One alternative is to use the crawling peg approach to setting the new US parity for gold; the authorities might reduce the parity if their gold purchases are too large and raise the parity if their sales are too large. In this case, the US authorities would change the dollar price of gold whenever changes in US official gold holdings are deemed too large.

Because of the risks of setting a parity that is too high, there may be a temptation to set a parity and attempt to insulate the parity from the market price through a parallel market arrangement. The evidence of the late 1960s is that there is difficulty in setting or maintaining a parity that would differ from the market price. Inevitably, if the prices diverge, then there will be efforts to arbitrage the two markets. And gold might again tend to be parked in official holdings, with the authorities reluctant to sell gold if the official price differs from the market price.

Determining the right parity for gold will prove elusive. One question is whether the changes in the US gold holdings, if the parity is less than perfect, will be so large as to complicate domestic monetary management. The implication of a positive answer is that the immediate approach toward changing the monetary role of gold should be directed at developing arrangements so that the monetary authorities are better able to trade gold at market-related prices.

CONCLUSION

The US Gold Commission punted on the key issues concerning the role of gold in the international monetary system. A large part of the

Administration's motive for establishing the Commission appears to have been to buy time while the pressures to go back 'on the the gold standard' abated. This objective appears to have been realized. The Commission recognized a potential monetary role for gold, but provided little if any guidance about the nature of this role.

Gold is an important international asset. That gold is an international reserve asset is implicitly recognized by both monetary authorities and market participants. A variety of measures might be undertaken to facilitate central bank trades in gold at market or market-referenced prices.

Some of these measures to enhance the monetary role of gold are straightforward, and could be readily negotiated between the United States and the other major gold-holding countries, probably as a series of bilateral arrangements. These measures would increase confidence that central banks owning gold might be able to use this gold as a basis for exchange market intervention without depressing the market price.

Central banks are likely to remain reluctant to deal in gold as long as the price is variable. One analogy is provided by the two-tier market: central banks were reluctant to deal in gold at the official price when the private price was higher. Yet a new parity for gold cannot be negotiated; if the US authorities believe that international monetary arrangements would be strengthened by establishing a parity for gold, then a unilateral decision must be made (a 15 August 1971, in reverse). Yet the views of others might be obtained on the value of this parity, and whether they would be buyers or sellers of gold at a series of possible parities.

As long as there remains a significant inflation premium in the gold price, establishing a new gold parity would be premature. Either the announcement of the parity might be delayed until this premium shrinks, or a crawling-peg approach toward establishing a parity might be developed.

REFERENCES

Commission on the Role of Gold in the Domestic and International Monetary Systems (1982) *Report to the Congress*, Washington.

Hicks, John (1969) *A Theory of Economic History* (Oxford: Oxford University Press).

Jastram, Roy W. (1977) *The Golden Constant* (New York: John Wiley and Sons).

10 Gold Monetization and Gold Discipline[1]

ROBERT P. FLOOD and PETER M. GARBER

Gold and its price have emerged as frequent topics of both academic and government debate.[2] Public attention, focused on the gold market since gold's price began fluctuating violently in 1980 and 1981, has turned to gold as a possible means of removing some discretion inherent in the current fiat money system. Since lack of adherence to monetary rules can lead to problems of dynamic policy inconsistency, academic economists have begun seriously to reconsider monetary standards based either on gold or on some other commodity as politically feasible methods of establishing rules.[3]

The political and intellectual resurrection of gold has coincided with the advent of three lines of thought concerning government gold market policy. First, Salant and Henderson (1978) have developed a partial equilibrium gold market model to analyze the interactions between rapid gold price rises, government gold auctions, and speculative attacks on government gold stocks. Salant (1981) places the possibility of a speculative attack on price stabilization schemes in a stochastic setting. Second, Barro (1979) has constructed a model based on an assumption of static expectations to study money and price dynamics under a version of the historical gold standard. Finally, others such as Laffer (1979) and Lehrman (1980, 1981) have proposed a new monetary gold standard under which the government would maintain a fixed nominal gold price while retaining the freedom to issue money without fixed gold backing.[4]

The purpose of the present paper is to provide a dynamic framework suitable for analyzing various gold monetization policies. We integrate the ideas in Salant and Henderson with those in Barro; and, as an example of the usefulness of the conceptual framework, we analyze both the functioning of and a transition to a gold standard. More generally, the methods developed here can be used to study a monetary system based on any storable commodity. In addition to analyzing a successful gold monetization, we study the possibility of an unsuccessful gold standard, i.e. a government's implementation of a gold standard destined to collapse either immediately or after a finite interval following implementation. Our results on the collapse of a gold standard draw from the work of Salant and Henderson (1978) (S–H hereafter), Salant (1981) and Krugman (1979). Finally, the analytical framework which we develop operates as a systematic means of categorizing the dynamic evolution of any commodity standard; using a simple graphical technique and given the policy environment, one can determine if a commodity standard will be permanent, temporary or immediately nonviable. We also seek to specify a method for determining the predictable time of a gold standard's collapse and to establish a terminology useful in discussing all of the potential evolutionary paths.

We organize the paper in four sections. In the first section we present an informal discussion of the effect of gold monetization on the money stock. In the second section we introduce the basic components of our model and study the paths of the relative gold price and the price level prior to a government's announcement that gold's nominal price will be fixed. In the third section we analyze the dynamics of the money and gold markets after the nominal gold price has been fixed, considering both a permanent gold standard and a gold standard which must ultimately collapse. We also examine the current effects of an announcement to fix gold's price at a given level in the future. In the fourth section we study the significance of the concept of the 'discipline of the gold standard'; we demonstrate that the notion lacks operational meaning if the alternative fiat money system is not also 'disciplined'. This section is followed by some concluding remarks.

THE EFFECT OF GOLD MONETIZATION ON THE MONEY STOCK

In this section we will informally discuss the nature of the gold monetization policies and the behavior of the public which we study in the rest of the paper. Our intention is to clarify the direction followed by our exposition, specifying explicitly the monetary nature of gold. Since we abstract away from a banking system throughout the paper, money will be either government-issued paper currency or, when gold is monetized, gold coins or bars held in private portfolios.

We wish to focus our attention on the money stock changes that will occur because of the nature of gold monetization. A policy of fixing its nominal price, allowing gold and currency to shift freely and instantaneously between private portfolios and government reserves, monetizes gold through its effect on the market for currency. The monetization policy may consist of a sudden, immediate shift to a gold standard, allowing no time for market prices to adjust to the new information before the gold price fixing. Alternatively, an announcement of a future monetization may be made with no current intervention into the gold markets.[5] Here we will ignore the aspect of the policy which pushes gold price fixing into the future and consider the effects of a permanently successful policy to fix gold's price immediately.

If a policy to fix gold's price is permanently successful, then either currency will dominate gold in private portfolios or portfolio gold and currency will be perfect substitutes. The first case hinges on currency's having a greater convenience than portfolio gold in making transactions. Since the two assets would be permanently fixed in price relative to one another, any purely speculative demand could be equally satisfied by currency balances. Since currency will therefore dominate portfolio gold after gold's price is fixed, agents will exchange all of their portfolio gold for currency at the fixed gold price. In the absence of sterilizing bond sales, the supply of currency will rise by the value of portfolio gold holdings, thus monetizing existing gold hoards.

Alternatively, if agents perceive that portfolio gold and currency are perfect substitutes, then both the amount of gold that the government must exchange for currency and the ratio of portfolio gold to currency held by the public are indeterminate.[6] However, this indeterminacy is inconsequential; to the extent that portfolio gold is held after price fixing, it exactly fulfils agents' demands for money. Thus the increase in both the supply of and the demand for nominal money at the time of gold's price fixing is identical in both cases.

In summary, when the government fixes the price of gold, the private sector monetizes portfolio gold by cashing in existing speculative hoards, by allowing hoards to fulfil money demands directly, or by a combination of the two. The nature of the government's commitment to exchange gold for currency at a fixed price produces an indeterminacy in the amount of gold exchanged between the government and the public.

Our discussion has neglected some important aspects of gold monetization. First, gold use in consumption and industry imposes specific dynamics on the gold market. Once gold is monetized, those dynamics are injected into the money market. What are the money market implications of gold's dynamics? Second, our discussion above assumes that the policy to fix gold's price will be permanently successful. However, it is possible that the fixed nominal price of gold is inconsistent with the permanent maintenance of a gold standard. Under what circumstances will a gold standard lack permanent viability and how will agents behave when they recognize this impending collapse? Third, how does a current announcement to fix gold's future price immediately affect the gold market and the nominal price level? Fourth, we will consider policies that involve announcing currently the future fixed gold price. How can we calculate the future gold price and currency issue compatible with price level stability? Finally, to what extent does a gold standard impose discipline or constraint upon a government? To study these questions we must turn to a formal analysis.

THE WORLD PRIOR TO GOLD MONETIZATION

To obtain results concerning the effects of an announcement to fix gold's price we must first characterize the world prior to the announcement. The concepts and methods we will use are very similar to those of S–H; however, there will be no government gold auctions, and we will modify their model to suit our problem. Specifically, we introduce a monetary sector, modify the nature of gold demand for private uses, and analyze a policy of nominal gold price pegging. Throughout the paper we employ a continuous time model in which agents have perfect foresight.[7] We present our ideas in the form of a linearized example in order to make the concepts involved as concrete as possible. We divide our economy into two explicit sectors, a gold sector and a monetary sector. The real rate of interest, ρ, is fixed at a constant level exogenously to the gold and monetary sectors.[8]

The Gold Sector

The operation of the gold market is partly described in equations (10.1)–(10.3):

$$\bar{I} = D(t) + G(t) + R(t) \tag{10.1}$$

$$D(t) = v[\{\delta/q(t)\} - D(t)] \qquad \delta, v > 0 \tag{10.2}$$

$$\dot{q}(t) = \begin{cases} \rho q(t) & \text{for } G(t) > 0 \\ 0 & \text{for } G(t) = 0 \end{cases} \tag{10.3}$$

$\bar{I}$ is a fixed total world stock of gold. $D(t)$ is the quantity of gold at time t which has been put into consumption and industrial uses. $G(t)$ is the quantity of gold held privately as ingots or coins in speculative hoards, and $R(t)$ is the quantity of gold in government reserves. Until gold is monetized, we will assume $R(t)$ to be the positive constant $\bar{R}$.[9]

Equation (10.2) describes the law of motion for the total stock of gold in consumption and industrial use. $D(t)$ is equal to current consumption and industrial gold purchases. When $D(t)$ is positive, speculative hoards are reduced to accomodate the flow of gold into consumption and industrial uses. The quantity $\delta/q(t)$ is desired stock of gold used in industry and consumption, where $q(t)$ is the relative price of gold in terms of other goods at time t. Central in generating any post-monetization price level dynamics, the form of (10.2) reflects a slow transformation of gold into and out of consumption and industrial uses. Equation (10.2) is similar to a gold sector equation set up by Barro (1979).[10] However, we ignore gold mining and the effect that capital gains on gold may have on demand for consumption and industrial use.[11] Also, we treat gold as a perfectly durable good, which allows the possibility that gold may be disgorged from other uses into hoards when the relative price of gold rises sufficiently.[12]

Equation (10.3) is the condition that gold's relative price must rise at the real rate of interest while gold is held in speculative hoards. The intuition behind this condition is that speculators price gold currently such that its relative price can be expected to rise at the rate ρ. If the relative price were expected to rise faster than ρ, then the current price would be bid up until $\dot{q}(t)/q(t)$ falls to ρ. If the price were expected to rise more slowly than ρ, then the current price would fall until $\dot{q}(t)/q(t) = \rho$.[13]

Equations (10.1)–(10.3) form a system of differential equations in $D(t)$ and $q(t)$. To solve this system explicitly, we require an initial value, $D(0)$, for the non-speculative gold stock. Below we will develop a terminal condition for $q(t)$ which will also prove useful. Equation (10.3) yields

$$q(t) = q(0)e^{\{\rho t\}}, \text{ when } G(t) > 0 \tag{10.4}$$

Substituting from (10.4) into (10.2) generates a differential equation in $D(t)$ whose solution is[14]

$$D(t) = D(0)e^{\{-vt\}} + ve^{\{-vt\}} \int_0^t [\delta/q(0)] e^{\{(v-\rho)\tau\}} d\tau \tag{10.5}$$

To complete the solution we must determine $q(0)$. If T is the date when $\dot{D}(t) = 0$, then we must have $G(T) = 0$. Since hoards of speculative gold are held only in anticipation of future consumption and industrial gold uses, the speculative gold stock must be exhausted when additional gold use in these areas ceases. Since $G(T) = 0$, equation (1) implies

$$\bar{I} - \bar{R} = D(T). \tag{10.6}$$

Combining equations (10.6) and (10.2) and rearranging, we find

$$q(T) = \delta/(\bar{I} - \bar{R}) \tag{10.7}$$

Equation (10.7) indicates the 'choke price' for new consumption and industrial gold use, which is the terminal condition required to solve for $q(0)$. To find $q(0)$, we employ (10.7) and (10.4) to yield

$$q(0) = [\delta/(\bar{I} - \bar{R})] \, e^{\{-\rho T\}} \tag{10.8}$$

Our solution for the gold sector will be complete once we have determined the unknown choke date, T, which is a function of the initial condition $D(0)$. T is determined by substituting from (10.8) into (10.5) for $q(0)$ and setting $D(T) = \bar{I} - \bar{R}$. While this sequence of steps produces a single equation in T, the solution is complicated, so we do not pursue it further.[15]

Determining $q(0)$ completes our solution of the gold sector. Given $q(0)$, equation (10.4) indicates the time path of $q(t)$ from 0 to T; and $q(t) = q(T)$ for $t > T$. Further, given the initial condition $D(0)$, equation (10.5) determines the time path of $D(t)$ from 0 to T with $D(t) = D(T) = \bar{I} - \bar{R}$ for $t > T$. Thus the gold sector alone determines gold's relative price path and the quantity of gold held in purely speculative hoards. To find the nominal price of gold, however, we must append a monetary sector to our model.

The Monetary Sector

The operation of the monetary sector has no real effects in the model prior to the monetization of gold. We introduce the monetary sector now, however, as a preliminary to the analysis of the next section.

We assume that equations (10.9) and (10.10) govern money market equilibrium, i.e.

$$M(t)/P(t) = \beta - \alpha i(t) \qquad \beta, \alpha > 0 \tag{10.9}$$

$$i(t) = \rho + [\dot{P}(t)/P(t)] \tag{10.10}$$

where $M(t)$ is the nominal quantity of money, $P(t)$ is the aggregate price level, $i(t)$ is the nominal rate of interest and $[\dot{P}(t)/P(t)]$ is the expected and actual rate of inflation. We view (10.9) as a linearization which is appropriate for $\beta - \alpha i(t) > 0$ and for $\rho + [\dot{P}(t)/P(t)] > 0$.

In this section we set $M(t) = C(t)$, where $C(t)$ is the quantity of currency in circulation. The price level solution to (10.9) and (10.10) which is consistent with market fundamentals is[16]

$$P(t) = e^{\{\phi/\alpha\}t} \int_t^\infty \frac{C(\tau)}{\alpha} e^{\{-\phi/\alpha\tau\}} d\tau \qquad \text{where } \phi = \beta - \alpha\rho \qquad (10.11)$$

We define the nominal price of gold as $Q(t)$, so $q(t) = Q(t)/P(t)$.[17] The path of the nominal price of gold in our model prior to the announcement of gold monetization is $Q(t) = q(t)P(t)$, with $q(t)$ given in the previous part of this section.

The model of this section is devoid of interesting interactions between the gold and monetary sectors. However, such interactions are introduced by a policy of gold monetization, the topic of the next section.

THE DYNAMICS OF A GOLD STANDARD

In this section we study the price level, money market and gold market dynamics generated when a government decides to fix gold's nominal price, commiting itself to buy and sell gold at a price $\bar{Q}$. Unless gold market operations are sterilized in other markets, such as the bond market, government gold intervention either creates or destroys high-powered money. Through this channel a government's decision to fix gold's price links the money and gold markets. The interaction may be permanent, transient or only momentary, depending upon the environment in which the gold standard is initiated. We will develop a general framework capable of defining the conditions that determine in which category the dynamics of a particular gold standard may fit.

Before exploring the money–gold linkage in detail, we will first establish the conditions under which a government gold price-fixing scheme is viable. A price-fixing scheme collapses when the government fails to maintain the announced price, which requires the exhaustion of the gold reserves earmarked for the defense of the system. In general the collapse of a price-fixing policy coincides with a speculative attack on government reserves. A price-fixing scheme may be permanently viable, temporarily viable or non-viable. A permanently viable gold standard need never collapse; a temporarily viable scheme will function for some positive, finite period, collapsing at a predictable time. A non-viable gold standard will collapse at the instant of its implementation.

Non-Viable Gold Monetization

We will first discuss a non-viable gold monetization scheme; later we will analyze price-fixing policies that are viable, if only for a transient period. Initially, we assume that the government announces suddenly that the nominal gold price will be fixed immediately at some level $\bar{Q}$. Prior to this surprise announcement, agents had expected a particular money growth path in determining their behavior. We assume that, given the non-viability of the gold monetization, the government will continue the money growth path according to these previous expectations. More precisely, suppose that $M(\tau)$, $\tau > 0$, was the anticipated money growth path prior to a surprise gold monetization at time 0 and that the gold standard terminates after a period of length z. Letting $M'(\tau + z)$, $\tau > 0$, be the post-gold standard money growth path, we assume $M(\tau) = M'(\tau + z)$ for all τ and for any $z > 0$. Under this assumption the fiat 'money growth clock' stops at the instant of gold monetization, restarting at its final fiat regime position instantly upon gold demonetization. That the government behaves in such a manner following the attempted monetization's collapse is a strong and arbitrary assumption which we make for ease of comparison of the pre- and post-announcement situations. Any alternative assumption concerning post-collapse monetary policy can be analyzed in a manner similar to that below.[18]

For our analysis we will presume that the pre-announcement supply of high-powered money is at least sufficient to purchase the government's gold reserve at the fixed price $\bar{Q}$, i.e. $M(0) = C(0) > \bar{Q}\bar{R}$, where time zero is the instant of implementation. If the money supply were less than $\bar{Q}\bar{R}$, the gold standard could not collapse because agents could not buy all of the government's gold.[19]

An attempt to fix the nominal gold price will fail if agents can profit by purchasing the government's gold stock, $\bar{R}$, at the government's price $\bar{Q}$ and reselling it at the immediate, post-collapse, market-determined price $\tilde{Q}(t)$. A sufficient condition to generate the immediate collapse of the price-fixing attempt is $\bar{Q} < \tilde{Q}(t)$, which follows from the infinite profit rate available to speculators who immediately attack the government's reserves.

To determine $\tilde{Q}(t)$ at any instant, we can employ the gold market model of the last section. Following the collapse of a non-viable price-fixing attempt, the stock of gold available to the private sector jumps from $(\bar{I} - \bar{R})$ to $\bar{I}$. Provided that there is no further attempt to monetize gold, the private sector will eventually absorb this augmented stock into consumption and industrial uses at some date T at a choke price

$\tilde{Q}(T)/\tilde{P}(T) = \delta/\bar{I}$. $\tilde{P}(T)$ is the price level at T, given that a collapse of the price fixing scheme has previously occurred.[20]

To establish dating, we define the current instant in time to be time 0. If, at time 0, a gold monetization scheme is suddenly attempted, it will be attacked immediately by speculators whenever

$$\bar{Q} < \tilde{Q}(0) = \tilde{P}(0)\,[\delta/\bar{I}]\,e^{\{-\rho T\}} \tag{10.12}$$

The equality in (10.12) follows because $\tilde{Q}(0)$ is simply the free market nominal gold price derived in the last section. To find $\tilde{P}(0)$, we must account for the linkage between gold and the money supply. Given that the government gold stock is run immediately at time 0, agents purchase the entire government stock at the abortive price $\bar{Q}$. Since the gold reserves are exchanged for currency, $\bar{Q}\bar{R}$ in nominal money balances is destroyed in the speculative attack. Consequently, the post-attack price level declines in accord with this once-and-for-all displacement in the money supply path. The price level change effected by this displacement is $-\bar{Q}\bar{R}/\phi$, so $\tilde{P}(0) = P(0) - [\bar{Q}\bar{R}/\phi]$. $P(0)$, given in equation (10.11), is the price level immediately prior to the abortive monetization attempt. Combining this result with (10.12), we obtain the explicit condition for

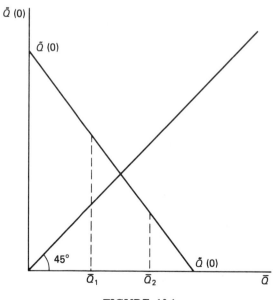

FIGURE 10.1

an attack

$$\bar{Q} < \tilde{Q}(0) = [P(0)\,\delta/\bar{I}]\,e^{\{-\rho T\}} - [\bar{Q}\bar{R}\,\delta/\phi\bar{I}]\,e^{\{-\rho T\}} \tag{10.13}$$

We re-emphasize that the form of the condition depends crucially on the assumed post-collapse money supply process. If the monetary effects of the collapse were sterilized or if the money growth process after the collapse were different from previous anticipations due to the abortive monetization attempt, then condition (13) would assume a different form.

In Figure 10.1, the line $\tilde{Q}(0)\tilde{Q}(0)$ is a graph of $\tilde{Q}(0)$ as a function of Q, based on (10.13). The slope of $\tilde{Q}(0)\tilde{Q}(0)$ is $-[\bar{R}\delta/\phi\bar{I}]\,e^{\{-\rho T\}}$, and the vertical intercept is $[P(0)\,\delta/\bar{I}]\,e^{-\rho T}$. In the figure the fixed price $\bar{Q}_1$ is not viable, while $\bar{Q}_2$ is either permanently or temporarily viable. Because an increase in $P(0)$ raises the vertical intercept of $\tilde{Q}(0)\tilde{Q}(0)$, there is a value of $P(0)$ high enough that any given $\bar{Q}$ is not viable.

Permanently Viable Gold Monetization

If the government sets $\bar{Q} > \tilde{Q}(0)$, the gold standard will function at least temporarily because there will be no profit from a speculative attack. We will now analyze the dynamics of a workable standard.

As mentioned previously, the key element integrating the monetary and gold sectors after price fixing is the money supply. After gold monetization the money supply is

$$M(t) = M(0) + \bar{Q}[R(t) - \bar{R}] + \bar{Q}G(t) \tag{10.14}$$

$M(0)$ is the quantity of high-powered money existing at the instant prior to gold monetization. $\bar{Q}[R(t) - \bar{R}]$ is the nominal value of government gold purchases after the price is fixed.

$\bar{Q}G(t)$ is the nominal value of gold used directly as money. Since gold's price is fixed in terms of currency, gold will yield the same nominal capital gain as currency. Since gold can also serve as money, those hoards remaining in private hands must, as perfect substitutes for currency, constitute part of the money stock. Since we cannot determine the split of monetary gold between government and private holding, it is convenient to define

$$X(t) \equiv R(t) + G(t) \tag{10.15}$$

Our framework allows us to keep track of $X(t)$ but not of its components.

Using the variable $X(t)$, the money supply can be written as

$$M(t) = M(0) - \bar{Q}R + \bar{Q}X(t) \tag{10.16}$$

Since we assume that the government's only open market operations occur in the gold market, only movements in $X(t)$ affect $M(t)$ after gold's price is fixed. Substituting from equation (10.16) for the money supply in (10.9), we obtain one of the equations of motion for the gold standard regime:

$$\dot{P}(t) = \phi P(t) - [\bar{Q}/\alpha]X(t) - [M(0) - \bar{Q}\bar{R}]/\alpha \tag{10.17}$$

The dynamics of the variable $X(t)$ are determined from those of $D(t)$ in equation (10.5). Since $D(t) = (\bar{I} - X(t))$ and $\dot{X}(t) = -\dot{D}(t)$, we substitute for $D(t)$ and $\dot{D}(t)$ in (10.2) to derive

$$X(t) = -[v\delta/\bar{Q}]P(t) - vX(t) + v\bar{I} \tag{10.18}$$

Equations (10.17) and (10.18) are the laws of motion of $P(t)$ and $X(t)$ under the gold standard. Since $D(t)$ is a slowly adjusting state variable, $X(t)$ also adjusts slowly. However, $P(t)$ is a jumping or currently determined variable.

In Figure 10.2 we depict the dynamics implicit in (10.17) and (10.18). The lines PP and XX are the loci of points $(P(t), X(t))$ such that $\dot{P}(t) = 0$ and $\dot{X}(t) = 0$, respectively. PP and XX intersect at the dynamic system's steady state price level and monetary gold stock, $\hat{P}$ and $\hat{X}$, whose values are

$$\hat{P} = \frac{\bar{Q}[\bar{I} - \bar{R}] + M(0)}{\phi + \delta} \tag{10.19}$$

$$\hat{X} = \frac{\phi\bar{I} + \delta[\bar{R} - (M(0)/\bar{Q})]}{\phi + \delta}. \tag{10.20}$$

The arrows in the figure indicate directions of motion of $P(t)$ and $X(t)$ in the various quadrants of the figure bounded by PP and XX. The dynamics imply that the steady state is a saddlepoint with a unique stable branch, indicated by the line SS.[21] For a permanently viable gold standard we assume that economic forces determine $P(t)$, given $X(t)$, such that $P(t)$ and $X(t)$ lie on the line SS.[22] For example, if $X(0) > \hat{X}$ as in the figure, then $P(0) > \hat{P}$; and both $P(t)$ and $X(t)$ will move along SS, approaching the steady state.

Figure 10.2 also contains the locus $\hat{P}(\bar{Q})\hat{X}(\bar{Q})$. We will refer to this locus, which indicates $\hat{P}\hat{X}$ combinations for all possible values of $\bar{Q}$, as the gold standard's *steady state locus*. Once we are given a fixed gold

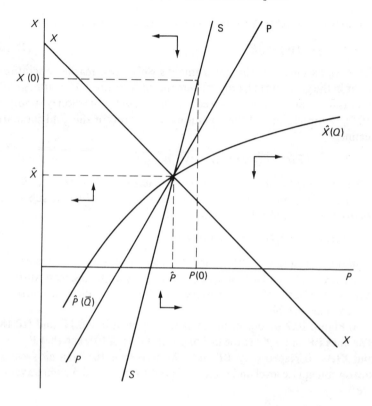

FIGURE 10.2

price $\bar{Q}$, we can determine the gold standard's entire future dynamics by reference to the steady state locus.[23] Associated with each possible choice of $\bar{Q}$, there is a steady state $\{\hat{P}(\bar{Q}), \hat{X}(\bar{Q})\}$; for each $\bar{Q}$ there is a single point on the steady state locus. The locus is non-linear and positively sloping; higher values of $\bar{Q}$ are associated with higher values of $\hat{P}$ and $\hat{X}$.

The steady state locus is not precluded from cutting the P-axis, a possibility that we shall exploit in some later analysis. Therefore, the dynamic model may imply negative values of $\hat{X}$ for sufficiently low values of $\bar{Q}$. More precisely, from equation (10.20) any $\bar{Q} < [\delta M(0)/(\phi \bar{I} + \delta \bar{R})]$ will yield a value of $\hat{X}$ which is less than zero. However, since $\hat{X} < 0$ implies $D(t) > \bar{I}$ for some t, the dynamic path of the system cannot lead to the steady state because $D(t)$ is constrained to be less than or equal to $\bar{I}$. Understanding that the dynamics of the system cannot lead to a negative $\hat{X}$, agents in the system will foresee an eventual end of the gold standard dynamics, i.e. a collapse of the gold standard. However, since $\bar{Q} > \tilde{Q}(0)$, the gold standard will be temporarily viable, with the collapse deferred to some future date. Again, the combination of a given $\bar{Q}$ and the steady state locus determines whether the gold standard evolves along this particular path. We shall study the notion of a forecastable collapse in more detail below.

In Figure 10.3 we integrate the elements of our gold standard model. The right-hand panel of the figure contains the steady state locus from Figure 10.2 and two examples of possible stable branches, the lines $S_1 S_1$ and $S_3 S_3$ positioned in accord with the possible fixed prices $\bar{Q}_1$ and $\bar{Q}_3$ respectively. In the left-hand panel we plot the curve $\hat{X}(Q)\hat{X}(Q)$, depicting the relation between $\hat{X}$ and $\hat{Q}$; this curve is based on equation (10.20).

Figure 10.3 is useful in analyzing the dynamics of a gold standard

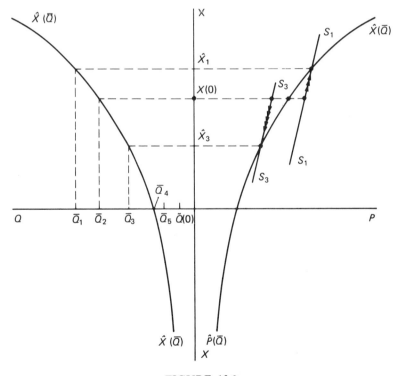

FIGURE 10.3

economy for which the initial value of X is given arbitrarily at $X(0) = (\bar{I} - D(0))$. A crucial assumption in employing the diagram is that $\bar{Q}(0)$ lies between the origin and that value $\bar{Q}_4$ such that $\hat{X}(\bar{Q}_4) = 0$. For many types of money growth paths, this will be a relevant assumption; however, for some paths $\tilde{Q}(0)$ will lie to the left of $\bar{Q}_4$. For such economies the gold standard is either permanent or it collapses immediately; a temporarily functioning gold standard is precluded.[24]

Given $X(0)$, Figure 10.3 presents us with a menu from which we can determine the dynamics of any gold standard for any choice of the fixed price $\bar{Q}$. For example, the price $\bar{Q}_1$ determines the value $\hat{X}_1 > X(0)$ and positions the stable branch $S_1 S_1$ through X_1 on the steady state locus. An economy with initial condition $X(0)$, confronted with a fixed gold price $\bar{Q}_1$, will determine the equilibrium price level such that it begins at point 1 along $S_1 S_1$. The gold standard dynamics are then completely determined, involving a movement along $S_1 S_1$ toward the steady state, with both $P(t)$ and $X(t)$ rising through time. If the fixed gold price is set relatively high, as at $\bar{Q}_1$, after the advent of the gold standard there will arise a gold inflation attributable to the disgorging of gold from consumption and industrial use into monetary use. For the price $\bar{Q}_2$, the associated steady state $\hat{X}_2$ equals $X(0)$. If $\bar{Q}_2$ is selected, the economy moves immediately to its steady state, point 2 on the steady state locus.[25] $\bar{Q}_2$ is the unique gold price at which agents are exactly satisfied to hold consumption and industrial gold stocks $D(0) = \bar{I} - X(0)$; therefore, no adjustments in the price level are required following the initial adjustment to the gold standard.[26]

The price $\bar{Q}_3$ yields $\hat{X}_3 < X(0)$. Accordingly, the initial position of the economy will be at point 3 on $S_3 S_3$; and both $X(t)$ and $P(t)$ will decline in their approach to the steady state. The gold deflation in this case results from setting a relatively low gold price, drawing the monetary gold stock into consumption and industrial uses.

The price $\bar{Q}_4$ is the lowest possible permanently viable gold price. At $\bar{Q}_4$, $\hat{X}(\bar{Q}_4)$ equals zero, implying that all gold will be driven from monetary uses in the steady state.[27]

Temporarily Viable Gold Standards

Gold prices below $\bar{Q}_4$ cannot yield permanently viable gold standards since they imply associated steady states with $\hat{X} < 0$. In particular, a gold price such as $\bar{Q}_6 < \tilde{Q}(0)$ produces a non-viable gold standard which collapses at its inception and obviates the gold standard dynamics portrayed in the right-hand panel. Gold prices like $\bar{Q}_5$ which lie between $\tilde{Q}(0)$ and $\bar{Q}_4$ are obviously not sustainable; however, at the outset these fixed prices are higher than the gold price, $\tilde{Q}(0)$, which would prevail following an immediate attack. Therefore the price $\bar{Q}_5$ will not generate an immediate collapse; but the dynamics that it initiates lead to a foreseeable future attack on government reserves. Prices like $\bar{Q}_5$ produce temporarily viable gold standards.

The notion of a transient, viable gold standard, implying a predictable future collapse, may seem alien to the economist who associates the collapse with foreseeable profit opportunities arising from discrete future gold price and price level movements. However, S–H, Krugman (1979) and Salant (1981) have shown that an anticipated collapse of a price-fixing scheme is barren of profit opportunities. In our gold standard example, the price level and gold accumulation rate will adjust immediately to preclude predictable speculative profit opportunities. Although it is an important development, the S–H result has received scant attention; hence we will spend some effort to present the concept in the context of our model.

It is possible to derive a method for determining z, the time of the collapse. However, since we were unable to construct a closed-form solution for z, we will present only a general analysis of the price continuity results necessary to approach a solution, leaving the complete discussion of the determination of z to the appendix. $\tilde{Q}(z)$ and $\tilde{P}(z)$ are the post-collapse gold price and price level respectively. If $\bar{Q}_5$ is the fixed gold price, the collapse will occur only if $\tilde{Q}(z) \geqslant \bar{Q}_5$. If agents forsee $\tilde{Q}(z) > \bar{Q}_5$, then they anticipate a profit opportunity at z. Competition among agents planning to arbitrage the collapse of the gold standard will lead some agents to purchase the government's gold stock just prior to z in order to reap the entire arbitrage profit. Since the collapse would then occur prior to z, a foreseeable collapse at time z can occur only if $\tilde{Q}(z) = \bar{Q}_5$.

Since goods are storable in our model, there can also be no anticipated price level jumps inherent in the gold standard's collapse, even though the money stock will discretely decline. Foreseeable price level discontinuities would open profitable arbitrage opportunities involving the storable good. For example, if, just prior to time z, agents expect that the price level will discretely fall at z, then they will seek to dispose of their goods prior to z. Consequently the price level must fall before time z until agents are satisfied with their holdings of the good. The equilibrium price level will be determined currently such that at time z its path is continuous.

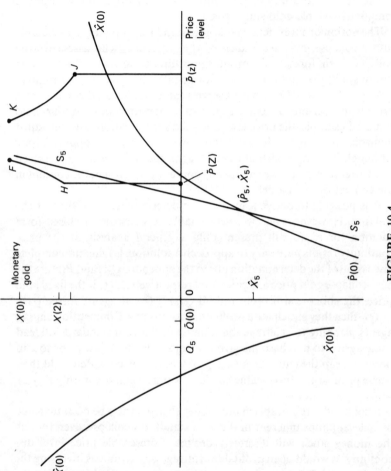

FIGURE 10.4

We can graphically analyze the dynamics of a temporarily viable gold standard using the concepts developed in Figure 10.3. In Figure 10.4 we have reproduced that section of Figure 10.3 for the region around $\bar{Q}_5$, a temporarily viable gold price, which is greater than $\tilde{Q}(0)$. In Figure 10.4, $\hat{X}_5$ is negative, so if this economy follows the dynamic path indicated by the saddle path, the gold standard must eventually collapse. Recognizing the coming collapse, agents foresee that afterwards the price level and relative gold price will be driven by the dynamic laws established in the last section. In particular, the price level $\tilde{P}(z)$ will be determined from equation (11) as a function of the future money supplies generated by the fiat money system. Therefore, since $\tilde{P}(z)$ rather than $\hat{P}(\bar{Q}_5)$ serves as the terminal condition for the gold standard dynamics, the price level and monetary gold stock cannot move along the saddle path during the gold standard's temporary existence. Instead, the system will follow an ostensibly unstable path like $FH\tilde{P}(z)$ and collapse when the monetary gold stock reaches $X(z)$, the gold hoard which agents are just willing to hold in the fiat system of the last section. The path $FH\tilde{P}(z)$ implies a deflation while the gold standard functions. Of course, if the post-collapse fiat money growth is expected to be great enough, the system may follow a path like $KJ\tilde{P}^*(z)$, implying a steady inflation prior to the collapse.

The Dynamics of Future Gold Monetization

Recent proposals to monetize gold involve a current announcement to fix gold's price on a given future date. Using the concepts already developed to study a policy of immediate gold monetization, we can readily analyze the case of future price fixing at some nominal $\bar{Q}$. We will discuss at a general level the transformations required of our previous arguments to encompass such a policy.

We assume that at time 0 the government announces that it will attempt to monetize gold at price $\bar{Q}$ starting at time w. The scheme will be permanently or temporarily viable only if $\bar{Q} > \tilde{Q}(w)$. $\tilde{Q}(w)$ can be determined from equation (10.12) with $\tilde{P}(w)$ replacing $\tilde{P}(0)$ where

$$\tilde{P}(w) = -[\bar{Q}\bar{R}/\phi] + e^{\{\phi/\alpha w\}} \int_w^\infty \frac{M(\tau)}{\alpha} e^{\{-\phi/\alpha\tau\}} d\tau \qquad (10.21)$$

Given that the scheme is either permanently or temporarily viable, the future gold standard can be analyzed using a diagram like Figure 10.3, except that the steady state locus and the $\hat{X}(\bar{Q})\hat{X}(\bar{Q})$ locus are repositioned to reflect the difference between $M(w)$ and $M(0)$. The only remaining unknown is the value of $X(w)$. With the immediate price-fixing policy, $X(0)$ is a pre-determined variable. However, for $w > 0$, the government policy will influence the value of $X(w)$ through the effect of the announcement on the relative gold price in the pre-monetization period. Using equation (10.5) we can determine $D(w)$, which equals $\bar{I} - X(w)$, from the time path of the relative gold price between times 0 and w. In (10.5) the relative price of gold immediately after the announcement is $q(0) = [\bar{Q}/P(w)]e^{\{-\rho w\}}$. For the permanently viable gold standard, $P(w)$ is restricted to lie on the relevant stable branch in the altered Figure 10.3, $P(w) = A(\bar{Q})X(w) + \hat{P}(\bar{Q}) - A(\bar{Q})\hat{X}(\bar{Q})$, where $A(\bar{Q})$ is a function of the parameters of the system.[28] If the system is only temporarily viable, then $P(w)$ will lie on a dynamic path such as $FH\tilde{P}$ $(w+z)$ in a revised Figure 10.4, which starts at $X(w)$ and attains $\tilde{P}(w+z)$ precisely at the moment of collapse $w+z$. Substituting expressions for either of these paths for $P(w)$ in the relative price formula for $q(0)$ and for $q(0)$ in equation (10.5) yields a single equation in the unknown $X(w)$.[29] Armed with a solution for $X(w)$, we can proceed with an analysis of the future gold standard's dynamics with exactly the same methods pursued in connection with Figure 10.3.

Price Level Effects of Gold Monetization

Since the proposed gold monetization is intended to provide a more stable price level than that provided by the current fiat system, we now employ our model to study the response of the price level to a monetary gold system.

If the gold price is set low enough that the system is non-viable, the government's gold stock is attacked immediately. Since the money stock falls discretely by an amount $\bar{Q}\bar{R}$, the price level path is instantly displaced downward by $\bar{Q}\bar{R}/\phi$ if there is no other alteration in the government's previous money growth plans.

If the gold standard is permanently or temporarily viable, its price level effects depend on the specific monetary growth path followed prior to the gold standard's announcement, the initial conditions and parameters of the model and the fixed gold price.

As an example we may consider the price level effects of a permanently viable system. In Figure 10.5 we plot monetary aggregates against time. Prior to the implementation of the gold standard at time 0, agents had expected the monetary policy given by $M(0)M(t)$, in which money

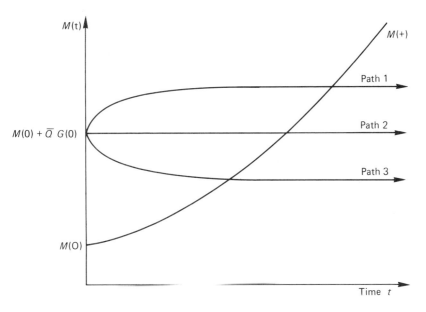

FIGURE 10.5

increases with time. When gold's price is fixed at $\bar{Q}$, the monetary aggregate immediately jumps from $M(0)$ to $M(0) + \bar{Q}G(0)$, where $G(0) > 0$ is the private gold hoard just prior to monetization. Once the gold standard begins, the money stock is driven by the movement of $X(t)$. If $\bar{Q}_1$ from Figure 10.3 is the gold price, the money stock will rise after time 0, asymptotically approaching a constant level, as in path 1 in Figure 10.5. If $\bar{Q}$ is such that $X(0) = \hat{X}(\bar{Q})$, the money stock will be constant as in path 2. Finally, if a price like $\bar{Q}_3$ in Figure 10.3 is set, then the money stock will decline asymptotically toward some constant level as in path 3.

Since the price level is a weighted average of future money stocks, it cannot be readily determined that the gold standard stabilizes prices relative to the fiat system. In order to determine the price level effects of the monetary system change, we must know the future money stock paths. Evidently, the money stock can evolve in any number of different ways, generating gold inflation, gold deflation, or price stability. The gold standard may be more or less stabilizing than the fiat system, depending on the initial speculative gold stocks, the parameters of gold and money demand, and the fixed gold price.

In practice, the price level can be stabilized by sterilizing the shift in the money growth path at the instant of monetization and choosing a gold price like $\bar{Q}_2$ in Figure 10.3 to place the system at its steady state. If prior notice of the monetization is given, the growth path of fiat money in the interim period must also shift to prevent immediate price jumps and price changes in the transition.

A Glossary for Commodity Standard Dynamics

In this section we wish to establish a terminology that will be useful in encompassing the concepts developed in previous sections and in categorizing particular types of commodity standard dynamics. The dynamic evolution of monetary standards developed thus far has been relatively uncomplicated. At most we have considered the possibility of two sequential switches in the dynamic laws which drive the money stock: from a fiat system there is a switch to a gold standard which may lead to a permanent return to a fiat system. In this dimension it is possible to imagine an *oscillating monetary standard* which fluctuates from a fiat base to a gold base with the transitions marked by runs on gold or by popular rejection of fiat. In another dimension the switches may consist of shifts from one commodity base to another, so that there are more than two possible dynamic laws that may drive the money stock in particular eras. The change in commodity base may occur directly with no intervening period of fiat money, or there may be a transitional period when the government does not attempt to fix the nominal price of any commodity. While such *compound commodity standards* are evocative of their own rich nomenclature, they can be analyzed by recursive application of methods employed in previous sections; so we will concentrate primarily on categorizing those dynamic phenomena which we have already considered.

First, we define a *main-sequence commodity standard* as any permanent commodity-based monetary standard which follows the dynamics associated with the stable saddle path of its dynamic system. For a commodity standard *on the main sequence*, the dynamic path can be completely determined from the steady state locus and the current value of $X(t)$ alone. Conversely, while a commodity standard *off the main sequence* follows the same general laws of motion as a main-sequence standard, it moves along an ostensibly unstable path whose track can be determined only from knowledge of the post-collapse money generation process. Thus, temporary commodity standards follow more eccentric dynamics than do main-sequence standards. Examples of main-sequence commodity standards are the gold standards associated with the gold prices $\bar{Q}_1, \bar{Q}_2, \bar{Q}_3$ and $\bar{Q}_4$ in Figure 10.3. The gold standard with price $\bar{Q}_5$ is a commodity standard off the main sequence.

The gold price $\bar{Q}_4$ in Figure 10.3 is the minimum fixed price for a main-sequence gold standard. We refer to $\bar{Q}_4$, which can be determined from equation (10.20) as $\bar{Q}_4 = [\delta M(0)]/[\phi \bar{I} + \delta \bar{R}]$, as the *main-sequence limit price*. Similarly, the phantom free market price $\tilde{Q}(t)$ establishes a minimum price bound on the very existence of a gold standard. At fixed prices below $\tilde{Q}(t)$, a commodity standard would explode, engendering a fiat system among its debris; in this sense, the fiat system is a corpse of a collapsed commodity standard. We refer to $\tilde{Q}(t)$ as a *commodity standard limit price*.

Using these definitions we can categorize the regions along the horizontal axis in the left panel of Figure 10.3. If the fixed price is greater than the main-sequence limit price, the commodity standard is on the main sequence. If the fixed price is less than the main-sequence limit price but greater than the commodity standard limit price, the commodity standard is off the main sequence. If the fixed price is less than the commodity standard limit price, the commodity standard instantly collapses.

Some Extensions of the Analysis

At this point we wish to discuss the implications of relaxing three important and rather arbitrary assumptions used in our previous analysis. The assumptions are: (a) $QR < M(0)$; (b) the only open market operations undertaken while the gold standard functions are gold market operations; and (c) the money growth path after a gold standard collapse is simply the pre-gold standard expected growth path displaced in time by the duration of the gold standard.

Given that the only open market operations occur in the gold market during the gold standard era, the assumption that $\bar{Q}\bar{R} < M(0)$ implies that $\bar{Q}R(\tau) < M(\tau)$ for all τ. There will always be enough currency to purchase all of the government's gold at the fixed price $\bar{Q}$, a necessary condition for a collapse of a gold standard. Alternatively, if we assume $\bar{Q}\bar{R} > M(0)$, the gold standard cannot collapse. When open market operations are allowed only in the gold market, further currency creation coincides with additions to the government gold stocks. Since the government's reserves, always maintaining a greater value than outstanding claims, will never be attacked, the analysis for a permanently functioning gold standard is applicable.

It is possible also to relax our assumption that open market operations occur only in the gold market during the gold standard era. If gold's price is set greater than the main-sequence limit price, the monetary authorities, though continually maintaining the fixed gold price, possess some discretion to increase the money stock through channels other than gold purchases. Such monetary expansions, unless expected to be transitory, raise both the main-sequence limit price and the shadow free market price, $\tilde{Q}(t)$. To determine the degree of discretion available to the monetary authorities we must find the maximum monetary issue during the gold standard such that $\bar{Q}$ exceeds the main-sequence limit price. In the definition of the main-sequence limit price, $\bar{Q}_4$, we showed explicitly the dependence between this price and the money stock, $\bar{Q}_4 = [\delta M(0)]/[\phi \bar{I} + \delta \bar{R}]$. Since the permanent existence of the gold standard requires that $\bar{Q}_4 \leqslant \bar{Q}$, the maximum permanent monetary issue during the gold standard is prescribed. In this limited sense, the gold standard may be said to impose some 'discipline' on the monetary authority.

Finally, we have assumed that money growth path following the collapse of a gold standard is the pre-gold standard path displaced in time by the gold standard's duration. Formally, this assumption is $\dot{M}(\tau) = \dot{M}'(\tau + z)$ for all $\tau > 0$, where $\dot{M}(\tau)$ is the pre-gold standard expected growth path, $\dot{M}'(\tau + z)$ is the post-gold standard growth path, and z is the duration of the gold standard. To illustrate the importance of this assumption, we consider an alternative in which we suppose that the post-gold standard money growth path corresponds exactly *in calendar time* to the pre-gold standard expected path. Formally, this assumption is $\dot{M}(\tau) = \dot{M}'(\tau)$ for all $\tau > 0$. If fiat money growth is always some constant μ, then $\dot{M}(\tau) = \dot{M}'(\tau) = \dot{M}'(\tau + z) = \mu$ and the altered assumption is immaterial. However, if the expected rate of fiat money growth were *growing* under the pre-gold standard regime, then the two assumptions are substantively different. When $\dot{M}'(\tau + z) = \dot{M}(\tau)$, accelerating money growth in the conditional fiat regime does not affect the value of $\tilde{Q}(t)$ while the gold standard exists. However, if $\dot{M}(\tau) = \dot{M}'(\tau)$, then accelerating conditional fiat money growth will continually raise $\tilde{Q}(t)$ during the gold standard era until it exceeds $\bar{Q}$, destroying the gold standard if $\bar{Q}\bar{R} < M(0)$.

THE DISCIPLINE OF THE GOLD STANDARD

Having studied a number of positive issues, we now turn to some normative questions associated with a gold standard. Any pressure to reestablish a commodity base for the monetary system rests on a conviction that the 'discipline' generated by such constraining rules yields beneficial price level stability or at least predictability. However, viewed in a dynamic context of periodic movements from commodity to fiat monetary systems, the 'discipline' of commodity systems is a mask obscuring the forces which drive the global dynamic money creation process. Since all commodity standard interludes eventually are superseded by fiat systems, the notion of 'discipline' can characterize only the underlying forces generating the entire dynamic monetary process. The application of this concept to only one facet of a general policy sequence, overlooking the empirical realization that all previous commodity standards have collapsed into fiat systems, may lead to misplaced confidence in prescriptions to return to a commodity base.

Behind the sequential transitions from one monetary scheme to another which we have analyzed must lie a political economy which we have ignored of necessity. Such political economic forces determine the complete dynamic panorama of the monetary process. Their nature can be gauged only by the *entire sequence* of monetary bases, not by the ephemeral monetary base that may operate currently. If the fiat segments of the money creation process are inflationary enough, then an existing commodity standard cannot be maintained, even though conditional on its continuation the money stock would grow according to the commodity standard's dynamic laws. A commodity system can be interpreted as a discipline-imposing rule only if the commodity standard's permanence is somehow guaranteed. Since there is absolutely no means of securing such permanence, the notion of a commodity standard as a stabilizing rule is a chimera. The monetary system is stable only if the global money generation scheme and agents' confidence in it produce stability, not if money is temporarily created according to some transitional rule.

To illustrate this point we focus on the gold standard limit price $\tilde{Q}(t)$ whose value, determined from equation (12), depends in part on the price level $\tilde{P}(t)$ which would prevail if the gold standard suddenly collapses. From equation (11) $\tilde{P}(t)$ itself depends on the correctly anticipated future path of fiat money creation, conditional on the end of the gold standard. We note that there exist many conditional fiat paths capable of determining $\tilde{P}(t)$ at any arbitrary level. In particular there are conditional paths that can raise $\tilde{Q}(t)$ above $\bar{Q}$, collapsing the system and causing the conditional paths actually to materialize.

If conditions arise which indicate that a government is likely to produce highly inflationary monetary policies in the absence of a gold standard, then the gold standard, even though maintained by a government conditionally and scrupulously obeying its rules, cannot survive. The gold standard is but one phase of an overall policy; if the entire constellation of conditional monetary standards is not relatively stable, the stability of any one of its conditional elements is precluded. When this result is contrasted with current policy discussions which prescribe a return to some type of commodity standard *because* conditional fiat systems are too unstable, it becomes apparent that simply comparing the price level dynamics of two permanent money generation schemes yields misleading results. The central political economic problem, that fiat systems are unstable, overrides any stabilizing properties of permanently viable commodity standards. Unless a political system somehow insures stability of the conditional fiat epochs of its money generation process, implementing a commodity standard will be a provisional, if not momentary, exercise. To conduct analysis of changes in monetary systems requires the recognition that all monetary generation rules are temporary, predictably to be replaced under some circumstances.

CONCLUSION

There are many possible commodities that can serve as monetary standards. However, the sequence of items upon which the monetary system has been based in modern times has been so limited that it can readily be characterized as a 'gold–paper–gold' cycle. Since the current 'paper' phase of the cycle has allowed price level instability, there has been some agitation to return to the gold standard. Proponents of such a return presume that simply allowing the market to determine the price at which gold will be fixed is sufficient to produce an 'appropriate' price, imposing discipline on the money generation process. A result of this paper is that such policies will lead to price level stability only in the presence of very specific, coincident monetary actions. To determine the nature of such policies requires detailed knowledge of the structure of the gold and money markets, the nature of expectations, and the dynamics of the price level and of private gold accumulation. In the absence of such monetary actions, implementing a policy to set the gold price according to a given day's market price may lead to a situation even more inflationary than that produced by the current system. Furthermore, the concept of the discipline enforced by a gold standard has no operational significance; 'discipline' is a meaningful concept only in the context of the full array of monetary standards that may conditionally materialize.

APPENDIX

In our perfect foresight model, an anticipation of an attack on government gold reserves, taking place at some time z, precludes jumps in the gold price or the price level at time z. Formally, this implies $P(z) = P(z_+) = \tilde{P}(z)$ and $\bar{Q} = Q(z_+) = \tilde{Q}(z)$, where z_+ is the instant after the run. With our money growth assumption, $\tilde{P}(z) = P(0) - [\bar{Q}\bar{R}/\phi]$. Since we know $\bar{Q} = \tilde{Q}(z)$, the relative price of gold at time z is $q(z) = \bar{Q}/\{P(0) - [\bar{Q}\bar{R}/\phi]\}$; this will serve as an initial condition for the relative gold price at time z. Furthermore, since the gold market model of section two above governs the gold price after the collapse, we also obtain the terminal condition $q(T) = \delta/\bar{I}$. Since $\dot{q}(t) = \rho q(t)$, we combine the initial and terminal conditions to find

$$T - z = [1/\rho]\ln(\delta/q(z)\bar{I}) \tag{10.A1}$$

According to (10.A1), gold will be held in speculative hoards for a period $\eta \equiv [1/\rho]\ln(\delta/q(z)\bar{I})$ after the collapse.

Knowing η allows us to determine $D(z)$ at the instant of the collapse. The accumulation requirement is

$$\bar{I} = D(z)e^{-v\eta} + e^{-vT}\int_z^T [v\delta\rho/q(z)]e^{\{-\rho(\tau - z) + v\tau\}}\,d\tau \tag{10.A2}$$

or

$$\bar{I} = D(z)e^{-v\eta} + \{v\delta\rho/q(z)(v - \rho)\}[e^{-\rho\eta} - e^{-v\eta}] \tag{10.A2a}$$

Equation (10.A2a) determines $D(z)$ as a function of $q(z)$, and since $\bar{I} = D(z) + X(z)$, we can determine $X(z)$.

Armed with the values $P(z)$ and $X(z)$, we can determine z by reference to the general solution for the price level and monetary gold given by the gold standard dynamics. That solution is

$$P(t) = c_1 A e^{\lambda_1 t} + c_2 B e^{\lambda_2 t} + \hat{P}, t < z \tag{10.A3}$$

$$X(t) = c_1 e^{\lambda_1 t} + c_2 e^{\lambda_2 t} + \hat{X}, t < z \tag{10.A4}$$

where $A = \bar{Q}/(\phi - \alpha\lambda_1)$, $B = \bar{Q}/(\phi - \alpha\lambda_2)$, λ_1 is the system's negative root, and λ_2 is the positive root.

To find z we first must solve for the constants c_1 and c_2 using our knowledge that (a) $P(z)$ in (10.A3) in $P(0) - [\bar{Q}\bar{R}/\phi]$ and (b) $X(0)$ is some value given by an initial condition as in the text. These constants will be functions of z and the parameters of the model. Next, since we know $X(z)$, we set $X(t)$ in (10.A4) equal to $X(z)$. This will produce a single non-linear equation in the unknown time of collapse z which, in principle, can be solved.

NOTES

1. The views presented in this paper are those of the authors and do not necessarily represent the views of the Governors of the Federal Reserve or other members of their staff. We would like to thank the National Science Foundation for financial support. Helpful comments were given by Dale Henderson, Jeff Frankel, Ken Rogoff and various participants in seminars at Rice University, the University of Florida, the University of Chicago, the University of Pennsylvania, MIT, the University of California at Berkeley, the Board of Governors of the Federal Reserve, and the University of South Carolina. The extensive comments of an anonymous referee proved enormously useful.
2. Congress decided to assess the role of gold in the domestic and international monetary systems through the establishment of a Gold Commission. While the Commission was generally hostile to the monetization of gold, its existence indicates that a return to a commodity base is a serious possibility.
3. For discussions of the time inconsistency problem, see Kydland and Prescott (1978) or Barro and Gordon (1981).
4. Laffer proposes to have the government announce that gold will be monetized at the market price prevailing on a certain future date. To prevent inflation in the interim, the government would follow an 'austere' monetary policy and sell a large portion of its gold holdings. Lehrman's proposal is somewhat different in that he requires that gold's price be fixed at its market-determined level as long as wages are not required to fall.
5. Recent proposals for government intervention in the gold market have suggested that the government should announce currently its intention to fix the nominal gold price at the market price prevailing on a fixed future date. Since this announcement alone would not produce a deterministic future market price in the absence of an explicit monetary policy, we will expand on some of the proposals, which are incomplete as presently specified. Lacking a specific policy for the money stock, the markets for gold and currency could not produce price solutions at the time of fixing. Otherwise stated, any market price for gold at the time of fixing is possible depending on which policy on government currency issue and gold reserves is selected. This includes the possibility of a market gold price which may be highly inflationary even after the price fixing.

6. In a stochastic model in which the gold standard may suddenly and unexpectedly collapse, there would be optimal portfolio reasons for holding monetary gold.

7. However, the switch to the gold standard itself will be treated as though it were a complete surprise. The perfect foresight assumption applies to the dynamics of prices *after* the advent of the gold standard.

8. Allowing for changes in the real rate of interest would greatly complicate our analysis; thus the development of our model is an exercise in partial equilibrium analysis. We presume that the real side of our model consists of gold and a storable good which can either be consumed or stored to produce more goods. One unit of the stored consumable produces more consumables at the rate ρ, given exogenously as in S–H. Our analysis is partial because we arbitrarily assume that the stock of the stored good is constant. In Barro, although demand and supply functions are explicitly dependent on ρ, for all of the conclusions ρ is exogenously set at a fixed value.

9. These assumptions preclude any gold mining activity, a specification similar to that of S–H. An inclusion of gold mining would produce a richer dynamics than those studied here; because of the exhaustible resource nature of gold, marginal cost curves for extraction would shift upward with cumulative increases in previously mined gold and anticipated capital gains would affect gold extraction rates. Indeed, an inclusion of the technical nature of extraction is necessary to make the monetization studied here specific to the gold commodity. However, we have chosen to ignore the gold extraction aspect of the problem because it apparently adds nothing to the *qualitative* results that we obtain while greatly increasing the technical complexity of the problem. On the other hand, a *quantitative* study, aimed at deriving explicit recommendations on money supply policies and on the price at which to fix gold, must account for the gold mining element since its parameters affect the steady state of the system.

10. Surprisingly, Barro worked out the dynamics of his gold standard model under an assumption of static expectations. This produced a stable dynamic system that is comparable only in its steady state to the system developed below.

11. In an early version of this paper we solved the model for a case in which capital gains enter into desired gold use. Since no substantive result depends on this assumption, we exclude it here to simplify our report.

12. While our methods are similar to those of S–H, our gold market model differs from theirs in some important respects. S–H interpret the variable which, in the context of their paper, is analogous to our $D(t)$ as a demand for a perishable good. Since this gold demand must always be non-negative in their paper, we have avoided using their form here; otherwise we would preclude the possibility of a post-monetization gold inflation and the disgorging of consumer gold which occurred on a large scale in 1980 and 1981. Also, we assume that the flow demand for gold depends negatively on $D(t)$, the existing gold stock already used in consumption and industrial forms. This reflects diminishing marginal utility and productivity associated with additional consumption and industrial gold uses, respectively.

13. The speculative pricing of such resources is discussed in more detail in S–H.

14. The differential equation is $\dot{D}(t) = -vD(t) + [v\,\delta/q(0)]e^{-\rho t}$, when $G(t) > 0$.

15. For the special case of $D(0) = 0$, equations (10.5) and (10.6) yield $D(t) = \bar{I}$
$- \bar{R} = ve^{-vT} \int_0^T [(\bar{I} - \bar{R})/e^{-\rho T}]e^{(v-\rho)\tau} d\tau$. The solution for T is T
$= \log(\rho/v)/[\rho - v]$, for $\rho \neq v$. Substituting for T in (10.8), we can determine the time zero relative gold price, $q(0)$.

16. In Flood and Garber (1980b) we estimate a model similar to (10.9) and (10.10) and cannot reject the hypothesis that only market fundamentals govern the price level.

17. Since $P(t)$ contains the rental price of gold in consumption form, our relative price $q(t) = Q(t)/P(t)$ is not equal to the price of gold divided by the price of goods other than gold. However, if we assume that the consumption rental price of gold is proportional to gold's price and that $P(t)$ is of the Cobb-Douglas form in gold's rental price and in the price of other goods, then our $q(t)$ is proportional to the price of gold divided by the price of goods other than gold raised to the power $(1 - \theta)$, where θ is gold's share in the price index. In our analysis we assume that θ is sufficiently small that it may be ignored without consequence. However, if θ were large then our equation (10.3) would become $q(t) = \rho(1 - \theta)q(t)$. This change would not alter our results substantively.

18. In the next section we discuss the implications of an alternative assumption about post-collapse money growth.

19. That $\bar{Q}\bar{R} < M(0)$ is an arbitrary assumption which we relax in our discussion in section III.

20. The post-collapse choke date T is not the same as the choke date discussed in the last section due to the addition of government gold reserves to the stock available for consumption. However, the logic used in the last section to determine T is also applicable in this case.

21. The equation of SS is $P(t) = AX(t) + \hat{P} - A\hat{X}$, where $A = \bar{Q}/[\phi - \alpha\lambda_1] > 0$, and λ_1 is the negative root of the equation system (10.17) and (10.18). To be precise, $\lambda_1 = (1/2)[-(\phi/\alpha - v) - \sqrt{(\phi/\alpha - v)^2 + 4(v/\alpha)(\phi + \delta)}] < 0$. For later use we also record the positive root of the system, $\lambda_2 = (-v/\alpha)[\phi + \delta]/\lambda_1 > 0$.

22. This assumption requires the absence of speculative bubbles.

23. The exact equation positioning the steady state locus is easy to determine. Using the equations for $\hat{P}$ and $\hat{X}$, (10.19) and (10.20), we solve for $\bar{Q}$ in (10.19) and eliminate $\bar{Q}$ in (10.20) by substitution. The resulting equation of the locus is $\hat{X} = (\phi + \delta)^{-1}[\phi\bar{I} + \delta\bar{R} - \{\delta(\bar{I} - \bar{R})/[\hat{P}/M(0) - (1/\phi + \delta)]\}]$.

24. The value of $\bar{Q}_4$ is $\delta M(0)/(\phi\bar{I} + \delta\bar{R})$. If, prior to monetization, agents had expected the fiat system to generate the constant money stock $M(0)$, then $\tilde{Q}(0) = \delta(M(0) - \bar{Q}\bar{R})e^{-\rho T}/(\phi\bar{I})$. This $\tilde{Q}(0)$ lies between the $\hat{X}(\bar{Q})\hat{X}(\bar{Q})$ locus and the axis. A similar positional relationship will hold for some range of conditional expected fiat money growth rates. However, for sufficiently high conditional expected money growth rates $\tilde{Q}(0)$ will exceed $\bar{Q}_4$, implying that a temporary gold standard with an expected future attack is not a possible outcome. Either the gold standard is permanent or it collapses immediately.

25. $\bar{Q}_2$ can be determined by equating $\hat{X}$ in equation (10.20) to $X(0)$ and solving for the implied value of $\bar{Q}$.

26. We will study the price level adjustments to gold monetization below.

27. Although our model is not constructed to facilitate welfare comparisons, it appears that a steady state such that $\hat{X} = 0$ is a prime candidate for an optimal monetary gold standard. In this case all gold is in productive private use, and the gold standard is permanently viable.
28. See note 21 for a discussion of the stable branch.
29. For a permanently viable gold standard we have determined that $X(w)$ is

$$X(w) = \frac{\bar{I} - D(0)e^{-vw} - \left[\hat{P}(\bar{Q}) - \dfrac{\bar{Q}\hat{X}(\bar{Q})}{\phi - \alpha\lambda_1} \right] \dfrac{\delta v(1 - e^{(\rho - v)w})}{\bar{Q}(v - \rho)}}{1 + \dfrac{\delta v(1 - e^{(\rho - v)w})}{(\phi - \alpha\lambda_1)(v - \rho)}}$$

REFERENCES

Barro, R. (1979) 'Money and the Price Level Under the Gold Standard', *Economic Journal*, March, pp. 13–33.

Barro, R. and D. Gordon (1981) 'A Positive Theory of Money in a Natural Rate Model', University of Rochester Working Paper, October.

Flood, R. and P. Garber (1980a) 'An Economic Theory of Monetary Reform', *Journal of Political Economy*, February.

Flood, R. and P. Garber (1980b) 'Market Fundamentals vs Price Level Bubbles: The First Tests', *Journal of Political Economy*, August.

Krugman, P. (1979) 'A Model of Balance-of-Payments Crises', *Journal of Money, Credit and Banking*, August.

Kydland, F. and E. Prescott (1977) 'Rules Rather than Discretion: the Inconsistency of Optimal Plans', *Journal of Political Economy*, 85, June, pp. 473–91.

Laffer, A. (1979) 'Making the Dollar as Good as Gold', *Los Angeles Times*, 30 October.

Lehrman, L. (1980) 'Monetary Policy, the Federal Reserve System, and Gold,' Working Paper, Lehrman Institute, New York.

Lehrman, L. (1981) 'The Case for the Gold Standard', Working Paper, Lehrman Institute, New York.

Salant, S. (1981) 'The Vulnerability of Price Stabilization Schemes to Speculative Attack', *Journal of Political Economy*, forthcoming.

Salant, S. and D. Henderson (1978) 'Market Anticipations of Government Gold Policies and the Price of Gold', *Journal of Political Economy*, August.

11 Gold in the Optimal Portfolio

DAVID A. HSIEH and JOHN HUIZINGA

INTRODUCTION

Along with the collapse of the Bretton Woods system in the early 1970s has come renewed interest of investors of gold. This has been stimulated by unprecedented large positive and large negative returns to holding gold. Figure 11.1 shows the time path of the monthly return to owning gold, expressed at annual rate. It is not uncommon to observe returns of 200 per cent per annum in either direction.

The purpose of the paper is to determine if a rational investor should have been, or should now be, investing a noticeable fraction of his portfolio in gold. We study the weight of gold in an optimal portfolio of assets which includes equities, short-term and long-term bonds, forward foreign exchange contracts, and real estate. Optimality, in this paper, means minimum variance for a given expected return.[2] Although gold is known to have a highly variable return, the covariance of its return with the return on other assets is also an important consideration. If the return to gold is strongly correlated with other asset returns, it may be a desirable investment despite its highly volatile return.

For some investors, gold may be seen as a hedge against inflation. Obviously gold is just one of a number of possible real assets that could serve this purpose, yet other logical choices such as equities may be inferior to gold. There is a large body of empirical work which seems to indicate that in the United States, inflation exerts a negative impact on stock returns.[3] Recent work by Gultekin (1981), however, shows that the relations between inflation and stock return varies greatly from country to country. Similarly, recent work by Mishkin (1982) indicates that the effect of domestic inflation on the real return to holding short-term offshore bank deposits varies substantially from country to country.

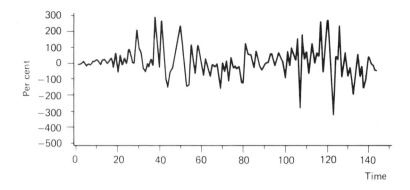

FIGURE 11.1   *Return to holding gold, 1970(1) to 1981(12)*

Thus it may be that gold should be an important part of the optimal portfolios in some countries, but of negligible importance in others.

To calculate optimal portfolios, we allow investors only the information available at the time the portfolio is created. At each point in time we form conditional means for the various asset returns and a conditional covariance matrix. The conditional means and covariances are continually updated period by period by use of the Kalman Filter. The next section describes the methodology in detail.

We construct optimal portfolios for six countries – Belgium, Canada, West Germany, Switzerland, the United Kingdom and the United States. We have two data sets: monthly returns of all six assets for the US and three-month returns of five assets (excluding real estate) for all six countries. The third section describes the data in detail and gives some summary statistics.

The fourth section presents the optimal portfolios for the first data set. The fifth section reports results for the second data set. The final section contains some summary remarks.

METHODOLOGY

Let $r_t = [r_{1t}, \ldots, r_{nt}]'$ be a vector of realized real returns on assets $i = 1, \ldots n$ from time t to time $t + 1$. r_t is unknown at time t, but we can denote its conditional mean by the vector μ_t and its conditional covariance matrix by Ω_t. The conditional mean and conditional covariance are conditional on the information set Z_t, which is known at time t. We represent a portfolio at time t by $Y_t = [Y_{1t}, \ldots, Y_{nt}]'$, a vector of portfolio shares of the n assets, where $Y'L = 1$ and $L = [1, \ldots, 1]'$. The portfolio Y_t has conditional mean $Y_t'\mu_t$ and conditional variance $Y_t'\Omega_t Y_t$.

At each point in time, we are interested in the mean-variance efficient portfolios $X_{\bar{r}t}$, where $X'_{\bar{r}t}L = 1$, $X'_{\bar{r}t}\mu_t = \bar{r}$ and $X'_{\bar{r}t}\Omega_t X_{\bar{r}t} \leqslant y_t'\Omega_t y_t$ for all y_t such that $y_t'\mu_t = \bar{r}$. Merton (1972) discusses how to solve for the portfolios $X_{\bar{r}t}$ given $\bar{r}$, μ_t and Ω_t, hence our goal in this section is to discuss how we form μ_t and Ω_t. We begin by postulating

$$r_t = Z_t\beta_t + U_t \quad t = 1, \ldots T \tag{11.1}$$

Z_t is an $n \times k$ matrix of predetermined variables. β_t is the unobserved $k \times 1$ coefficient vector of the equation at time t, and U_t is an unobservable vector white-noise process with zero mean and constant covariance matrix R.

In order to forecast r_t, we need to estimate β_t. This is done by adding to equation (11.1) a law of motion for β_t:

$$\beta_{t+1} = A_t\beta_t + V_t \quad t = 1, \ldots, T \tag{11.2}$$

Here A_t is a $k \times k$ transition matrix and V_t is an unobservable $k \times l$ vector white-noise process with mean zero and constant variance Q. V_t and U_t are assumed to be uncorrelated. A_t and Q are assumed to be known in advance. We also have a prior distribution for β_0 with $k \times 1$ mean vector b_0 and $k \times k$ covariance matrix P_0.

The model set out above is the standard Kalman Filter model.[4] At each point in time we use only information available at that time, and our priors, to generate a posterior mean and covariance for β_t, denoted b_t and P_t. We also update our estimate of R, denoted $\hat{R}_t$. The forecast, or conditional mean, of r_t is then $\mu_t = Z_t b_t$ and the conditional covariance matrix is $\Omega_t = [Z_t P_t Z_t' + \hat{R}_t]$. The term $Z_t P_t Z_t'$ represents uncertainty about the value of β_t, and $\hat{R}_t$ represents the estimated variation in U_t.

The Kalman Filter can be thought of as a generalization of the rolling regression, which considers the coefficient vector β_t to be a constant over time and estimates it every period by running an ordinary least squares regression with all past information. In terms of the Kalman Filter, the rolling regression species A_t to be the identity matrix, Q to be the zero matrix, and β_0 to have a diffuse prior.

In our empirical work we try several versions of the Kalman Filter. The exact specifications for A_t, Q, b_0 and P_0 for each model are given in sections four and five. For each model we calculate the time series of four efficient portfolios. The first picks the minimum variance portfolio at each point in time. Portfolios 1, 3 and 4 are the minimum variance plus

0.5 per cent, plus 2 per cent and plus 10 per cent respectively. More than two efficient portfolios need to be created, since we assume there is no riskless real asset and therefore the efficient portfolios do not lie along a straight line in mean-standard deviation space.[5]

DATA

There are two data sets used in this study. The first is for monthly holding returns in the United States. This includes six assets: gold, short-term US Treasury securities, long-term US Treasury securities, equities, real estate, and forward contracts in foreign exchange. All returns are expressed as annual, continuously compounded rates.

The return for gold is based on end-of-month observations for the 3:00 p.m. US dollar fixing price of gold at the London Bullion Market. Gold price data are available in the *International Monetary Market Yearbook* and the *Bank of England Quarterly Bulletin*. The returns for equities are the monthly return for a value-weighted portfolio of the New York Stock Exchange, taken from the data base of the Center for Research in Securities Prices (CRSP) at the University of Chicago. The return includes both dividend payments and capital gains.

The return on short-term US Treasury securities is taken to be the return on a Treasury bill with thirty days to maturity. The returns are computed from end-of-month Treasury bill prices available on the CRSP data files. When a thirty-day bill was not available, the returns on the two bills with days to maturity closest to thirty were used to form a linear interpolation. It was not necessary to use bills with a maturity of under twenty-five days or over thirty-five days. The return on the long-term US treasury securities is the one-month holding period return, including coupon payment, on a five-year US Treasury bond. The bonds used are described in Fisher and Lorie (1977).[6]

The return for forward contracts in foreign exchange is based on selling US dollars for West German Deutsch marks in a one-month forward contract, and since no transactions take place at the time of the contract, the investor is assumed to invest for thirty days at the nominally riskless rate on US Treasury bills. Upon purchase of Deutsch marks at the forward rate, there is a conversion back to dollars at the spot rate. Exchange rates are from Harris Bank and are the last Friday of the month or first Friday of the next month, whichever is closest to the end of the month.

The return on real estate is measured by the home purchase price component of the US Consumer Price Index (CPI). The series was taken from the Citibank data base. The same series has been used by Fama and Schwert (1977), Ibbotson and Fall (1979) and others. Although the series has some defects, it appears to be the best series available for our time period.[7] The inflation rate used to deflate all nominal returns is the CPI. None of the series used is seasonally adjusted.

Summary statistics for the six assets are reported in Table 11.1. Stocks have had the highest return, with gold having the only other positive real rate of interest. Gold has the most variable rate of return by a substantial margin, having a standard deviation which is close to twice that of stocks and foreign exchange speculation. Real estate is shown to have a negative real rate of return, and a small amount of variation. The small variation must in large part be explained by the fact that the CPI home purchase price series is reported as a three-month moving average. Short-term US Treasury securities have outperformed long-term securities in terms of mean rate of return; they have also had the smallest variation of real returns for any of the six assets we studied.

The second data set used in this study contains five assets per country for six countries. The countries are Belgium, West Germany, Switzerland, Canada, the United Kingdom and the United States. The returns are three-month holding period returns for three-month bank deposits, long-term government bonds, equities, forward foreign exchange contracts, and gold. The three-month holding period was necessary to make countries comparable. Only in the United States could we find data for a one-month fixed nominal rate assets. All returns are expressed as annual rates, continuously compounded.

The returns for equities are computed from dividend yields and end-of-month stock market indices reported in *Capital International Perspective*, a monthly publication of a Swiss investment firm. We use this series for the US, and therefore have a different series from the first data set, for the purpose of comparability across countries. The three-month bank deposit rates are from *World Financial Markets*, published by Morgan Guaranty Trust. The return on holding gold is calculated using the dollar price of gold described for the first data set and converting to domestic currency using the end-of-period exchange rate reported in *International Financial Statistics*.

Constructing three-month holding returns on long-term bonds was possible only for the US. Therefore, for all other countries, the long-term bond return was taken to be an uncovered position of holding the US long-term bond – that is, the US bond return minus the rate of depreciation. The forward foreign exchange investment for all countries

TABLE 11.1 *Real monthly asset 'returns and inflation rcte in the US, 1975(1) to 1981(12)*

Asset	Mean return	Min return	Max return	Standard deviation of return	Autocorrelation at lag											
					1	2	3	4	5	6	7	8	9	10	11	12
Gold	-0.24	-3.192	2.665	0.982	0.05	0.01	-0.08	0.18	0.26	-0.09	0.14	0.00	-0.18	-0.08	0.21	0.01
STB	-0.006	-0.071	0.104	0.034	0.78	0.55	0.42	0.32	0.24	0.18	0.19	0.25	0.22	0.20	0.19	0.14
LTB	-0.038	-1.205	1.249	0.303	0.15	-0.26	-0.18	-0.00	0.06	-0.02	-0.06	0.07	-0.07	0.09	0.12	0.08
NYSE	0.060	-1.523	1.448	0.538	0.01	-0.16	-0.03	0.02	-0.13	-0.20	-0.08	0.05	0.02	0.02	0.05	0.12
FXWG	-0.021	-1.087	1.082	0.357	0.03	0.16	0.03	-0.09	-0.04	-0.19	0.07	0.07	-0.03	0.17	0.07	0.01
RE	-0.004	-0.224	0.134	0.064	0.76	0.35	-0.02	-0.28	-0.35	-0.25	-0.03	0.20	0.36	-0.40	0.34	0.21
PI	0.085	0.029	0.167	0.034	0.85	0.62	0.46	0.36	0.29	0.28	0.34	0.41	0.45	0.44	0.41	0.34

Note

All returns and the inflation rate are expressed as annual, continuously compounded rates. Gold: based on London Bullion Market; STB: Short-Term (30-day) US Treasury Bill; LTB: Long-Term (5 years) US Treasury Bond; NYSE: Value-Weighted New York Stock Exchange; FXWG: selling US dollars for West German DM in 1 month forward contract; RE: real estate as measured by home purchase price of US CPI; PI: US CPI inflation.

TABLE 11.2 Real Three Month Asset Returns and Inflation for Six Countries 1975(1) to 1981(9)

Asset	Mean return	Min return	Max return	Standard deviation of return	Autocorrelation at lag											
					1	2	3	4	5	6	7	8	9	10	11	12
Belgium																
Gold	0.069	−0.930	1.937	0.524	0.68	0.32	0.12	0.21	0.27	0.20	0.24	0.26	0.32	0.21	0.11	−0.07
STB	0.029	−0.054	0.116	0.036	0.90	0.75	0.62	0.49	0.42	0.37	0.31	0.26	0.24	0.22	0.21	0.22
LTB	−0.015	−0.715	0.667	0.245	0.62	0.38	0.01	0.02	−0.04	−0.03	−0.02	0.06	0.09	0.20	0.19	0.27
STK	−0.006	−0.512	0.634	0.236	0.61	0.25	−0.07	−0.05	0.02	0.03	0.05	0.11	0.15	0.21	0.12	0.11
FX	0.032	−0.635	0.562	0.240	0.68	0.51	0.18	0.12	0.07	0.08	0.13	0.16	0.20	0.21	0.14	0.06
FI	0.067	0.015	0.119	0.024	0.83	0.63	0.48	0.35	0.37	0.42	0.39	0.36	0.36	0.34	0.36	0.36
Canada																
Gold	0.062	−1.034	1.965	0.610	0.69	0.41	0.20	0.29	0.32	0.20	0.18	0.11	0.18	0.15	0.17	0.01
STB	0.009	−0.073	0.107	0.031	0.82	0.63	0.41	0.23	0.13	0.04	−0.00	−0.06	−0.11	−0.13	−0.16	−0.16
LTB	−0.022	−0.550	0.642	0.177	0.53	−0.06	−0.34	−0.13	0.00	0.02	−0.06	−0.14	0.10	0.27	0.23	0.02
STK	0.052	−0.984	1.129	0.356	0.60	0.20	−0.06	0.06	0.20	0.16	0.14	0.14	0.20	0.20	0.16	0.07
FX	0.027	−0.210	−0.213	0.082	0.53	0.15	−0.05	0.09	0.12	−0.05	−0.14	−0.06	0.08	0.11	−0.02	−0.24
PI	0.091	0.046	0.139	0.023	0.84	0.67	0.46	0.27	0.23	0.19	0.22	0.23	0.24	0.25	0.18	0.12
Germany																
Gold	0.076	−0.869	1.915	0.521	0.68	0.30	0.11	0.20	0.27	0.19	0.21	0.21	0.28	0.20	0.11	−0.08
STB	0.012	−0.037	0.074	0.027	0.84	0.62	0.33	0.04	−0.14	−0.23	−0.18	−0.02	0.19	0.38	0.50	0.53
LTB	−0.008	−0.649	0.686	0.237	0.62	0.40	0.05	0.07	0.02	0.04	0.03	0.09	0.10	0.19	0.19	0.25
STK	0.019	−0.349	0.767	0.219	0.54	0.09	−0.09	−0.03	−0.08	−0.20	−0.12	0.07	0.17	0.13	0.07	0.02
FX	0.043	−0.572	0.597	0.230	0.66	0.50	0.18	0.16	0.12	0.14	0.19	0.20	0.23	0.22	0.14	0.03
PI	0.044	−0.008	0.088	0.023	0.84	0.59	0.23	−0.11	−0.30	−0.38	−0.29	−0.11	−0.14	0.37	0.52	0.56

Switzerland

Gold	0.051	−0.869	2.116	0.559	0.73	0.40	0.21	0.26	0.28	0.20	0.20	0.19	0.22	0.13	0.05	−0.10
STB	−0.003	−0.072	0.059	0.024	0.76	0.57	0.41	0.22	0.20	0.16	0.01	−0.05	−0.08	−0.10	−0.02	0.01
LTB	−0.032	−0.667	0.599	0.268	0.67	0.45	0.08	0.04	−0.01	−0.02	0.05	0.03	−0.01	0.01	0.03	0.14
STK	0.014	−0.454	0.982	0.253	0.58	0.14	−0.20	−0.23	−0.15	−0.06	0.08	0.19	0.14	0.01	−0.08	0.00
FX	0.018	−0.652	0.696	0.279	0.66	0.42	0.11	0.07	0.03	0.03	0.08	0.02	0.03	0.04	0.08	0.05
PI	0.032	−0.015	0.110	0.027	0.85	0.70	0.57	0.41	0.38	0.35	0.29	0.22	0.20	0.18	0.20	0.23

United Kingdom

Gold	0.024	−1.134	1.627	0.523	0.61	0.17	−0.05	0.07	0.14	0.03	0.05	0.10	0.20	0.14	0.05	−0.12
STB	−0.027	−0.251	0.868	0.067	0.82	0.56	0.31	0.07	0.01	0.04	0.04	0.06	0.10	0.09	0.09	0.11
LTB	−0.060	−0.696	0.559	0.272	0.74	0.41	0.13	0.12	0.18	0.26	0.27	0.21	0.14	0.09	0.06	0.04
STK	0.076	−0.976	2.023	0.465	0.56	0.12	−0.16	−0.19	−0.11	−0.06	−0.03	−0.02	0.02	−0.02	−0.15	−0.22
FX	−0.019	−0.515	0.669	0.251	0.72	0.43	0.16	0.16	0.19	0.16	0.10	0.06	0.12	0.11	0.08	0.05
PI	0.137	0.048	0.353	0.068	0.83	0.59	0.34	0.09	0.00	0.01	0.00	0.02	0.05	0.03	0.02	0.01

United States

Gold	0.039	−1.075	2.000	0.595	0.66	−0.35	0.13	0.24	0.29	0.19	0.19	0.13	0.20	0.14	0.12	−0.05
STB	0.001	−0.047	0.115	0.032	0.80	0.55	0.33	0.20	0.16	0.21	0.24	0.27	0.25	0.21	0.15	0.09
LTB	−0.044	−0.530	0.578	0.174	0.56	0.17	−0.26	−0.14	−0.03	0.00	−0.03	0.02	0.07	0.18	0.20	0.14
STK	0.021	−0.574	0.800	0.272	0.56	0.15	−0.10	−0.07	−0.06	−0.15	−0.07	0.00	0.07	0.12	0.07	0.01
FX	−0.031	−0.551	0.591	0.232	0.63	0.41	0.03	−0.03	−0.07	−0.03	0.05	0.09	0.14	0.15	0.10	−0.01
PI	0.086	0.031	0.163	0.032	0.92	0.76	0.60	0.49	0.44	0.42	0.44	0.48	0.53	0.53	0.49	0.43

Note

All returns and the inflation rate are expressed as annual, continuously compounded rates. Gold: based on London Bullion Market; STB: domestic bank deposits; LTB: uncovered holding (except for US) of 5-year US Treasury Bond; STK: domestic stocks; FX: selling domestic currency for US dollar in 3-month forward contract; for US, selling US dollars for German DM in 3-month forward contract; PI: CPI inflation.

but the US is selling domestic currency for US dollars in a three-month forward contract. Since no outlay is needed at the time of the contract, it is assumed that funds are invested for three months domestically at the bank deposit rate. This can also be thought of as collateral or margin. For the US the return is based, as in the first data set, on selling dollars in a forward contract for German Deutsch marks. No real estate series was available for countries other than the US.

Summary statistics for the second data set appear in Table 11.2. In all countries, gold has the most variable rate of return. Only in the UK is any asset even close to having as much variation in its return as gold does. Gold also typically outperforms all other assets in terms of mean rate of return.[8] The sole exception is again the UK, where stocks have had a higher rate of return. The real return to gold has been positive in all countries.

Stocks have earned a positive real rate of return in all countries except Belgium. The UK shows the highest return for stocks as well as the highest and most variable inflation rate. Switzerland has the lowest inflation rate. In all countries, the 'riskless' nominal asset has the lowest variation of real returns. Results reported for the forward foreign exchange asset reveal that the forward market for all currencies considered has, on average, underestimated the value of the US dollar.

UNITED STATES MONTHLY RETURNS

For the monthly returns in the US we constructed several prediction models. The first is Model RW, a random walk specification. In the Kalman Filter notation of equations (11.1) and (11.2),

$$\begin{aligned}
\text{\emph{Model RW}:} \quad r_t &= Z_t \beta_t + U_t = r_{t-1} + U_t \\
\beta_{t+1} &= A_t \beta_t + V_t = 1 \\
b_0 &= 1, \; P_0 = 0
\end{aligned}$$

That is, β_t is a constant and equal to unity so that A_t is the identity matrix, I, and V_t is identically equal to zero. Z_t, the information set relevant for predicting returns, is r_{t-1}. The prior mean for β_0, b_0, is set equal to one and the prior variance P_0 is set to zero. This specification obviously uses the forecast $\mu_t = r_{t-1}$ and uses the updated covariance matrix $\Omega_t = \hat{R}_t$, since there is no parameter uncertainty. $\hat{R}_t$, the estimated covariance matrix of U_t at time t, is given by,

$$R_t = (1/t - 1) \sum_{s=0}^{t-1} (r_s - \mu_s)(r_s - \mu_s)' \tag{11.3}$$

We consider Model RW to be our base-line model, due to its popularity and simplicity.

The second model used is a multivariate second-order autoregressive model with fixed, but unknown, coefficients and is denoted AR2F1. We also include a constant, time and time squared as regressors.

Model AR2F1: $r_t = Z_t\beta_t + U_t = I \otimes [1 \; t \; t^2 \; r'_{t-1} \; r'_{t-2}]\beta + U_t$
$$\beta_{t+1} = A_t\beta_t + V_t = \beta$$
$$b_0 = 0, P_0 = I$$

Here $\otimes$ is the Kronecker product. This specification is similar to the rolling regression; the only difference is our use of the prior $b_0 = 0$ and $P_0 = I$ instead of the rolling regression's use of the diffuse prior. We chose this specification so as to be as totally agnostic as possible. At time t Model AR2F1 uses the forecast $\mu_t = Z_t b_t$ and covariance matrix $\Omega_t = (Z_t P_t Z'_t + \hat{R}_t)$. The method of combining sample and prior information to form b_t and P_t is described by Kalman (1960) and $\hat{R}_t$ is formed according to equation (11.3).

Model AR2F2 is the same as Model AR2F1 with the exception of Ω_t. In Model AR2F2 $\Omega_t = \hat{R}_t$, so that uncertainty about the value of β is ignored when forming the estimated covariance matrix of returns. At each point in time Model AR2F2 will have the same expected return vector, μ_t, as Model AR2F1.

Summary statistics and some model diagnostics for estimating Models RW, AR2F1 and AR2F2 over the sample period January 1975 to December 1981 appear in Table 11.3.[9] The sample period was chosen based on a desire to get as much data as possible, yet to minimize the effect of the transition from fixed to flexible exchange rates. By beginning in 1975, we allow investors over a year to observe the workings of flexible exchange rates and fully fluctuating gold prices. As described in the last section, we constructed four portfolios for each model. Portfolio 1 is picked to be the minimum variance portfolio. Portfolios 2, 3 and 4 are created so that the expected return is that on portfolio 1 plus 0.5 per cent, 2.0 per cent and 10 per cent respectively.

In the first column of Table 11.3 we report the cumulative expected returns for each portfolio in each model. The results are very similar across models, with the minimum variance portfolio always expected to earn a negative real rate of return. In the second column of Table 11.3 we report the cumulative actual return on the various portfolios. If the sample of returns is large enough and the model chosen to predict returns is correct, the expected and actual returns will coincide. Column 4 of Table 11.3 presents one way of summarizing the deviations of

TABLE 11.3 *Estimation of Models RW, AR2F1 and AR2F2, six assets, 1975(1) to 1981 (12)*

	Port-folio	Cumulative expected return	Cumulative actual return	Standard error of actual return	Root MSE of expected return	Min actual return	Max actual return
Model RW	1	−0.0060	−0.0014	0.0337	0.0381	−0.087	0.087
	2	−0.0010	0.0017	0.0333	0.0374	−0.074	0.090
	3	0.0140	0.0109	0.0340	0.0374	−0.050	0.100
	4	0.0940	0.0600	0.0676	0.0751	−0.100	0.240
Model AR2F1	1	−0.0058	−0.0018	0.0379	0.0329	−0.077	0.123
	2	−0.0008	0.0003	0.0386	0.0328	−0.073	0.127
	3	0.0142	0.0067	0.0430	0.0369	−0.076	0.137
	4	0.0942	0.0405	0.0963	0.1041	−0.359	0.267
Model AR2F2	1	−0.0048	−0.0039	0.0340	0.0279	−0.071	0.097
	2	0.0002	−0.0016	0.0345	0.0279	−0.065	0.100
	3	0.0152	0.0053	0.0389	0.0328	−0.074	0.112
	4	0.0952	0.0423	0.0912	0.0993	−0.353	0.259

Note
All returns expressed at annual rates. The six assets used to form these portfolios are short-term US Treasury securities, long-term U.S. Treasury securities, equities, real estate, foreign exchange contracts, and gold. Root MSE is the square root of the mean squared error for forecasting actual portfolio returns with the expected returns.

expected returns on a portfolio from the actual returns. Model AR2F2 appears to be the most accurate for predicting portfolio returns.

A persistent pattern across models is that low-expected return portfolios earn a higher return than predicted and vice versa for high-expected return portfolios. This could indicate consistently under-predicting (overpredicting) the return to an asset which is relatively important in the high- (low-) variance portfolio. Alternatively, it could indicate a poor estimate of the true covariance matrix for the asset returns. There does not seem to be any simple way to distinguish between these two possibilities.

Column three of Table 11.3 presents the standard deviation of the actual returns on the various portfolios. If the mean-variance frontier does not move over time and we have a large sample, the actual returns in column two and the standard deviations in column three give us four points along the efficient frontier. If the frontier moves over time we cannot make this assumption but can still use the two columns to compare the *ex post* performance of the models.

We conclude that Model RW is superior to the other models. The high-return portfolio in model RW had a return of 6.00 per cent with a standard deviation of 6.76 per cent, while the same portfolio in Model AR2F2 had a lower return, 4.23 per cent, and a higher standard deviation, 9.12 per cent. Model AR2F1 is even worse than AR2F2. For the lower-expected return portfolios Model RW again dominates Model AR2F2, having an expected return of −0.10 per cent with a standard deviation of 3.33 per cent, compared to a return of −0.48 per cent with a standard deviation of 3.40 per cent.

Before turning to a description of the role of individual assets in the various portfolios, one last point needs to be made. Based on the lower root MSE and the better *ex post* performance of Model AR2F2 compared to Model AR2F1, it seems that ignoring parameter uncertainty is a desirable thing to do. Allowing for the uncertainty about the parameter vector β gives the investor a distorted picture of the true covariance matrix of returns and leads him into undesirable investments. Recall that the forecasts of individual asset returns is the same for Models AR2F1 and AR2F2. This result is consistent with a view of asset markets which stresses new information, rather than parameter uncertainty, as the dominant source of randomness.

Figure 11.2 shows the weight of gold in portfolios 1 and 4 for all three models. It is not possible to show the weights for portfolios 2 and 3 since they are indistinguishable from the weight in portfolio 1. For Model RW the mean absolute fraction of portfolio held in gold is 0.007, 0.007 and 0.008 for portfolios 1, 2 and 3 respectively. For portfolio 4 it is 0.023. From January 1976 on, it is only in the highest risk portfolio that gold is given a truly noticeable weight in the optimal portfolio. The largest roles for gold in Model RW are a 0.128 long position in April 1976 and a 0.123

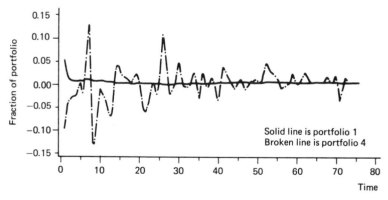

FIGURE 11.2a *Weight of gold in Model RW, 1975(9) to 1981(12)*

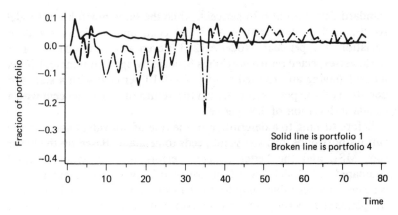

FIGURE 11.2b   *Weight of gold in Model AR2F1, 1975(9) to 1981(12)*

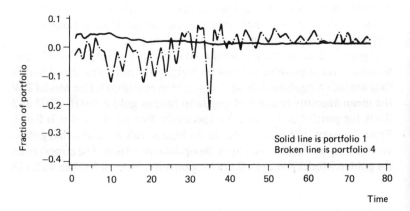

FIGURE 11.2c   *Weight of gold in Model AR2F2, 1975(9) to 1981(12)*

short position in May 1976. There is also a 0.107 long position in October 1977.

For all but the high-variance portfolio, gold is given only a slightly more important role in Models AR2F1 and AR2F2. For Model AR2F1 the mean absolute fraction in portfolios one through three are 0.021, 0.020 and 0.019, while for Model AR2F2 they are 0.020, 0.019 and 0.018. The high-variance portfolio of these models assigned gold a noticeable, but far from dominant, role with a mean absolute share of 0.042 in Models AR2F1 and 0.038 in Model AR2F2. The two autoregressive models exhibit a clear pattern of taking a short position in gold in the early part of our sample, while going long in the latter part.

To help explain why gold is assigned the role it is, Figure 11.3 shows the time series of expected return to gold calculated in both Model RW and Models AR2F1 and AR2F2. The figure shows large swings in expected returns for both forecasts. In Model RW, the expected return on holding gold reaches a high of 266.5 per cent and a low of − 319.2 per cent; the portfolio weights of gold in the high variance portfolio are 0.011 and − 0.002 for these two periods. For the autoregressive models the expected return ranges from 183.9 per cent to − 147.2 per cent. For the high-variance portfolio in these periods gold gets weights of 0.046 and − 0.003 in Model AR2F1 and weights of 0.044 and − 0.004 in Model AR2F2. The failure of gold to achieve an important role in making up an optimal portfolio is clearly not due to our models generating a series of low expected returns.

The reason gold is given so little importance is shown in Table 11.4, where the estimated standard errors and correlation coefficients of the six asset returns are presented. Diagonal elements of the matrices report the conditional standard error for each asset at the end of the sample. Off-diagonal elements are conditional correlation coefficients. The most striking feature of Table 11.4 is the unpredictability of returns to holding gold. Gold's return is almost twice as hard to predict as the return on the stock market, according to Model RW, and remain the hardest to predict according to Models AR2F1 and AR2F2. Taken together, the results of Tables 11.1 and 11.4 show that not only does the return on holding gold have the most variance, but it is also the hardest to predict. The gold

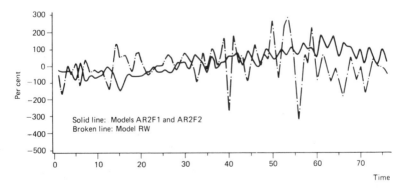

FIGURE 11.3 *Expected return to holding gold, 1975(9) to 1981(12)*

TABLE 11.4   *Standard errors and correlation coefficients of monthly asset returns, 1981(12)*

	STB	LTB	NYSE	FXWG	RE	GOLD
Model RW	0.0207					
	0.41	0.3811				
	0.11	0.32	0.7611			
	0.28	0.29	0.24	0.4945		
	0.40	0.18	0.13	0.03	0.0422	
	−0.03	0.22	−0.00	0.58	−0.00	1.3505
Model AR2F1	0.0374					
	0.11	0.3375				
	−0.10	0.18	0.9048			
	0.10	0.40	0.04	0.4352		
	0.51	0.12	0.14	0.24	0.0467	
	−0.19	0.25	−0.32	0.45	−0.03	1.2488
Model AR2F2	0.0327					
	0.12	0.3019				
	−0.08	0.19	0.8118			
	0.11	0.38	−0.02	0.3827		
	0.52	0.11	0.14	0.22	0.0565	
	−0.20	0.23	−0.32	0.47	−0.03	1.1566

Note
Diagonal elements are the conditional standard errors. Off-diagonal elements are conditional correlation coefficients.

market is too volatile to allow gold an important role in the optimum portfolios we have constructed.

The importance of the five assets other than gold in various portfolios is illustrated by Figures 11.4–11.6. The figures deal exclusively with Model RW, but we will describe where Model AR2F2 differs. Figure 11.4 shows that long-term bonds, equities and forward foreign exchange are assigned negligible weights in the minimum variance portfolio. The weights for any of these three assets rarely goes above 5 per cent. For the high-return and high-variance portfolio, long-term bonds are the most important, followed by forward foreign exchange and then stock. The long-term bonds obtain a portfolio share of 0.445 in June of 1976 and a share of − 0.250 in October 1977. The magnitude of the position appears to be diminishing somewhat over time, but as late as May 1980 there is a 0.108 long position and in May 1981 a 0.175 short position. Stocks hardly ever exceed a 5 per cent weight and show a diversity of long and short positions. Model AR2F2 differs slightly from Model RW here in

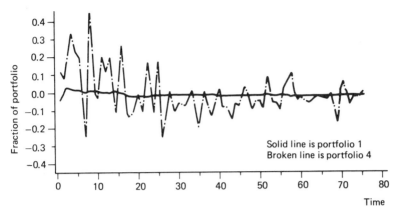

FIGURE 11.4a   *Weight of LTB in Model RW, 1975(9) to 1981(12)*

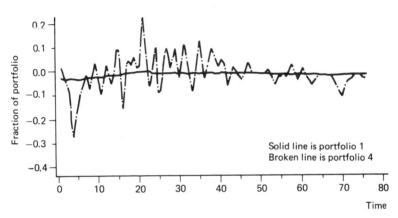

FIGURE 11.4b   *Weight of FXWG in Model RW, 1975(9) to 1981(12)*

that the former model has a distinct tendency to be long in stock in the earlier periods and short in stock in the latter periods. The magnitude of the positions is only slightly larger than pictured in Figure 11.4. For most periods, selling US dollars for German Deutsch marks takes a larger share of the optimal portfolio 4 than does investing in stocks. Foreign exchange speculation receives less weight in the latter periods; and as was the case with stock, Model AR2F2 shows a clearer pattern of long and short positions than Model RW does in Figure 11.4. In Model AR2F2

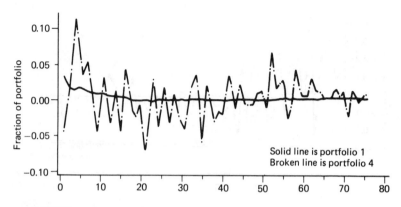

FIGURE 11.4c   *Weight of NYSE in Model RW, 1975(9) to 1981(12)*

the investor is consistently long dollars from the start of the sample until January 1977 and short dollars thereafter.

Figure 11.5 shows the portfolio weights given to short-term US Treasury bills and real estate. Clearly the minimum variance portfolio is dominated by the T-bills. For much of the sample real estate occupies a 5–15 per cent share in the minimum variance portfolio. Model AR2F2 differs in this regard with real estate consistently given a short position of approximately 5 per cent. Figure 11.5 shows that for most of the period, higher expected return and higher variance portfolios give a noticeably smaller weight to T-bills and larger weight to real estate. This point is

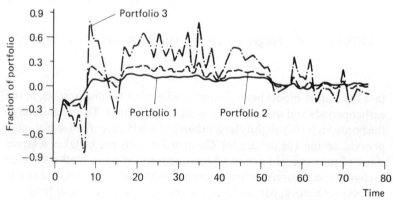

FIGURE 11.5a   *Weight of RE in Model RW, 1975(9) to 1981(12)*

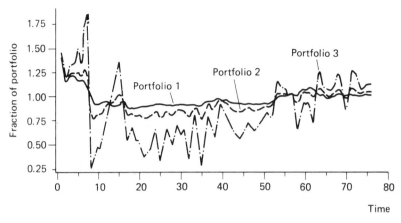

FIGURE 11.5b   *Weight of STB in Model RW, 1975(9) to 1981(12)*

most clearly made in Figure 11.6, which shows the portfolio weights for the highest risk portfolio. To obtain a high expected return, enormous positions are taken in real estate with almost identical offsetting positions in T-bills.

The forces underlying this result are best undestood by returning to Table 11.4, where it is shown that the returns in real estate and T-bills have very low conditional variances. Thus whenever the predicted return to real estate exceeds the predicted short-term interest rate, the model wants the investor to take out a one-month mortgage and buy a house. Obviously the reverse happens when the predicted rate for T-bills exceeds that for real estates.

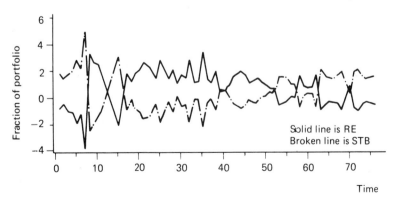

FIGURE 11.6   *Weights of STB and RE in portfolio 4, 1975(9) to 1981(12)*

It is our opinion that Figure 11.6 may cast doubt on the reliability of the estimation in the six asset models considered so far. The data that are used to construct the real estate returns are certainly the most suspect of all our data, yet real estate is a dominant force. For that reason, and others, we have estimated Models RW, AR2F1 and AR2F2 for the same data as above but dropping real estate. This also allows comparison with the international three-month holding period returns taken up in the next section.

For analyzing the five-asset framework we added an additional model which allows the coefficients to vary randomly over time, Model AR2V1.

$$\text{Model } AR2V1 \quad r_t = Z_t\beta_t + U_t = I \otimes [1 \ t \ t^2 \ r'_{t-1} \ r'_{t-2}]\beta_t + U_t$$
$$\beta_{t+1} = A_t\beta_t + V_t = \beta_t + V_t$$

We choose the prior b_0 on β_0 so as to start r_t as a random walk. The prior covariance matrix for β_0, P_0, is again set as the identity matrix. The variances of the elements of V_t are set so that in each equation the variance of $Z_t\beta_t$ has the same order of magnitude as the variance of U_t. Changes in the individual elements of β_t are assumed to be independent. The updated conditional variance matrix Ω_t ignores parameter uncertainty.[10]

Table 11.5 gives the diagnostics for the four models using five assets. In

TABLE 11.5   *Estimation of models, five assets, 1975(1) to 1981(12)*

	Port-folio	Cumulative expected return	Cumulative actual return	Standard error of actual return	Root MSE of expected return	Min actual return	Max actual return
Model RW	1	-0.0058	-0.0044	0.0363	0.0237	-0.122	0.092
	2	0.0008	-0.0033	0.0360	0.0233	-0.111	0.091
	3	0.0142	-0.0002	0.0374	0.0294	-0.079	0.097
	4	0.0942	0.0165	0.0813	0.1092	-0.128	0.429
Model AR2F1	1	-0.0049	-0.0036	0.0460	0.0350	-0.104	0.187
	2	0.0001	-0.0024	0.0454	0.0351	-0.101	0.192
	3	0.0151	0.0011	0.0466	0.0415	-0.101	0.201
	4	0.0951	0.0202	0.1000	0.1260	-0.226	0.365
Model AR2F2	1	-0.0040	-0.0053	0.0396	0.0338	-0.098	0.110
	2	0.0010	-0.0040	0.0387	0.0341	-0.092	0.096
	3	0.0160	0.0001	0.0392	0.0404	-0.099	0.072
	4	0.0960	0.0217	0.0929	0.1224	-0.192	0.350
Model AR2V1	1	-0.0058	-0.0055	0.0356	0.0253	-0.0770	0.1030
	2	0.0008	-0.0045	0.0353	0.0259	0.0722	0.1028
	3	0.0142	-0.0016	0.0361	0.0327	0.0578	0.1056
	4	0.0942	0.0141	0.0663	0.1042	-0.0938	0.2298

agreement with our findings in the six-asset framework, portfolios from Model RW outperform those from Models AR2F1 and AR2F2. Model AR2F2, which ignores parameter uncertainty, again outperforms Model AR2F1, which includes parameter uncertainty in its estimate of the estimated covariance matrix of returns. Model AR2V1 generates portfolios which perform the best, although Model RW generally has the lowest root MSE.

In contrast to our earlier findings, almost every portfolio in our models now earns below its expected rate of return. Only in portfolio 1 is the actual return close to the expected return. The difference between expected and actual returns is greatest for the high-return and high-variance portfolio. Without the option of playing the spread between two low variance returns (real estate and T-bills) none of our models can successfully predict how to earn a high rate of return.

Figure 11.7 shows the portfolio weights assigned to gold in the minimum variance portfolio and the high variance portfolio for Models RW, AR2F2 and AR2V1. Portfolio 1 gives practically no weight to gold in any of our models. Portfolios 2 and 3 are indistinguishable from portfolio 1, and so are not represented in this figure.

If we compare the weight of gold in portfolio 4 across models, we find substantial divergence. At times Model RW gives gold quite a large weight, reaching 0.332 in March 1976. This may be due to the instability of our parameter estimates at the start of the sample, however. In the later period, gold holdings in RW are usually positive but do not exceed a 0.100 share of the portfolio. Portfolio 4 in Model AR2V1 does not take

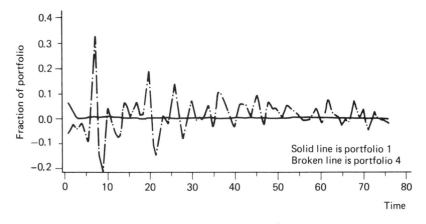

FIGURE 11.7a   *Weight of gold in Model RW, 1975(9) to 1981(12)*

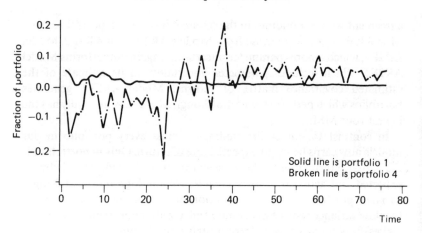

FIGURE 11.7b *Weight of gold in Model AR2F2, 1975(9) to 1981(12)*

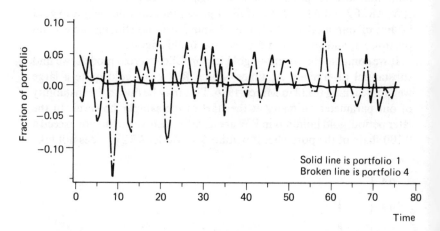

FIGURE 11.7c *Weight of gold in Model AR2V1, 1975(9) to 1981(12)*

as large a position in gold as the same portfolio in Model RW. The maximum never exceeds an absolute value of 0.150 and usually it stays within ± 0.100. AR2F2 gives gold the least weight. The mean absolute share of gold in portfolio 4 is 0.030 for Model AR2F2, 0.048 for Model RW and 0.056 for Model AR2V1. The mean absolute share of gold in portfolios 1, 2 and 3 does not exceed 0.018 in any of the models.

It is also interesting to note that RW and AR2V1 fluctuates between long and short positions in gold over the entire period, but AR2F1 tends to short gold in the first half of our sample and go long in gold in the second half.

For the discussion of the portfolio weights assigned to the other assets, we shall concentrate on AR2V1 since it performed best. Results are presented in Figures 11.8 and 11.9. The minimum variance portfolio assigns almost all the weight to the short-term asset, and negligible amounts to the other assets. The mean absolute share for STB is 0.950, for LTB is 0.047, for NYSE is 0.023 and for FXWG is 0.037, all of which exceed the share given gold. Portfolios 2 and 3 are very similar to the minimum variance portfolio.

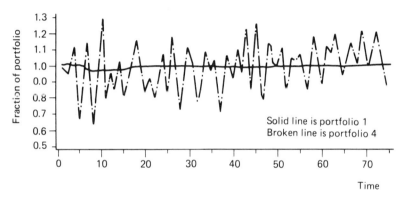

FIGURE 11.8a   *Weight of STB in Model AR2V1, 1975(9) to 1981(12)*

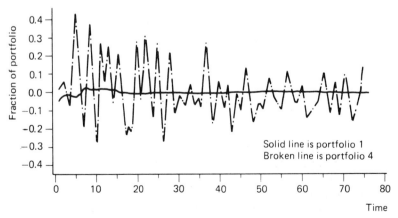

FIGURE 11.8b   *Weight of LTB in Model AR2V1 1975(9) to 1981(12)*

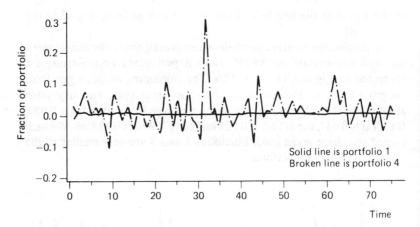

FIGURE 11.9a *Weight of NYSE in Model AR2V1, 1975(9) to 1981(12)*

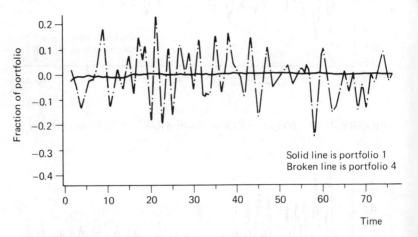

FIGURE 11.9b *Weight of FXWG in Model AR2V1, 1975(9) to 1981(12)*

The high-return and high-variance portfolio also assigns a lot of weight to the short-term asset and the variation is substantial, ranging from 0.665 in January 1976 to 1.283 in May 1976. The weight assigned to LTB in portfolio 4 tends to move in the opposite direction of the weight of STB. This exhibits the effect of 'playing the spread' in order to get a higher expected return. We either borrow long to lend short, or vice versa. Hence in the five-asset version, the long-term bond has replaced real estate as the second most important asset in portfolio 4. Its mean absolute weight is 0.188, which is higher than that of stocks (0.056) and forward foreign exchange (0.129). For foreign exchange and long-term bonds, the long and short positions tend to cancel out over the sample, resulting in mean weights of 0.002 and 0.024 respectively. For stock, the mean weight is 0.010.

Table 11.6 gives the conditional standard errors and correlation coefficients for the five assets at the end of the sample. We report results for AR2F2 and AR2V1, but not for RW, which are the same as in Table 11.4. As expected, gold returns continue to have the largest standard error of prediction, which is almost one and a half times that of stock returns in Model AR2V1.

The results for Model AR2F2 are essentially unchanged from those reported in Table 11.4. None of the models shows gold returns to be strongly negatively correlated with other asset returns. In Models RW and AR2V1 the largest negative correlation is −0.03. All models agree that the return to holding gold in most strongly positively correlated with forward foreign exchange speculation. Even with a correlation coefficient of 0.58 with FXWG, gold is still not an important part of the optimal portfolio.

Thus far, we have tried various models to forecast returns, and have consistently found that all portfolios hold very little gold. This result does not change even if we drop real estate, making gold the only real

TABLE 11.6 *Standard errors and correlation coefficients, monthly asset return,
1981(12)*

	STB	LTB	NYSE	FXWG	GOLD
Model AR2F2	0.0388				
	0.01	0.3042			
	−0.05	0.11	0.8867		
	0.08	0.34	0.08	0.3759	
	−0.21	0.17	−0.26	0.46	1.1708
Model AR2V1	0.0265				
	−0.11	0.4249			
	−0.05	0.22	0.8221		
	0.10	0.05	0.13	0.5411	
	0.14	−0.03	−0.02	0.39	1.4127

Note
Diagonal elements are conditional standard errors. Off diagonal elements are conditional correlation coefficients.

asset in the models. The explanation is probably that gold return is much harder to predict than any other asset, and that it lacks strong correlation with other returns. This makes gold unattractive to hold in the US. In the following section, we examine whether this is also true for other countries.

INTERNATIONAL THREE-MONTH RETURNS

Our data for Belgium, Canada, West Germany, Switzerland and the United Kingdom consist of three-month returns on the five assets described in the third section above. We include the United States to allow comparison with our earlier results.

Three models were used to obtain conditional means and variances of returns for all six countries. We again use a random walk model, but the specification changes slightly due to the fact that we have monthly data and three-month returns. If r_t is now used to denote the three-month return from time t to time $t+3$, then r_{t-1} and r_{t-2} are not in the investor's information set at time t. It is now necessary to generate three period-ahead forecasts, i.e. forecast r_t with r_{t-3}. This lead to our first model.

$$\text{Model RW} \quad r_t = Z_t\beta_t + U_t = r_{t-3} + U_t$$
$$\beta_{t+1} = A_t\beta_t + V_t = 1$$
$$b_0 = 1, P_0 = 0$$

This specification has the simple forecast $\mu_t = r_{t-3}$ and uses as its conditional covariance matrix

$$\Omega_t = (1/t - 3) \sum_{s=0}^{t-3} (r_s - r_{s-3})(r_s - r_{s-3})' \tag{11.4}$$

Both the second and third models used in this section are second-order autoregressive models with fixed, but unknown, coefficients. As in the random walk case, the fact that we have monthly data and three-month holding returns to forecast creates a complication that was not present when we had one-month holding returns. The complication can be illustrated as follows.

Suppose y_t is a scalor first-order autoregressive process

$$y_t = \alpha y_{t-1} + \varepsilon_t \tag{11.5}$$

where α is between 0 and 1, and ε_t is a white-noise error with zero mean and constant variance. Then the three-month-ahead forecast of y_{t+3} at time t is $\alpha \hat{y}_{t+2} = \alpha^3 y_t$. If α is unknown, we can estimate α^3 by estimating α in equation (11.5). Alternatively we can estimate α^3 by the equation

$$y_t = \alpha^3 y_{t-3} + U_t \qquad (11.6)$$

where U_t is a moving average of order two:

$$U_t = \varepsilon_t + \alpha \varepsilon_{t-1} + \alpha^2 \varepsilon_{t-2} \qquad (11.7)$$

When the sample is large, the two procedures yield equivalent forecasts. We select the second procedure, because of its simplicity in forecasting, especially in a multivariate system.

To use the Kalman Filter formula, we would then rewrite (11.6) as:

$$y_t = [y_{t-3} \ \varepsilon_{t-2} \ \varepsilon_{t-1}] \begin{bmatrix} \alpha^3 \\ \alpha^2 \\ \alpha \end{bmatrix} + \varepsilon_t \qquad (11.8)$$

The ε's prior to the sample period assumed to be zero. Starting with a prior b_0 on β_0, which is also assumed to be $(\alpha^3, \alpha^2, \alpha)'$, we can compute the posterior mean $b_t = (\alpha_t^3, \alpha_t^2, \alpha_t)'$ and covariance P_t. The ε's are updated each point by the prediction errors in the previous two periods. The three-period forecast of y_{t+3} will then be $\alpha_t^3 y_t$.[11]

The multivariate second-order autoregressive models we estimate, AR2F1 and AR2F2, both have the following Kalman Filter specification:

Models AR2F1 and AR2F2

$r_t = Z_t \beta_t + \varepsilon_t$

$Z_t = \text{diag} \{X_{1t}, \ldots, X_{5t}\}$, i.e. Z_t is block diagonal

$X_{it} = [1 \ t \ t^2 \ r'_{t-1} \ r'_{t-4} \ \varepsilon_{it-1} \ \varepsilon_{it-2}]$

$\beta_{t-1} = \beta_t + V_t = \beta$

$b_0 = [0\,0\,0\,1\,0 \ldots 0\,1\,0 \ldots 0\,1\,0]'$, $P_0 = I$

The prior on b_0 has a mean such that V_t follows a random walk. The difference between AR2F1 and AR2F2 is the construction of Ω_t. In AR2F1, Ω_t takes into account the parameter uncertainty, i.e. $\Omega_t = [Z_t P_t Z'_t + \hat{R}_t]$. In AR2F2, Ω_t ignores the parameter uncertainty, i.e. $\Omega_t = \hat{R}_t$.

Table 11.7 presents the diagnostics for the best models in each country. For Belgium, AR2F2 is the best. For Germany, AR2F1 is the best. In all the other countries, RW is the best. The results are similar across countries. The actual returns of the low-variance portfolios are usually close to or above the expected returns, while those for the high-variance portfolios are below the expected returns.

As in Table 11.5, the US still expects a negative real rate of return on

TABLE 11.7   *Estimation of models, five assets, 1975(1) to 1981(12)*

Country (Model)	Port-folio	Cumulative expected return	Cumulative actual return	Standard error of actual return	Root MSE of expected return
Belgium	1	0.0333	0.0339	0.0329	0.0335
(*AR2F2*)	2	0.0383	0.0354	0.0330	0.0326
	3	0.0533	0.0399	0.0370	0.0358
	4	0.1333	0.0638	0.0958	0.1115
Canada	1	0.0060	0.0158	0.0354	0.0381
(*RW*)	2	0.0110	0.0170	0.0351	0.0381
	3	0.0260	0.0206	0.0391	0.0418
	4	0.1060	0.0396	0.0764	0.1038
Germany	1	0.0018	0.0149	0.0283	0.0412
(*AR2F1*)	2	0.0068	0.0172	0.0295	0.0412
	3	0.0218	0.0244	0.0378	0.0463
	4	0.1018	0.0625	0.1162	0.1246
Switzerland	1	−0.0062	−0.0063	0.0249	0.0249
(*RW*)	2	−0.0012	−0.0043	0.0246	0.0251
	3	0.0138	0.0018	0.0274	0.0309
	4	0.0938	0.0341	0.0801	0.1009
United Kingdom	1	−0.0233	−0.0183	0.0601	0.0716
(*RW*)	2	−0.0183	−0.0171	0.0596	0.0710
	3	−0.0033	−0.0135	0.0595	0.0715
	4	0.0767	0.0057	0.0846	0.1159
United States	1	−0.0008	0.0045	0.0358	0.0308
(*RW*)	2	0.0042	0.0062	0.0356	0.0298
	3	0.0192	0.0114	0.0380	0.0327
	4	0.0992	0.0392	0.0895	0.1038

the minimum variance portfolio. The same is true in Switzerland and the UK. Belgium, Canada and Germany, however, expect a positive real rate of return. Four of the six countries earn a positive return on the minimum variance portfolio. Figure 11.10 illustrates the mean-standard deviation frontiers of all countries. The risk-return tradeoff is the best for Belgium, and the worst for the UK, with Germany, Canada, the US and Switzerland in between.

Figures 11.11 and 11.12 give the weight of gold in the minimum and high-variance portfolios for all six countries. For most of these countries, the weight of gold in portfolio 1 is consistently small, with very little change, especially towards the end of the sample period. The mean

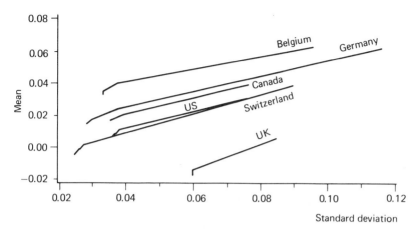

FIGURE 11.10 *Mean–standard deviation frontiers*

absolute weight of gold in portfolio 1 is 0.006 in Belgium, 0.010 in Canada, 0.011 in Germany, 0.005 in Switzerland, 0.033 in the U.K., and 0.006 in the US.

Portfolio 4 assigns more weight to gold. The mean absolute share in portfolio 4 is 0.073 in Belgium, 0.069 in Canada, 0.087 in Germany, 0.088 in Switzerland, 0.082 in the UK and 0.076 in the US. These portfolios are still quite low, similar to our findings in the previous section. After the first ten time periods, there seems to be an upward trend of gold holdings in Belgium and Germany. They tend to short gold in the early period, and go long in gold toward the end. Canada, Switzerland, the UK and

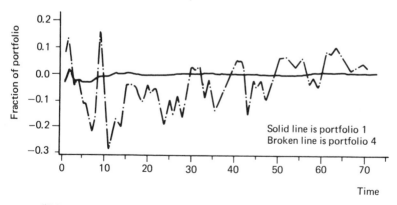

FIGURE 11.11a *Weight of gold in Belgium, 1975(9) to 1981(9)*

240

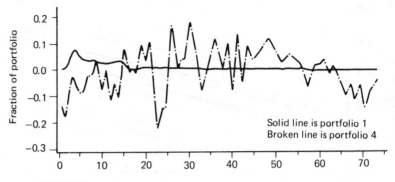

FIGURE 11.11b   *Weight of gold in Canada, 1975(9) to 1981(9)*

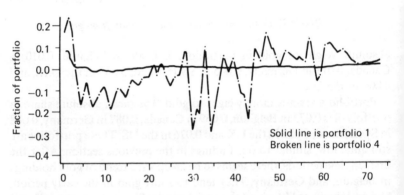

FIGURE 11.11c   *Weight of gold in West Germany, 1975(9) to 1981(9)*

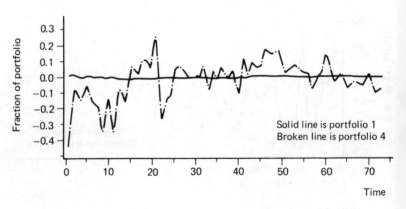

FIGURE 11.12a   *Weight of gold in Switzerland, 1975(9) to 1981(9)*

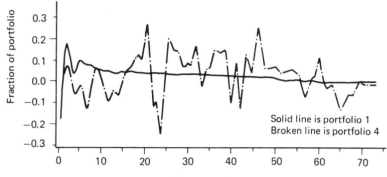

FIGURE 11.12b   *Weight of gold in United Kingdom, 1975(9) to 1981(9)*

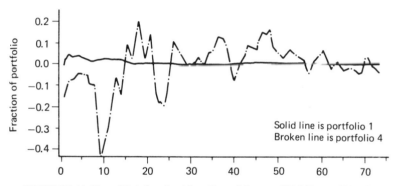

FIGURE 11.12c   *Weight of gold in United States, 1975(9) to 1981(9)*

the US tend to short gold in the early period, then go long in the middle period, and short again towards the end.

The small positions taken in gold can be explained by Table 11.8, which reports the conditional standard errors and correlation coefficients for the assets in each country. Similar to our early finding, gold is still the hardest return to predict, except in the UK where it is the second to the stock market. This comes from the fact that UK stock returns are much more volatile than those in other countries, and does not mean that gold returns in the UK are less volatile than elsewhere. Gold is not correlated with other assets in Switzerland or the UK, but is correlated with LTB in Belgium and Germany, with FX in Belgium and the US, and with STK in Canada. No correlation coefficient has an absolute magnitude greater than 0.51, which is too low to make gold an important asset in view of its large variance.

TABLE 11.8 *Standard Errors and Correlation Coefficients, Three-Month Asset Returns, 1981(12)*

Country (Model)	STB	LTB	STK	FX	Gold
Belgium	0.0315				
(AR2F2)	−0.05	0.3000			
	−0.24	0.01	0.2969		
	−0.26	0.84	0.07	0.3132	
	0.05	−0.47	−0.05	−0.37	0.7308
Canada	0.0282				
(RW)	0.19	0.2816			
	0.23	−0.26	0.5159		
	0.20	0.48	−0.26	0.1160	
	0.20	−0.10	0.46	0.0005	0.7589
Germany	0.0043				
(AR2F1)	−0.04	0.2938			
	0.41	−0.12	0.4267		
	−0.06	0.80	−0.11	0.2905	
	−0.11	−0.51	−0.09	−0.23	0.6682
Switzerland	0.0311				
(RW)	−0.18	0.3613			
	−0.003	−0.11	0.3982		
	0.01	0.77	−0.06	0.3675	
	0.12	−0.18	0.17	0.03	0.6911
United Kingdom	0.0719				
(RW)	0.07	0.3503			
	0.16	−0.40	0.8129		
	0.19	0.73	−0.27	0.3010	
	0.14	−0.01	−0.01	0.17	0.7544
United States	0.0305				
(RW)	0.50	0.2598			
	0.20	0.13	0.3868		
	0.55	0.37	0.20	0.2962	
	0.21	−0.08	0.29	0.47	0.7727

Note
Diagonal elements are conditional standard errors. Off-diagonal elements are conditional correlation coefficients.

Without exception, the short-term asset (STB) is the easiest to predict. Its standard errors are usually more than five times lower than the other assets. STK is harder to predict than LTB or FX in all countries except Belgium. There is substantial correlation between LTB and FX, especially in the four European countries. This is probably due to the dominance of exchange rate changes in these variables.

It is interesting to compare the results for the US in Table 11.8 with those in Table 11.6. The reader should note, however, that there are important differences in the data, as discussed in the second section above. The short-term asset used in Table 11.8 is the three-month time deposit rate, and in Table 11.6 it is the one-month Treasury bill return. Also, STK in Table 11.8 comes from *Capital International Perspective*, while NYSE in Table 11.6 comes from a value-weighted portfolio of the New York Stock Exchange from CRSP. Furthermore, the returns in Table 11.8 are annualized three-month holding yields, while those in Table 11.6 are annualized one-month holding yields. Hence the standard errors in Table 11.8 should be lower by a factor of $\sqrt{3}$. Indeed, this is approximately true for the variables which remain unchanged in the two tables (i.e. LTB, FX and Gold). This is even true for stock returns, although the variables are different.

However, this is not true in the short-term assets. The short-term deposit rate in Table 11.8 has a higher standard error than the Treasury bill rate in Table 11.6. In general, the variables in Table 11.8 for the US are more correlated with each other than those in Table 11.6.

Figures 11.13 and 11.14 present the weights of assets other than gold for Belgium. LTB receives little weight in the minimum variance portfolio. In portfolio 4, the weight is consistently negative and fairly large in magnitude. The propensity to short the long-term assets could be the result of a desire to hedge against domestic inflation (higher US interest rates appreciating the dollar and raising Belgium import prices), although LTB has a generally negative expected return and hence a short position may be taken based on expected return considerations. Further, the large negative positions in LTB need not mean speculation in foreign exchange since one can attempt to cover the open position created by shorting the US bond with a positive position in FX. A positive position in FX means holding Belgium francs now and buying dollars in the forward market. The sum of the weights given LTB and FX is therefore a better measure of the net open position in US dollars than either FX or LTB separately. Figure 11.13 shows that for the high-return and high-variance portfolio in Belgium there is generally a short position in US dollars.

Figure 11.14 shows the weights for STB and STK in Belgium. Since FX requires holding short-term domestic assets, the weight of STB and FX is the total position in this asset. For portfolio 4 the weight of STB + FX is almost exclusively greater than one, indicating a net short

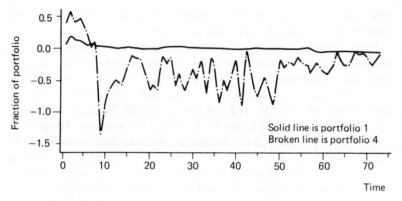

FIGURE 11.13a   *Weight of LTB in Belgium, 1975(9) to 1981(9)*

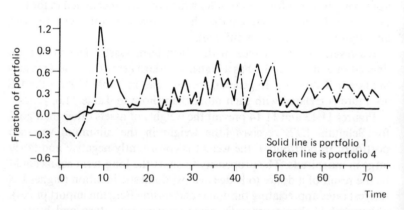

FIGURE 11.13b   *Weight of FX in Belgium, 1975(9) to 1981(9)*

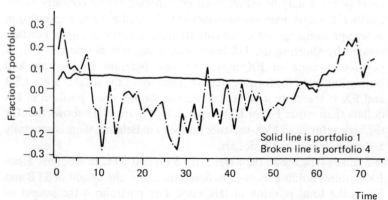

FIGURE 11.13c   *Weight of LTB + FX in Belgium, 1975(9) to 1981(9)*

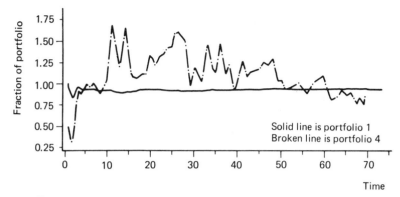

FIGURE 11.14a   *Weight of STK in Belgium, 1975(9) to 1981(9)*

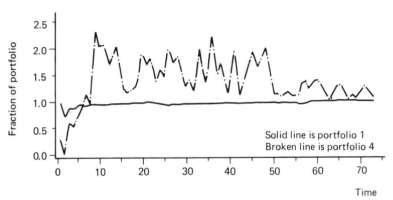

FIGURE 11.14b   *Weight of STB + FX in Belgium, 1975(9) to 1981(9)*

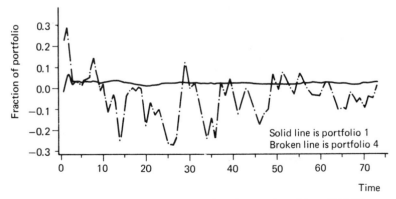

FIGURE 11.14c   *Weight of STK in Belgium, 1975(9) to 1981(9)*

position in all other assets. For the minimum variance portfolio the weight is usually close to one, as was true for the US. Stock, STK, receives a small but positive weight in the minimum variance portfolio, but a consistently negative weight in portfolio 4.

Figure 11.15 shows that for Canada the LTB position is again close to zero for portfolio 1. Unlike Belgium, however, portfolio 4 gives a positive weight to LTB in the early periods and only gives negative weight in the latter periods. The short positions of LTB in portfolio 4 are smaller in magnitude for Canada tan they are for Belgium. In addition, Canada differs from Belgium because the Canadian portfolio 4 assigns LTB + FX a positive weight in a variety of periods.

Figure 11.16 shows that from January 1976 on, the minimum variance

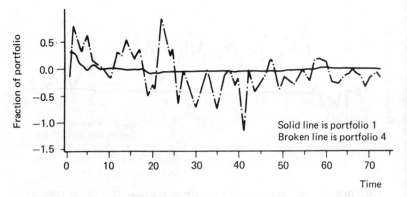

FIGURE 11.15a   *Weight of LTB in Canada, 1975(9) to 1981(9)*

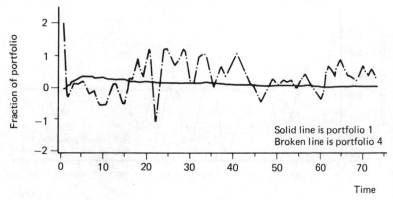

FIGURE 11.15b   *Weight of FX in Canada, 1975(9) to 1981(9)*

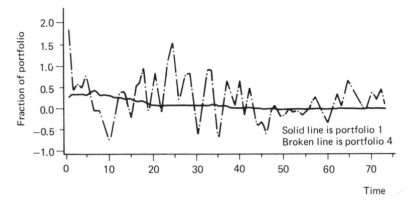

FIGURE 11.15c   *Weight of LTB + FX in Canada, 1975(9) to 1981(9)*

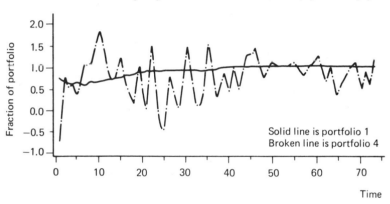

FIGURE 11.16a   *Weight of STB in Canada, 1975(9) to 1981(9)*

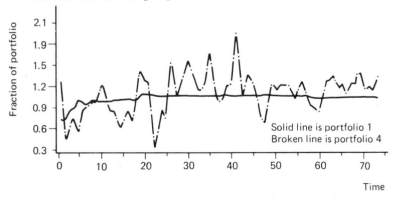

FIGURE 11.16b   *Weight of STB + FX in Canada, 1975(9) to 1981(9)*

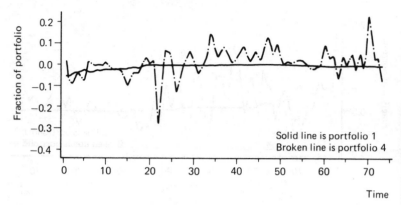

FIGURE 11.16c   *Weight of STK in Canada, 1975(9) to 1981(9)*

portfolio in Canada has the weight of the short-term asset above 0.900. This is shown in the plot for STB + FX; the plot for STB understates the share of the short-term asset due to the positive holdings captured in FX. Stock receives almost no weight in the Canadian minimum variance portfolio. For the high-return and high-variance portfolio stock typically gets a small positive weight.

In West Germany, Figures 11.17 and 11.18 show the minimum variance portfolio to be composed almost exclusively of STB. The German portfolio 4, like the Canadian, exhibits a clear pattern for the use of LTB; go long from September 1975 to December 1977, then take a

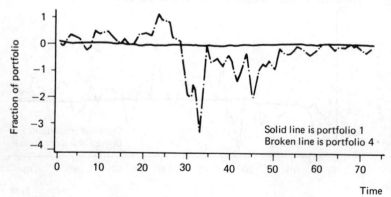

FIGURE 11.17a   *Weight of LTB in West Germany, 1975(9) to 1981(9)*

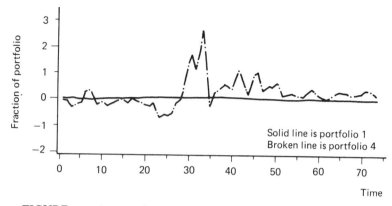

FIGURE 11.17b   *Weight of FX in West Germany, 1975(9) to 1981(9)*

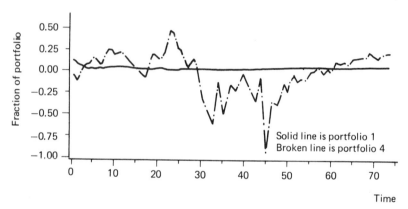

FIGURE 11.17c   *Weight of LTB + FX in West Germany, 1975(9) to 1981(9)*

short position from January 1978 to December 1981. The expected return series for LTB does not exhibit this pattern, however; for example, in June 1981 the expected return for LTB is 0.099 yet its portfolio weight is −0.104. The plot of LTB + FX in Figure 11.17 shows that in the early and middle periods the open position in US dollars created by the use of LTB is not completely hedged. In the last time periods, from the beginning of 1981 on, the German portfolio 4 is selling Deutsch marks in the forward market in excess of its short position in LTB.

The plot of STB + FX in Figure 11.18 shows that when the German

250

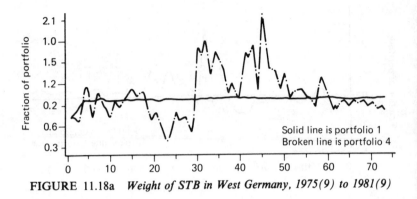

FIGURE 11.18a   *Weight of STB in West Germany, 1975(9) to 1981(9)*

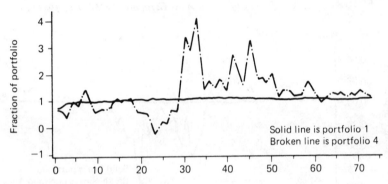

FIGURE 11.18b   *Weight of STB + FX in West Germany, 1975(9) to 1981(9)*

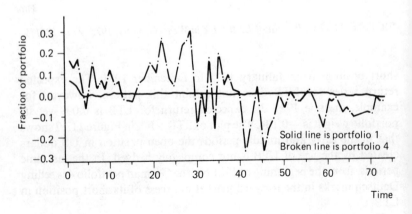

FIGURE 11.18c   *Weight of STK in West Germany, 1975(9) to 1981(9)*

portfolio 4 takes a short position in LTB, it is largely offset by, investing in the domestic short-term asset. To the extent that short-term interest rates in the US and Germany move together, the Germany portfolio 4 appears heavily involved in speculating on interest rate changes. Stock, like LTB, receives positive weight in first part of our sample and negative in the latter part. The magnitude of the positions in stock are much smaller than those in LTB, however.

Figure 11.19 shows the role of LTB in Switzerland to be similar to that of West Germany and Canada: no weight in the minimum variance portfolio, a positive weight for portfolio 4 in the early periods, and a negative weight for portfolio 4 in the later periods. The magnitude of the positive position is somewhat larger in Switzerland than in Germany, with the reverse holding true for the negative positions. The pattern of

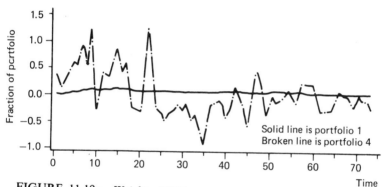

FIGURE 11.19a   *Weight of LTB in Switzerland, 1975(9) to 1981(9)*

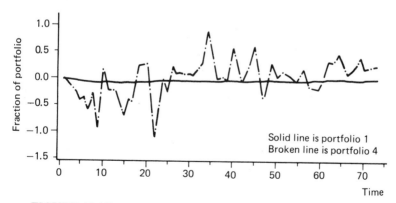

FIGURE 11.19b   *Weight of FX in Switzerland, 1975(9) to 1981(9)*

FIGURE 11.19c   *Weight of LTB + FX in Switzerland, 1975(9) to 1981(9)*

foreign exchange rate hedging, illustrated by LTB + FX, is also similar in Switzerland and Germany.

Figure 11.20 shows that, as in all other countries, the Swiss minimum variance portfolio is dominated by the short-term bank deposit asset. For the high-return, high-variance portfolio we again see the total share of the short-term asset, shown as STB + FX, moving to offset the position of LTB. Swiss stocks rarely exceed a weight of 0.020 and show several swings of positive and negative positions.

The portfolio weights for assets other than gold in the UK are shown in Figures 21 and 22. In the early period there is an unusually large negative weight for LTB in the minimum variance portfolio.

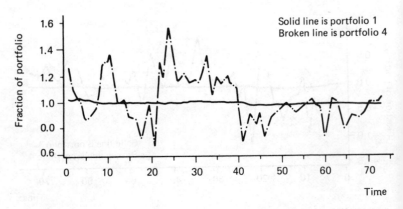

FIGURE 11.20a   *Weight of STB in Switzerland, 1975(9) to 1981(9)*

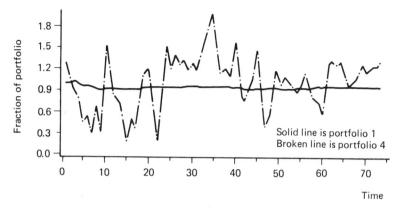

FIGURE 11.20b   *Weight of STB + FX in Switzerland, 1975(9) to 1981(9)*

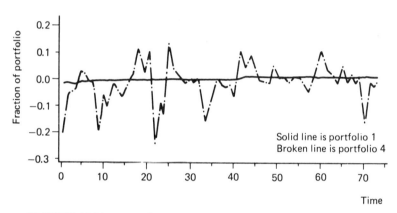

FIGURE 11.20c   *Weight of STK in Switzerland, 1975(9) to 1981(9)*

Presumably this is due to the instability of estimated parameters in the early time period, since from early 1977 to the end of the sample LTB reviews a share of close to zero in portfolio 1. The role of LTB in portfolio 4 is reminiscent of the role of this asset in Canada, West Germany and Switzerland – positive weight in the beginning of our sample followed by negative weight for the majority of the remain time. There does not appear to be a stable pattern of covering the open position in US dollars created by use of LTB. Positive positions in LTB + FX, indicating a net short position in the British pound, reach as high as 0.593 in February 1979 and negative positions reach − 0.392 in

254

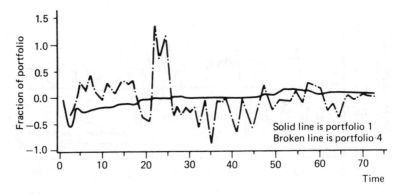

FIGURE 11.21a   *Weight of LTB in United Kingdom, 1975(9) to 1981(9)*

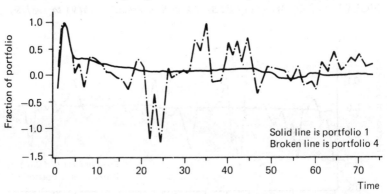

FIGURE 11.21b   *Weight of FX in United Kingdom, 1975(9) to 1981(9)*

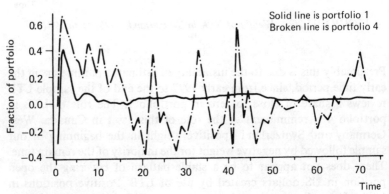

FIGURE 11.21c   *Weight of LTB + FX in United Kingdom, 1975(9) to 1981(9)*

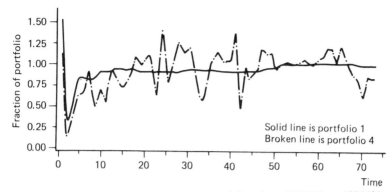

FIGURE 11.22a *Weight of STB in United Kingdom, 1975(9) to 1981(9)*

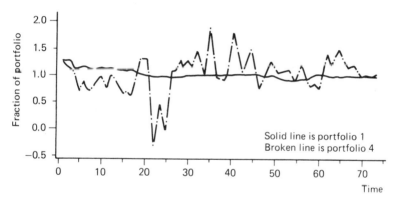

FIGURE 11.22b *Weight of STB + FX in United Kingdom, 1975(9) to 1981(9)*

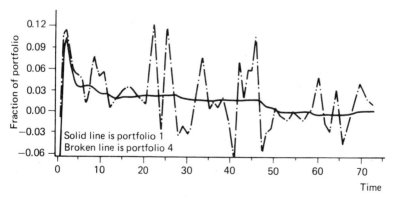

FIGURE 11.22c *Weight of STK in United Kingdom, 1975(9) to 1981(9)*

May 1977. LTB + FX shows the same early instability in portfolio 1 as was seen for LTB.

The plot of STB + FX in Figure 11.20 shows that by the time the UK model seems to have stabilized, the share of domestic short-term assets in the minimum variance portfolio is near one. Like other countries who have a distinct time path for LTB, in the UK portfolio 4 the weight of STB + FX generally stays below one in the pre-1978 period and exceeds one in the post-1978 period. Given the degree of volatility present in the UK stock market described earlier, it is not surprising that stock is less important in the UK portfolio 4 than in any other country's portfolio 4. The fact that UK stock has a higher return is insufficient to make it

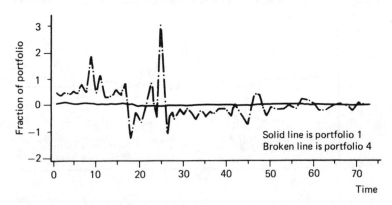

FIGURE 11.23a　*Weight of LTB in United States, 1975(9) to 1981(9)*

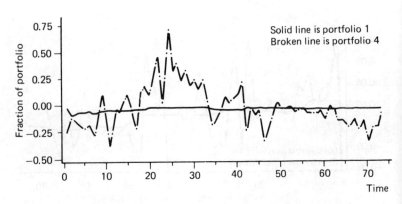

FIGURE 11.23b　*Weight of FX in United States, 1975(9) to 1981(9)*

attractive to hold in light of the highly variable nature of its return. Portfolio 4 in the UK actually assigns gold a more important role than stock.

The final two figures of this section present portfolio weights for assets other than gold in the US. Figure 11.23 shows that the magnitude of the weight given to LTB in Portfolio 4 is larger in the US than in any other country. Again the pattern of a long position early, which changes to a short position in the latter periods, is present. The role of foreign exchange in the US portfolio 4 is very close to that of West Germany; the weights are reversed, since for all countries FX represents selling domestic currency in the forward market. FX is noticeably important in portfolio 4 for the US, achieving a portfolio share of 0.702 in August

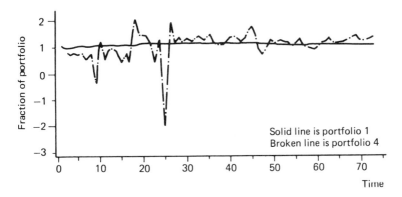

FIGURE 11.24a   *Weight of STB in United States, 1975(9) to 1981(9)*

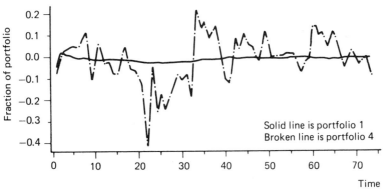

FIGURE 11.24b   *Weight of STK in United States, 1975(9) to 1981(9)*

1977. The minimum variance portfolio does not involve any significant use of FX or LTB.

Figure 11.24 shows that the US repeats the pattern of other countries by devoting all of the minimum variance portfolio to STB. For the high-return and high-variance portfolio the US also shows the standard result for all countries except Belgium: draw down the holdings of STB when a long position is taken for LTB and deposit the proceeds of a short sale of LTB into STB. The weight of stock in portfolio 4 for the US is generally positive, with the exception of the period from early 1977 to early 1978. Stocks never receive a weight above 0.207, which occurs in May 1978.

SUMMARY OF RESULTS

In this paper we have analyzed the weight assigned to gold in the optimal portfolio. First, we used monthly data on six assets in the US – T-bills, long-term bonds, stocks, forward foreign exchange, real estate and gold. We observed that gold received a small weight in all the portfolios for various models of returns. This result remained unchanged when we dropped real estate from our menu of assets.

Next we used three-month returns for five assets (short-term deposits, long-term bonds, stocks, forward exchange and gold) in six countries (Belgium, Canada, West Germany, Switzerland, the UK and the US). Gold continued to be assigned a small weight across countries. This is probably due to the large unforecastable variance in gold returns, as well as the lack of strong correlation with other assets. We noted that the small positions in gold were not a result of our forecasting low returns to gold, since we obtained predictions of 100 per cent or more in gold price changes.

Several observations are worth emphasizing. First, in all the models the realized cumulative return on the minimum portfolio was usually near or above the expected return. However, in the high-variance portfolio the realized return was always lower than expected. This could have resulted from incorrect predictions of returns, or incorrect estimation of the covariances between returns.

Second, the random walk model performed very well in all the cases we considered, ranking first or second in every country. This may indicate parameter instability in our models. However, the random walk model usually led to wide swings in asset positions from period to period, which happened less frequently in the other models.

Third, in the minimum variance portfolio in all countries the short-term assets carried a weight close to or above 0.95. Other assets had little weight. This was due to the predictability of its return, which had by far the smallest forecast error of all assets.

Fourth, in the high-variance portfolio, the short-term asset continued to carry a lot of weight. However, the long-term bond (LTB) also became important. Most countries were long in LTB in the early period but short in the middle and in the end. The exception was Belgium, which shorted LTB throughout the sample period. These positions in LTB correlated negatively with the total position in short-term assets (STB + FX), indicating that we were 'playing the spread' in order to earn a higher expected real return than the minimum variance portfolio. Also, the exchange risk in holding LTB could be partially offset by selling forward foreign exchange (FX). We observed that the net open position in foreign exchange (LTB + FX) consistently diverged from zero, indicating that we were not completely hedging our foreign exchange risk.

Fifth, stocks were rarely important in our models. The unpredictability of stock returns was second only to gold for most countries. In the UK stock returns were harder to predict than the return to holding gold.

NOTES

1. We thank Robert Cumby and Robert Holthomsen for helpful discussion.
2. Gold may be held for reasons other than standard portfolio investment. People may use gold as a hedge against hyperinflation, as a hedge against the collapse of the existing financial system, or as a consumption good. This paper is not concerned with these uses of gold.
3. See Bodie (1976), Fama and Schwert (1977), Firth (1979), Modigliani and Cohn (1979), and Nelson (1976).
4. See Kalman (1960).
5. See Merton (1972).
6. For the most recent time periods, the bond series was updated using unpublished information obtained from Lawrence Fisher.
7. A good description of the home purchase price component of the CPI is found in Greenless (1982). He concludes that the series underpredicts the return to holding real estate. He presents an alternative series, but it ranges only from 1973 through 1978. A major problem with the series for use in our work is the fact that it is a three-month moving average. Fama and Schwert (1977) also discuss the series.
8. The return to gold is higher for the US in Table 11.2 than in Table 11.1 because it is a three-month return and therefore stops in September of 1981. Thus it does not assign as much weight to the returns of -0.391 in November 1981 and -0.466 in December 1981 as does Table 11.1.

Similarly, the long-term bond returns were 0.666, 0.658 and −0.294 in the last three months of 1981, which raises the real return over the longer sample. The stock, short-term bond and foreign exchange series differ for the US between Tables 11.1 and 11.2. Table 11.2 is based on a three-month forward foreign exchange contract compared to a one-month contract in Table 11.1. The stock series is the CRSP series in Table 11.1 and the series from *Capital International Perspective* in Table 11.2. CRSP stock returns are 0.648, 0.499 and −0.374 in the last three months of 1981, which accounts for some of the differences between the results of Tables 11.1 and 11.2. For the short-term bond, Table 11.2 is based on a three-month bank deposit rate and Table 11.1 on a one-month US Treasury bill.

9. We form expected returns and covariances beginning in January 1975 but our first portfolio is not formed until August 1975. This is done to let the model settle down and to ensure that the priors for b_0 and P_0 are not overly important.

10. Although we do not report the results, we have estimated variable parameter models which include the $Z_t P_t Z_t'$ component and which increase the variance of V_t above what is used in Model AR2V1. The portfolios formed in these models performed much worse than those reported in Table 11.5. In addition, we added the nominal risk-free rate for STB as an explanatory variable, but obtained no noticeable improvement. Predicting returns and estimating covariances with higher than second order, single-equation autoregressions also provided little change in the results.

11. We do not constrain the elements of β_t due to the difficulty in imposing nonlinear constraints. Furthermore, in a multivariate system, these constraints are more complicated than the univariate example used here.

REFERENCES

Bank of England Quarterly Bulletin, Bank of England, various issues.

Bodie, Z. (1976) 'Common Stocks as a Hedge Against Inflation', *Journal of Finance*.

Capital International Perspective, Capital International SA, various issues.

Fama, E. F. and G. W. Schwert (1977) 'Asset Returns and Inflation', *Journal of Financial Economics*, pp. 115–146.

Firth, M. (1979) 'The Relationship between Stock Market Returns and the Rate of Inflation', *Journal of Finance*.

Fisher, and J. Lorie (1977) *A Half Century of Returns on Stocks and Bonds: Rates of Return on Investments in Common Stocks and US Treasury Securities, 1926–1976*, University of Chicago Graduate School of Business.

Greenless, J. S. (1982) 'An Empirical Evaluation of the CPI Home Purchase Index, 1973–1978', *Journal of American Real Estate and Urban Economics Association*, pp. 1–24.

Gultekin, N. B. (1981) 'Stock Market Returns and Inflation Evidence from Other Countries', mimeo, University of Pennsylvania.

Ibbotson, R. G. and C. L. Fall (1979) 'The United States Market Wealth Portfolio', *Journal of Portfolio Management*.

International Financial Statistics, International Monetary Fund, various issues.

International Monetary Market Yearbook, Chicago Mercantile Exchange, various issues.

Kalman, R. E. (1960) 'A New Approach to Linear Filtering and Predicting Problem', *Journal of Basic Engineering*, Trans, ASME, Series D, Vol. 82, No. 1, pp. 35–45.

Merton, R. C. (1972) 'An Analytic Derivation of the Efficient Portfolio Frontier', *Journal of Financial and Quantitative Analysis*, pp. 1851–1872.

Mishkin, F. S. (1982) 'The Real Interest Rate: A Multi-country Empirical Study', Parts I and II, University of Chicago, mimeo.

Modigliani, F. and R. A. Cohn (1979) 'Inflation, Rational Valuation, and the Market', *Financial Analyst Journal*.

Nelson, C. R. (1976) 'Inflation and Rates of Return on Common Stocks', *Journal of Finance*.

World Financial Markets, Morgan Guaranty Trust Co. of New York, various issues.

12 An Analysis of the Management of the Currency Composition of Reserve Assets and External Liabilities of Developing Countries[1]

MICHAEL P. DOOLEY

SUMMARY

Analyses of developing countries' financial positions have generally focused on the growth and currency composition of their reserve assets. The theory of portfolio selection, however, is clearly relevant to net positions rather than to assets alone. For this reason it is inappropriate to interpret changes in developing countries' net currency positions as having resulted from independent decisions concerning the currency composition of foreign exchange reserves and external debt. Such a decision-making process would be suboptimal, and we see no reason to ascribe such behavior to the countries studied.

In this paper estimates of the currency composition of developing countries' foreign exchange reserves and external debt are presented and analyzed. Our interpretation of data on net positions suggests very different conclusions concerning the financial policies of developing countries, compared with conclusions based on reserve assets alone. In particular, the share of developing countries' foreign exchange reserves denominated in US dollars varied over a narrow range in recent years, and changes that occurred can be largely accounted for by fluctuations in dollar exchange rates. This finding, which is consistent with previous work in this area,[2] is not maintained when net positions are examined. Net positions showed a substantial shift from 1974 to 1979 as the share of net liabilities denominated in US dollars increased from 25 per cent to nearly 60 per cent.

Analysis of net positions of analytical sub-groups of developing countries shows that this large shift toward net dollar liabilities for all developing countries did not result from changes over time in the preferences for dollar positions by the sub-groups studied. For three of the five sub-groups, shares of net positions denominated in US dollars showed even less variation than was the case for shares of foreign exchange reserves denominated in dollars. Rather the shift toward net dollar liabilities resulted from changes in the relative size of financial positions of sub-groups of developing countries that displayed different currency preferences throughout the period 1974 to 1979. Since data on the currency composition of reserve assets are not available for individual developing countries but only for country groups, this finding suggests that great care should be taken in drawing conclusions from aggregate data about a 'typical' government's financial policies or currency preferences. Nevertheless, the fact that preferences vary across sub-groups of countries suggests that changes in the structure of international reserve and debt holdings will continue to exert an important influence on the aggregate net currency positions of developing countries.

INTRODUCTION

The scale of international financial transactions of governments of developing countries has grown rapidly in recent years. Moreover, the greater variety of financial arrangements entered into by these governments, particularly transactions involving private credit markets, has generated fundamental changes in their financial positions. In this paper we present estimates of the size and currency denomination of international financial assets and liabilities for this diverse group of countries and for analytical sub-groups over the 1974–79 period. Our main objective is to determine whether conclusions drawn from traditional analysis of the behavior of individual balance sheet items, such as the stock of foreign currency reserves, are maintained when management of these items is viewed as part of a more comprehensive financial strategy.

Analysis of overall balance sheet positions rather than individual items is based on the assumption that some objectives for financial management are met by manipulation of a number of different types of assets and liabilities. There would be little point in examining the interaction of balance sheet items in a world where each item was constrained by factors beyond the control of the government. If, for example, developing countries did not have access to private credit markets, so that currency composition of their debt was determined by official donors, and if these countries held reserve assets exclusively in the form of a key currency, the currency denomination of international reserves and debt positions would be independent of one another. It is roughly this institutional environment for which the traditional analysis of the financial management of these countries was developed.

In recent years institutional changes have increased the incentives, and have provided governments with the means, to carry out more comprehensive management of their countries' financial positions. The variability of exchange rates among major currencies that has marked the floating rate period has certainly created strong incentives for more active management of the currency composition of both international reserves and foreign currency debt. Moreover, changes in oil and commodity prices and other shocks to the international economy have resulted in unprecedented growth in the size and variability of external assets and liabilities of oil-producing and other developing countries. Finally, the expansion of international credit markets has allowed developing countries greater flexibility in managing their international financial portfolios.

A better understanding of developing countries' adaptation to these circumstances would facilitate analysis of a number of policy issues. In an earlier paper by the author,[3] it was shown that the financial policies of developing countries had generated substantial changes in the supplies of net official debt denominated in US dollars and other major currencies. It was argued that this may have played a role in determining exchange rates among reserve currencies in recent years. Other policy issues for which the analysis presented in this paper might be important include the appropriate growth of international liquidity, the stability of a multi-currency reserve system, the role of the SDR and other reserve assets, and the role of private and official credit in the adjustment process.

Discussion of each of these questions depends in part on our understanding of how governments of developing countries have adapted their policies of financial management to changes in the international monetary system. We cannot begin to evaluate these policies until we have a clear idea as to which set of balance sheet items is manipulated by governments in order to meet their objectives. It should be noted that constraints on developing countries' financial policies undoubtedly continue to influence a variety of individual balance sheet items. However, as long as all positions are not constrained, optimal net positions can be attained by marginal adjustments of unconstrained financial assets and liabilities.

PORTFOLIO THEORY AND FINANCIAL MANAGEMENT OF DEVELOPING COUNTRIES

The financial management of governments can be analyzed using well-known principles of optimal portfolio selection. This theory posits that an individual decision-maker, in this instance a government, attempts to manipulate his portfolio in order to maximize the expected utility of consumption over time. The utility, or desirability, of a portfolio depends on both the expected value of the financial assets and the variability of the value of the financial assets in terms of some basket of goods. Thus a rational government would not put all of its wealth in one currency that has the highest expected yield, since this would, in general, imply a highly variable outcome for its wealth depending on how exchange rates actually change. This theory also suggests that countries producing or consuming different goods and services would optimally hold different portfolios of financial assets.[4]

An application of portfolio theory to an analysis of developing countries' financial policies encounters several problems of measurement and interpretation. First, it is clear that predictions drawn from portfolio theory apply to net wealth positions. Changes in exchange rates affect the value of both financial assets and liabilities, and for this reason it is not sensible to evaluate separately holdings of reserve assets or official liabilities. Second, data on reserve assets and official liabilities do not encompass all important financial positions. Agreements to sell commodities forward or to purchase intermediate inputs are equivalent to financial assets and liabilities but are not included in the balance sheets we study. Third, the expected patterns of trade in goods and services that in part determine the demand for financial positions in different currencies, include not only relatively stable final consumption patterns but also receipts arising from exports and payments associated with the import of intermediate goods. For this reason it would not be surprising to find that currency preferences varied among groups of countries with different patterns of international trade. Moreover, changes in currency preferences over time for groups of similar countries must be interpreted cautiously and may be better explained by changes in the expected patterns of production and consumption than by changes in expected yields and covariances of financial assets denominated in various currencies. Finally, while the natural unit for analysis is an individual country, data on the currency composition of reserve assets are available only for groups of countries that are in some respects similar but which may have different preferences for the financial assets included in the balance sheets studied. To the extent that behavior is not uniform within a group of countries, changes in the compositions of the balance sheets studied might reflect changes in the relative size of the positions of different countries.

The primary objective of this paper is to evaluate the importance of the distinction between net and gross financial positions denominated in different currencies. It seems likely that the desired currency composition of reserve assets is largely independent of the optimal disposition of net wealth over currencies. For example, reserve assets denominated in US dollars might be attractive because of the dollar's role as a 'vehicle' currency in most foreign exchange market transactions. As for liabilities, it might be the case that some countries can issue debt denominated in a given currency on relatively favorable terms because of familiarity with financial institutions in the country whose currency is the denominator, the lending policies of international organizations such as the World Bank, or the policies of creditor countries that regulate access to their credit markets.

Although such considerations can be expected to influence the size of gross asset and liability positions in various currencies, it would, in general, be possible to attain a desired net position in each currency. The problem can be compared to a hedging strategy of a private firm engaged in international trade. Such a firm acquires asset and liability positions in foreign currency that expose the firm's net worth to exchange rate changes. It might be very costly to attempt to eliminate the exposure by constraining gross positions, for example, by limiting the liquid assets held in order to facilitate payments. The firm can, however, eliminate the exposure generated by its liquid assets by borrowing in the same currency or through a number of other financial arrangements. In this manner the net worth of the firm is protected while the advantages of holding gross asset or liability positions in different currencies are preserved.

A government faces essentially the same problem. It might want to protect its net worth, which depends upon its net position by currency. But it also is a 'going concern' that holds liquid assets denominated in different currencies in order to facilitate expenditures and that faces a number of constraints on the currency denomination of debt issues. There are, of course, limitations to the process of transforming a portfolio in which gross positions are constrained so that net positions by currency are optimal. An obvious limitation is the fact that reserve and debt management are often not controlled by the same decision-maker within the government. As a working hypothesis, however, it may prove useful to interpret data for governments' net positions in different currencies as though they were able to obtain desired net positions.

One complication faced by most developing countries and non-financial firms in reaching their desired net positions is that the average maturity of financial assets is much shorter than for financial liabilities. In these circumstances the *means* available for adjusting net currency positions are to some extent constrained by the inability to alter the currency denomination of long-term debt. This is, however, just one of the many constraints on an individual balance sheet item that must be taken into account in managing net currency positions. In general, the *objectives* for net currency positions are not affected by the maturities of financial assets and liabilities. Although capital gains or losses resulting from changes in interest rates in assets and liabilities of different maturities may complicate hedging strategies, such gains and losses are unlikely to be systematically related to gains and losses related to exchange rate changes. The basic point remains, therefore, that exposure to exchange risk depends on stocks of assets and liabilities of all maturities.

The balance sheet items that can be manipulated at least cost will be determined by considerations that change over time and are largely unrelated to the factors determining the desired net position in each currency. For developing countries, the rapid growth of Eurocurrency credits in recent years may have provided an efficient vehicle for managing net currency positions. These credits are typically priced in terms of a spread over an interbank deposit interest rate. The borrower can normally choose to denominate the debt in a variety of major currencies or in several multicurrency baskets. Debt service payments need not be made in the currency in which the credit is denominated. The lender does not have a direct interest in which currency is chosen since it can fully cover its exchange and interest rate risk in the well-developed

Eurocurrency deposit market. Thus a country with a growing stock of Eurocurrency liabilities can conveniently manipulate its net position in different currencies by drawing credits denominated in a number of major foreign currencies.

CURRENCY COMPOSITION OF EXTERNAL ASSETS AND LIABILITIES OF 93 DEVELOPING COUNTRIES

The analysis in this section is largely descriptive, in that no model of portfolio behavior is tested. Nevertheless, two tentative conclusions seem warranted. First, the currency composition of reserve assets is not highly correlated with the currency composition of net positions of developing countries. This is the case both for the entire sample of countries and for analytical sub-groups. This lack of correspondence calls into question analysis of the currency composition of reserve assets based on the assumption that reserve assets taken by themselves are optimal portfolios. Second, the currency composition of net positions of various sub-groups of developing countries is quite different throughout the sample period. As noted earlier, this finding is consistent with the fact that the sub-groups studied have different expected patterns of receipts and payments for traded goods. By way of contrast, the net positions of sub-groups of countries are relatively stable over the time period studied. It follows that the large shifts in the net currency positions for developing countries as a whole are due to changes in the composition of net financial positions among groups of countries with different currency preferences rather than changes in currency preferences of groups of similar countries over time.

Data for the combined balance sheets of developing countries are shown in Table 12.1.[5] These data reveal little concerning the behavior of a 'typical' government, since it is clear that there were large differences among individual countries with regard to the direction and size of changes in net positions. It does, however, provide a rough measure of the net impact this group of countries has had on the outstanding supplies of assets and liabilities denominated in various currencies. In the following section we will examine various sub-groups of countries.

As shown in the top panel of Table 12.1, there were sizable shifts in the currency composition of developing countries' foreign exchange reserves over the six years for which we have data. A remarkable feature of the change in the share of dollar-denominated assets is that it closely mirrors changes in the dollar exchange value as measured by the SDR/$

TABLE 12.1 *Ninety-three developing countries (end of period)*

Year	Total (millions of $)	Per cent denominated in:						Memo SDR/$ (1974 = 100)
		US	DM	STG	FF	JY	Other	
	Foreign exchange reserves							
1974	67,677	67	10	11	2	0	11	100
1975	72,439	70	9	7	2	1	11	104.5
1976	89,925	72	10	3	2	1	12	105.4
1977	107,412	68	13	3	2	0	14	100.1
1978	106,550	62	15	3	2	1	17	94.0
1979	128,415	62	16	3	2	4	12	92.9

Year	Total (millions of $)	Per cent denominated in:							
		US	DM	STG	FF	JY	SF	Multi	Other
	Foreign currency debt								
1974	88,446	50	9	9	4	4	1	11	12
1975	107,320	52	9	8	4	4	1	11	12
1976	128,358	56	7	7	4	4	1	11	11
1977	157,532	58	7	6	4	4	1	10	10
1978	196,980	57	8	5	4	5	1	9	10
1979	249,705	55	9	4	4	7	1	9	10

Year	Total (millions of $)	Per cent denominated in:					
		US	DM	STG	FF	JY	Other
	Net foreign currency debt[1]						
1974	20,769	25	13	7	16	18	21
1975	34,881	37	12	14	10	11	15
1976	38,433	44	4	18	13	12	9
1977	50,120	59	−1	14	10	14	5
1978	90,430	65	2	9	8	12	5
1979	121,290	58	5	7	8	12	10

1. In order to account for the sizable share of multi-currency liabilities in the data, liabilities to individual currencies are allocated in a manner proportional to the actual shares for each currency for that year.

rate shown in the last column of Table 12.1. That is, if we held exchange rates at their 1974 levels and recalculated the shares shown in Table 12.1, there would be little change in the dollar share of the portfolio. Such a result would seem to suggest that this large group of countries on balance passively accepted changes in the share of assets denominated in different currencies resulting from changes in exchange rates. Such behavior would be difficult to reconcile with portfolio theory because it is unlikely that the preferences of this group of countries for currencies always coincided with exchange rate changes.[6]

An alternative explanation is that reserve assets are held for transactions and precautionary reasons, and the currency composition of such assets is denominated by the consideration that they can be easily liquidated and used to make payments. Adjusting the currency mix of transactions balances following an exchange rate change might not be called for, particularly if nominal prices and payment patterns do not change along with exchange rates. Thus a country with a given pattern of payments in, for example, US dollars and Deutsch marks might expect little change in the nominal level of those payments in each currency following a change in the dollar–mark exchange rate.

The middle panel of Table 12.1 shows estimates of size and currency composition of external debt for developing countries. The data show that external debt positions were larger and grew more rapidly compared with reserve assets throughout the six-year period. Moreover, exchange rate changes did not dominate changes in the share of liabilities denominated in different currencies. In particular, the 10 per cent fall in the dollar's exchange value between 1976 and 1978 was associated with a 1 per cent rise in the share of dollar-denominated liabilities for this group of countries.

The evolution of net positions in various currencies is shown in the bottom panel of Table 1.[7] The very different appearance of the information in this part of the table serves as a reminder that when assets and liabilities are growing at different rates, inspection of data on either assets or liabilities alone is likely to give a misleading picture of changes in net positions.

A striking feature of these data is the very large shift toward net dollar-denominated liabilities from 1974 to 1978. It follows that investors other than developing country governments absorbed a substantial net supply of dollar-denominated debt issued by the governments of developing countries. As opposed to the picture of financial management for developing countries that emerges from an inspection of reserve asset data, we would conclude from these more comprehensive measures that the combined actions of this diverse group of governments has resulted in a substantial shift away from net dollar asset positions.

The share of net liabilities denominated in Deutsch marks fell rapidly from 1974 to 1977 as the share of reserve assets denominated in marks increased and the share of liabilities denominated in marks fell. The 14 per cent fall in the Deutsch mark's share of net liabilities over this three-year period is consistent with efforts of many governments to increase the share of their net wealth denominated in marks in the early years of the floating rate system. If we look only at reserve assets this trend continues in 1978 and 1979. However, the share of mark-denominated liabilities increased after 1977, more than offsetting the continued build-up of reserve assets and, by 1979, reversing about half of the early fall in net mark liabilities.

The behavior of net positions denominated in pound sterling is also quite interesting. The share of net liabilities denominated in sterling rose rapidly from 1974 to 1976 as the decline in sterling-denominated liabilities was overwhelmed by a rapid decline in sterling-denominated reserve assets. However, after 1976 the continued decline in the share of sterling liabilities was accompanied by an unchanged share of sterling assets, so that by 1979 the net position in sterling had returned to its 1974 level.

The French franc presents another picture. In this case the share of both franc-denominated assets and liabilities remained unchanged during the entire sample period. However, because the share of liabilities denominated in francs exceeded the share of assets denominated in francs, and because liabilities grew more rapidly than assets, the net liability position in francs fell throughout the sample period.

Finally, net liabilities denominated in yen were quite small and their share in total net liabilities changed little after 1975, in spite of a fairly rapid increase in both assets and liabilities during 1978 and 1979.

CURRENCY COMPOSITION OF EXTERNAL ASSETS AND LIABILITIES OF ANALYTICAL SUBGROUPS OF DEVELOPING COUNTRIES

In order to examine the external financial policies of groups of countries that are in some respects similar, Tables 12.2–12.6 show foreign currency assets, liabilities and net positions for analytical sub-groups. A full discussion of the recent experience of these groups of developing countries can be found in the *World Economic Outlook*.[8]

Detailed discussion of gross asset and liability positions is limited to only two groups of countries because such discussion is not helpful in understanding the evolution of net positions over time. In a mechanical sense the difficulty is that the evolution of net positions depends upon

TABLE 12.2   *Major oil exporters*

Year	Total (millions of $)	Per cent denominated in:					
		US	DM	STG	FF	JY	Other
	Foreign exchange reserves						
1974	39,488	76	4	15	0	0	3
1975	46,875	77	6	8	2	1	7
1976	52,330	78	8	4	1	1	8
1977	59,780	72	12	2	2	0	11
1978	44,901	67	15	2	2	1	12
1979	59,870	68	16	2	2	4	8

Year	Total (millions of $)	Per cent denominated in:							
		US	DM	STG	FF	JY	SF	Multi	Other
	Foreign currency debt								
1974	7,895	47	6	5	10	0	1	13	17
1975	8,103	43	5	6	11	0	1	13	20
1976	9,138	44	4	5	10	0	0	17	20
1977	11,128	47	4	5	10	1	0	15	19
1978	15,619	47	8	4	10	5	1	11	16
1979	21,405	45	10	3	9	9	1	8	14

Year	Total (millions of $)	Per cent denominated in:					
		US	DM	STG	FF	JY	Other
	Net foreign currency assets[1]						
1974	31,593	81	4	18	−2	0	0
1975	38,773	82	6	7	0	1	4
1976	43,192	83	9	3	−1	1	5
1977	48,652	75	14	2	0	0	9
1978	29,282	75	18	1	−2	−1	9
1979	38,465	78	18	1	−2	1	4

1. In order to account for the sizable share of multi-currency liabilities in the data, liabilities to individual currencies are allocated in a manner proportional to the actual shares for each currency for that year.

the levels and growth rates of both shares and amounts of assets and liabilities denominated in different currencies. The economic interpretation of this is that the rational management of the currency denominations of net positions need not result in consistent patterns over time for either assets or liabilities. For example, a financial strategy to reduce

TABLE 12.3   *Middle-income net oil importers*

Year	Total (millions of $)	Per cent denominated in:					
		US	DM	STG	FF	JY	Other
		Foreign exchange reserves					
1974	8,912	54	24	5	3	0	13
1975	8,695	57	20	4	3	0	15
1976	10,883	62	20	2	2	1	13
1977	12,218	59	20	2	2	2	14
1978	16,027	53	23	3	4	2	16
1979	18,702	53	24	4	2	5	12

Year	Total (millions of $)	Per cent denominated in:							
		US	DM	STG	FF	JY	SF	Multi	Other
		Foreign currency debt							
1974	31,463	60	8	4	4	2	1	12	8
1975	42,032	63	7	4	4	2	1	11	7
1976	52,250	66	6	3	3	3	1	11	7
1977	65,592	67	6	3	3	3	1	10	7
1978	82,501	65	8	3	3	4	1	10	7
1979	105,494	63	9	2	3	5	2	8	7

Year	Total (millions of $)	Per cent denominated in:					
		US	DM	STG	FF	JY	Other
		Net foreign currency debt[1]					
1974	22,551	75	4	6	5	3	7
1975	33,337	76	5	5	4	3	6
1976	41,367	78	3	4	4	4	6
1977	53,373	79	4	3	3	4	6
1978	66,475	77	5	3	3	5	7
1979	86,792	73	6	2	4	6	8

1. In order to account for the sizable share of multi-currency liabilities in the data, liabilities to individual currencies are allocated in a manner proportional to the actual shares for each currency for that year.

the share of net worth denominated in dollars might call for a reduction in the share of reserve assets denominated in dollars in one time period but an increase in level of liabilities denominated in dollars in the next time period.

The behavior of foreign currency reserves of developing countries that

TABLE 12.4   *Low-income countries*

Year	Total (millions of $)	Per cent denominated in:					
		US	DM	STG	FF	JY	Other
	Foreign exchange reserves						
1974	2,517	45	20	17	9	0	9
1975	2,397	49	18	13	10	0	9
1976	4,607	63	14	6	7	0	11
1977	7,430	57	14	11	4	0	14
1978	8,325	51	17	11	5	0	16
1979	9,365	43	17	14	5	11	10

Year	Total (millions of $)	Per cent denominated in:							
		US	DM	STG	FF	JY	SF	Multi	Other
	Foreign currency debt								
1974	22,504	33	10	23	4	5	1	11	14
1975	25,621	33	11	22	5	4	1	10	15
1976	28,324	37	10	19	5	4	1	10	15
1977	32,246	39	10	17	5	4	1	9	15
1978	38,021	38	10	16	6	5	1	9	15
1979	45,195	39	10	14	7	5	1	8	15

Year	Total (millions of $)	Per cent denominated in:					
		US	DM	STG	FF	JY	Other
	Net foreign currency assets[1]						
1974	19,987	36	11	27	4	6	15
1975	23,223	37	11	26	5	5	16
1976	23,717	37	10	25	6	5	17
1977	24,816	39	10	22	7	6	17
1978	29,695	40	9	20	7	7	17
1979	35,829	43	9	16	8	5	19

1. In order to account for the sizable share of multi-currency liabilities in the data, these liabilities to individual currencies are allocated in a manner proportional to the actual shares for each currency for that year.

are major oil exporters is marked by rapid growth and substantial changes in currency denomination (Table 12.2). The dollar share of the asset portfolio fell sharply after 1976, following closely the decline in the exchange value of the dollar. The rise throughout the period in the share of mark- and yen-denominated assets and the decline in sterling-denominated assets reflects both valuation changes and a redistribution

TABLE 12.5 *Manufacturing exporters*

Year	Total (Millions of $)	Per cent denominated in:					
		US	DM	STG	FF	JY	Other
	Foreign exchange reserves						
1974	11,880	50	14	3	1	0	31
1975	9,609	56	11	5	0	0	27
1976	15,697	63	9	2	0	1	26
1977	19,884	65	12	2	0	0	21
1978	28,110	61	11	2	0	0	26
1979	28,924	64	12	2	1	2	20

Year	Total (millions of $)	Per cent denominated in:							
		US	DM	STG	FF	JY	SF	Multi	Other
	External debt								
1974	12,313	49	10	3	3	9	1	9	17
1975	14,680	52	11	2	3	8	1	9	15
1976	18,092	56	9	2	4	8	1	9	11
1977	22,091	56	10	2	4	8	1	9	11
1978	26,750	54	10	2	4	9	1	9	11
1979	32,660	51	11	2	4	11	1	10	10

Year	Total (millions of $)	Per cent denominated in:					
		US	DM	STG	FF	JY	Other
	Net foreign currency debt[1]						
1974	433	170	− 54	10	49	280	− 354
1975	5,071	60	14	− 2	8	27	− 7
1976	2,395	59	22	5	29	62	− 78
1977	2,207	35	7	3	41	90	− 76
1978	− 1,360	65	15	− 3	− 83	− 195	302
1979	3,736	7	21	− 1	35	94	− 55

1. In order to account for the sizable share of multi-currency liabilities in the data, liabilities to individual currencies are allocated in a manner proportional to the actual shares for each currency for that year.

of portfolios among the non-dollar currencies. In general, this data taken by itself would suggest active management of the non-dollar part of the portfolio, but a passive policy toward changes in the dollar share of the portfolio.

However, when the information on external debt (shown in the

TABLE 12.6   *Net oil exporters*

Year	Total (millions of $)	Per cent denominated in:					
		US	DM	STG	FF	JY	Other
Foreign exchange reserves							
1973	4,880	64	10	7	5	0	15
1974	4,862	68	8	4	4	0	16
1975	6,408	70	9	2	3	0	16
1976	8,100	73	9	1	1	0	15
1977	9,187	67	11	1	2	1	18
1978	11,554	63	13	2	2	3	16
1979	15,000	63	13	2	2	3	16

Year	Total (millions of $)	Per cent denominated in:							
		US	DM	STG	FF	JY	SF	Multi	Other
External debt									
1974	14,270	55	9	2	4	3	1	13	13
1975	16,884	57	8	2	4	4	1	12	11
1976	20,553	62	7	2	3	4	0	12	10
1977	26,475	65	7	2	3	4	0	11	9
1978	34,089	64	6	2	3	6	1	9	9
1979	44,952	59	9	2	3	8	1	9	9

Year	Total (millions of $)	Per cent denominated in:					
		US	DM	STG	FF	JY	Other
Net foreign currency debt[1]							
1974	9,391	64	10	1	5	6	14
1975	12,022	66	11	2	4	6	11
1976	14,145	72	8	2	4	7	7
1977	18,375	74	7	2	4	6	7
1978	24,902	74	5	2	4	9	6
1979	33,398	67	9	2	4	12	7

1. In order to account for the sizable share of multi-currency liabilities in the data, liabilities to individual currencies are allocated in a manner proportional to the actual shares for each currency for that year.

middle panel) is taken into account, these conclusions are substantially affected. Perhaps the most interesting feature of the debt data is the relatively low share of dollar-denominated liabilities issued by these countries throughout the sample period. As the growth of liabilities accelerated after 1976, the practice of denominating less than half of these liabilities in dollars acted as an important offset to the decline in the share of dollar assets discussed above. Thus, while the share of gross assets denominated in dollars, shown in the top panel, declined by 10 per cent from 1976 to 1979, the share of net assets denominated in dollars fell by only 5 per cent, considerably less than the fall in the dollar's exchange value over the period. One interpretation of these data is that as the dollar's exchange value fell after 1976, this group of countries 'rebalanced' their portfolio by issuing non-dollar liabilities rather than substituting dollar for non-dollar reserve assets. Such a strategy may also account for the fact that the very large change in the relative share of mark and sterling assets was even more pronounced in the net asset position, shown in the bottom panel of Table 12.2. However, the fairly sharp increase in the share of yen-denominated assets in 1979 was largely offset by increases in yen liabilities.

The foreign currency debt of 'middle income' developing countries that are net oil importers accounted for about half the total for all developing countries (Table 12.3). The currency composition of both assets and liabilities of this group of countries showed less variability than that of the major oil exporters over the six-year period. An exception was the fairly large increase in the dollar share of reserve assets from 1974–76, which, however, was completely reversed by 1979. The share of net liabilities denominated in dollars was quite stable over the period and was virtually unchanged in 1979 compared with 1974.

The stability of this group's net liability position during a time of very large exchange rate changes and a threefold increase in their foreign currency debt is consistent with the view that net positions are managed in order to maintain a desired net portfolio allocation. The fact that these countries have held about three-quarters of their net debt in dollar-denominated positions would indicate a fairly strong preference for maintaining a predictable stream of dollar payments. The concentration of net liabilities in dollars would also suggest that these countries' net worth position are unusually sensitive to changes in dollar exchange rates and interest rates.

Data for low-income countries (Table 12.4) show a very different portfolio as compared to the two groups discussed above. The dominant difference is the comparatively low share of dollar-denominated net debt. With the exception of a significant decline in the share of net liabilities denominated in pound sterling, these countries' policies have also resulted in a remarkably stable balance sheet. It would also appear that this group prefers a more diversified portfolio than do the other groups.

Data for manufacturing exporters (Table 12.5) indicate that these countries have maintained a roughly balanced position in total assets and liabilities, so that their net liability or asset position has remained small. The net position by currency has been quite erratic and shows no particular trend. Finally, the group of net oil exporters (Table 12.6) shows an unusual pattern in that the net liability position denominated in dollars rose from 1974 to 1978 to about the level prevailing for other 'middle income' countries, but fell sharply in 1979 as liabilities denominated in marks and yen increased.

FUTURE RESEARCH

In this paper we have only begun to draw conclusions from a comprehensive approach to analyzing the financial management of developing countries. It has been shown that changes in the currency composition of reserve assets of developing countries as a group, and for several analytical sub-groups, are not reliable guides to the behavior of net financial positions in various currencies. In several instances, inferences drawn from analysis of assets alone are significantly modified or reversed by more careful analysis of net positions.

A topic for further research is the possibility that tests of propositions drawn from portfolio theory concerning the optimal size of reserve asset holdings might also be materially affected by a more comprehensive evaluation of assets and liabilities. It seems likely that the growth of Eurocurrency credits and lines of credit also influenced the gross stock of reserve assets held by developing countries. An unconditional line of credit may be a good substitute for a liquid asset. Since most non-oil developing countries are net debtors, their international reserves are financed by external liabilities. The cost of carrying such reserve assets is the difference between the government's marginal borrowing rate and the rate of return on their reserve assets. If, as is sometimes the case, the commitment fee for a line of credit is less than this differential, it might be rational to hold only a very small transactions balance in the form of reserve assets. The difficulty in testing this hypothesis is in measuring a government's access to credit. The amount or maturity structure of the stock of a country's debt is probably of little help in constructing such a measure.[9] This line of argument suggests that an analysis of the demand for growth reserve assets should consider measures of off-balance-sheet agreements that ensure a government's access to credit on prearranged terms.

NOTES

1. This paper was prepared while Mr Dooley was Assistant Chief, Developing Country Studies Division, Research Department. The author wishes to thank V. Sundararajan for helpful comments on an earlier draft. S. Jelencovich performed the calculations. The paper represents the views of the author and should not be interpreted as reflecting the views of the Board of Governors of the Federal Reserve System or other members of its staff.
2. For an empirical analysis of the currency composition of foreign exchange reserves, see Heller and Knight (1978).
3. Dooley (1982).
4. A theoretical and empirical literature has developed relating international asset demand to principles of expected utility maximization. Theoretical papers include Kouri (1976, 1977), Kouri and Macedo (1978), Frankel (1979), Krugman (1981) and Dornbusch (1982). Empirical work includes Roll and Solnik (1977), Cornell and Dietrich (1978), Kouri and Macedo (1978), Macedo (1980), Dornbusch (1980), Healy (1981) and von Furstenberg (1981). Asset demand functions derivable from expected utility maximization have been employed to estimate the effects of changes in the relative supplies of assets on exchange rates and rates of return. See Bramson, Halttunen and Masson (1977), Frankel (1981), and Dooley and Isard (1982).
5. Data on foreign-currency-denominated debt are from the World Bank Debtor Reporting System and include public debt, publicly guaranteed debt, and a small amount of private external debt, all of which have original maturities of more than one year. Data on foreign currency reserve assets are from *International Financial Statistics*. The currency composition of foreign exchange is based on the Fund's currency survey and on estimates derived mainly, but not solely, from official national reports.
6. It is, of course, true that exchange rates reflect all wealth holders' preferences for net positions in various currencies. It seems unlikely, however, that the preferences of this group of wealth holders would consistently correspond to changes generated by exchange rates.
7. In order to account for the sizable share of multi-currency liabilities in the data, we allocated these liabilities to individual currencies in a manner proportional to the actual shares for each currency for that year.
8. See International Monetary Fund (1981) pp. 108–9 for a list of countries and a brief discussion of the sub-groups discussed in this section.
9. See Eaton and Gersovitz (1981) for a discussion of possible linkages between external debt and gross international reserves.

REFERENCES

Branson, William, Hannu Halttunen, and Paul Masson (1977) 'Exchange Rates in the Short Run: The Dollar-Deutschemark Rate', *European Economic Review*, Vol. 10, pp. 303–24.
Cornell, Bradford and J. K. Dietrich (1978) 'The Efficiency of the Market for

Foreign Exchange Under Floating Exchange Rates', *Review of Economics and Statistics*, Vol. 60, No. 1, February.

Dooley, Michael P. (1982) 'An Analysis of Exchange Market Intervention of Industrial and Developing Countries', International Monetary Fund, *Staff Papers*, Vol. 29, July, pp. 233–69.

Dooley, Michael and Peter Isard (1983) 'The Portfolio-Balance Model of Exchange Rates and Some Structural Estimates of the Risk Premium', International Monetary Fund, DM/83/20, March.

Dornbusch, Rudiger (1980) 'Exchange Rate Economics: Where Do We Stand?', *Brookings Papers on Economic Activity*, No. 1, pp. 143–94.

Dornbusch, Rudiger (1982) 'Exchange Risk and the Macroeconomics of Exchange Rate Determination', in *The Internationalization of Financial Markets and National Economic Policy by* R. Hawkins, R. Levich and C. Wihlborg (eds) (JAI Press).

Eaton, Jonathan and Gersovitz, Mark (1981) 'Poor Country Borrowing in Private Financial Markets and the Repudiation Issue', *Princeton Studies in International Finance*, No. 47, June.

Frankel, Jeffrey (1979) 'The Diversifiability of Exchange Risk', *Journal of International Economics*, Vol. 9, August, pp. 379–93.

Frankel, Jeffrey (1982) 'A Test of Perfect Substitutability in the Foreign Exchange Market', *Southern Economic Journal*, Vol. 49, October, pp. 406–16.

Healy, James (1981) 'A Simple Regression Technique for the Optimal Diversification of Foreign Exchange Reserves', International Monetary Fund, DM/81/64, August.

Heller, Robert and Malcolm Knight (1978) 'Reserve Currency Preferences of Central Banks', Princeton University International Finance Section, *Essays in International Finance*, No. 131, December.

International Monetary Fund (1981) *World Economic Outlook*, Occasional Paper No. 4.

Kouri, Pentti (1976) 'The Determinants of the Forward Premium', ILES Seminar Paper 62, University of Stockholm, August.

Kouri, Pentti (1977) 'International Investment and Interest Rate Linkages Under Flexible Exchange Rates', in *The Political Economy of Monetary Reform*, Robert Aliber (London: Macmillan).

Kouri, Pentti and Jorge Braga de Macedo (1978) 'Exchange Rates and the International Adjustment Process', *Brookings Papers on Economic Activity*, Vol. 1, pp. 111–50.

Krugman, Paul (1981) 'Consumption Preferences, Asset Demands, and Distribution Effects in International Financial Markets', NBER Working Paper No. 651, March.

Macedo, Jorge Braga de (1980) 'Portfolio Diversification Across Countries', International Finance Section Working Paper, Princeton University, November.

Roll, Richard and Bruno Solnik (1977) 'A Pure Foreign Exchange Asset Pricing Model', *Journal of International Economics*, Vol. 7, No. 2, pp. 161–80.

von Furstenberg, George (1981) 'Incentives for International Currency Diversification by US Financial Investors', International Monetary Fund *Staff Papers*, Vol. 28, September, pp. 477–94.

13 The Theory of the Lender of Last Resort and the Eurocurrency Markets[1]

JEFFREY R. SHAFER

PROLOGUE

The paper that follows was written several months ago. Comments from several readers and further reflection have convinced me that some matters warrant clarification.[2] I have not revised the body of the paper, but will address some of these matters in this prologue.

One is the use of the term liquidity. In the paper, I discuss the concept of liquidity at some length following the tradition of Hicks and Tobin. I define liquidity as a characteristic of the financial position of an economic entity relative to other entities. In my usage, an entity is more or less liquid if it can transform future receipts into means of payment on more or less favorable terms than other entities. I adopted this usage in an attempt to make an objective distinction between illiquidity and insolvency – a distinction that is central to the theory of the lender of last resort. But the term has enjoyed far too much freedom of usage to be contained by my efforts. In the end I found this usage too confining myself. And some readers have understood me to be arguing that the role of the lender of last resort is to alleviate the problems of individual institutions rather than systemic problems. In fact, my view is emphatically the opposite.

One alternative would have been to define liquidity as the terms on which future claims can be converted into means of payment relative to the terms that would be available in normal times. (The benchmark of normal times appealed to Bagehot.) Then solvency becomes a test of what the net worth of a balance sheet would be in 'normal times', while liquidity is a test of what can be realized under prevailing market conditions. There are two problems with this usage. First, one must accept the view that, except in periods of financial distress, real rates of return and even inflation rates are constant. There is a risk in practice that 'normal' will be taken to be what has prevailed in the past. Most entities with financial problems would have some basis for claiming lender-of-last-resort assistance. Moreover, this approach would lead directly to the proposition concerning monetary policy that real or even nominal interest rates should never be permitted to rise.

Perhaps it is impossible to set forth purely objective criteria for distinguishing liquidity problems from solvency problems. The case of a general liquidity problem in a financial system may also be difficult to distinguish in its manifestations from a case of monetary conditions that are in some normative sense 'too tight'.

This observation leads me to the view that the theory of the lender of last resort, is, at root, a theory of the conduct of monetary policy under extremely disturbed conditions. As such, it is both more than and less than a theory of the conduct of discount window operations. Indeed, in the paper I emphasize the role of open market operations and exchange market operations in dealing with problems of financial distress. And discount window operations are important in the routine conduct of monetary policy for many central banks.

Thinking back over the analysis of historical episodes considered by Bagehot and Kindleberger, they consistently argue implicitly or explicitly that these were times when monetary conditions suddenly became inappropriately tight because of rapidly changing expectations or perceptions, especially about creditworthiness. Either a central bank lost reserves under a fixed exchange standard and could not maintain its domestic monetary policy; or financial institutions sought to compensate for a perceived loss of liquidity by curtailing the internal creation of money and credit; or others sought to do so and increased their demand for money. Often all three occurred. My argument that the current international financial system is essentially a closed system is an argument that the first of these occurrences is not a potential problem today. The first problem, then, for the lender of last resort is to identify when the second or third is happening – that is, when the monetary mechanism is not operating as it normally does.

The second problem is to deal with it. This leads me back to the need to emphasize, if not rest exclusively on, my original characterization of a liquidity problem as describing conditions in part of a global market rather than conditions generally. So long as an excessive liquidity squeeze is general, whether it is caused by a rush for liquidity under conditions of financial distress or by 'monetary policy' that needs rethinking, authorities can respond using normal monetary policy techniques. It is when the problem is localized that special discount window activities become important, distinctions between solvency problems and liquidity problems become crucial, and the need for carefully orchestrated action under confused and uncertain conditions becomes important. I stand by my analysis of what needs to be done under these conditions, my evaluation of the problems of doing it well, and the importance of being as clear as possible about what would and would not be done before the problem presents itself.

INTRODUCTION

The literature on the lender of last resort is informal and heuristic. I am unaware of a formal theory in the sense of a widely accepted mathematical framework that is based on fundamental axioms of the behaviour of economic agents.

Bagehot provided a statement of the issues in his *Lombard Street* (1873), which continues to be the context in which lender-of-last-resort questions are discussed. He also provided an analysis that economists ever since have found difficult to refine. Bagehot approached his subject from a practical rather than a theoretical perspective. It is not surprising that a man who was closely involved in the financial affairs of his day would take this approach. But even recent writers such as Kindleberger (1978) and Solow (1979), who have solid credentials as theorists, have eschewed formal models, equations and graphs when they have turned to the subject of the lender of last resort.

Undoubtedly one reason that authors have tended to approach issues relating to the lender of last resort informally is that they wish to reach a broad audience that includes central bankers and government officials, as well as economists who have achieved and maintained proficiency in mathematical analysis. But the potential audience for work on the theory of monetary policy is probably much broader than the audience for the more arcane topic of the lender of last resort. And yet monetary theory has had an extensive formal development. A more likely explanation is that some of the essential concepts relevant to the theory of the lender of last resort are difficult to formalize, despite their strong intuitive appeal.

The absence of a rigorous theory can be invoked to cast doubt on the need for a lender of last resort. Those who believe strongly in the optimality of private markets tend to attribute problems to events which a lender of last resort could not control or to mismanagement by monetary authorities. Indeed, even Bagehot said: 'Under a good system of banking, a great collapse, except from rebellion or invasion, would probably not happen' (p. 52). The hypothetical system he goes on to describe would be comprised of many banks and be self-regulating – characteristics the Eurocurrency markets possess. But theoretical work on the subject has not been pursued intensively enough to conclude that private markets will be stable under all conditions.

I will not fill the gap in the formal theory in this paper. But I will outline what I think are the essential elements of a theory and suggest what such a theory might have to say about (a) whether there is a need for a lender of last resort in the Eurocurrency market, and (b) when and under what terms and conditions its resources should be available to a bank or banks in the market. Someone of a thoroughly practical nature might consider the first question frivolous. An uncontrolled financial panic would have awesome costs. The direct costs of making arrangements for a lender of last resort are small. So it would seem a version of Pascal's wager presents itself: unless those who have a stake in or are responsible for the survival of world banking are convinced beyond all doubt that a lender of last resort is unnecessary, they should seek to provide for it. And no theoretical argument could remove all doubt from practical minds. I have another motivation for examining this question. By examining what, if any, features of the Eurocurrency market might make it necessary to provide lender-of-last-resort assistance, we can understand better when and how the assistance could best be provided. Moreover, as has been recognized at least as far back as Bagehot, the existence of a lender of last resort and public perceptions of how it will act may affect its own need to act. Under some conditions, awareness that a lender of last resort is standing by may maintain financial confidence and make it unnecessary to do anything. On the other hand, the existence of a lender of last resort may encourage excessive risk-taking, thereby increasing the likelihood of financial distress.

The second section of this paper provides a discussion of the sources of financial distress. It focuses particular attention on the nature of liquidity and liquidity problems. The third section draws on this analysis to discuss disturbances that might occur in the Eurocurrency markets and how central banks might respond to them. The fourth section offers some principles suggested by the analysis that might be considered in practical discussions of how central banks should respond to difficulties in the Eurocurrency markets.

SOURCES OF FINANCIAL DISTRESS

At an abstract level it is helpful to distinguish three sources of financial distress:

1. Distress resulting from a decline in aggregate real wealth.
2. Distress resulting from a redistribution of wealth associated with changing relative prices of assets.
3. Distress resulting from insufficient liquidity.

As a practical matter, financial distress may and often does result from a combination of these factors, and even if an initial disturbance is of one kind, it may induce elements of the others. In particular, a decline or redistribution of real wealth that threatens the solvency of some financial or non-financial institutions may become an acute problem because it impairs the creditworthiness of those institutions and hence their liquidity. And a widespread liquidity problem may often generate relative price changes that reduce the net worth of financial or non-financial institutions. I will return to these complications after assessing the role of a lender of last resort in dealing with each kind distress.

A decline in aggregate wealth within a closed economic and financial system may render some individuals and non-financial institutions bankrupt. Losses that exceed the net worth of borrowers would then fall on their creditors, including their bankers. A large and widespread loss of wealth may threaten the solvency of these banks – bank depositors as well as equity holders would share in the loss.

A decline in net worth and resulting financial distress may be the result of a large natural disaster or human catastrophe – earthquake, flood, crop failure or war. Physical productive capacity would be impaired. The losses may affect only some or be widespread. In either case, there is nothing a lender of last resort can do to restore the lost wealth. Loans to cover a negative net worth position of financial institutions whose prospects for recovery are so poor as to preclude their being acquired or their raising new capital are unlikely to be repaid. Support would mean that ultimately the losses would be transferred to taxpayers. This would be an indirect way of socializing the losses. Other mechanisms would also transfer or spread the losses: national governments or international organizations might wish to redistribute the losses by direct relief to those most seriously affected, and government deposit insurance, where it is in force, represents a commitment to insulate depositors from loss. None of these mechanisms would eliminate the loss.

But the function of socializing losses is different from the usual lender-of-last-resort function. Both the literature and practice from Bagehot till now have been built on a principle of lending only to solvent institutions or advancing only on good security. A catastrophe destroys good security. The role of a central bank, if any, in assisting with politically directed relief efforts must be distinguished from its lender-of-last-resort function.

Large, sudden changes in relative prices may generate financial distress, even without a loss of aggregate real resources. This was the first stage of many of the financial panics chronicled by Kindleberger.

A change in the relative prices of real assets may result from a variety of causes. They may occur because new resources are discovered – that is, aggregate wealth may actually increase. New deposits of minerals may be found, or new technologies may be discovered that render old productive equipment or old skills obsolete. In these cases, certain individuals and institutions may be hard pressed, even though aggregate wealth increases. Changes in tastes may also occur, which raise the value of some firms and reduce the value of others. Or one economic agent or group of agents may develop a corner or monopoly position in some market.

Changes may also occur in the relative price of money claims relative to real assets (inflation or deflation) or between different money claims (exchange rate changes or changes in long-term interest rates that alter the present value of existing long-term interest-bearing assets). These changes may directly threaten the solvency of financial institutions that were unfortunately positioned before the change, as well as threaten them indirectly if their borrowers fail.

The relative price changes that create a fundamental reallocation of wealth must be presumed to have lasting effects on asset prices. Otherwise, the problems that may arise are better classified as liquidity problems. Determining which price changes are lasting and which are transitory may be difficult in practice, and hence it may be difficult to distinguish between a relative price problem and a liquidity problem. I will return to this issue after discussing the nature of liquidity problems below.

A relative price change must also be sudden and unanticipated if it is to create widespread financial distress. A gradual trend in relative prices permits time for adjustment. Most sudden changes seem to follow periods during which markets ignored underlying economic developments. Either prices are pushed increasingly out of line with long-term fundamentals until a correction occurs (a speculative bubble), or prices fail to track a trend in its fundamental economic determinants, and then, during a sudden reassessment, market prices jump to a new equilibrium level. Whether preceded by a bubble or not, sudden large price changes are generally viewed by writers on manias and panics as movements towards equilibrium. The rational expectations school would consider *any* price change as a movement towards a new equilibrium reflecting new information. Others may be more skeptical that markets are always wise. But even those who are agnostic or skeptical concerning the rationality of market expectations tend to view most sudden large price changes as corrections – movements towards equilibrium, whether they reverse a previous speculative trend in prices or not.

Central banks may be tempted or pressured to assist financial institutions that are placed in difficulty as a result of large relative price changes. Unlike the first kind of distress, when a central bank is obviously unable to counter a loss of resources, the community as a whole may be prosperous even though some institutions are hard pressed. And if the distress comes in a period of tight monetary policy, the central bank may be blamed for the problems. But by assumption, the central bank would be making loans that are unlikely to be repaid in full in real economic terms (although book-keeping practices might obscure this fact). In effect, the central bank that made loans under such circumstances would socialize the losses. Since governments in most countries have a claim on central bank earnings – if not year-by-year, then at least in the long run – a reduction would ultimately be felt by taxpayers. Of course, when restrictive monetary policy has contributed to the problem, it is especially important that the degree of restraint be warranted by the extent of inflationary pressures. But effective restraint entails squeezing many in the economy. If the pressure on some is relieved by lender-of-last-resort assistance, the pressure on others will be correspondingly greater.

There are other reasons, besides the dubious propriety of a central bank assuming the responsibility for redistributing wealth, which suggest that losses arising from large relative price changes *per se* ought not to trigger lender-of-last-resort operations. First, if banks know that such losses will be made up, they may not exercise sufficient caution during the period that disequilibrium is building up. Their lending may support a speculative price trend or forestall necessary adjustment. Alternatively the banks may participate in a bandwagon themselves or maintain excessively large exposures to interest rate or exchange rate changes. Thus a lender of last resort that responded to such problems could become necessary only because it existed. This moral hazard problem has always been recognized as one of the dilemmas faced by lenders of last resort.

Central banks have been advised to maintain uncertainty about the availability of lender-of-last-resort credit in order to minimize the moral hazard problem. It is a false hope that banks could maintain their credibility if they commonly provided support after expressing doubt about its availability. Moreover, if banks are uncertain about what behaviour would disqualify them from support, they will not know what activities they should avoid. Central banks have also been advised to maintain strict supervision over banks' risk-taking. Supervision is necessary if the risks that banks take are going to be socialized, either by the lender of last resort, a deposit insurance fund or other arrangements. Supervision may also be desirable for other reasons. But supervision migh reasonably be conducted so as to leave room for enough risk-taking, so that banks might occasionally become insolvent. Such risk-taking would be tempered but not stifled by a policy of not lending to banks whose net worth has been eaten away by bad loans or poor portfolio management.

Liquidity problems are difficult to characterize, but these are the problems that a lender of last resort ought to deal with. Before discussing how such problems arise, it is necessary to try to get a handle on the elusive concept of liquidity.

The term liquidity is applied to assets, institutions, individual financial markets and financial systems. Although it is widely used in financial writing, it is rarely defined in a way that would permit a measure of liquidity. Even when liquidity measures are used, they are only loosely related to the intuitive concept of liquidity. I will argue that liquidity is essentially a concept that applies most directly to an economic entity – an individual, a commercial or industrial enterprise, or a financial institution. From the concept of the liquidity of an entity one can identify attributes of assets, markets or financial systems that contribute to their liquidity.

Liquidity is that which allows flexibility in the management of financial affairs. Hence it has meaning only in an environment of risk and uncertainty, but liquidity preference and risk aversion ought not be used synonymously.

Flexibility may be desired for defensive reasons: in order to permit an entity to discharge its responsibilities and avoid default. Or it may be desired for offensive reasons: to permit an entity to take advantage of unanticipated opportunities. Since this paper deals with issues related to financial distress, it will focus on the defensive utility of liquidity.

Any economic entity has to make certain payments in order to continue in existence.

1. An individual must pay for food, clothing and shelter and meet its contractual debt obligations.
2. A non-financial business must pay wages, pay for supplies, and meet its contractual debt obligations.
3. A bank must pay deposits at maturity or on demand and meet other debt service payments.

Payments means unconditional transfer of ownership of an asset. In any financial system, law and custom govern what assets are accepted in payment of obligations. In modern developed financial systems, individuals and non-bank businesses generally make payments by transferring the demand liabilities of banks or by transferring currency (the liabilities of central banks). Banks may make most payments to non-banks and some payments to banks by transferring ownership of demand liabilities of another bank (with a name acceptable to the payee). Ultimate payment among banks requires the transfer of central bank liabilities (usually a book-keeping entry, but sometimes currency). The central banks of major financial countries today have few absolute obligations to make payments by transfer of assets. Obligations to redeem central bank currencies for gold no longer exist. EMS central banks commit themselves to exchange their liabilities for those of other central banks at fixed exchange rates, but these obligations can be suspended or modified at any time. Major central banks do incur obligations to make payments in foreign currencies if they borrow from the market or from other central banks, but it will be useful to distinguish between these obligations and central banks' monetary liabilities, the transfer of which by other parties represents ultimate payment in the modern world, both by law and by custom.

Let us now consider the liquidity of a single economic entity. It faces a need to make payments from now into the future according to some schedule. This need may be fixed or it may be uncertain, as with a bank's need to make payments on demand deposits. The need may be an absolute contractual one or failure may have a lesser opportunity cost (as when an attractive investment opportunity must be foregone). The resources available to the entity to meet these obligations may include:

1. cash (its stock of assets that constitute means of payment);
2. future receipts of cash from financial claims on others or from its ongoing sale of goods and services;

3. sale of assets (by which it can receive cash sooner than by waiting for the stream of payments from the asset);
4. borrowing power (which permits the entity to realize cash but obligates it to make subsequent payments).

If these resources are sufficient for the entity to meet its obligations into the indefinite future, it is both solvent (has positive net worth) and liquid. If it cannot, it is insolvent, and at the time in the future when it can no longer make payments it will become illiquid and will fail. The interesting question for a discussion of liquidity problems is: can an entity be characterized as illiquid but solvent?

The difficulty in dealing with this question is that it involves a counterfactual hypothesis: the illiquid entity could survive and have positive net worth if it could obtain resources sooner. But whether the entity can pull through or not depends on the terms on which it can acquire means of payment now to meet its obligations. At some interest rates it may be able to sell assets or borrow on terms that leave it solvent. At higher interest rates it may not.

An example may help to illustrate this difficulty. Assume an entity is obligated to make payments of $100 in every period from now until three periods from now. It has resources of $200 in cash and an asset that will pay $210 three periods from now. If the entity can neither sell the asset nor borrow new money, its economic future can be traced out as follows:

Period	Cash at beginning of period	Receipts	Payment requirement	Cash at end of period
0	200	0	100	100
1	100	0	100	0
2	0	0	100*	failed
3	—	210*	100*	—

* Creditors would not receive payment in period 2. If assets can be transferred to creditors through bankruptcy without loss (as with a debt instrument), they would accrue to the creditors. If the assets represent anticipated receipts from the conduct of business, they would be lost.

If, however, the entity can borrow at an interest rate of less than 10 per cent in period 2, it can wind up its affairs with a positive net worth. For example, at an interest rate of 5 per cent its future would be:

Period	Cash at beginning of period	Receipts	Payment requirement	Cash at end of period
0	200	0	100	100
1	100	0	100	0
2	0	100	100	0
3	0	210	205	5

If a part of the asset could be sold at a discount equivalent to an interest rate of 5 per cent, the outcome would be the same.[3] However, if the rate of interest that was required by a buyer of an asset was greater than 10 per cent, the entity would fail and have a negative net worth, but the day when it became illiquid could be postponed until period 3. (The entity would be unable to borrow from a lender that knew the true situation if the interest rate was above 10 per cent.)

This analysis allows us to distinguish between the liquidity and the solvency of an individual entity if there is a market interest rate that prevails generally, but is not available to the entity. Clearly, quantitative limits on credit available to an entity may constitute a liquidity problem in the absence of a solvency problem: if it could obtain more resources at the same rate that prevails in the market, it could survive. In the presence of borrowing constraints, an entity's ability to remain liquid will depend on how large a discount it must take to convert future receipts into cash by selling assets. Means of payment (which often but not always earn a zero rate of interest) always set the lower bound on the rate of return (in terms of the means of payment numeraire) that must be foregone if another asset is sold to raise cash. An asset that offered less would not be held. The extent to which a higher return must be foregone is a measure of the liquidity of an asset. Because of transactions costs and thinness of markets some real assets may be very illiquid – the rate of return foregone by having to dispose a piece of specialized equipment compared with using it in production may be very great. And labor services, with relatively few exceptions, cannot be sold for cash up front (but one can borrow against earning power, within limits). It is worth noting that an illiquid asset generally offers the prospect of a somewhat higher return than a liquid asset when it is acquired as compensation for its illiquidity. But the rate of return to one who already holds it is likely to be higher still because the transactions costs of acquiring it have already been paid. It cannot be sold quickly for what was paid for it.

The liquidity of an asset may also depend on just how quickly cash is needed. A bank may not be able to sell a loan immediately at all, or at least not for anywhere near its full value at prevailing interest rates, but given time for a buyer to review the documentation and the creditworthiness of the obligor, the selling back might realize a price somewhat near the present value of the loan at market interest rates.

Some would argue further that the liquidity of an asset may be affected by relative price changes. If the relative price of an asset drops sharply, holders may feel that, over time, its price may rise again. Essentially, holders would be expecting an above-normal rate of return on the asset from continuing to hold it rather than selling it. In this sense, the asset would be illiquid. One case where such views might be held would be when long-term interest rates rose, depressing bond prices, but interest rates were expected to fall in the future by more than the implicit expectations contained in the yield curve. Accepting such a situation as a liquidity problem rather than a solvency problem requires one to accept an optimistic view that interest rates will decline in the future, rather than the implicit view of the market imbedded in the term structure of interest rates. Those who believe markets are efficient and expectations are rational would argue that there is no basis for such an assessment. But markets for some assets, including long-term bond markets, show evidence of price behavior that is inconsistent with the hypothesis that the term structure of interest rates is based on rational expectations of expected future interest rates. Thus there is some basis for concluding that, at times, an economic entity may reasonably anticipate having to forego a higher return by disposing of long-term assets than the expected cost of borrowing to an entity with access to credit at present and anticipated short-term rates. But a good deal of skepticism is warranted toward claims that the market is wrong and therefore that viable entities are threatened. If lender-of-last-resort assistance is offered readily in response to such claims, the failure of the borrower will often be found to be merely delayed, not avoided.

Three conclusions follow from this discussion. First, the concept of liquidity is intrinsically related to the heterogeneity of rates of return implicit in various opportunities faced by an economic agent (including infinite borrowing costs beyond some borrowing capacity, and the impossibility or difficulty of obtaining an amount of cash for some assets that is close to their present value as calculated using market interest rates).

Second, a liquidity problem can only be distinguished from a net worth problem for a hypothetical interest rate that in some sense ought to apply. These conclusions point ahead to the proposition that, while it is relatively easy to think of the liquidity of an individual entity or a group of entities in terms of the liquidity of its assets, its payment obligations and its borrowing opportunities, it is difficult to give meaning to the concept of the liquidity, as contrasted with the net worth, of a closed financial system.

Finally, it should be apparent why liquidity is not easily measured, even though it can be defined with some precision. It involves an evaluation of the cash flows from assets held, relative to their market value or hypothetical value. It has a time dimension, which makes it impossible in principle to summarize with one number. And it involves unused borrowing power, which does not appear on balance sheets. The discussion above suggests that it is meaningful to say that a solvent entity could fail because of a liquidity problem when it is unable to transform receipts due in the future into cash needed to meet present payments on terms that compare with the terms facing others. But it is also important to consider how an entity might find itself in such a situation and what are the economic consequences.

I suggested earlier that liquidity is synonymous with financial flexibility. In a world where all future payments and receipts could be contracted with certainty, liquidity would not be a concern. An entity would be able to acquire assets and liabilities of such maturities that known receipts in each period would exactly match known payments. Cash would only be held between periods if it paid a rate of return at least as great as the highest yielding asset for that period (net of transactions costs). All assets, including cash, would be held for their investment return, not for their liquidity. But since future cash receipts or payments, or both, are generally uncertain, an entity needs to guard against illiquidity by holding cash and other liquid assets and by assuring itself of access to credit. It is willing to accept a lower expected return on cash and liquid assets and pay for lines of credit in order to guard against a possible cash drain, which it might be unable to meet or could force it to sell off less liquid assets and lose the higher return on them.

In a smoothly functioning competitive financial system the cost of remaining liquid will be small. Liquid assets, if not cash itself, will offer rates of return near those on less liquid assets. Efficient secondary markets will enhance the liquidity of a wider range of assets. Moreover, an entity will not need to hold large cash balances, because it will be able to borrow at a narrow spread to cover temporary cash drains if it can maintain good long-run prospects – that is, remain solvent. Liquidity problems could arise because an entity incurred unanticipated payments needs that exceeded those it had been willing to protect against (given the cost of doing so) and it faced limits on what it was able to borrow. Of course, the most likely reason a well established entity such as a large international bank would face borrowing limits is that its solvency had been called into question, perhaps because it had suffered negative publicity that depositors or other lenders were unable to assess precisely, and they held back. Or perhaps regulations limiting interest that can be paid or amounts that may be loaned meant that an entity was short of credit that it needed and would be able to pay for in the absence of the regulatory constraints.

In an underdeveloped financial system, an entity may also incur liquidity problems because credit is simply not available or an entity may be vulnerable to being squeezed by one or a few creditors. Entities would guard against illiquidity by holding larger cash balances and foregoing investment opportunities. Economic growth would be retarded. And since the cost of avoiding liquidity problems would be higher, entities would take greater risks of having a cash shortfall. Failures of fundamentally sound entities would occur more frequently, with accompanying disruptions of commerce and industry.

The question naturally arises whether an ideal financial system would be one in which there was no cost to maintaining liquidity. The answer to this question appears to be no. A theoretically optimal exchange economy would involve contingent contracts for the receipt and delivery of all commodities in any future period under each state of nature, with no constraints on entities other than net worth constraints. But the determination of the price level in a modern monetary economy rests on preserving some cost to entities of maintaining liquidity. The techniques of monetary policy have an influence on the price level because entities demand a real quantity of what the central bank supplies or controls. Central banks create liabilities that are defined in terms of themselves and are monetary units of account. They regulate monetary conditions by controlling the supply of these liabilities and in several other ways. (They may restrict nominal magnitudes on banks' balance sheets through reserve requirements or quantitative limits. They may also enforce interest rate restrictions on means of payment, thus driving a wedge between the rate of return on the most liquid assets and other assets in the economy.) But the only distinctive attribute of the quantities influenced by central banks is their extreme liquidity. A demand for them in real terms exists because the cost of maintaining liquidity in other forms has not been driven to zero. The ratio between the real demand for the assets supplied or controlled by the central bank, given the liquidity needs of entities that cannot be satisfied by other means, and the nominal supply of these assets determines the equilibrium price level. If the financial system could satisfy its liquidity needs costlessly by creating liquid assets, by operating in frictionless secondary markets or by having unlimited access to private or central bank credit at market rates, there would be no specific demand for the assets that central banks supply or control. Then the price level could rise without limit.

Seen in this way, the goal of monetary policy is to control the nominal liquidity of economic entities in the aggregate, relative to their desire to become more or less liquid. When entities' liquidity desires are more or less freely satisfied, the prices of less liquid assets, goods and services come under upward or downward pressure. Monetarists reduce the problem of monetary policy to that of stabilizing the nominal supply of particular liquid instruments, although they differ among themselves about what instruments are important. Historically, the real demand for some monetary magnitudes has been relatively stable, although not so stable as monetarists have often claimed. Moreover, *ex post* stability has been found, in part, by defining monetary aggregates with the benefit of hindsight, which is not available to the policy-maker. And there have been episodes in history when the real demand for outside liquid assets (central bank liabilities or precious metals) has increased sharply, owing to an actual or feared breakdown of the process by which liquidity is generated within the private economy: borrowing power has been called into doubt or the marketability of assets has become questionable. Under such circumstances maintaining monetary stability requires central banks to create more liabilities to satisfy the desires of entities to become more liquid, or at least to make their liabilities potentially available by being willing to lend freely to banks.

One strand of the lender-of-last-resort literature deals with the appropriate behavior of central banks under such circumstances. Indeed, discount window lending is one way that central banks can meet an increased demand for their liabilities. But more generally this issue should be examined from the perspective of monetary policy, not the lender-of-last-resort function alone. In particular, the question is how to gauge and respond to changing demands for central bank liabilities in the midst of financial distress, so that monetary conditions appropriate to economic stability can be maintained.

THE LENDER OF LAST RESORT IN THE INTERNATIONAL BANKING MARKETS

The foregoing discussion of the sources of financial distress, liquidity and monetary policy should provide a basis for considering the role of the lender of last resort in international banking markets. One more piece of background is necessary, however: the present international financial system must be related to the abstract concepts that have been discussed.

One important aspect of Eurocurrency banking (perhaps the most important way in which international banking is conducted today) is its reliance on internally generated liquidity and its relative freedom from regulation, including monetary policy controls that central banks may establish for domestic banking. It is important to stress, however, that central banks do exercise considerable prudential supervision over the Eurocurrency operations of their banks, and that the trend is towards greater prudential supervision.

A second aspect of the present international financial system (including both Eurocurrency banking and national banking systems) is that it is essentially a closed system. As a whole, it is not subject to either internal or external drains of liquid assets of the sort that occurred in the nineteenth century. Indeed, an attempted flight into precious metals or other commodities would create an excess supply of central bank liabilities since the central banks would not exchange reserves for commodities. Maintaining monetary stability in such an event would require the active contraction of reserves.

Banks may experience real economic losses as a result of natural catastrophe or relative price changes that impaired the economic prospects of their loans customers. Such developments could be associated with serious economic distress and threaten the solvency of many or a few institutions. But no liquidity problems (in the sense I have defined them) would *necessarily* appear as a result of such developments, since a distinction between a liquidity problem and a solvency problem can only be made by comparing opportunities available to individual entities with some market cost of funds. What is often described as a generalized liquidity problem could emerge because the demand for the liabilities of central banks increased sharply, and this increase was not accommodated by an increased supply. Market interest rates would rise. As indicated before, it is really a question of monetary policy whether the increased market cost of funds should be accepted. And the normal techniques of monetary policy, including discounting, can be used to supply more reserves if that is desirable.

Nevertheless, the potential for shifts among banks or types of deposits within the closed system suggests a need to consider a lender-of-last-resort function apart from monetary policy. It is conceivable that a sector of the market could face a loss of liquidity. Such a loss could threaten solvent institutions in that sector. Moreover, it could trigger relative price changes that could compound liquidity problems with solvency problems. I will discuss several types of shifts of funds, why they might occur, and what difficulties they might pose for central bankers. I will also consider what response would maintain stability. Three kinds of shifts cover the range of possibilities:

1. Shifts out of a single bank or group of banks into deposits at other banks in the same currency within the Eurocurrency market.
2. Shifts from a Eurocurrency into the domestic deposits in the same currency.
3. Shifts from Eurodeposits in one currency to deposits in another currency.

Any of these shifts might be initiated by non-bank depositors in banks, or involve interbank placements, or both. Actual events might involve a combination of these shifts, e.g. a shift from Eurodollar deposits in non-US banks to domestic dollar deposits in US banks would combine shifts of the first and second kind. A shift from Eurodollar deposits in US banks to Euromark deposits in German banks would combine shifts of the first and third kind. Dealing with these composite problems would require policy responses that are composites of the appropriate responses to the pure shifts.

Shifts out of a Single Bank or Group of Banks into Deposits at Other Banks in the Same Currency in the Eurocurrency Market

One recurring concern about the Eurobanking system is that an outflow of deposits from some Eurobanking offices could create liquidity problems. Loans to non-banks appear to have a longer maturity structure than deposits from non-banks and could not be run off by a bank as quickly as deposits matured. Under normal conditions, the liquidity provided by the interbank market would provide protection for banks that lost deposits: banks losing deposits would be able to bid for interbank funds or withdraw their own interbank placements as they ran off. With some time to react, a bank could also sell off loans. If the withdrawn deposits were placed with other Eurobanks in the same currency, those banks would have excess funds to place in the interbank market or to buy loans. Banks may also be able to tap the domestic market for the currency involved, e.g. the Federal funds market to replace a Eurodollar drain, if they have a well developed presence in that domestic market.

Banks losing deposits would be likely to face an unmanageable liquidity problem only if their solvency were also in question on account of problems with loan portfolios, losses incurred because of interest rate or exchange rate mismatches, or fraud. The most commonly talked about worry is that loans to developing countries could turn bad, but concentrated lending by a bank or group of banks to a particular international industry that became depressed might conceivably be a source of difficulty.

I suggested earlier that providing lender-of-last-resort assistance to banks in these circumstances would be undesirable. If banks thought assistance would be available, they would be inclined to be less cautious than would be desirable. Moreover, central bank assistance could not reverse the losses; it would only result in their being redistributed.

There are two reasons why central banks might want to act when there is a question of solvency, however. First, in an atmosphere of uncertainty and heightened concern, fundamentally solvent institutions could find their credit standing impaired. This is the most widely expressed fear about the stability of banking. Banks could lose deposits and face tight quantitative limits on borrowing in the interbank market. A central bank that has been exercising prudential supervision over a bank may be better placed than market participants to assess its true condition. By supporting a bank that it found to be solvent, the central bank could avoid a propagation of liquidity problems.

It is important to note, however, that an outflow of deposits from one Eurobank will generally improve the liquidity position of the receiving bank. Lending by a central bank to the bank in difficulty, without an offsetting reduction in central bank liabilities through open market operations or reduced lending to others, could result in an undesirable relaxation of monetary conditions.

It may not be possible to gauge the exact amount of offset that is needed. For example, assume that assistance is provided to a bank in the Eurodollar market by the central bank with primary supervisory responsibility – the central bank in the best position to judge its true condition. Dollars are obtained by the central bank from the sale of Treasury bills, either by the Federal Reserve through open market operations or by another central bank by reducing its foreign exchange reserves. Thus no change occurs in the monetary liabilities of the Federal Reserve or any other central bank. The domestic bank deposits and loans that could be supported in the United States and elsewhere would be unchanged. If the problem in the Eurocurrency market were isolated in a few small banks, other banks would tend to use the inflow of funds to expand their Eurocurrency activities, and no change would occur in global monetary conditions. But if heightened liquidity concerns in the Eurodollar market led those banks in a position to expand to hold back (for instance, to hold more short-term liquid assets because they could not count on being able to raise funds through borrowing or selling loans) global monetary conditions could become tighter. How this tightness would fall on different economies and different currencies would depend on the extent to which the Eurodollar market was used as a substitute for different domestic markets as a place to make deposits and borrow. Domestic money and credit aggregates would be poor guides for policy, and a quantitative picture of what was going on in the Eurodollar market would not be available on a timely basis. The signal that conditions had changed would be a rise in interest rates. Greater weight would have to be given to interest rates and exchange rates to steer through the disturbance. The appropriate response to a generalized increase in the demand for liquid assets, then, is to adjust monetary policies. Activating the lender-of-last-resort function is only one way of doing this.

A second reason for central bank action is that when an insolvent bank closes, its depositors and creditors may experience at least a temporary impairment of liquidity during reorganization and bankruptcy proceedings, when the assets of the bank are tied up. This loss of liquidity is additional to the ultimate loss of wealth that will remain after the affairs of the failed institution have been sorted out. This problem points to the need to deal with bank failures quickly and smoothly. But some interim liquidity assistance may be necessary. Such assistance could take the form of slightly relaxed money and credit conditions in the markets to which those with problems are likely to turn. As with the situation created by a cutting back of banks' Eurodollar activity, central banks would not be able to measure directly the size of the aggregate need for central bank liabilities.

Assistance might also be targeted to the depositors of the institution: a central bank might advance funds (against the collateral of the depositors' claims) to depositors with maturing deposits up to an amount that is relatively certain to be ultimately recovered. If such operations were to be undertaken, a number of practical issues would arise: which central bank should lend? The supervisor of the failed institution would be best able to judge how much would be recovered, but it may not consider the need to lend to be urgent if the depositors are of another nationality. Moreover, constraints on various central banks' lending powers may preclude lending to those directly in need. Arrangements might need to be worked out to channel funds through private banks. Targeted lending may be difficult to execute in the event of a failure of an international bank, but it would most directly deal with the difficulty and reduce the likelihood of distorted money and credit conditions.

Shifts from a Eurocurrency into Domestic Deposits in the Same Currency

This second kind of shift, to the extent that it also involved a shift out of particular banks, would pose the same sort of problems for central banks as the first kind of shift. Two distinctive difficulties could arise, however. These can be seen by assuming a deposit shift occurs, but the banks losing deposits are not suffering from impaired credit standing in the interbank Eurocurrency market.

First, there would be a need for reflows of funds from the domestic market to the Euromarket. If there were no barriers to flows between domestic offices and foreign offices of banks operating in both the domestic market and the Euromarket, such a reflow would occur naturally. One could expect only small and transitory interest rate distortions between the two markets. The unexciting way in which large shifts in the net due-to-foreign-affiliate positions of US banking offices have occurred since 1974 gives reason to be complacent about this. But if there are barriers to outflows from domestic offices, Eurocurrency rates may be bid up relative to domestic rates. Eurocurrency banks would face a liquidity problem in not being able to raise funds at rates that are available to others. Authorities may need to consider relaxing restrictions on capital flows if such rate differentials develop and money is flowing to the market where rates are lower. It would make little sense for a central bank to lend to Eurobanks in order to alleviate their liquidity difficulties, thereby bypassing the capital controls, while maintaining them.

Second, an increase in demand for domestic deposits would require an adjustment of monetary policy to maintain unchanged macroeconomic conditions. Balance of payments data and data on foreign deposits, if they are timely, might give some indication of the change in deposits that needed to be accommodated. But an indication of the extent to which domestic residents are moving deposits from the Eurocurrency market back to the domestic market might not be timely. Once again, a broad assessment of monetary conditions, including the behavior of interest rates, would be required to keep domestic monetary policies on course.

Shifts from Eurodeposits in One Currency to Deposits in Another Currency

This third kind of shift may also take place when some banks are losing deposits while other banks are gaining them. But independently of such problems, a shift of currency preferences would create exchange market pressures and perhaps alter interest rates in the two currencies. This kind of shift and the effects of different central bank responses is studied in detail in a recent paper by Truman and Shafer (1981). In brief, the central banks of issue of the two currencies could accept the changes in exchange rates and interest rates and their implications for domestic and international macroeconomic equilibrium, or they could offset them by undertaking sterilized exchange market intervention. Once again, the policies necessary to keep the global financial system on track need not involve assistance to the directly affected institutions unless they are cut off from access to the interbank market in the currency they are losing.

Exchange rate pressures may be associated with international financial distress for two other reasons. First, if banks suffered loan losses that were concentrated in one currency, their currency positions would be shifted out of balance. They might seek to shift the currency composition of new lending or new deposits to restore a desired currency position. If the losses were large and the bank failed, its creditors would face the same need. These portfolio adjustments would put upward pressure on the currency in which the loans were denominated.

Second, banks that suffered an outflow of Eurocurrency deposits (say, dollars) and did not have strong credit standing in the Eurodollar market or the domestic market for the currency involved, might nonetheless remain able to attract funds in their own home market or borrow domestic currency from their central bank. They would need to sell their currency to obtain dollars. If they did not cover the resulting currency exposure (they could be precluded by their poor credit standing from covering in the forward market), their currency would be forced down against the dollar. Such a situation could lead to sizable exchange rate movements and be misdiagnosed as a currency problem.

SOME PROPOSITIONS ABOUT CENTRAL BANK ACTIONS TO DEAL WITH DISTURBANCES IN INTERNATIONAL MARKETS

This paper reaffirms the traditional doctrine of the role of the lender of last resort: lending should be restricted to institutions that are solvent and for the purpose of maintaining their liquidity. Applying this doctrine requires one to distinguish between liquidity and solvency – not an easy task in practice, or even in theory, but a task that is essential to attempt. One must also take into account the nature of the present international financial system and how liquidity problems might be manifested in it. It is essentially a closed system that, as a whole, is not prone to an outflow of funds, which was the hallmark of nineteenth-century financial panics in individual markets. Moreover, central banks are not generally committed to exchanging their liabilities for reserve assets and so individual markets are not so susceptible to a loss of liquidity. But Eurocurrency banking, which is in the center of the system, depends heavily on liquidity in the form of borrowing power rather than assets. Some banks could find themselves cut off from borrowing even though they are solvent and have liquidity problems. This is the most likely problem for which a lender of last resort is the solution. Or a more general cutting back of credit lines could increase the demand for central bank liabilities to serve as a reserve. In this case, the most important need would be to counter the tendency for monetary conditions to become undesirably restrictive. If the breakdown of the interbank market had progressed to a serious stage, however, it might be necessary to target an increase in central bank liabilities to institutions in difficulty by lending directly to them.

Depending on one's view of the intrinsic stability of markets, these problems may be viewed as likely to present themselves or as remote possibilities. But it is a responsibility of central banks to contain the risks of serious disruption of banking and to be prepared to deal with even small probability events if mishandling them would have very large costs. The foregoing discussion of the issues suggests several principles that could be useful in practical discussion of lender of last resort responsibilities in international banking markets.

1. Lender-of-last-resort assistance ought not be available to institutions with no net worth.
   (a) Otherwise excessive risk-taking would be encouraged.
   (b) Such lending can redistribute but not eliminate the losses.
2. Lender-of-last-resort assistance should not be too freely available. Easy access to assistance (an implicit subsidy) would make banks in the Eurocurrency market more comfortable with their liquidity and stimulate the growth of the unregulated Eurocurrency markets relative to controlled domestic markets. Among other consequences, the effectiveness of anti-inflationary monetary policies would gradually erode.
3. Making access to the lender of last resort uncertain is a poor way of restricting availability. Some uncertainty is inevitable if a solvency proviso is maintained, but failure to keep markets informed of true intentions may increase the instability of liquidity management by banks and their customers.
4. Making assistance available at an interest rate somewhat above prevailing interbank interest rates is a better way of discouraging dependence on a lender of last resort.
5. Widespread difficulties may require an adjustment of domestic reserve and monetary targets as interest rates deviated sharply from what would normally be expected to be the result of the policies that were being followed. Indeed, these market-oriented policies (as contrasted with institution- or sector-oriented policies) may be all that are needed to ensure the survival of institutions that are not endangered by loan losses or fraud.
6. Exchange rate pressures may be associated with financial problems. Such pressures could be alleviated either by giving assistance in a strong currency or by undertaking parallel exchange market intervention.
   (a) Depending on the form in which difficulties manifest themselves, the currency most directly involved may be strengthened or weakened.
   (b) Concerns about credit availability to support Eurocurrency operations in a currency will increase the demand for liquid assets in that currency and put upward pressure on exchange rates.
   (c) Shifts out of one Eurocurrency into another will depress the value of the currency that depositors wish to get out of.

These principles suggest the need for close consultation both within central banks and among central banks to prepare for possible financial distress in international markets. Within central banks, an appropriate response may involve a domestic monetary policy response and an exchange market intervention response, as well as (or perhaps in place of) action by the lender-of-last-resort function. Among central banks, a division of responsibility will have to reflect both differing policy interests (the extent to which a central bank's own nationals are in difficulty) and different capacities to act (a central bank's knowledge of the true condition of a bank that asks for help and the resources that each central bank commands). Indeed, it is likely that effective measures to deal with financial distress will require co-ordinated actions by several central banks.

NOTES

1. The views expressed in this paper are the author's alone. They do not represent official views of the Federal Reserve Bank of New York or the Federal Reserve System.
2. I have received insightful comments from G. Aubenel, P. H. Kent, C. P. Kindleberger and R. S. Masera. I have not dealt with all of their criticisms in this prologue, nor would they necessarily endorse what I have written.
3. It is interesting to note that if the asset was indivisible and had to be sold in its entirety at the same discount and the balance had to be held in cash, the net worth of the entity would be eliminated.

REFERENCES

Bagehot, Walter (1873) *Lombard Street: A Description of the Money Market* (New York: Scribner, Armstrong and Co.), reprinted by Richard D. Irwin, 1962.

Kindleberger, Charles P. (1978) *Manias, Panics, and Crashes: A History of Financial Crises* (New York: Basic Books).

Solow, Robert (1979) 'On the Lender of Last Resort', processed, March.

Truman, Edwin M. and Shafer, Jeffrey R. (1982) 'International Portfolio Disturbances and Domestic Monetary Policy', in Cooper, *et al.*, *The International Monetary System Under Flexible Exchange Rates (Essays in Honor of Robert Triffin)* (Boston, Massachusetts: Ballinger Publishing Company).

14 The Endogeneity of International Liquidity[1]

PETER M. OPPENHEIMER

This paper argues that the volume of international liquidity, as well as its composition and distribution, is the outcome of the operation of the international monetary system over time. It is, in other words, endogenous, and is not something which it makes sense to try to control *a priori*. Policies for the monetary system cannot usefully aim to achieve, by any direct or simple means, control over the aggregate amount of liquidity. The first section of the paper outlines the scope of the argument and its relation to some basic economic principles. The second section sketches a selective analytical history of international monetary arrangements from pre-1914 to 1980. The third section discusses the functions of international liquidity and liquidity creation in relation to the economic debates which began around 1960. The final section is a brief re-statement and conclusion.

THE SUPPLY OF RESERVES

One might have thought that the endogeneity of world liquidity was obvious after the events of the past decade. In 1971–3 a monetary system supposedly threatened with a *shortage* of liquidity collapsed amid a mushrooming of reserve creation that left a legacy of concern about the 'dollar overhang' for several years afterwards. Since 1973 the pace of reserve creation has been determined to a large extent by non-monetary factors, notably the price of oil and its balance of payments consequences, to which world monetary arrangements have had to adapt themselves in a more or less passive manner. Yet the issue continues to be debated. For example, at the IMF Memorial Conference for Marcus Fleming in 1976 there was a heated discussion, led by Triffin on one side and Haberler on the other, over whether control of world liquidity should be seen as a policy objective.[2]

For those wishing to argue that international liquidity ought to be centrally controlled in some way, there is an acute preliminary problem of definition. What is to be included under the heading of international liquidity? Table 14.1 in the Appendix gives an overview of global *reserves* in the years 1979–81. Even on their own terms the significance of these figures – especially the year-to-year changes – is difficult to interpret. First, in the absence of an official monetary gold price, gold reserves are readily mobilizable only in part and perhaps indirectly (as collateral for borrowing). Their valuation is thus bound to be somewhat arbitrary. Second, for certain important asset-holders such as Saudi Arabia, the dividing line between reserves and other overseas assets is also arbitrary. But even if one takes the reserve figures at face value, they are not the whole of *liquidity*, meaning official financing possibilities for balance of payments disequilibria. These include credit facilities actually or potentially available through the IMF, the central bank swap network and private markets, and accompanied by widely varying degrees of pressure on the deficit country to reduce its rate of borrowing in the future. In these circumstances, one might be forgiven for concluding at once that attempts to control any part of this profusion would succeed only in eliciting substitute mechanisms elsewhere.

Less hastily, some observers may suppose that my proposition about the endogeneity of world liquidity has to be accepted in the special circumstances of the 1970s and 1980s, with their OPEC surpluses and floating exchange rates, but not in more tranquil and ordered times. I believe, on the contrary, that it is quite generally applicable. It certainly applied, for example, under the Bretton Woods system. To a large extent the proposition stems from the fact that there is no central sovereign authority in the international system. Policy is made by national governments and central banks in – to correct Hedley Bull's mistitled volume – a polyarchical society.[3] That fact, however, does not make the proposition a 'purely political' one, any more than consumer sovereignty is a purely political concept on account of its roots in liberal philosophy. Economists take pride in having developed a comprehensive analysis of resource allocation under decentralized decision-taking. Similarly, a satisfactory analysis of the international monetary system must incorporate decentralized decision-taking among governments.

There is, admittedly, an important difference; but it is a difference of degree rather than in kind. Decentralized socio-economic systems exhibit two kinds of interaction among their participants: arm's-length interaction through the market place and co-operative interaction designed to formulate or influence the market parameters themselves.[4] In the theory of production and consumption direct co-operative interaction is welcome in the presence of particular types of externality; but it may not come about, because of the cost or difficulty of organizing it, particularly when a large and diffuse group of consumers is involved. At other times, direct interaction may be unwelcome and public policy called in to prevent it, e.g. in the case monopoly and restrictive practices enforced by producers. In short, collusion and co-operation are desirable or not, according as they remove or generate instances of 'market failure'; and they are feasible or not, depending on the number of agents involved and on the institutional mechanisms available.

In the international monetary domain, a good deal of co-operation is both feasible and desirable. It is feasible because of the small number of major authorities involved as well as the availability for the past twenty years of appropriate institutional arrangements. And it is desirable because of the common interest in stability, which contains important externality or public-good elements. For example, the commodity price inflation of 1971–3 clearly owed something to the expansionary credit policies pursued simultaneously by nearly all countries in the wake of the 1971 dollar devaluation. More generally, countries have a common interest in minimizing (*ceteris paribus*) both price and exchange rate volatility, because it tends to undermine the efficacy of the price mechanism as a guide to resource allocation. And just as monetary and exchange rate targets have both been employed as policy guidelines by various national authorities in the past decade, so there may be scope both for co-operative exchange-market intervention and for co-operative pursuit of monetary targets by two or more countries acting in concert.[5]

Thus the importance of co-operative relative to market-place interaction is higher in international monetary affairs than in many other areas of economic life; but that still leaves most of the job to be done by the market place at various levels, their relative importance depending on the prevailing institutional arrangements. One level is that of domestic credit, commodity and labour markets; a second is that of foreign exchange markets; and a third is that of markets in international credit and reserve assets, where national sovereign authorities are essential participants. The non-existence of a global sovereign means, in particular, that market-place interaction plays a more pervasive part in determining international liquidity than in determining domestic money stocks. The analogy that, because we claim to control domestic money supplies, we should readily be able to establish control over international liquidity is false (quite apart from the fact that the extent of our control over domestic money is disputable).[6] The following sections are intended to illustrate and substantiate these points.

THE SHORTAGE OF INTERNATIONAL RESERVES

Before 1914, the gold standard constituted a monetary system in which market forces – namely, those affecting the supply of and demand for gold – were entirely responsible for the accrual of international reserves.[7] At the same time, these forces were exogenous to the monetary system itself, because currency values were supposed to be *permanently* fixed in terms of gold. (Only in the ultra-long run could the supply of monetary gold be seen as endogenous, because if world output grew faster (or slower) than the world's gold-based money supplies, then the world price level would fall (or rise), thereby encouraging a greater (or smaller) accrual of monetary gold, whose price in terms of currencies was unchanging.) The system was acceptable because the price level in each country was supposed to adjust itself to reconcile full employment with whatever size money stock was permitted by the current volume of reserves. Given the nominal amount of reserves, price changes produced the required real amount. Thus no question of inadequacy of global reserves should arise – nor did it, although, as is well known, a number of commentators in Britain worried about the low level of the Bank of England's reserves.

Nevertheless, the way in which the system operated – even where exchange-rate stability was maintained – did not quite match the theoretical model. As Triffin has shown, the variable which in practice adjusted to keep the system going was not so much the price level as the relationship between gold stocks and national money supplies.[8] There was growing use of bank deposits, while monetary gold was gradually withdrawn from circulation and concentrated at central banks. This was tantamount to an endogenous stretching of the stock of monetary gold itself. The United Kingdom's external portfolio preferences (see below) also helped.

The process could not be repeated after the First World War on the domestic front because there was no gold left in circulation. At the same time, money wages and at least some prices were felt to have become less flexible than formerly (at any rate in a downward direction). Consequently, the notion of global reserve inadequacy made its appearance for the first time – at the Genoa Conference of 1922, which looked to the restoration of the fixed-rate system partly with the help of a further organized stretching of monetary gold reserves, this time on the international front through the gold exchange standard. The restoration lasted only a few rather unhappy years. Its collapse in the 1930s led, by way of floating exchange rates, to an endogenously generated increase in the value of monetary gold stocks. As has frequently been emphasized, the relative prices of the major currencies were not very different after 1936 from what they had been in 1930. The main change was the more or less uniform increase in the currency price of gold. But it had been achieved in a disorderly way, involving major economic loss and hardship.

One aspect of the disorder was that the collapse of the inter-war gold standard involved an initial shrinkage of international liquidity, as currency (particularly sterling) reserves were presented for conversion into gold. The shrinkage could have been prevented in either of two not mutually exclusive ways. One was to generate a new credit mechanism, to forestall or offset the strain on the key-currency countries' gold reserves. Such a 'quantity' mechanism was propounded by Keynes, who in *The Means to Prosperity* (1933) advocated the issuance of international gold notes to replenish the world's stock of reserves. (The wartime Keynes Plan, which preceded the Bretton Woods discussions, was simply an updated version of these proposals first advanced ten years earlier.)

The other route by which the liquidity collapse of 1930–1 could have been prevented would have been to increase the price of gold, i.e. devalue sterling and subsequently other currencies, before currency holders decided to convert. Provided the rise in the gold price was large enough to rule out the prospect of further increases in the foreseeable future, it would have boosted world liquidity in three ways. First, it would have increased the value of existing monetary gold stocks, notably those of the key-currency or reserve-centre countries. Second, it would have made reserve currencies (which can be held in interest-bearing form) more attractive assets, thereby encouraging their retention and subsequent growth. Third, it would have enlarged the currency value of the annual inflow of gold to the monetary system from the market, mainly because output would have been worth more per ton and private buyers would have taken a smaller proportion of it. This 'price' mechanism may be contrasted with the quantity mechanism noted above. As was shown by the Tripartite Agreement of 1936, currency devaluations required minimum international co-operation by comparison with the quantity mechanism of printing new forms of international money.

When it came to the Bretton Woods discussions and the drafting of the IMF Articles of Agreement in 1944, which was, after all, an explicit attempt to prevent recurrence of the inter-war monetary disorder, both the above means of promoting reserve adequacy were incorporated. The Articles established the new conditional lending mechanism of IMF quota-based drawing rights, to assist countries in coping with particular payments deficits. At the same time they provided for adjustments in the currency price of gold, either through an agreed uniform change in par values or alternatively through a series of par value changes undertaken on account of successive 'fundamental disequilibria' in national balances of payments.

Although the rules of the Bretton Woods system were symmetrically drawn up as between currencies, the US dollar was always *primus inter pares*; and in practice the system operated with the dollar as centrepiece, the United States handling its own exchange rate directly in terms of gold, while other countries intervened in the exchange markets, buying and selling their own currency in exchange (usually) for dollars. Unfortunately, when it came to the crunch, the United States proved unwilling, for reasons mainly of short-term political expediency but partly also of defective analytical vision, to abide by the rules of the Bretton Woods system and devalue the dollar to the extent necessary to maintain its convertibility into gold. The result, as in 1931, was the collapse of the fixed-rate system, triggered by large-scale disruptive movements of liquid funds – which, precisely as in 1931, were misdiagnosed by many people as being responsible for the monetary debacle when in fact they merely reflected deep-seated imbalances in the system.[9]

The movement of total world reserves and the global monetary environment were radically different on the two occasions. Whereas 1931 witnessed reserve shrinkage and all-round deflation, in 1971 there was an unprecedented explosion of global reserves and massive inflation. It is scarcely plausible to attribute the former collapse to a shortage and the latter to an excess of total liquidity! What was common to the two situations was a *gold* shortage and a fundamental disequilibrium in international payments affecting the main reserve-currency country. Both the reserve shrinkage in 1931 and the reserve explosion in 1971 resulted from policies pursued by *other* countries reacting to that disequilibrium – selling sterling in 1931, buying dollars in 1971.

Thereafter the 1970s, like the 1930s but much more so, saw international liquidity being generated on a large scale by the pattern of world payments. It was a matter of, on the one hand, the low-absorbing OPEC countries deciding on the disposition of their vast accumulation of external assets, and, on the other hand, the oil-consuming world choosing an acceptable structure of borrowing and reserve-holding. In addition, there was the puzzle of how to treat gold, official holdings of which remained largely dormant while inflation and speculation drove its market price to between ten and twenty times the Bretton Woods level of $35 an ounce. There was no acquisition of gold reserves from new production in the 1970s. Indeed, there was net movement from official into private hands, as the IMF and the US Treasury auctioned off parts of their holdings during the years 1975–9. (The US Treasury, of course, had earlier sold almost $3,000 millions worth of gold to the market indirectly at $35 an ounce in 1967–8, in the aftermath of the 1967 devaluation of sterling; that episode came to an end with the introduction of the two-tier gold system in March 1968.) Official sales then ceased, and the early 1980s saw a modest revival of central bank purchases of gold.

LIQUIDITY AND ADJUSTMENT

The re-emergence of interest and concern about the volume of international liquidity after 1945 owed more to Robert Triffin than to any other single analyst. Triffin had observed at first hand the establishment of the European Payments Union in 1950 – at the time by far the most important addition to international credit and reserves ever brought about by co-operative policy, and much more important than the quota mechanism of the IMF, which was semi-voluntarily precluded from lending to countries in receipt of Marshall Aid. But the EPU was not a paradigm for the creation and control of international liquidity in normal circumstances. It was an exception, a transitional scheme designed specifically to hasten the liberalization of international trade in Western Europe. And it was promptly abolished in favour of exchange-market mechanisms as soon as sufficient liberalization was agreed to be possible. Triffin's account of the EPU (in his *Europe and the Monetary Muddle*) provided a stepping stone to his more celebrated contribution, which appeared in book form in 1960 under the title, *Gold and the Dollar Crisis*. Triffin deserves every credit for being well ahead of the field in seeing which way the wind was blowing for the dollar. Nonetheless, his work contained a crucial analytical error, which helped to direct economists down false paths in the 1960s.

The error lay in the supposition that correction of the US external payments deficit in the 1960s would expose a global liquidity problem, which would thereafter have to be overcome by one of a number of means (floating exchange rates, raising the gold price or establishing a world central bank was Triffin's menu, which may be regarded as complete apart from the possibility of a pegged-rate system based on an inconvertible dollar, i.e. a pure dollar standard). In reality there was no liquidity problem apart from the problem of the dollar itself. These were two sides of the same coin. And the two sides could not be treated sequentially. No monetary reform menu was available to the rest of the world, because the choice of dish would be pre-empted by the eventual US decision on what to do about the dollar. A world central bank not being in the realm of possibility, the choice for the United States lay between increasing the dollar price of gold or abrogating the dollar's gold convertibility; and the latter would sooner or later mean floating rates between the dollar and other major currencies. There were also evident implications for the composition of official reserves.

Triffin's contribution thus gave rise at the next stage of debate to the bogus threefold distinction, first formulated, I believe, by Fritz Machlup and his Group of 32, between *liquidity, adjustment* and *confidence* as separate aspects of the international monetary problem.[10] This distinction influenced not only a vast academic literature, most of it as dead as the dodo, but also the official negotiations on monetary reform which took place in the Group of Ten and elsewhere from 1963 onwards.[11] IMF Special Drawing Rights were designed in 1967–8 as a means of overcoming the *liquidity* problem, and also ultimately the *confidence* problem inasmuch as they might become the dominant asset in the monetary system and eliminate the desire on the part of central banks to switch between alternative forms of reserve. Once this negotiation was out of the way, the United States turned its attention to what it regarded as the *adjustment* problem – which had proved obdurate in the face of restrictions on capital outflow from the US and of the various *ad hoc* devices introduced to defend the US gold stock – by stepping up pressure on the Federal German authorities to upvalue their currency. The floating of the Deutsch mark in May 1971, however, only triggered a run on the dollar which led to the final abrogation of gold convertibility in August. Even if the Deutsch mark had been upvalued to a new fixed parity, thereby giving the fixed-rate system a further respite, it would basically have intensified and not relieved the long-run pressure on the US gold stock. This is first because, even with a reduction in the German current and overall surplus, the counterpart balance of payments gain would have fallen largely on countries other than the United States, including some whose marginal reserve preference for gold rather than dollars was stronger than Germany's. Secondly, upvaluation of any currency would have lowered the average price of gold and therefore ultimately *increased* pressure on the United States as *de facto* buffer-stock manager for the world's monetary gold.

The agreement among the Group of Ten to establish SDRs – activated for the first time in 1970–2 – was precarious, in the sense that it glossed over basic differences of purpose. The US authorities were trying to avoid a rise in the dollar price of gold, while acquiring leverage over the dollar's effective exchange rate by influencing the par values of other currencies. US enthusiasm for SDRs waned after the downfall of Bretton Woods. The other countries, notably the EEC Six under French inspiration, wanted to reduce the latitude previously available to the United States for running deficits through the rest of the world's accumulation of dollars. In other words, the United States saw SDRs mainly as a substitute for monetary gold, the others mainly as a substitute for dollars.

Failure to recognize the so-called liquidity problem for what it truly was, a problem of adjustment involving the composition of reserves rather than their total, also helps to explain the persistent search in the 1960s for operational criteria of global reserve adequacy. Two main types of criteria were proposed in the literature, statistical and qualitative. The statistical category in turn subdivides into two. One approach looked at the ratio of reserves to some indicator of economic activity, such as world merchandise trade or the aggregate of national money supplies. The other approach sought to estimate countries' 'demand for international reserves' econometrically. The qualitative approach was based on the idea that a shortage or an excess of reserves would influence macroeconomic management. A shortage would be indicated by a global tendency towards unemployment or deflation, by a preponderance of currency depreciations over appreciations, and by increasing controls or fiscal penalties on imports and other external outlays; and *mutatis mutandis* for an excess. The 1970s combination of inflation together with unemployment and vague protectionist noises was not envisaged.

The efforts of the Committee of Twenty in 1972–4 to re-establish a pegged-rate system on the basis of SDRs rather than gold were the earlier debates of 1963–71 writ large. The United States sought to impose stringent requirements on countries to limit reserve increases by upvaluing their currencies, while the European countries sought to prevent 'uncontrolled' accumulations of dollar reserves in the future by imposing 'asset settlement' of US external payments deficits beyond clearly specified limits. For the asset-settlement proposal to be even remotely realistic, the United States had to have at its disposal a reliable and acceptable adjustment mechanism for its balance of payments; yet since the abrogation of gold convertibility, this was precisely what it did not have. In the gold–dollar system there was a strong and direct link between the exchange rate policy and the international liquidity position of the United States; a reduction in the dollar's par value could always be made large enough to produce a decisive impact on US reserves. It is highly doubtful whether this feature could be reproduced in an SDR-based system, because SDRs are a fiduciary asset and not a commodity; in any case the Committee of Twenty's plans did not even consider the need to reproduce it, because they failed to recognize that creation of appropriate international liquidity is itself *part of the adjustment process.*

This point needs to be spelled out more fully, especially because it applies under floating no less than under fixed rates. A common view of international liquidity is that its prime function is to finance payments deficits (which must obviously be limited in duration), and that countries wish accordingly to possess a certain stock of reserves both for direct use in financing possible future deficits and for its indirect value as a sign of financial strength and creditworthiness. On this view it is a matter of indifference how countries, or *a fortiori* the system as a whole, acquire reserves, although it does matter that the global addition to reserves year by year should be large enough to prevent a competitive scramble for them by way of leapfrogging devaluation or trade restrictions. This view, however, while not in itself false, overlooks an important part of the truth. An additional purpose of reserves is to finance normal or structural *surpluses* in international payments, and this is accomplished only to the extent that the system generates a flow of reserves, appropriate in amount and composition, to surplus countries.

In the gold–dollar system of Bretton Woods this was a matter of securing a modest annual growth of reserves, appropriately divided between dollars and gold. Since 1973, by contrast, gold has played little active part and exchange rates have floated; but there has been a need to satisfy the portfolio preferences of the low-absorbing OPEC countries. In both cases, equilibrium was attainable through a combination of official policies and market mechanisms. Under Bretton Woods, the operation of the gold market and official policy towards the price of gold played a key role. In the OPEC-surplus system the private international banking network has performed the central function; official policy is important both in allowing banks to operate freely and in safeguarding the stability of the banking network through prudential supervision and last-resort lending where necessary. To be sure, not all the external surpluses of the low-absorbing OPEC countries are an equilibrium phenomenon. Some fraction of them represents disequilibrium – abnormal surplus positions expected to diminish or even disappear in the near future. But this qualification does not alter the basic argument, especially as the disequilibrium itself called forth additional reserve creation of an interim nature.

It is particularly instructive to notice the importance of the OPEC countries' portfolio preferences. Before 1914 the United Kingdom ran a very large annual surplus on current account, but this did not give rise to increases in international reserves because the claims on foreign economies were taken up in the form of long-term bonds. No doubt this facilitated the working of the gold standard. Can it in turn be attributed to the influence of the gold standard itself? If so, this would shed a startling new light on the allegedly self-stabilizing character of the system. No conclusive answer can be given; but the savings and investment habits of the British bourgeoisie seem likely to have been determined for the most part by other, less specifically monetary factors. The OPEC countries today, alas, happen to prefer bank deposits, which are liquid assets and count as reserves; and it is far-fetched to suggest that this preference could have been decisively altered by handing OPEC a lot of SDRs as the latter-day equivalent of nineteenth-century gold reserves.

The counterpart of OPEC's bank deposits consists of claims on borrower countries, including some of the OPEC states themselves, as well as other less developed and industrial nations. Deficit countries have tended to borrow more than they needed to finance their current account deficits, and have added the difference to their own foreign exchange reserves; the motives were precautionary and perhaps in part speculative (to benefit from an expected rise in world interest rates). All in all, gross official foreign exchange reserves have risen since the early 1970s by an average of $30–40 billion a year. But when one takes into account the corresponding international debts and the doubts that have emerged about the soundness of some of them, one might argue that by this process net liquidity has increased little or not at all or has even declined. As already mentioned, variations in the gold price and institutional innovations such as the credit arrangements in the EMS add further complications.

Gold reserves have the merit of being net liquidity, and not the counterpart of somebody else's debt. The absence of an official monetary gold price makes it difficult to exploit this valuable characteristic effectively. But it remains an obvious point that if the OPEC countries had been willing and able to finance a measurable fraction of their external surpluses since 1974 in the form of gold, the volume of international debts and the financial anxieties which they are generating could well have been reduced.[12] The same could be said, perhaps, of various types of non-liquid asset, such as real estate, or commodities other than gold. But gold, had it not been three-quarters expelled from the monetary system on US and IMF insistence, would have had the special merit of presenting a unique addition to the range of *liquid* assets available. Moreover, the economic side-effects of investment purchases of real estate or primary commodities tend to be much more questionable than in the case of gold. The commodity price inflation of 1971–3, fuelled by investment demand from officially sponsored institutions trying to dispose of excess dollar holdings, is a case in point.

Reckoned at market price, aggregate official gold reserves in 1980–1 were approximately equal in value to aggregate reserves in other forms. This is much the same relationship as obtained in 1968–9, when the two-tier gold market had been introduced and the Bretton Woods system was sliding towards its end. How far the identity is coincidental is a nice question. (In a rational-expectations world almost nothing is coincidental.) The price of gold and the nominal value of foreign exchange reserves have both shown a much larger rise since 1970 than the general price level. And there are some specific positive connections between the gold price and foreign exchange reserves, albeit not of the first order of magnitude. Countries, e.g. in Eastern Europe, using their gold reserves as collateral for foreign loans are able to borrow larger amounts (adding them either to their own or to other countries' foreign exchange holdings) when the gold price goes up. In 1981 high US interest rates helped to cause a shrinkage both of foreign exchange reserves (via the reflux of private funds to New York) and in the market value of gold reserves (via the decline in the gold price) (see Appendix).

On the other hand, the valuation of official gold reserves at the market price remains arbitrary. It overstates their present liquidity value. But it could be said to understate their potential value, since if gold were again to become a fully active asset in the monetary system, a higher price would probably be necessary to accommodate the increased central bank demand. Furthermore, there would be a corresponding reduction in demand for foreign exchange reserves, the two being to some extent substitutes rather than complements. The proposition that international liquidity is endogenous implies precisely that an exogenous change in the availability of any one established reserve asset will tend to generate offsetting changes in the amounts of other assets employed in the system.[13]

To restore gold to a fully active role would require some country or group of countries to re-establish an official monetary price by setting up as residual buyer and seller of gold, like the United States in the Bretton Woods system. No such initiative can be contemplated until global inflation has been convincingly halted; without this proviso a declared attempt to hold the gold price constant for an indefinite period would lack all conviction. Restoration of price stability is thus a prerequisite for return to a gold-based system, and not something to be achieved by means of it. But if the prerequisite were fulfilled, it is questionable whether the political wish to resuscitate gold would be present then, any more than it is now. Such resuscitation could help to strengthen and preserve balance-of-payments discipline thereafter. But it is doubtful whether countries would wish to view it in that light.

CONCLUSION

From time to time circumstances arise in which the efficiency and stability of the international monetary system require strengthening by means of some new initiative among governments and central banks. The creation of the European Payments Union, the development of the central bank swap network in the 1960s and the establishment of prudential supervision of international banking in the 1970s are all good examples. But the sum total of such initiatives does not amount to a policy for the control of international liquidity. Such control is not a realistic objective. The volume and composition of liquidity in the international system is the outcome of numerous and varied decisions by national sovereign authorities. The viability of an international system depends on the behavior of those authorities, or at least on the behavior of the small number of them who really 'matter'. What is important is that national authorities should be committed, in theory and practice, to the pursuit of equilibrating policies. This may sometimes involve conditionality of access to finance for disequilibria, and even arbitrary limits on such finance to the individual country. But to conclude from this that aggregate international liquidity can likewise be directly determined by some central decision-taking body is to commit a fallacy of composition.

Even if money wages and prices were much less sticky than in fact they are, countries would hardly think it advantageous to tie their own hands in the matter of foreign-asset holding and balance of payments finance by submitting either to the restoration of a nineteenth-century gold standard or, *a fortiori*, to the establishment of an SDR standard with reserve portfolios controlled by some supranational body. Individual governments who might favor schemes of this kind could not be confident that other governments, including their own national successors, would adhere to them. The limited willingness of sovereign governments to internationalize stabilization policy and balance of payments financing is one of the exogenous elements of the international monetary system, along with trading patterns, national savings propensities and the location of investment opportunities. Given these factors, an appropriate distribution, mix and volume of liquidity will result from the combined pursuit of equilibrating policies by sovereign members of the international system.

NOTES

1. A previous version of this paper was presented in June 1982 to a Study Group on International Monetary Relations at the Royal Institute of International Affairs in London.
2. R. A. Mundell and J. J. Polak (eds) (1977) *The New International Monetary System* (New York: Columbia University Press).
3. H. N. Bull (1977) *The Anarchical Society* (London:
4. This distinction is related to, though not identical with, Albert O. Hirshman's distinction between 'exit' and 'voice'. See his *Exit, Voice and Loyalty* (New York: Columbia University Press).
5. The desirability of a joint monetary growth rule for the United States, Japan and West Germany has been argued for some years by Ronald McKinnon. See, for instance, his 'Sterilization in Three Dimensions: Major Trading Countries Euro-currencies and the United States', in R. Z. Aliber (ed.) (1974) *National Monetary Policies and the International Finance System* (London: University of Chicago Press); and more recently, 'The Foreign Exchanges, Gold and Monetary Control in the United States', mimeo, 1981.

   The case for co-operative policy formulation must not be confused with a preference for discretionary rather than rule-based stabilization policies, or with a belief in the superior wisdom of governments over private market agents. On the contrary, the object is to try to establish a less volatile environment in which stability will be further enhanced by the expectations and actions of private agents.

6. For an uncompromising advocacy of the view that in a credit- (i.e. non-commodity) based system domestic money stocks are basically endogenous, see N. Kaldor (1982) *The Scourge of Monetarism* (New York: Oxford University Press).
7. Parts of what follows draw on my paper written for the Bank of England Academic Panel, *International Monetary Arrangements: the Limits to Planning* (1979).
8. R. Triffin (1964) *The Evolution of the International Monetary System: Historical Reappraisal and Future Perspectives* (Princeton: Princeton University Press).
9. For the best short history of the dollar 1945–71, see Bank for International Settlements, *Annual Report*, 1972, Chapter 1. The key point is that by 1970 (though not much earlier) the dollar was suffering *both* from a (major) undervaluation of gold in terms of all currencies and from a (modest) overvaluation of itself *vis-à-vis* a few other currencies.
10. F. Machlup and B. G. Malkiel (eds) (1964) *International Monetary Arrangements: The Problem of Choice* (Princeton: Princeton University Press).
11. Students and others whose interest in international monetary affairs began after the mid-1970s will find it difficult and scarcely profitable to come to grips with the mountain of earlier literature. Fortunately some very helpful surveys are available, notably Fritz Machlup, *Plans for the Reform of the International Monetary System*, Princeton Special Papers in International Economics, No. 3, revised edn 1964; H. G. Grubel (1971) 'The Demand for International Reserves: A Critical Review of the Literature', *Journal of Economic Literature*, and J. H. Williamson (1973) 'International Liquidity', *Economic Journal.*
12. It is difficult to be categorical about this, because the major post-1973 debtors in the third world and in Eastern Europe are not major gold holders; so one has to envisage a good deal of reshuffling of balance of payments positions.
13. Offsetting changes, but not perfectly matching ones, since that would imply that different assets were *perfect* substitutes.

APPENDIX: STATISTICS OF RESERVES

TABLE 14.1 Changes in global reserves, 1979–81

Areas and periods	Gold (in millions of ounces)	*(in billions of US dollars)[1]*	Foreign exchange	IMF reserve positions	SDRs	ECUs	Non-gold total
Group of Ten countries and Switzerland							
1979	− 95.1	199.2	− 31.2	− 2.2	3.7	42.1	12.4
1980	− 1.1	47.9	9.6	3.1	− 0.9	20.9	32.7
1981	− 0.6	− 140.4	− 11.0	2.3	2.3	− 13.6	− 20.0
Amounts outstanding at end-1981	*739.0*	*295.6*	*107.6*	*14.4*	*12.5*	*49.4*	*183.9*
Other developed countries							
1979	0.7	28.2	1.1	− 0.2	0.3	0.7	1.9
1980	2.5	7.7	3.4	0.6	− 0.1	− 0.1	3.8
1981	− 2.6	− 19.3	− 2.2	− 0.2	0.4	− 0.2	− 2.2
Amounts outstanding at end-1981	*94.1*	*37.6*	*34.7*	*1.7*	*1.6*	*0.4*	*38.4*
Developing countries other than oil-exporting countries							
1979	1.8	21.4	8.7	0.4	1.1		10.2
1980	2.9	6.3	− 0.9	1.0	− 0.6		− 0.5
1981	1.0	− 13.5	0.6	− 0.3	0.8		1.1
Amounts outstanding at end-1981	*74.4*	*29.8*	*70.5*	*1.9*	*2.8*		*75.2*

Total oil-importing countries							
1979	-92.6	248.8	-21.4	-2.0	5.1	42.8	24.5
1980	4.3	61.9	12.1	4.7	-1.6	20.8	36.0
1981	-2.2	-173.2	-12.6	1.8	3.5	-13.8	-21.1
Amounts outstanding at end-1981	*907.5*	*363.0*	*212.8*	*18.0*	*16.9*	*49.8*	*297.5*
Oil-exporting countries							
1979	0.4	11.2	15.5	-1.8	0.8		14.5
1980	3.4	4.4	19.4	1.3	0.2		20.9
1981	1.6	-7.1	-0.2	1.5	0.5		1.8
Amounts outstanding at end-1981	*42.2*	*16.9*	*89.8*	*6.8*	*2.2*		*98.8*
All countries							
1979	-92.2	260.0	-5.9	-3.8	5.9	42.8	39.0
1980	7.7	66.3	31.5	6.0	-1.4	20.8	56.9
1981	-0.6	-180.3	-12.8	3.3	4.0	-13.8	-19.3
Amounts outstanding at end-1981	*949.7*	*379.9*	*302.6*	*24.8*	*19.1*	*49.8*	*396.3*

[1] Gold reserves valued at market prices

TABLE 14.2 *The pattern of investment of exchange reserves, 1977–81*

Items	End-1977	End-1978	End-1979	End-1980	End-1981
			(amounts outstanding, in billions of US dollars)		
1. Deposits with banks in European countries.[1] Canada and Japan:					
(a) In national markets	7.6	9.3	8.8	17.6	16.3
Deutsche Mark	2.2	3.1	3.4	4.8	3.3
Swiss francs	1.3	0.6	0.6	1.6	2.7
Yen	0.9	2.7	0.9	4.6	5.4
Pounds sterling	1.6	1.2	1.9	3.0	2.2
Other currencies	1.6	1.7	2.0	3.6	2.7
(b) In Euro-markets	71.0	80.1	115.0	122.4	104.5
Dollars	53.0	52.8	73.3	79.4	70.5
Deutsche Mark	12.0	16.8	24.1	24.5	19.1
Swiss francs	3.2	4.6	6.0	8.0	6.9
Yen	0.9	2.2	4.2	2.2	2.2
Pounds sterling	0.3	0.7	1.5	2.2	1.1
Other currencies	1.6	3.0	5.9	6.1	4.7

2. Deposits with certain offshore branches of US banks[2]	4.4	5.7	6.4	5.6	5.0
Total 1+2	83.0	95.1	130.2	145.6	125.8
of which: in dollars	57.2	58.2	79.0	84.4	75.0
in non-dollar currencies	25.8	36.9	51.2	61.2	50.8
3. Exchange reserves identified as being held in the United States (= reported US liabilities to foreign official institutions)	126.0	157.0	143.3	157.1	161.1

Notes

The figures in the table include changes in the dollar value of reserves held in other currencies resulting from movements in exchange rates.

[1] Austria, Belgium-Luxembourg, Denmark, France, Germany, Ireland, Italy, the Netherlands, Sweden, Switzerland and the United Kingdom.

[2] In the Bahamas, the Cayman Islands, Panama, Hong Kong and Singapore.

SOURCE Bank for International Settlements, *Annual Report*, 1982, pp. 162 and 166.

Index

The abbreviations *I* and *F* following a page reference indicate respectively *Table* and *Figure*.